THE ILLUSTRATED COMPENDIUM OF
MAGIC TRICKS

THE ILLUSTRATED COMPENDIUM OF
MAGIC TRICKS

THE COMPLETE STEP-BY-STEP GUIDE TO MAGIC, WITH MORE THAN 375 FUN AND SIMPLE-TO-LEARN TRICKS

EVERY CONJURING TRICK IS SIMPLY EXPLAINED IN MORE THAN 2500 EASY-TO-FOLLOW COLOUR PHOTOGRAPHS

NICHOLAS EINHORN
GOLD STAR MEMBER OF THE INNER MAGIC CIRCLE

PHOTOGRAPHY BY PAUL BRICKNELL

LORENZ BOOKS

In loving memory of my brave auntie, Jean Cohen.

This edition is published by Lorenz Books,
an imprint of Anness Publishing Ltd,
Hermes House,
88–89 Blackfriars Road,
London SE1 8HA;
tel. 020 7401 2077; fax 020 7633 9499

www.lorenzbooks.com; www.annesspublishing.com

If you like the images in this book and would like to investigate using
them for publishing, promotions or advertising, please visit our website
www.practicalpictures.com for more information.

UK agent: The Manning Partnership Ltd;
tel. 01225 478444; fax 01225 478440;
sales@manning-partnership.co.uk

UK distributor: Grantham Book Services Ltd;
tel. 01476 541080; fax 01476 541061; orders@gbs.tbs-ltd.co.uk

North American agent/distributor:
National Book Network; tel. 301 459 3366;
fax 301 429 5746; www.nbnbooks.com

Australian agent/distributor:
Pan Macmillan Australia;
tel. 1300 135 113; fax 1300 135 103;
customer.service@macmillan.com.au

New Zealand agent/distributor:
David Bateman Ltd;
tel. (09) 415 7664; fax (09) 415 8892

ETHICAL TRADING POLICY
Because of our ongoing ecological investment programme, you, as our
customer, can have the pleasure and reassurance of knowing that a tree is being
cultivated on your behalf to naturally replace the materials used to make the
book you are holding. For further information about this scheme, go to
www.annesspublishing.com/trees

contents

history of mystery 14

close-up magic 32

card magic 56

string and rope magic 224

silk, thimble and paper magic 258

party tricks 300

stunts and puzzles 352

introduction

If you have never before had an interest in learning the art of magic, then be warned. You are at the beginning of a journey that could and often does last a lifetime!

I became interested in magic while watching a magician on my fourth birthday and knew at that very moment what I was going to do for the rest of my life. That was more than 25 years ago and I have been performing, creating and learning ever since.

Those of you who have already learnt a few magic tricks know how much fun it is to amaze and amuse people. Magic as a hobby is unique in that it not only fascinates the person studying it, but family and friends also. This is one reason why magic is such a wonderful pastime. Another is the sense of achievement from mastering any of the skills you undertake to learn.

Magic is also universally recognized as a wonderful form of entertainment. If you ever get the opportunity to visit one of the many magic conventions that take place all over the world, you will see a wide mixture of people. Every ethnic background is represented – young and old, amateurs and professionals, students and people in every career imaginable – but all of them share one thing in common. They all love magic.

Many of the routines and magic tricks in this book can be performed at a moment's notice with whatever objects happen to be lying around. You may want to break the ice at a meeting in the office, entertain at a dinner party or show a few tricks to your children. Whatever the situation, you will be in a position to perform something amazing.

Within this book you will find over 380 miracles to learn and perform. Many are very simple and are what magicians call "self-working tricks". Despite this term, do not expect that the tricks will work themselves. However simple a trick may appear to be, practice and rehearsal are always required to enable the performer and performance to look polished and professional. You may only wish to learn one or two of these magic tricks, but if you perform them with confidence you will be amazed at the reaction you will receive, and may well be inspired to learn more.

As you progress though the book, you will be introduced to a number of moves and sleight-of-hand techniques. Many of these are not particularly difficult to learn, but again require practice in order to reach a point where you will feel comfortable using them.

If you learn everything in this book, you will have an excellent grounding in the basics of the art of magic. If you want to learn more, you will find details of your nearest magic shop at the back of the book.

Above: Many hours of practice and rehearsal are necessary in order for you to attain a level of ability that will leave your audiences speechless at your skill and stunned by your magic.

The methods for all the tricks are clearly explained, with photographs showing each step. For convenience, the explanations are from a right-handed person's point of view; left-handed readers can reverse the left and right hands, as necessary.

Professional magicians use many of the tricks in this book, and very soon you will be performing them too. You may be surprised at just how simple some of these tricks are to perform, but do not be disappointed. The easier the method the less there is to go wrong.

Remember how you felt the first time you saw a magician make a coin vanish right before your eyes? Or that time your card was found, even though you shuffled the deck and told no one what it was? Well, in learning magic you are about to give up some of that sense of wonder in order to allow others to experience and appreciate the art. This brings us on to a very important point.

keeping the secret

A magician's golden rule is always to keep the secret. There are several reasons for this. You are investing time and effort in learning the magic tricks in this

Left: For centuries audiences have marvelled and puzzled over how a woman can be sawn in half. If the audience saw how the illusion was achieved, they would be far from impressed. Luckily for professional illusionists there is more than one method to saw someone in two! Guarding your secrets is fundamental to your success.

Below: Magicians are a regular feature at children's parties, and many of the world's greatest magic stars were inspired from a very early age.

book. When you perform them properly, the first thing people will say is "How did you do that?" which is the ultimate compliment because it means that they were amazed. Some of the tricks are very simple to perform, so you would disappoint people by letting them in on the secret. If you tell your friends how a trick works you become nothing more than a presenter of clever puzzles and they will no longer give you the credit you deserve. If they are amazed, baffled and entertained, they will want to see you perform over and over again.

People often think the secret to a trick is very complicated and involves mirrors, wires and trapdoors. Allow their amazement to continue. To take this sense of wonder away is like telling someone how a film ends before they have watched it. Keeping the secret is also fundamental to the continuing success of magic as an art form. If everyone knew all of the secrets, then magic could eventually cease to exist.

Learning magic has long been a "chicken-and-egg" scenario because if magicians do not tell people their secrets, how is it possible to learn? You are holding the answer in your hands. This book has been written to introduce you to the basics of the art of magic, and a little beyond. Whether you choose to continue further is entirely up to you.

You are taking the time to learn something that can make you memorable and popular for all the right reasons. If you keep the secrets, the secrets will keep you.

We hope that regardless of whether you learn or perform any of the magic inside this book, you will respect the art of magic by keeping the secrets to yourself.

fooling people

There is a big difference between fooling someone and making someone look a fool. Some people will feel threatened when they realize that you are going to be "doing a trick on them". They may respond with a line such as "Oh! Please don't pick on me."

They assume that you are going to make them feel silly or make them look foolish. Always be aware of this. There is a fine line between amazing someone and frustrating or offending them. The best route to success is to win your audience over by creating a rapport with them – a feeling of mutual respect. This will become second nature if you are aware of it from the outset.

"Magic" is created by the magician, not by the trick. What does this mean? Simply that a trick with a poor performance is merely a puzzle. Combine a fun presentation with a great performance and you can create miracles.

misdirection

Read the sentence in the triangle. Read it again. Did you notice that the word "the" is printed twice? Chances are you did not. This is an example of how you can look directly at something and yet fail to see the whole picture.

Misdirection is a very important part of magic and is in itself a subject that could fill the whole of this book. All you need to know for now is that misdirection is the name given to the technique of directing someone's attention away from what you don't want to be seen. This may mean diverting their eyesight away from your right hand as it secretly places an object in your pocket, or making them think something is going to happen to a coin when it was the glass they should have been watching.

There is an art to making misdirection subtle and difficult to detect. When used correctly, it becomes invisible. Later on in the book we will be discussing the basics of misdirection in more detail, with particular relevance to some of the tricks you will learn. As you begin to use this psychological tool with confidence, you will be amazed at how much you can get away with!

Above: Practising can sometimes be very frustrating, especially when you are attempting some of the effects that require manual dexterity. Do not give up. Just like learning to ride a bicycle, the more you practise, the better you will get.

practice, patter and style

It is vital to practise if you wish to succeed with any of the tricks in this book. The best way to learn is to read through the instructions of a trick from beginning to end and then try it out step-by-step, as shown.

Once you have learnt the order of the moves, put the book to one side and practise by talking out loud and looking at yourself performing the trick in a mirror. You may feel silly doing this initially, but a mirror is the perfect way to see what your audience will see. Often you can correct your own mistakes by following this technique.

Patter is the term used to define the words that will accompany the trick. It is a very important aspect of your overall presentation and should be considered carefully. Plan everything you will say and how you will say it, even if the words seem obvious. You will create a more polished performance by doing this. Some tricks require you to talk through what you are doing; others may need a simple story to accompany the routine. Remember to put your personality into the performance.

Think about the kind of style you wish to create. Do you want it to be fun and comical, or serious? If you make the style an extension of your personality, you will find this easier.

magic shops

There are shops dedicated to selling magic all over the world, in places you would never imagine. Have a look in your local business directory to find out where your nearest shop is located. Magic shops usually keep fairly quiet about their existence, and only a few of them advertise widely in order to stop the merely curious from learning too many secrets.

Some magic shops are like Aladdin's cave – small, dark and mysterious. Others are modern, bright and spacious. There will be experienced demonstrators behind the counter ready to show you what each trick does, and they will be able to recommend certain tricks to you, depending on your ability. As well as individual tricks, you will see magic books not to be found on the shelves of your local bookstore. Many of the books written by leading experts in the field of magic will be too advanced for a beginner, but there are others written for the aspiring amateur. Videos and DVDs are the latest way of learning magic.

You will find all of these things and more inside a magic shop. You may also be surprised at who you meet in such places. I have often bumped into famous magicians who I recognized from their performances on television.

watch and learn

Next time you watch a professional magician, even if you know the secrets of each trick, admire the performance and try to see beyond the trick in order to understand what really makes the magic work. By now you will have realized that there is far more to being a good magician than you first thought, but many of the things we have discussed will eventually become second nature.

If this book inspires and encourages you to learn more about the art of magic, you will find a hobby that will fascinate you for the rest of your life. You are already on your way to learning some of the greatest secrets ever kept, and to creating moments of happiness and amazement for people everywhere. Your journey is just beginning…enjoy!

Below: The audience here is seen waiting to watch a magic show. It is often difficult for a lay person to appreciate how much time has been spent on planning and rehearsal in order to put together such a performance. In a theatre, atmospheric music and carefully designed lighting can change the mood and help to add drama to the performance. These theatrical tools are a vital ingredient for a full show of magic, where a variety of performance styles can often make the whole experience far more dynamic and therefore more enjoyable to watch.

magicians' equipment

Most of the magic tricks in this book require very little in terms of special props. Nearly all of the items needed will be found at home, and the special props that are required for certain effects can be made very easily, as will become apparent.

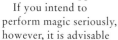
books

If you intend to perform magic seriously, however, it is advisable that you visit a local magic shop and invest in a few essential items. In a shop you will be able to talk to the experienced demonstrators behind the counter, and find out about tricks that involve the use of specially made props. Magic shops are also a good source for books, videos and DVDs about magic.

There are hundreds of magic shops all over the world that you may wish to visit in person or on the Internet; you will find some of these listed at the back of the book. If your area is not listed, take a look in your local business directory.

playing cards

These are available in many shapes and sizes. The two most common sizes are bridge size, approximately 56 x 87mm (2 x 3½in), which tend to be more popular in Europe, and poker size, approximately 63 x 88mm (2½ x 3½in), which are fairly standard in casinos and throughout the USA. It is essential that you purchase a good deck of playing cards. In several of the routines in this book you will require more than one deck, and to make the special gimmicks you will be required to destroy a number of duplicate cards.

playing cards

close-up mat

close-up mat

Your first purchase might be a close-up mat. This is basically like a large computer mouse pad with a rubber base and a spongy felt top which makes spreading cards and picking up objects much easier than other surfaces such as a wooden table. Close-up mats are available in a range of different colours and sizes. Once you have a close-up mat, you can perform magic anywhere and will not have to worry about finding a nice surface on which to work. In the event that a close-up mat cannot be found, then it is advisable to work on a soft surface such as a tablecloth.

silks, cups and balls

Colourful silk handkerchiefs, together with attractive props such as the Cups and Balls, may be worth your serious consideration. The aluminium cups shown here are specially manufactured for this one trick, and there are many different styles and sizes available.

brightly coloured silks

cups and balls

rope and string

For the magic tricks in this book, most types of rope or string will suffice. If you would like a more professional rope, magic shops will be able to supply you with hanks of specially made soft "magicians' rope". This is relatively inexpensive, and available in a wide range of colours. Try to find a rope that has a high cotton content, and one that is soft and flexible.

blue and white rope
and ball of string

stationery

In order to make some of the special props, you will need a few items of stationery, such as envelopes, paper, scissors, a scalpel, pen and pencils, and adhesives. Professional equipment is always available from your local magic shop, but it is fun to make up the various props. Also, constructing props yourself can often help you to understand how they operate.

envelopes, post-it notes, scissors,
scalpel, pencil, pen, glue stick,
reusable adhesive and adhesive tape

household items

General household items – such as silverware, napkins, glasses, matches, dice, thimbles and sugar cubes – are useful for many magic tricks. They are especially suited to "impromptu magic" because performances can be off-the-cuff, with little or no preparation necessary.

silverware, napkin, glass, matches,
dice, thimbles and sugar cubes

money

Banknotes and coins are props that are easy to find, and can be used for an enormous range of magic tricks. You do not need to have new banknotes – many routines require folding or even gluing them – but shiny new coins create the best impression and are easier to see than old coins.

banknotes
and coins

history of mystery

The story of magic dates back so far and is so interesting it could easily fill every page in this book. This chapter is not intended as a definitive account, however, but as a brief introduction to some of the most important events and names in magic's rich history, showing how the skills they developed and, in many cases, invented, helped to move the ancient art forward.

magic and magicians through the ages

It is difficult to pinpoint with accuracy exactly when magic began. To start with, we need to define what we mean by "magic". Man's ability to create fire could be described as a "magical" happening, but we are only concerning ourselves here with the type of magic used as a form of entertainment.

The earliest documented evidence to suggest a performance of magic was found in the Westcar Papyrus, written about 1700BC, which tells a story that goes back to about 2600BC. Dedi, an Egyptian magician, was summoned to entertain King Cheops. One of his tricks involved cutting off an animal's head and then bringing it back to life unscathed. Dedi was asked to do the trick again using a prisoner. Much to the king's disappointment, he declined to do so, but repeated the effect with an ox instead.

The Cups and Balls is often mistakenly considered to be the earliest magic trick. It features in what was once thought to be the earliest known illustration of a magical performance. Egyptologists have dated a painting on a wall at an Egyptian tomb at Beni Hasan as being between 2500BC and 2200BC. It depicts two people playing with four cups. Recently there has been much speculation whether the absence of balls in the painting nullifies the claim that it is indeed the Cups and Balls. It certainly is an ancient trick, however, and is still popular today. There are many variations, but the basic effect is that of balls magically passing from cup to cup, appearing and disappearing at the magician's will.

Above right: *Le Joueur de Gobelets* is an early engraving which suggests that the Cups and Balls has been a popular trick for street performers for a very long time.

Right: This late fifteenth-century painting by Hieronymus Bosch is called *The Juggler*. It is another example which highlights the popularity of the famous Cups and Balls. Magicians were often referred to as "jugglers", which explains the title of the painting. Did you notice the man in the back row stealing the purse of the person in front of him?

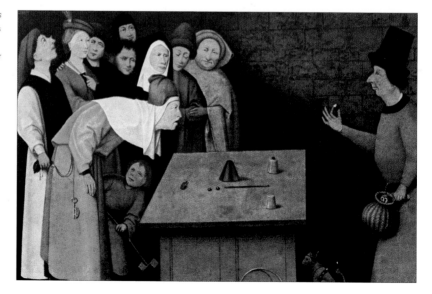

frequently performed for royalty. In 1783, while he was performing in Paris, Henri Decremps, a Parisian lawyer and amateur magician, exposed Pinetti's methods in a book. Ironically, the exposure only helped Pinetti's fame to spread, and he became even more popular. In 1784 he performed at the Haymarket Theatre in London, an important event because it marked the move of magic from the streets and fairgrounds to the theatre, inspiring a whole new generation of performers.

John Henry Anderson (1814–74) was a Scottish magician, often known as "The Wizard of the North". He was popular in Europe, America and Australia and was, prior to Harry Houdini, the most successful publicist in magic. Anderson was known for his large props, which were often made of solid silver. He amassed a fortune but lost it after several theatres in which he was working burnt to the ground, leaving him bankrupt.

By now, society had recognized magic as an art form. Its popularity and success continued into the next century as a steadily increasing number of magicians performed to larger audiences. In the days before motion pictures and television, magic was one of the most popular forms of live entertainment and performers generated enthusiastic responses wherever they went.

Left: John Henry Anderson became known as "The Wizard of the North". His daughter Louise accompanied him on stage.

Below: Isaac Fawkes was a regular performer at London's annual Bartholomew Fair. He is seen here producing many objects from an apparently empty bag.

The trick often finishes with the surprise production of large objects from beneath the cups – sometimes even live chicks and mice! HRH Prince Charles became a member of The Magic Circle in London in 1975 after visiting the society and performing this classic trick.

By the eighteenth century magic was a very popular form of entertainment. Isaac Fawkes (1675–1731) was responsible for generating much of the interest in Britain. He worked at large fairgrounds and gathered huge crowds for his incredible tricks, many of which relied on spectacular mechanical principles that were well ahead of their time. One of these mechanical marvels was an apple tree which blossomed and bore fruit in less than a minute. He became very famous, amassing a fortune before his death.

Giuseppe Pinetti (1750–1800), born in Italy, was another of the most important figures in the history of magic. Inspired by the success of Isaac Fawkes, he also displayed mechanical marvels. He was hugely successful wherever he appeared, and is known to have

magical inventors

Inventors are vital to the continuation of the art of magic and their revolutionary ideas often bring about great changes. Some inventors are also great performers, but many take a back seat and prefer to watch someone else breathe life into their creations. Here we take a look at some of the most important inventors in magic's history and those who are leading the field today.

Jean-Eugène Robert (1805–71) was born in France. He later added his wife's name to his own, becoming Robert-Houdin, and will forever be known as "The Father of Modern Magic". Robert-Houdin was a pioneer and innovator who opened his own Theatre of Magic in Paris in 1845, where he performed and thrilled audiences with his original work and amazing automata, including a version of Isaac Fawkes's tree that grew and bore fruit. He also wrote several books on magic, which were undoubtedly the best available at the time. His style and ideas were often copied by others but never equalled.

A century after Robert-Houdin's death, the French government issued a commemorative postage stamp to celebrate the life of their most famous magician.

Another French inventor was Buatier De Kolta (1847–1903). Although he performed frequently, his real strength was his ability to create and invent. He was responsible for some of the most incredible illusions of the time, some of which are still being used today. One example is the Vanishing Lady, or the

Above: Jean-Eugène Robert-Houdin was a mechanical genius and successful performer whose literary works inspired the young Harry Houdini.
Above left: This postage stamp was commissioned by the French government 100 years after Robert-Houdin's death in recognition of his achievements and as France's finest magician.

Right: Buatier De Kolta, one of magic's greatest inventors and also a fine sleight-of-hand magician. Many of his creations are used to this very day by the world's leading illusionists.

De Kolta Chair, as it is now known. A woman would sit on a chair in the centre of the stage. A sheet of newspaper was laid on the floor to show there was no trapdoor, and the woman was covered with a large cloth. As the cloth was whipped away, she vanished. This remains one of the most beautiful illusions to watch. Another of De Kolta's famous tricks was the Vanishing Bird Cage, in which a small cage containing a bird would be made to disappear without a trace. This particular trick was performed by illusionist Carl Hertz in 1921, who created a sensation when he vanished a bird cage for members of the House of Commons in England.

Servais Le Roy (1865–1953) was born in Belgium but moved to England at an early age. He was well known for his rendition of the classic Cups and Balls trick, and even more so for some of his inventions. These were revolutionary at the time, and are still used in one form or another by many large illusion acts all over the world. If one had to single out a particular illusion, it would have to be the Asrah Levitation. An assistant is covered in a thin sheet and made to levitate slowly from the ground to a position high in the air. The sheet is pulled away and the assistant melts away in mid-air.

The English magician Percy Tibbles (1881–1938) spelt his family name backwards, leaving out one "b", to become known as Selbit. He created many superb and widely used illusions. In about 1921 he performed a new invention of his that started a wave of excitement which was to spread around the globe. Sawing Through a Woman became the most famous illusion of all time. Selbit's American contemporary Horace Goldin was inspired by this illusion and quickly developed a variation called Sawing a Woman in Half. Since then, countless versions have been invented with a surprising number of different methods – with or without boxes, using large or small saws, and most recently using lasers.

Guy Jarett (1881–1972), born in Ohio, USA, was one of the most important inventors of the twentieth century. He was an odd man with many antisocial habits, but his knowledge of magic and his ability to create new and fresh methods for illusions remain unmatched. His 21-person cabinet became legendary. A small cabinet, barely large enough to hold five people, was

Left: Selbit was the creator of Sawing Through a Woman and many more wonderful illusions which are still in use today. He toured the British Isles and the USA, showcasing his incredible inventions.

shown empty. Despite the cabinet being isolated in the centre of the stage and off the floor, 21 people were made to appear from within. As a special effects consultant, Jarett provided illusions for several Broadway shows and for the most popular magicians of the time, who were thankful for fresh ideas. It was his idea to make an elephant appear on stage, and a similar method was used by modern superstars Siegfried and Roy. In fact, many of today's illusions work on principles devised and developed by this genius in magic.

Robert Harbin (1910–78) was born Ned Williams in South Africa. He moved to England and created a huge impact with his numerous inventions. Harbin is perhaps best known for the incredible Zig-zag Girl illusion. An assistant stands inside a small cabinet, which is then divided into three sections by two large, imposing blades. The middle section of the box is pushed over to one side, creating a sight that simply defies explanation. This is still one of the most popular illusions among performing magicians. Harbin was also a busy cabaret performer, working on cruise ships all over the world and at private events in London hotels.

Magicians today are as inventive as ever. Pat Page, Ali Bongo, Jim Steinmeyer, John Gaughan, Paul Osborne, Tommy Wonder, Juan Tamariz, Eugene Burger, Max Maven, Paul Harris and Michael Ammar are just a few of those who have helped to move the art of magic forward thanks to their incredible knowledge and sheer originality.

Left: Robert Harbin presenting his most famous illusion, the Zig-Zag Girl. It was to become one of the most popular and most performed illusions of all time. The original cabinet is currently on display at The Magic Circle Museum, London.

literary experts

Until the relatively recent introduction of videos and DVDs, magicians relied heavily on books for information about the art of magic. The first English book to include magic was published in 1584 and since then tens of thousands of books have been written covering every aspect of this ancient art. A plethora of new material continues to appear at an almost daunting rate, but a few literary works stand out as being particularly important to magicians of their time and to today's students and performers.

During the sixteenth and seventeenth centuries people who performed magic were often feared to be working in league with the Devil. As history books tell us, witchcraft was heavily frowned upon and was considered a crime punishable by death. In 1584 Reginald Scot published *The Discoverie of Witchcraft*, the first English book to expose the methods of magicians and to reveal how they used sleight of hand rather than evil powers to perform their magic. The book even contained the method used for decapitating animals as performed in Egypt by Dedi in about 2600BC. It caused huge controversy, and King James I ordered it to be publicly destroyed.

In the same year, 1584, a less well-known French book was published – *Clever and Pleasant Inventions* by J. Prevost. Unlike *The Discoverie of Witchcraft*, this book completely focused on the performance of magic as entertainment rather than denouncing witchcraft.

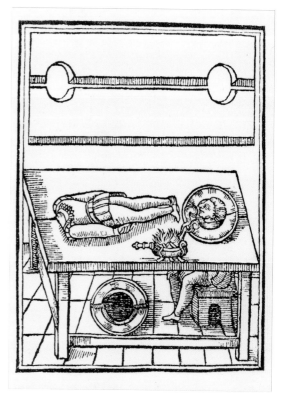

Above right: This diagram, taken from Reginald Scot's *The Discoverie of Witchcraft*, clearly shows the workings of a decapitation illusion. When the trick was performed, a curtain would cover the trestlework to hide the secret. It is just one of the many illusions exposed within this famous book.
Right: The original title page of Reginald Scot's book, which was fiercely condemned during the reign of King James I.

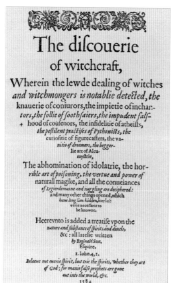

Between 1876 and 1911 Professor Louis Hoffmann (1839–1919) wrote numerous books. These included *Modern Magic*, *More Magic* and *Later Magic*, as well as English translations of earlier books by Robert-Houdin. It is said that Hoffmann's books have had more influence on the art of magic than any others. They revealed many secrets and were responsible for a whole new wave of magicians. His English translation of the *Memoires of Robert-Houdin* captured the imagination of a young man who was later to become the most famous magician of all time and whose name is synonymous with magic – Harry Houdini.

S.W. Erdnase wrote *The Expert at the Card Table*, published in 1902. This exposed the underhand methods of card cheats and introduced many of the sleight-of-hand techniques that today's card sleights are based on. His name spelt backwards is E.S. Andrews but the true identity of Erdnase still remains a mystery.

In 1910 the French magician J.B. Bobo wrote *Modern Coin Magic*, which is still regarded as one of the best reference books concerning this branch of the

Ricky Jay and Edwin A. Dawes, together with the late Milbourne Christopher and Walter B. Gibson, are all recognized for their important literary works which unveil many interesting and significant facts about magic's history. These names represent some of the leading experts in the field of magic history. Gibson was also known for having written a vast number of magic books for the amateur.

Many other magicians have written books and essays discussing the psychology of magic and "misdirection". They include Dariel Fitzkee, Eugene Burger, Tommy Wonder, Michael Ammar and Darwin Ortiz. With the exception of Fitzkee, who died in 1977, they continue to be major authorities in magic.

Today there is a steady stream of new magic books being published. Most of these can only be bought at magic shops and will not be found on the shelves of your local bookstore. Reading the ideas, philosophy and psychology of respected magicians is a rewarding experience, and a great opportunity to increase your knowledge and develop your skills.

Left: British-born Professor Louis Hoffmann wrote many books on the subject of magic, several of which became legendary.

Below: Harlan Tarbell was thought by many to be the most influential writer on the subject of magic after Professor Hoffmann. His huge *Course in Magic* continues to be recognized as one of the finest sets of books available. Tarbell was also a superb illustrator and fine performer.

art. The American Harlan Tarbell (1890–1960) was the author of *The Tarbell Course in Magic*. Originally designed as individual lessons which were sent regularly to subscribers, they were eventually bound in six volumes. The contents form one of the most comprehensive references to magical effects and methods, and include every type of magic imaginable. This huge set of books is highly regarded among professionals and amateurs alike. After Tarbell's death more volumes were added, and there are now eight volumes in total.

In 1949 Jean Hugard and Frederick Braue published *The Royal Road to Card Magic*. This book teaches a huge range of card techniques and an array of card tricks that would be received as well now as when they were written. It was considered to be the foremost book on basic card magic, though it has now been superseded by the work of the Swiss, Roberto Giobbi. Giobbi expertly documented advances in modern card handling in a later set of books, *Card College Volumes 1–4*, published from 1998 onwards.

magical venues

In 1873 the Egyptian Hall in London was the venue for regular performances by John Nevil Maskelyne (1839–1917) and George Alfred Cooke (1825–1905). These performers were known for their ability to weave their magic into short plays, which gave their tricks and illusions meaning and helped to provide a context for the magic. This clever concept can be seen in the work of some of today's great illusionists such as David Copperfield, who brings together music, dance, theatre and magic to incredible effect.

Maskelyne and Cooke's original show was due to last for three months, but Maskelyne went on to become a regular fixture at the Egyptian Hall for some 30 years, during which time he became part manager. Many of the world's great magicians had performed at this venue before him, but during this period it became synonymous with magic. He would invite singers, pianists and jugglers as well as other magicians to perform, thus making every show unique and therefore watchable over and over again. The Egyptian Hall became known as "England's Home of Mystery". It closed in 1905 but Maskelyne's success enabled him to buy a new theatre in which to continue his shows. St George's Hall, only a few minutes away from the old site, became "The New Home of Mystery". Shortly after the new venue opened, Cooke died and Maskelyne found a new partner, David Devant (1868–1941). Devant was considered one of the best magicians of the time and the duo became an even more successful team than Maskelyne and Cooke. After Maskelyne's death the theatre remained a magical showcase for the greatest performers of the day. St George's Hall was finally sold in 1933. It is now a hotel.

In 1905 a group of 23 magicians decided to start a magic club in London. The Magic Circle is now one of the world's most exclusive and famous magic societies. Early meetings took place in a room above St George's Hall, with David Devant as the society's first president. Its Latin motto "Indocilis Privata Loqui" roughly translates as "Not apt to disclose secrets", and any member who breaks this rule stands to lose their membership.

Above: The Egyptian Hall in London was originally a museum. It was built in 1812 and later became known as "England's Home of Mystery" when Maskelyne and Cooke became regular performers. It was a popular venue for many of the leading magicians of the time, until its demolition in 1905.

Left: The enchanting and awe-inspiring spiral staircase at The Centre for the Magic Arts, London. This is The Magic Circle headquarters, one of the most prestigious magic societies in the world. It houses a library, museum and theatre.

In 1998 The Magic Circle bought an old office block near London's Euston Station and transformed it into The Centre for the Magic Arts. Meetings are held every Monday evening, and the facilities include a library which boasts Europe's largest collection of books on the subject and a museum that houses some of the most important artefacts in magical history. The theatre is used regularly and often features shows that are open to the general public.

In 1963 the Academy of Magical Arts was established in Hollywood by William Larsen Snr. The Magic Castle, erected as its headquarters, is possibly the foremost magic building in the world today. It remains a private members' club and showcases leading magicians from around the world, who perform nightly. Soon after its opening, the Magic Castle became a mecca of magic and many of the great magicians relocated just to be near this home of mystery. More than a few of today's magic stars owe a great deal to the Larsen family, who continue to run this incredible club and to promote the good name of magic.

comedy magicians

Arthur Carlton Philps (1881–1942), known simply as Carlton, performed mostly in London's music halls in the early 1900s. He developed a unique style which made him a hit with his audiences. Carlton was incredibly skinny and his skin-tight black tights made him look even thinner; he also wore a bald wig and increased his height with platform shoes. He was known as the "Human Matchstick" and later as the "Human Hairpin". His very presence on stage was enough to set the audience laughing, and his comical throwaway lines made him into a commercial act that would be received as well in today's theatres as then. When the music halls began to close during the late 1930s and trade became slack, Carlton put on a lot of weight, which destroyed the very thing that made him so funny. Sadly his final years contained little to laugh about and he died having lost everything he once had.

Tommy Cooper (1922–84) was without doubt one of England's funniest men. After discovering early on in his career that his audiences found him more entertaining when he made mistakes, he created a character that will never be forgotten. Like Carlton before him, Cooper could make an audience howl with laughter without saying a word. The fact that he was a big, tall man with a face made for comedy probably helped. Always wearing his trademark fez, Cooper was a superb comedian who wrote some of the funniest lines and sketches, for example:

> I went to the dentist. He said, "Say aaah."
> I said, "Why?" He said, "My dog died!"

On 15 April 1984 Cooper collapsed on stage at Her Majesty's Theatre, London, and soon afterwards he died of a massive heart attack. The show was being broadcast live to viewers all over Britain. Most of the audience thought it was part of an elaborate joke and bellowed with laughter until the curtain dropped and it became clear something was very wrong. It was perhaps how he would have liked to have died – in front of his adoring fans. Britain, however, had lost an incredible comedian and magician.

American comedy magician Carl Ballantine (born 1922) became a well-known actor and magician throughout the United States after television catapulted his name across the nation in the 1950s. "The Great Ballantine", as he is known, performed on many of the top shows of the time including "The Ed Sullivan Show", "The Steve Allen Show" and "The Johnny Carson Show". Like Tommy Cooper, Ballantine realized early on in his career that his magic and style was best suited to comedy, and his act is a catalogue of disasters from start to finish. His superb timing and hysterical sight gags have made him a legend among comedy magicians.

The well-known American duo Penn and Teller (born 1955 and 1948 respectively) have been together since 1975. After ten years performing on and off Broadway, they shot to fame following many television appearances. They became known within the industry as "the bad boys of magic" due to their offbeat brand of humour and their apparent exposure of magical methods. Although their style would not be to everyone's taste, they have extended the boundaries of magic and comedy, and their numerous television specials have won several industry awards. Penn and Teller's busy schedule of live shows continues to amaze and amuse huge audiences wherever they perform.

Above: Tommy Cooper was one of Britain's funniest magicians and best-loved comedians. His trademark fez and recognizable laugh, together with many hysterical routines and sketches, left his audiences bellowing with laughter.

close-up magicians

The term "close-up" is used to describe the type of magic performed intimately for small groups of people. Compared to the other areas of the art, it is a fairly recent branch of magic which has become hugely popular and has seen a sharp increase in bookings for magicians at private parties, banquets and corporate events. Its popularity among magicians is probably due to the fact that expensive props are not necessary and there is no need for a stage or particular lighting. The beauty of "close-up" is that it can be performed anywhere and with virtually anything.

Nate Leipzig (1873–1939) was a Swedish-born magician who moved to America and became an important authority in close-up magic. Perhaps best known for tearing up a cigarette paper and restoring it in a very magical way, his techniques and effects are still studied today and remain in constant use.

The great Max Malini (1873–1942) was of Polish-Austrian descent but moved to America at a young age, where he became a wonderful performer of intimate magic. He was also very highly paid for his larger shows and became famous throughout the world during the 1920s when he gave many prestigious performances for royalty and heads of state. His astounding magic is still talked about and there is much to be learnt from his methods and philosophy. There is more information about Malini and his magic in the introduction to the chapter on Dinner Table Magic.

Fred Kaps (1926–80) was an outstanding Dutch magician who became famous within the magic fraternity in the 1950s. He was a role model for many future magicians – his skill and style were impeccable and his ability to change his performance to suit his audience was outstanding. As well as performing wonderful close-up magic, Kaps was known as a superb manipulator with a great sense of humour. His incredible sleight of hand ensured a faultless act that was enjoyed by millions of people all over the world.

Canadian Dai Vernon (1894–1992), famous for his rendition of the Cups and Balls, was a legend of magic affectionately known among his peers as "The Professor". He was quite simply regarded

Above: The great Max Malini performed for some of the most important people of his time. Several US Presidents, as well as royalty throughout Europe, enjoyed his magic. Many of Malini's tricks are still talked about, and even today one wonders how he could make such large objects appear from under his hat without anyone seeing how it was done.

as the absolute master. His close-up magic, at which he excelled, was of a quality rarely seen, and it is doubtful whether the close-up magic of today would be where it is without this wonderfully talented man, whose influence on magicians everywhere was substantial. Another of the most influential magicians of the twentieth century was Tony Slydini (1901–91). Originally from Italy, Slydini lived in New York and was the East Coast's answer to Vernon. Magicians would travel from all over the world to see him and to persuade him to teach them his techniques for "misdirection", which are still largely recognized and used to this day.

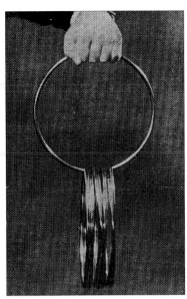

American Albert Goshman (1920–91) should be noted for two reasons. He was an exceptional performer who understood "misdirection" in a way very few people do. To watch a performance of his legendary coin under the salt shaker routine was an unforgettable experience. Despite two people watching as closely as they could, Goshman made coins continually vanish and reappear under the salt shakers, which were right in front of the spectators. He also built a factory which manufactured sponge balls for magicians. Sponge balls have become incredibly popular because of the interest they generate with audiences, and more importantly because of their ease of manipulation. The development of sponge-ball magic owes a great deal to Albert Goshman, but sadly it is believed that constant exposure to the fumes of the factory contributed to his death.

Today the field of close-up magic is led by the likes of Eugene Burger, Paul Harris, Juan Tamariz, Michael Close, Guy Hollingworth, Lennart Green, Daryl Martinez, David Williamson, Michael Ammar, Tommy Wonder, Ricky Jay, John Carney, Harry Lorayne and many more wonderful performers.

Left: Nate Leipzig, a true master of sleight of hand, travelled the world with his act. Leipzig would perform only for a small crowd he had invited upon the stage. The reactions of this lucky few were apparently enough to delight the rest of the audience – only a true showman could manage that.

illusionists

As well as illusionists such as De Kolta, Selbit and Servais Le Roy, there are others who were known predominantly for their incredible showmanship and dramatic presentations.

Born in France, Alexander Herrmann (1844–96) was the youngest of 16 children. His father Samuel and his brother Compers were both magicians, and by the time Alexander decided to build a career in magic, his brother Compers was already known as one of the best magicians of the day. However, the style Alexander adopted was well ahead of his time. Instead of the usual presentations associated with magicians, he injected a great deal of humour and fun into his shows. He quickly became the foremost magician of the mid-to late nineteenth century. "Herrmann the Great", as he became known, worked extensively in America, and later in England he performed large illusions regularly at the Egyptian Hall. By the time of his death he was so famous that he was regarded as a living legend.

The American Harry Kellar (1849–1922) belonged to the same era as Herrmann, and there was a bitter rivalry between them. Kellar filled the gap in the market after Herrmann died, touring his show all over the world. He was heavily influenced by England's master magician Maskelyne, and tried to purchase the method and rights to perform Maskelyne's levitation illusion. Maskelyne declined to sell, but this was the first of many effects to appear suddenly in Kellar's repertoire with remarkable similarities to Maskelyne's creations. After Kellar's retirement in 1908, he announced Howard Thurston as his successor. Thus Howard

Above: Alexander Herrmann had a huge family and a background steeped in entertainment. He was the most famous of the Herrmanns, and created a sensation with his act. He toured successfully around the globe, often performing for royalty.

Above: Harry Kellar was regarded by many as America's leading magician. He toured his illusion show all over the world.

Right: Howard Thurston's impressive illusion show assured him of rapid success.

Thurston (1869–1936) became America's leading magician. He updated Kellar's show and added fresh illusions, including the vanish of a motor car. He was a huge success, and his repertoire became so extensive that it took ten railway carriages to transport all of the necessary props and scenery.

William Ellsworth Robinson (1861–1918) was born in New York. After a fairly uneventful beginning to his magical career he decided to create a Chinese act, influenced by the famous Chinese magician of the time, Ching Ling Foo. Robinson chose the "oriental" name Hop Sing Loo but soon changed it to Chung Ling Soo, the name that was to make him famous. Soo's act was as colourful and visual as it was entertaining, and proved very successful with his audiences. He made bowls full of goldfish materialize from nowhere and caused money to appear in abundance.

Although Soo was considered a competent illusionist, it is not this for which he is famous. The one trick that will forever be associated with Chung Ling Soo is the notorious Bullet Catch, in which a bullet is marked for later identification and shot from a gun aimed at the magician. The marked bullet is, incredibly, caught before it has a chance to do any harm and the markings on it are then verified. On 23 March 1918 at the Wood Green Empire in London, Chung Ling Soo was shot on stage after the gun misfired. He was rushed to hospital but died the following morning. He was not the first magician to lose his life performing the Bullet Catch, but he was certainly the most famous.

Above: A poster depicting Chung Ling Soo performing the famous Bullet Catch which finally killed him after the gun misfired.

German-born Sigmund Neuberger (1872–1911), later known as "The Great Lafayette", was a superb and very dramatic performer who worked all over the world. He was famous for incorporating large animals into his illusions. The scale of these shows had never been seen before and he was one of the highest-paid performers. Beauty, one of the dogs he used in his act, was a gift from Houdini. Lafayette's love for his animals, especially Beauty, was obsessive and frequently mocked. He died on 4 May 1911 when the Edinburgh theatre he was performing in burnt to the ground during a performance.

Horace Goldin (1873–1939) was born Hyman Goldstein in Poland. He moved to America in his teens and became known as "The Whirlwind Illusionist" because of the speed at which he rushed through his repertoire. Goldin's most famous illusion was Sawing a Lady in Half. In his first version, his assistant was placed inside a box which was then sawn in half and split down the middle before being reassembled. In 1931 he presented a new version which disposed of the boxes and gave the audience a clear view of a huge circular saw ripping through the lady's midriff. The publicity generated by this spectacular illusion was incredible, and Goldin travelled the world with his show. He died suddenly after a performance at the Wood Green Empire in London, on the same stage where 21 years earlier Chung Ling Soo had been shot dead during his bullet-catching routine.

Above: The Great Lafayette, one of the highest-paid performers of his time, with his beloved dog Beauty, a gift from his friend Harry Houdini.

Bess, tied and bound. It was, as you can imagine, a staggering illusion and one that has stood the test of time. Modern versions of it are still performed frequently by many of today's illusionists. One particular act, The Pendragons, are able to effect the change faster than anyone else in the world, in under half a second!

Before long Houdini was known specifically for his escapology, and often offered large monetary rewards to anyone who could produce a pair of cuffs from which he could not escape. His escapes from milk cans, safes and prison cells excited, amazed and thrilled audiences the world over. Another of his most famous illusions was the Chinese Water Torture Cell, in which he was shackled and placed upside down inside a tall glass-walled cabinet filled with water. Despite the impossibility of the situation, Houdini was able to escape from the confines of the tiny cabinet. The publicity he generated was huge, and he sustained a continued and successful performing career until 22 October 1926. One of his incredible abilities was to withstand punches to the stomach without discomfort, but on this occasion he was struck without warning and suffered a ruptured appendix. Houdini bravely continued his engagements until he could no longer stand the pain. Peritonitis had set in and a week after being punched, at the age of 52, one of the greatest showmen on earth passed away. In death he became even more famous.

Harry Houdini (1874–1926) was born Ehrich Weiss in Budapest. Soon after his birth the Weiss family moved to Appleton, Wisconsin, USA, and it was here during his teens that Ehrich developed a keen interest in magic after reading the *Memoires of Robert-Houdin*. Adding an "i" to the end of this great magician's name, he changed his name to become Houdini. He married Wilhelmina Beatrice Rahner, known to all as Bess, and together they toured Europe with an act that quickly established Houdini as a sensation wherever he went. One of the illusions most associated with Houdini is Metamorphosis. Houdini would be handcuffed and tied up inside a sack, then placed in a large trunk which was locked shut. A curtain would be pulled around the trunk and Bess would tell everyone to watch carefully as she entered the curtained enclosure. Within seconds the curtains would open and Houdini would be seen standing free of the shackles, ropes and cuffs that had bound him only moments earlier. The trunk was unlocked, the sack opened and there inside would be

Above left: An early Houdini poster showing the master escapologist bound by chains. He was possibly the greatest publicist in the history of magic. Almost a century after his death, he remains famous all over the world. **Right:** Harry Blackstone Snr was a popular illusionist whose name became synonymous with magic throughout the USA during his lifetime and continued to remain known as a result of the highly successful career of his son, Harry Blackstone Jnr.

In 1918 Henri Boughton (1885–1965) changed his name to Harry Blackstone. He was America's next greatest illusionist after Thurston. As his show grew so did his repertoire, which included the incredible vanish of a horse and Sawing a Lady in Half with a huge circular saw (similar to Goldin). He was also a master of more intimate magic, which he would perform in front of the stage curtains while the next big illusion was being set up. Two of the smaller illusions associated with him were the Dancing Handkerchief, in which a borrowed handkerchief was caused to come to life, bouncing, squiggling, squirming and floating across the stage before being handed back to its startled owner, and the vanish of a canary from a bird cage held by several children from the audience.

The name Blackstone continued to be associated with magic for many years thanks to his son, Harry Blackstone Jnr (1934–97). Harry toured a smaller show in the 1960s and 70s before reproducing his father's show with some new illusions and touring it across America. He became a prominent magician on American television and a well-known and respected celebrity. He is remembered for his incredible Floating Light Bulb, which glowed, levitated and floated across the stage before sailing out just above the heads of the audience.

Few dispute the assertion that American Channing Pollock (born 1926) was one of the greatest manipulators of the mid-1900s. This suave, handsome man handled cards, coins, billiard balls and doves with a style and panache never seen before. His incredible production of doves started a whole line of copycat acts, but although many magicians strive to reach the standard of Pollock's dove productions, few succeed. It is Channing Pollock we have to thank for one of today's top manipulators and illusionists. Lance Burton (born 1960) was inspired by the work of Pollock, and is one of the few magicians who have managed to equal his incredible skill. Burton's shows in the theatre built especially for him at the Monte Carlo in Las Vegas continue to astound audiences twice daily. His repertoire includes a version of the act that won him the FISM Grand Prix in 1982. FISM is the biggest and most important magic convention in the world and the enormous competition held every three years is the Olympics of magic. Burton's illusion show enables a modern audience to appreciate what audiences in the days of Thurston, Kellar, Goldin and Blackstone Snr must have felt. He is one of the leading showmen of magic today.

Siegfried and Roy (born 1939 and 1944 respectively) were perhaps the most successful megastars and illusionists in the history of magic. Their incredible show was the main attraction at the Mirage, one of the biggest hotels in Las Vegas, and their performances were always sold out. At one time it was the most expensive show ever to be produced, with a cast of hundreds. The two German-born magicians met in the early 1960s and worked on cruise ships around the world before landing their very own show in Vegas in the mid-70s. Their sensational illusions used large white tigers and there was no shortage of lions, elephants, cheetahs and other exotic animals, which were made to appear and vanish close to and often directly above the audience. Siegfried and Roy were one of the highest-paid acts in the world, but their show closed in 2003 when Roy Horn was attacked on-stage by a white tiger.

television magicians

David Nixon (1919–78) became Britain's first regular television magician. He was a kind, gentle and popular man whose weekly show made him famous throughout Britain from the 1950s to the 70s. Meanwhile, across the Atlantic the American Mark Wilson (born 1929) also became a television legend. His show "The Magic World of Allakazam" featured many top magicians, and ensured a future of stardom and fame which continues to this day.

Doug Henning (1947–2000) was born in Canada and became a magical superstar of the 1970s and 80s. Having studied under the greatest (Dai Vernon and Slydini), he developed several stage shows that changed the face of magic with a style never before seen. He did not look like the typical magician; in fact he looked as if he had just stepped out of the 60s in full Woodstock regalia, including tie-dyed tops and flared trousers. His journey in magic began to take off when he appeared in the 1974 Broadway show "The Magic Man" and he followed this debut with eight television specials which were, and still are, among the greatest shows ever caught on camera. The fact that the shows were filmed live is testimony to Henning and his team's incredible skill. Doug Henning became a

sensation in America, touring with an awesome illusion show until he decided to leave his life of showbiz to live in India, where his religious studies became the focus of his life. He had begun work on designing a transcendental meditation theme park in Ontario, but sadly died before his dream could be realized.

David Copperfield (born 1956) was born David Seth Kotkin in New Jersey. After developing an interest in magic at the age of ten, he knew there was only one thing he wanted to do. He started his career on stage in the Chicago version of "The Magic Man" and was soon signed up for his own television special, the first of many which catapulted him to fame. His sensational style and stage presence, together with his groundbreaking illusions, keep audiences on the edge of their seats. He is one of the world's highest-paid entertainers and also one of the busiest, performing over 500 shows a year.

Copperfield made a name for himself by performing illusions that captured the world's imagination. In 1981 he vanished a Lear jet and two years later he caused the Statue of Liberty to disappear. This illusion was the biggest ever performed at the time and attracted huge television audiences. These grand-scale illusions became a necessity to Copperfield's television specials and fans were eager to see what he would do next. Among other stunts, he walked through the Great Wall of China and levitated and vanished an Orient Express railway carriage. David Copperfield has become one an icon in magic and will always be regarded as a leader in the field.

Above right: Doug Henning was famous for his live television shows, tours and his trademark wacky 60s-style outfits, such as the flamboyant one worn here.
Below: David Nixon became Britain's first successful resident television magician. His show "It's Magic" featured many top magical acts from around the world.

David Blaine (born 1974) represents a new wave of magicians. Breaking with tradition, he successfully stripped magic of its glamour and pretentiousness, showing the world that magicians do not need a stage with trapdoors, expensive sets and careful lighting to perform miracles. Blaine takes his magic on to the streets and performs for unsuspecting members of the public. The television crew captures the surprise of his spectators, and this unique approach has made him immensely successful in a relatively short time. He is currently creating the kind of publicity and awareness that has not been seen since the likes of Houdini. Blaine is known around the world thanks to the power of international media and repeats of his television specials, which are aired across the globe. He is known for his ability to read people's minds, for levitating himself off the ground and for publicity stunts such as being buried alive for five days, standing in a block of ice for over 60 hours, standing on top of a pole for 35 hours and starving himself inside a suspended perspex box for 44 days. One thing is certain – his image is fresh and his style unique. Trends in magic will change, but for now David Blaine is one of the most talked-about magicians of our time.

Paul Daniels (born 1938) became Britain's most famous magician shortly after he hit the television screen in 1970. His cheeky banter was a huge contrast to the style of David Nixon, and his catchphrase "You'll like it, not a lot but you'll like it!" was an instant success with the public. In 1979 he appeared in the Royal Variety Show and his weekly television slot "The Paul Daniels Magic Show" pulled in huge viewing figures for over ten years, winning many industry awards including the Golden Rose of Montreux. He later married his long-term assistant Debbie McGee and the husband-and-wife team became a celebrity couple recognized all over Britain. Daniels was without doubt one of the most talented magicians of the late twentieth century and a major influence on British magic.

Although not publicly famous worldwide, Luis de Matos of Portugal, Juan Tamariz of Spain and Silvan of Italy are all superb magicians, well known in their own countries for their television shows. De Matos is a suave and elegant performer of close-up magic and larger illusions, often creating mini-playlets complete with incredibly designed sets comparable in style to David Copperfield's. Tamariz is one of the most talented card magicians in the world today. His regular television shows are popular with his audiences, who recognize him as one of Spain's top television personalities. Silvan, like Luis de Matos, is an all-rounder, performing huge illusions as well as incredible close-up magic.

Above left: Paul Daniels is one of Britain's most successful television magicians, responsible for inspiring a new generation of conjurors during the 1980s and 90s.
Below: American street magician David Blaine stood inside a block of ice for over 60 hours as one of his feats of endurance.

close-up magic

In this chapter you will find over 40 magic tricks. Most of these routines use ordinary objects that can be found around the house, and several of them can be performed without any preparation at all. While some use simple sleight-of-hand, others require a minimum amount of skill. Once you have learnt a few of these close-up tricks, you'll be able to perform to an audience in no time.

up close and personal

Performed directly in front of the spectator, close-up magic uses small, familiar props such as banknotes, coins, handkerchiefs, pens, fruit, keys, playing cards, string, and lots more besides. As soon as magicians learnt to manipulate these small objects they began using them in tricks, although the term "close-up magic" did not come into use until the 20th century, when its rise in popularity was assisted by several magicians who inspired a generation of magic artistry.

Dai Vernon (1894–1992) was a Canadian-born magician who moved to the USA and worked as a silhouette cutter before his magic began to impress all who saw him. Early in his career he baffled Harry Houdini, who used to boast that he could not be fooled, with one of his sleight-of-hand tricks. Even though he repeated it over and over again (some say seven times) Houdini could not see how Vernon accomplished his miracle. During the 1960s Vernon moved to Los Angeles to spend as much time as possible at the Magic Castle in Hollywood, and people travelled from all over the world in the hope of spending even a small amount of time with this master of magic, who became affectionately known as "The Professor". His most famous tricks were his versions of the classic Chinese Linking Rings and the legendary Cups and Balls. The urn containing his ashes remains on display at the Magic Castle, and he will always be one of the most important names in magic's history.

The Expert at the Card Table by S. W. Erdnase, published in 1902, explained many previously unknown card moves and secret ways of cheating at card games. The biggest mystery of all, however, is the identity of the author, since S. W. Erdnase never existed. Spelling the name backwards gives E. S. Andrews, which could be a clue, but to this day no one knows who really wrote the work.

This revolutionary book gave fresh insights to many card tricks and among the many people who may have been inspired was Ed Marlo (1913–91). Marlo could perform magic with all kinds of objects but specialized in playing cards. His techniques were so far ahead of their time that he quickly became a major authority in his chosen area, publishing over 2,000 of his sleights and tricks. It is worth noting that many gambling cheats have used similar moves, and in the early 20th century crooked gamblers and magicians sometimes exchanged ideas. In fact, Dai Vernon searched extensively for notorious card cheats in order to learn their secrets and apply them to his magic tricks.

Another legendary name in close-up magic is Tony Slydini (1901–91). Originally from Italy, this famous magician moved to the USA around 1930 and was the East Coast's answer to Dai Vernon. Slydini was a master of misdirection and applied layers of psychology to his magic to enhance his illusions. He was one of the first to teach his use of psychology as part of his overall strategy for bringing out the artistry in magic, and his methods are still used and respected today. One of his most important messages was to *be natural* when executing a sleight. Your hand may be secretly holding a coin, but if you hold your hand in a natural way no one will guess. Of course, when you think about doing this it is actually quite difficult: if you try too hard it inevitably looks unnatural. Try it. Rest a coin on the tips of your curled fingers and hold your hand in such a way that it looks empty. Not easy, is it?

Above: Ricky Jay is of the world's finest exponents of sleight-of-hand. He is also an established actor and has appeared in many classic films, including as the villain Henry Gupta in the James Bond blockbuster *Tomorrow Never Dies*.

Slydini inspired a whole generation of magicians to increase the power of their magic by acting naturally and applying psychology. In a sense, his work is the antithesis of the popular notion that the hand is quicker than the eye. Slow moves can be just as deceptive if they are performed well.

Today, close-up magic is the most popular area of magic. This is because it costs very little to learn a simple trick – the only real investment is time – and opportunities to perform are increasing. In an age in which people frequently spend vast sums on entertaining there is scope to make a decent wage performing close-up magic at private parties and corporate events.

Advances in techniques and technology over the past 50 years have led to a massive growth in the magic industry. Almost daily there are new tricks to learn and buy, but far too many are simply poor copies or so-called improvements of existing tricks.

The reality is that many are not improvements at all, but backward steps. It is too easy for anyone to blitz the magic fraternity with a never-ending stream of inferior products. But while hobbyists and even some professionals are happy to perform tricks using specially made gimmicks in place of sleight-of-hand, there are still those who prefer to do things the old-fashioned way.

There are many brilliant close-up magicians around the world today. It would be impossible to name them all, but among the most respected are Ricky Jay, Bill Malone, Michael Ammar and David Roth from the USA, Juan Tamariz from Spain, Guy Hollingworth from Britain, Lennart Green from Sweden and, until his death, Holland's Tommy Wonder.

Every three years the world's finest magicians gather at a convention called FISM (Fédération Internationale des Sociétés Magiques). Held in a different country each time, this is the Olympics of the magic world. Among the most exciting events are the competitions, at which the top talents compete for the FISM Grand Prix. Competing in The Hague in 2003 was one of the most nerve-wracking experiences of my own performing career. I was placed joint second in the micro magic category with Shawn Farquhar from Canada. The winner was America's Jason Latimer.

Some of the greatest magicians in the world will have performed many of the wonderful magic tricks in this chapter. Now it is your turn to learn them and begin your journey as a close-up magician. Practise hard and – who knows? – maybe *you* will be a future FISM award winner. After all, everybody has to start somewhere.

pen-go

A pen is wrapped up in a piece of paper and the paper is slowly torn into pieces, the pen having vanished into thin air! Actually it doesn't disappear into thin air – it flies up your sleeve, but no one sees it go.

The pen is on a special gimmick known to magicians as a "pull". It's best to use this trick as part of a longer sequence or routine that requires the spectator to write something.

1 Attach the lid of a pen to a piece of elastic approximately 30cm (12in) long (depending on the length of your arm). At the other end tie a safety pin. You will also need a piece of paper a little longer then the pen.

secret view

2 Fasten the pin inside the top of your right sleeve, so that when the elastic is loose the pen hangs just below your elbow. When you are ready to begin you will need to pull the pen down your sleeve secretly and hold it by the lid. Pull the pen out of the lid when handing it out for use. When it is returned, re-cap the pen, ensuring the elastic stays hidden behind your right wrist.

secret view

3 Begin to wrap the paper around the pen, making sure that the elastic is still hidden from view from the front. This picture shows the starting position as seen from behind, with the pen at one corner of the paper.

4 From the spectators' point of view the elastic is completely hidden by the back of your hand.

secret view

5 Wrap up the pen by rolling the paper loosely around it.

secret view

6 Hold the pen and paper loosely in your right hand.

secret view

7 Allow the pen to slip out of the paper and up your sleeve. The tube of paper will hold its shape.

8 Rip the paper tube in half and then tear it into smaller pieces. Finally, throw the pieces of paper up in the air for a dramatic finish.

let there be light

You show the spectators an ordinary light bulb, which you then screw into your empty fist where it immediately begins to glow. After a few seconds it "switches" off and you hand the light bulb to the spectators *so that they can check it has not been prepared in any way. You show your empty hands and take your well-deserved applause. This trick also requires a "pull".*

1 Prepare a pull by tying one end of a piece of elastic approximately 30cm (12in) long (depending on the length of your arm) to a safety pin and the other end to a miniature flashlight. The flashlight needs to be one that operates at the push of a button rather than with a switch that needs to be pushed up or down. You will also require a frosted light bulb.

2 Fasten the pin inside the top of your right sleeve so that when the elastic is loose the flashlight hangs just below your elbow. Hand the light bulb out for examination. Meanwhile, secretly position the flashlight in your right hand, as shown above. It is important that you practise doing this in such a way that no one sees what you are doing.

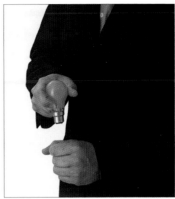

3 Retrieve the light bulb from the audience and hold it in your right hand, as shown. Show everyone that your left hand is empty and then hold it in a fist under the bulb.

4 This secret view shows how the tip of the flashlight is resting against the side of the light bulb. From the front the audience will not be able to tell what is really happening.

5 Slowly pretend to screw the bulb into your left hand. As you do so, activate the flashlight by covertly pushing the button with the fingers of your right hand. The bulb will glow just as if it were screwed into a light fitting.

6 Unscrew the light bulb from your fist, meanwhile turning off the flashlight, and show that your left hand is still empty. ▶

7 As you are showing your left hand, release the flashlight from your right hand, allowing it to shoot up your sleeve and out of sight.

tip *This could also make a great stage trick, and if you wear the special pull at all times you can even remove a bulb from a table lamp to do the trick at a moment's notice. Of course, if you do this you must make sure the lamp is switched off and unplugged before you remove the bulb and always replace it afterwards. Also remember that if the light has been on for a while the bulb will be extremely hot!*

8 Finally open both hands wide, showing the audience that there are no secret gadgets to be seen in your hands.

rising ring on pencil

A borrowed ring is placed over a pencil that is held vertically by the magician. Slowly and eerily the ring begins to climb the pencil until it reaches the top. Considering how easy this trick is to do, it is incredibly effective and will fool most people.

1 To set up the trick, take a pencil with an eraser on the end and with a sharp knife carefully make a slit in the middle of the eraser.

2 Take a length of very thin fishing line or thread (the thinnest you can find) and tie a small knot in one end, wedging this knot into the slit. (Thick black thread was used in these pictures so that you can see how the trick works.)

3 Attach the other end of the thread to a safety pin and fasten the pin to your belt loop or waistband. The thread should be approximately 50cm (20in) long, but you will need to experiment to find a length that suits you.

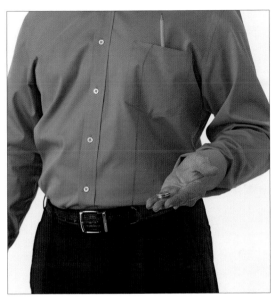

4 Put the pencil into your breast pocket. Carrying it in this fashion means the thread will not get in the way.

5 Remove the pencil from your pocket, borrow a ring and drop the ring over the top of the pencil and the thread. The fine thread will remain unseen.

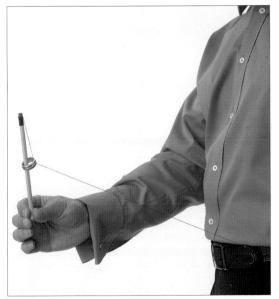

6 Make a magical gesture with your left hand while you slowly move the pencil away from you, tightening the thread. The ring will rise up the pencil.

7 When the ring reaches the top remove it and hand it back to the owner. Either replace the pencil in your pocket or move the pencil away from you, secretly pulling the thread out of the eraser in order to use the pencil for something else.

gravity-defying ring

A rubber band is broken and a borrowed ring is threaded on to it. The band is held between both hands at an angle of approximately 45 degrees. The ring slides up to the top of the band, uncannily defying the laws of gravity. You must try this out, as it is one of the most convincing illusions you are ever likely to see; the first time I saw it I was completely fooled.

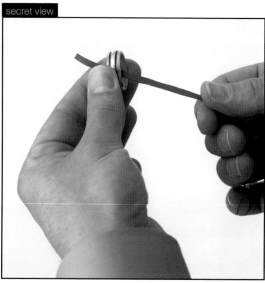

1 Choose a medium-sized rubber band with no imperfections, and break it. Hold the ring in the fingertips of your left hand and insert the top 2cm (¾in) of the band through the ring.

2 Notice how the band is pinched between the left forefinger and thumb, with the back of the hand towards the spectators, while the ring also remains pinched.

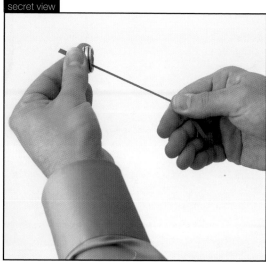

3 Now pinch the band just under the ring with your right finger and thumb.

4 Pull the band taut. Most of the band is hidden in your right hand.

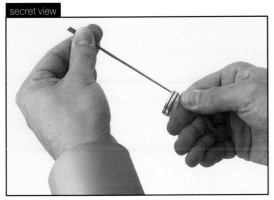

5 Allow the ring to drop down the band to rest on the index finger of your right hand.

6 From the front it looks as if you are holding the band by the two ends. In fact, what the spectators are seeing is about 2cm (¾in) of the band stretched to look like the entire band.

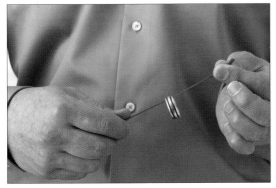

7 Hold the band at an angle of 45 degrees and slowly release the pressure of the right finger and thumb. The ring will adhere to the band and as the band retracts the illusion is that the ring is climbing up the band.

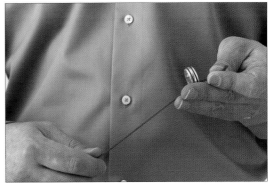

8 As soon as the band has been allowed to retract as much as possible the fingers of the left hand complete the illusion by reaching for the ring, sliding it off the band and handing it back to the owner.

9 Finish by displaying the ring and the band held in your fingertips and handing them out for examination.

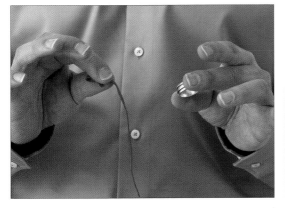

tip *The band must be released slowly and smoothly for the ring to climb steadily. Experiment with different thicknesses and sizes of rubber band, as some work better than others for this trick. The weight of the ring can also make a difference, so try using different ones, then use the combination of ring and rubber band that works best.*

the Bermuda triangle

Three pencils are laid on the table in the shape of a triangle. A small ship placed in the middle and covered with a glass mysteriously disappears, as does the glass. The whole trick is presented as a demonstration of how things seem to disappear inside the famous

Bermuda triangle. This trick is actually two tricks put together. You can do just the first part if you wish, but running the two together makes a really great routine. The story about the Bermuda triangle turns a basic trick into an engaging presentation.

1 To set up the trick you will need several sheets of card (stock), three pencils, glue, double-sided adhesive tape, scissors, a pen, a glass and a sheet of paper.

2 Draw around the top of the glass on the card and cut out a disc that exactly matches the size of the rim.

3 Glue this to the rim of the glass, making sure that no edges stick out. This special addition to the glass is known as a "gimmick".

4 Place a small piece of double-sided tape in the middle of the the card disc and press down firmly.

5 Draw a small ship on another piece of card and carefully cut it out using a pair of scissors. The ship must be smaller than the surface area of the base of the glass you are using.

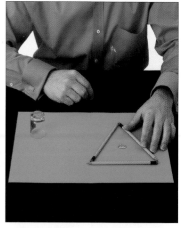

6 To set up the trick, arrange three pencils in a triangle on a piece of card that is exactly the same colour as your gimmick and place the ship in the middle. Place the glass, mouth down, on the card. (Notice how the gimmick becomes invisible.) Tell your spectators the legend that anything passing through the Bermuda triangle disappears.

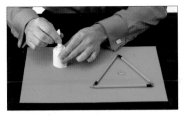

7 Take a sheet of plain paper and, being sure to keep the glass absolutely flat on the table, cover it as shown. The paper should not be wrapped too tightly around the glass.

8 Grip the glass through the paper and place both on top of the ship in the middle of the triangle.

9 Lift up the paper, leaving the glass on the table. The ship will have totally disappeared from view, perfectly hidden by the gimmick on the bottom of the glass. Explain that the glass represents a tornado passing through the Bermuda triangle, and that when the tornado was directly over the ship it disappeared.

10 Re-cover the glass with the paper, then lift up the glass, gripping it through the paper. The ship will stick to the double-sided tape on the gimmick and will be lifted up with the glass.

11 Explain that when the tornado moved away the ship was never seen again. Notice how the glass has been moved near the back edge of the table. While you are speaking, secretly allow the glass to slip out of the paper and into your lap. These are examples of techniques called misdirection and lapping.

12 The paper will retain the shape of the glass, even though it is no longer covering the glass. Replace this empty shell in the centre of the triangle, explaining that hurricanes sometimes come back.

13 Slam your hand down on the paper, flattening it and revealing that the glass has disappeared! Pick up the paper and explain that even a tornado can disappear in the Bermuda triangle.

14 If you have a small box of props on a chair to your side you can secretly take the glass off your lap and put it away as you pick up the other props from the table. Be sure to hold the sheet of card so that it masks the glass being secretly removed from your lap.

tip *You must practise the misdirection and lapping until you can do it without thinking about it or making it obvious.*

unlinking safety pins

*Two safety pins are clearly linked together but, amazingly, unlink
three times in a row under challenge conditions. This little routine is
an excellent one to learn as it can be performed impromptu or as part*
*of a larger set, perhaps with some of the other safety pin tricks in this
book, such as Pin-Credible and Safety Pin-a-tration. Although quite
difficult to follow initially, once you have the knack it is simple.*

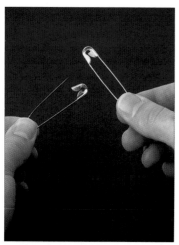

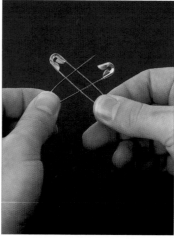

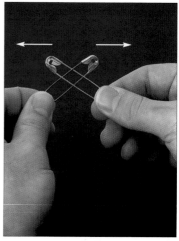

1 Hold one safety pin in your right hand
and open the other. Notice how the
open pin is oriented so that the head is to
the right and open at the top. (For clarity,
this pin has been coloured red.)

2 Thread this pin through the other.
Make sure that the head of the pin in
your left hand goes behind the other pin,
while the open part goes through the
middle. Close the pin.

3 Now hold the pins by their ends and
pull in opposite directions, as shown
by the arrows.

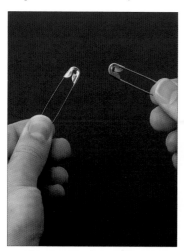

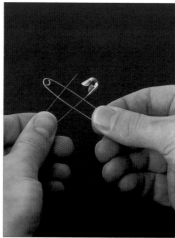

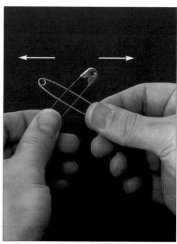

4 The spectator will be astonished that
they come apart.

5 You can repeat this trick with a small
change. Turn the pin in your right
hand the other way up, as shown.

6 Link the pins in the same fashion as
before and pull them apart.

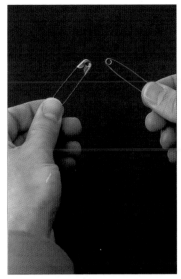 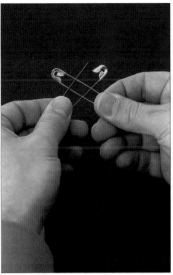 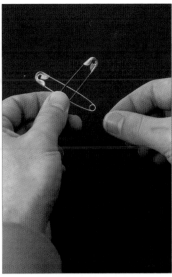

7 The safety pins will miraculously separate again! You can end the trick here, if you like, and hand out the safety pins for inspection, but it is a more impressive sequence if you continue and perform the grand finale.

8 For a finale, link the pins together one last time. However, as you can see, you don't actually link them together at all. The pin in your left hand goes over both sides of the other one, rather than going through the middle.

9 Pinch both pins between the tips your left thumb and fingers so that the pins stay together.

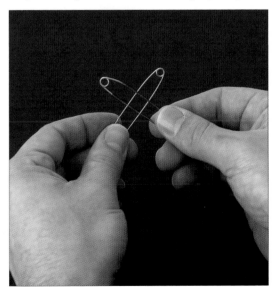 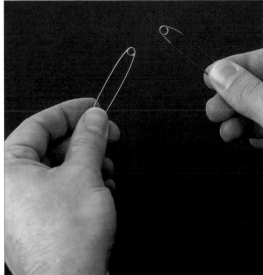

10 Turn the pins upside down, explaining that for the final time you will make the pins penetrate at the bottom instead of the top.

11 Pull them apart as the two pins apparently pass through one another one last time.

pin-credible

Five safety pins each have a different coloured bead attached. You turn your back on a volunteer and hold out your hands behind your *back. The volunteer places one of the pins in your hand and hides the rest. You are magically able to divine which colour was chosen.*

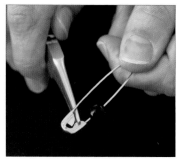

1 Find five beads of the same size but of different colours. You will also need five large safety pins and a pair of pliers.

2 Open all five pins and thread on the five beads. Now you need to prepare each of the pins in a special way that you will be able to recognize.

3 Clamp shut the head of the pin with the black bead, using the pliers.

4 Bend the tip of the pin with the white bead threaded on to it.

5 Bend the tip of the pin with the green bead in several places, to create a distinct surface.

6 Cut off the tip of the pin with the blue bead. Each pin now looks the same when closed but, when opened, is distinct enough for you to feel which is which .

secret view

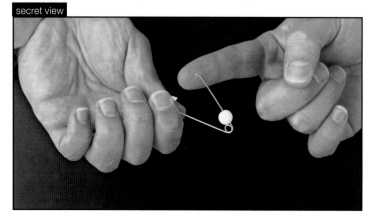

7 With the chosen pin behind your back, secretly open it as you turn to face the spectators again. Depending on what you can feel you now know which colour was chosen. Reveal it in a dramatic fashion and offer to repeat the trick.

safety pin-a-tration

A safety pin travels along the edge of a handkerchief before being removed without unfastening the pin. Practise this with an old *handkerchief until you understand the principles behind the trick. It will work consistently once you have mastered the moves.*

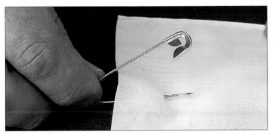

1 Secure a safety pin in the corner of a handkerchief, as shown in the picture above.

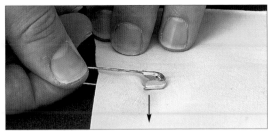

2 Hold the pin with the free top bar flat against the handkerchief, facing towards you. Slide the pin down to the far corner and the material will slip through the pin's fastener without damage. This is the first phase.

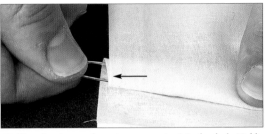

3 Turn the pin over three times, wrapping it in the cloth. Hold the cloth below the pin and pull it out with your right hand.

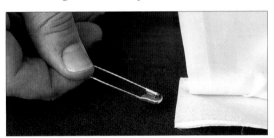

4 The safety pin will come free, still firmly closed, and the handkerchief will remain undamaged in every way.

domi-no-way

You show the audience that a prediction has been placed in a sealed envelope and set it to one side. Now you give two people a set of dominoes and tell them to arrange all the dominoes in any order they desire, ensuring that (just as in a proper game) each number matches *the number next to it. At the end you ask them to make a note of the two numbers at the end of the line of dominoes. When they open the envelope they discover, to their astonishment, that your prediction was correct; a baffling demonstration of your psychic abilities!*

1 The swindle is really very easy to carry out. Just remove one domino from a full set and make a note of the numbers. Then write this out as a prediction and seal it in an envelope.

2 Set the envelope on the table in full view and ask two people to set out the dominoes as described above.

3 So long as they adhere to the rule that numbers next to each other must match they will always end up with the two numbers in your prediction at the ends of the line. Show that your prediction matches.

escaping jack

You display a card with a hole punched through its centre, along with a small envelope with a matching hole. You place the card inside and secure it with a ribbon running through all the holes. Despite being secured with the ribbon, the card is pulled free and proves to be completely unscathed. If you like you could substitute the card with a cut out figure of Harry Houdini to add an extra element to the trick.

1 You will need an old playing card, a hole punch, a 50cm (20in) length of thin ribbon, a pair of scissors and an envelope that is just larger than the card.

2 Prepare the envelope by cutting a tiny sliver off the bottom so that the envelope is bottomless.

3 Punch a small hole in the centre of the envelope.

4 Punch or cut a small hole, using scissors or a knife, exactly in the centre of the playing card.

5 Show both sides of the card and the envelope to the spectators and slowly insert the card into the envelope until it is completely inside.

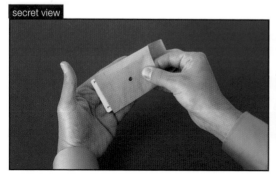

secret view

6 Give the playing card an extra push so that it starts to emerge from the bottom of the envelope, as shown. The left hand hides this from the front.

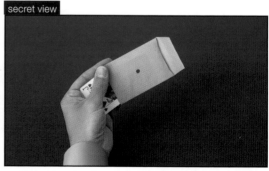

secret view

7 The card needs to be pulled out far enough to clear the hole in the centre of the envelope.

8 From the front everything looks as it should. Thread the ribbon through the holes in both sides of the envelope.

9 As soon as the ribbon is through the hole, push the card completely back into the envelope.

10 This view inside the envelope shows how the ribbon runs over the top of the card.

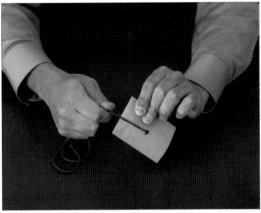

11 Seal the envelope and show both sides to the spectators so that they can see that the ribbon goes through it.

12 Grasp the envelope firmly in one hand and both ends of the ribbon in the other.

13 With a quick tug, tear the ribbon through the envelope.

14 Remove the card and show that it is totally unharmed.

tip *You will need to rehearse this trick several times before you attempt to perform it to an audience. It would be a good idea to prepare a number of envelopes at the same time as you can use each one only once.*

spooky matchbox

A matchbox on the back of your hand stands up and lies back down all on its own. Although this is one of the first tricks most magicians ever learn, very few realize just how good it looks. Try it, practise it *and you will have another great trick to perform with no extra props beyond the matchbox. As you gain skill you can make the box stand and lie down with minimal movement and under your control.*

1 Remove the cover of a matchbox and replace it upside down.

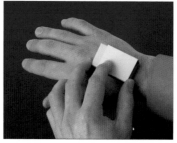

2 Hold out your right hand, palm down, and put the matchbox (partially opened) on the back of your hand. The open part of the box should be just behind your knuckles.

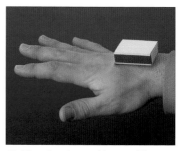

3 Now shut the matchbox, pushing down as you close it and trapping a small piece of your skin in the drawer. This looks painful but does not hurt at all. You may need to arch your fingers upward to facilitate the action. At the very least the fingers should be absolutely straight when you do this.

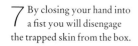
secret view

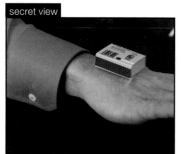

4 The view from this side clearly shows the flap of skin trapped in the drawer of the box.

5 By stretching open your fingers and flexing them as far apart as possible you will stretch the skin and the box will slowly stand up on its own.

6 Make a mystical pass with your left hand as it stands up, to add some misdirection and mystery.

7 By closing your hand into a fist you will disengage the trapped skin from the box.

tip *The trick looks much better when you turn your hand so that the box is viewed from the end opposite the trapped skin. Remember this when showing it to others.*

swapping checkers

On the table are a column of white checkers and a column of brown checkers. Each column is covered with a paper tube and the two are moved around so that no one knows which colour is under which tube.

A spectator makes a guess and the magician shows everyone whether they were correct. Regardless, with a magical wave the two piles change places instantaneously.

1 You will need seven brown checkers, seven white checkers and two sheets of paper. Paint the bottom of one brown checker white and the bottom of one white checker brown.

2 Create two piles of checkers, with the double-sided checker on the bottom of each pile.

3 Use a piece of paper to wrap each column of checkers. The paper should not be too tight.

4 Move the two columns around, sliding the two paper tubes on the surface of the table. Explain that if you don't watch closely it is difficult to know where each colour is. Ask someone to guess where the brown pile is.

5 Whichever pile they point to tilt both backwards and show the colours. Of course, what they actually see is the painted undersides of the prepared checkers.

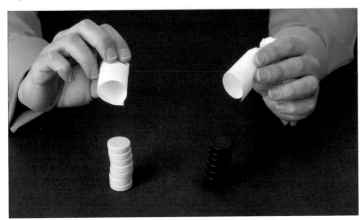

6 Make a magical gesture as you say that you are going to make the two columns of checkers change places. Lift the paper tube off each pile to show that this has happened.

tip *For an even better effect, scan one of each colour of checker on a computer, print them out at life size in colour, then cut around them and stick them to the bottom of the checkers.*

magnetic cards

Rubbing your hand on your sleeve to generate static, you proceed to stick over a dozen playing cards to your palm-down, outstretched hand. This trick may require a bit of practice in order to perfect it, *but once you get used to how the cards are positioned you will find it an easy matter to succeed every time. There are many different ways of performing this famous and popular trick.*

secret view

1 You will need to be wearing a ring for this trick. Place a toothpick under the ring and keep it hidden as you rub your hand on your sleeve, supposedly to generate static.

2 Hold your hand flat on the table and take the first card, placing it sideways in between the toothpick and your fingers.

3 Now add two more cards, as shown, sliding them between the first card and your fingers.

secret view

4 This view from underneath shows the configuration of the first three cards.

5 Carefully add more and more cards, making a haphazard petal-like pattern, until about twelve cards have been used.

6 Finally, slowly lift your hand into the air and all the cards will cling to your palm as if magnetized!

secret view

7 The secret view shows how the cards remain trapped by the toothpick against the palm of your hand.

8 Place your hand back on the table and use your other hand to separate the cards, disengaging the toothpick and leaving the normal cards to be examined by your now amazed spectators.

picture perfect

A sheet of paper is torn into nine pieces. Eight pieces are left blank and a spectator draws a simple picture on the ninth. The magician is blindfolded and by touch alone – apparently from psychic vibes – is able to find the piece of paper with the picture on it. To finish, the magician makes a quick sketch, still blindfolded, and the picture matches that drawn by the spectator.

1 Tear a sheet of thin card (stock) or paper into nine pieces along the lines shown here.

2 Ensure that the tears are not too neat – they should be as rough as possible.

3 Notice that the central piece of card or paper is the only one that has four torn sides. This is the key to this trick. Hand out this piece of card or paper and ask someone to draw a simple picture on it, keeping it hidden from you.

4 Meanwhile, blindfold yourself using a handkerchief.

secret view

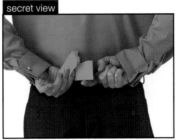

5 After the spectator has drawn the picture, ask them to mix all the papers together and then to hand them to you behind your back. Take each piece of paper in turn and feel the edges to determine which piece has four torn sides. This is the one with the picture on it. Bring it to the front and show that you found it.

6 If you are blindfolded with a handkerchief you will find that you can still see down the side of your nose, even if the blindfold is quite tight. Glance at the picture when you bring it to the front.

7 Make a quick sketch of the same subject while you are still blindfolded.

8 Finish by removing your blindfold and revealing that the pictures match!

sweet tooth

A small paper bowl is shown to contain four candies. It is covered with a second bowl and shaken. The candies are shown to have *somehow multiplied so that now there are seven. When the bowls are shaken once again only four remain.*

1 You will need two paper bowls, some double-sided adhesive tape, seven candies and a pair of scissors.

2 To prepare the trick, cut three small pieces of tape and stick three candies to the base of one of the bowls.

3 The positioning of these candies should look random.

4 In performance, hide the three taped candies by holding that bowl upside down on a surface. Show the other bowl, which contains four loose candies, to the spectators.

5 Cover the bowl containing the loose candies with the inverted bowl.

6 Now turn the bowls over three or five times. As you do so, the candies will rattle inside for all to hear. Because you have turned the bowls an odd number of times the bowl with the fixed candies will now be at the bottom.

7 Lift the top bowl, showing it to be empty and at the same time asking someone to count how many candies are in the bowl now. Of course there will be three more than before, as the ones that are glued to the base are now included in the count.

8 Finish by either nesting the empty bowl under the other one and removing and eating a candy, or placing the empty bowl over the one containing the candies, and turning the bowl an odd number of times so that the bowl with fixed candies is at the top. When you lift it off, only the four loose candies will be visible.

zero gravity

The mouth of a bottle of water is covered with a small piece of paper and inverted. The water remains inside the bottle. The paper is removed but the water still defies gravity. Finally, toothpicks are fed into the neck of the bottle, proving there is nothing to stop the water from gushing out. This trick takes practice to execute confidently and it's a good idea to practise over a sink.

1 You will need to make a special gimmick: a disc of clear plastic just a fraction larger than the mouth of the bottle you are using.

2 Punch a hole in the middle of the plastic and the gimmick is ready.

3 Take a small square of paper and dip it into a glass of water to wet it.

secret view

4 You must secretly hold the plastic disc under this piece of paper.

5 Place the wet plastic disc and paper against the mouth of the bottle and hold it tightly as you turn the bottle upside down.

6 Very carefully let go and you will find the paper and water remain suspended. Now remove the paper, leaving the disc in place.

secret view

7 This close-up view shows how the gimmick keeps the water in.

8 Insert a toothpick into the hole in the disc.

9 Watch as the toothpick floats to the surface of the water. This sight is incredible and it looks like real magic.

10 Finally, turn the bottle upright again.

11 As you do so, secretly remove the gimmick from the mouth of the bottle and hide it in your hand.

tip *This trick can be done close-up with care, as the disc is invisible at very close quarters. If you want extra reliability you can purchase a relatively cheap gimmick from a magic shop.*

card magic

Playing cards are internationally recognized symbols and there is a universal familiarity with them. For this reason, card tricks are one of the most popular forms of magic. The scope for creating illusions with a deck of cards is huge. As you will learn in the following pages, they can be made to appear, disappear, change colour, multiply, defy gravity and a lot more besides.

luck of the draw

Playing cards have a rich history of their own. The origins of the playing card are as mysterious as the beginnings of magic itself, and much of their history can only be speculated because of lack of evidence.

The first playing cards are thought to have been invented in the twelfth century in China, and from there their popularity spread quickly throughout the East. Playing cards probably began to appear in Europe at the end of the fourteenth century. They changed drastically as the original Eastern designs were replaced by European designs, which evolved as they passed from country to country.

It seems it was some time before it occurred to anyone that playing cards could be used for magic. A Spanish magician by the name of Dalmau performed card tricks for Emperor Charles V in Milan at the turn of the sixteenth century, and there is evidence to suggest that by the seventeenth century card magic was a popular form of entertainment. Queen Elizabeth I apparently enjoyed watching card tricks, and in 1602 paid an Italian magician 200 crowns to perform for her.

One of the greatest playing-card manipulators of the twentieth century was the Welshman Richard Pitchford (1894–1973), known as Cardini. His act involved the incredible manipulation of playing cards, billiard balls and cigarettes. The character he chose to adopt was that of a very elegant, well-dressed but slightly drunk English gentleman to whom strange things tended to happen. With his trademark monocle, Cardini acted as if he were as amazed at his antics as his audience. His act relied heavily on the Back Palm, which can be found at the end of this chapter. However, rather than producing just a single card, Cardini was able to produce a seemingly endless supply, one by one, several at once and in beautiful fans – even while wearing gloves.

Playing cards are available in many shapes and sizes. The two most common sizes are bridge size, approximately 56 x 87mm (2 x 3½in), which tend to be more popular in Europe, and poker size, approximately 63 x 88mm (2½ x 3½in), which are pretty much standard in casinos and throughout the USA. The other variant is the quality of the card itself. Different boards are used by different manufacturers – some are very hard-wearing and long-lasting, but others can be ruined in a matter of minutes. A poor-quality card will crack if you bend it; a good-quality card will bend out of shape but can usually be bent back again. It is recommended that before you begin this chapter you purchase several good-quality decks of cards.

Top: Cardini shown here with his wife Swan, who became part of his act. Many tried to imitate Cardini's style and repertoire but no one could equal the artistry of this master magician.

Above: Playing cards and tarot cards are universally recognized, but designs differ from country to country.

As well as the "you pick a card, I'll find it" type of effect, many illusions can be created using cards. You can predict which card will be chosen (Magic Time, Face Value), vanish cards (Back Palm, Card through Tablecloth), change cards (Changing Card, Card under Glass, Card to Matchbox, Find the Lady) and move cards without any visible means (Rising Card from Box, Versions 1 and 2).

Playing cards can generally be found in most homes and in many public places. It always pays to know a few card tricks so that when the opportunity arises you can be ready to spring into action!

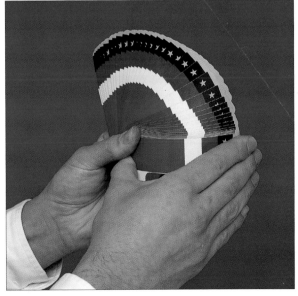

Above: Croupiers are trained to handle cards with incredible manual dexterity. Some of their skills are similar to those of a magician.

Right: A specially printed deck of magicians' fanning cards. The designs are bold and colourful, and every time the deck is fanned in a different way the pattern changes. Cardini used a similar deck for a sequence within his card act.

basic card techniques

For many of the techniques you will learn in the following pages it is important for you to hold the deck in the correct way so that you can accomplish the moves with ease and success. The grips shown below *are simple to master and should feel very very natural after just a little practice. Do not let the names of the various grips worry you. They sound more complicated than they really are!*

the hand

In order to fully understand how to handle a deck of cards, it is vital that you know which part of the hand is which.

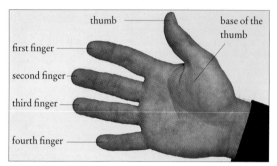

Although mostly self-explanatory, you may find that some of the terms used to describe the parts of the hand are unfamiliar to you. Therefore, before you continue, take a moment to check that you know which part of the hand is which.

dealing grip

In most instances you will be holding the deck as shown below. It is likely that you would hold a deck of cards like this instinctively.

The deck is clipped by the thumb in the left hand. All the fingers are located along the other long edge. Notice how the thumb is positioned on the top of the deck and how the cards bevel slightly. In this position it is possible for the thumb to push off cards singly from the top of the deck in readiness to be dealt to the table.

mechanics' grip

This variation of the Dealing Grip will allow certain moves to become possible. However, in most cases these two grips are interchangeable.

The difference between this and the Dealing Grip is that the cards are held more firmly, with the left first finger curled round the top short edge of the deck and the thumb positioned straight along the left edge of the deck.

biddle grip

This is another simple grip that you will need to become familiar with in order to perform many of the sleights in this book.

Hold the deck from above in the right hand. The thumb holds the deck at the short edge nearest you. The first finger is curled gently on top of the deck and the second and third fingers hold the deck at the short edge furthest from you.

dribbling cards

This is a simple flourish with a deck of cards. Learning to dribble will help you to become familiar with handling a deck comfortably. Aside from a simple flourish, the dribble can also be used to help make controlling a card more deceptive (see In-Jog Dribble Control).

1 Hold the deck in the right-hand Biddle Grip position with the left hand in an open position below.

2 With the right first finger (curled on top of the deck), apply pressure as the right fingers and thumb simultaneously release pressure, allowing the cards to fall rapidly, one after the other, into the waiting left hand. Try experimenting with varying distances between your hands.

3 Cradle the cards in the left hand and square them to complete the flourish.

two-handed spread

This is simply a neat way to offer cards for a selection. It is a very basic technique, but one with which you should become familiar from the outset. A nice spread of cards can be an early indication to your spectators that you are a polished performer.

1 Hold the cards using the left-hand Dealing Grip or Mechanics' Grip. The left thumb pushes the top few cards to the right.

2 The right hand approaches, gripping the spread of cards in the crotch between the thumb and base of the fingers. The left fingers and thumb begin to push several more cards over to the right, the right fingers providing support from beneath.

3 Continue to push the cards with the left thumb as your hands stretch into an arc. The result is a neat and uniform spread of cards.

4 From underneath the spread, you can see how the cards are supported by the outstretched fingers of both hands.

squaring the cards

This is a simple procedure to ensure that the cards are neat, tidy and perfectly square. Very often working with a deck of cards that have *been neatly squared will make the learning process easier and facilitate general card handling.*

1 Hold the untidy deck in the left hand. Start to square the cards so that you hold the deck in a loose Mechanics' Grip.

2 Approach the deck from above in the right-hand Biddle Grip position. Squeeze the short ends of the deck together. Slide the right hand back and forth along the short edges, then support the deck in the Biddle Grip position while your left hand moves up and down.

3 The result is a deck of cards squared neatly in the left hand.

swing cut

This is a very useful cut that is simple to learn and is referred to in many of the routines in this book. The top card of the deck has *been marked with a black border so that you can follow the sequence of the cut more clearly.*

1 Hold the deck in the right-hand Biddle Grip position.

2 Extend the first finger so that it rests near the corner of the deck furthest from you.

3 With your first finger, lift half of the cards and pivot them out to the left. (Your right thumb is the pivot point.)

4 With your left hand, pinch the top half of the deck in the crotch of the thumb.

5 With your right hand, place the original bottom half on top of the left-hand cards. Square the deck to complete the cut.

Charlier Cut

This is a pretty, one-handed cut. It is relatively easy to master with just a little practice. If you experience difficulty with it, try altering *your grip at the first stage. Through trial and error, the Charlier Cut will become second nature to you.*

1 Hold the deck high up at the left fingertips. Notice how the deck is held from all sides.

2 Releasing pressure from your thumb, allow approximately half of the deck to fall down towards the palm of your hand.

3 Your first finger should now curl under the deck and push the bottom stock of cards towards the thumb.

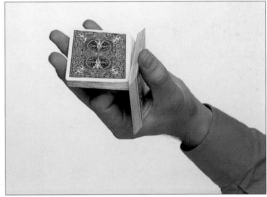

4 Let the bottom stock clear the top stock, which drops on to the curled first finger.

5 Close your thumb and fingers together to complete the cut. You can now use your right hand to help square the cards.

the glimpse

It is often necessary to secretly look at and remember a particular card in the deck. This secret move is known as a "glimpse". There are many ways to do this, depending on how the cards are being held.

Two "glimpses" are explained here, enabling you to learn the bottom card of the deck secretly, in an unsuspicious fashion. You may be able to think of other subtle ways too.

out of the box glimpse

An ideal time to "glimpse" a card occurs when you are removing the cards from the card box. Simply ensure that the deck is orientated so that it is pulled out of the box face up. Absolutely no attention should be drawn to the deck at this stage. If required, a casual Overhand Shuffle gives you an extra opportunity to move the "glimpsed" card to another location such as the top of the deck.

square and glimpse

This is another way to secretly look at the bottom card of the deck while handling the cards in a natural way. The "glimpse" takes place during the innocent action of squaring the deck. All the movements occur in one smooth action. Essentially you are squaring the deck while turning it from end to end. It is so subtle, your audience will never suspect a thing!

1 Hold the deck face down in the left hand, with the right hand supporting the deck in the Biddle Grip. The deck is squared.

2 With the right hand, lift the deck and turn it palm up by twisting at the wrist. Simultaneously turn the left hand palm down so that it can continue the squaring action along the long sides of the deck. The bottom card of the deck will now be facing you, and this is when you "glimpse" the card.

3 Almost immediately, lift the deck with the left hand and turn it palm up again as the right hand turns palm down, back to the start position. The hands square the cards one final time.

the Braue Reversal

A magician called Frederick Braue created this simple way to reverse a card in the centre of the deck. It is assumed the top card is to be reversed. Performed at speed, the Braue Reversal simply looks like a series of quick cuts and should not arouse any suspicion.

secret view

secret view

1 Hold the deck in right-hand Biddle Grip with a Thumb Break under the top card. For ease of explanation, there is a black border on the top card.

2 With the left hand, take the bottom half of the deck and turn it face up, flipping it on top of the right-hand cards.

3 Allow all the remaining cards below the break to fall into the left hand. These are again reversed and replaced under the right-hand cards.

4 Spread the deck between your hands. The result will be that the top card of the deck has been reversed in the centre.

tip *This method of reversing a card can also be used to reveal a selected card. Have a card returned to the deck and controlled to the top. Now perform the Braue Reversal and spread the deck on to the table to display one card reversed. It will be the one selected.*

the glide

This is a useful move, creating the illusion that the bottom card of the deck has been removed when in reality the second from bottom card is removed. This simple procedure is worth learning if only for Gliding Home, which is a wonderful trick.

secret view

secret view

secret view

1 Hold the deck in the left hand from above. The deck should be held by the long edges, thumb on the right side and fingers on the left. Ensure the cards are held high enough to allow the first joints of the fingers to bend around the deck and rest on the bottom card.

2 This view from underneath shows how the extreme tips of the fingers are positioned on the face of the card.

3 Drag the bottom card back about 5–10mm (¼–½in) by pulling the second, third and fourth fingers backwards. (The first finger remains stationary.) The bottom card remains aligned against the left thumb.

4 The right hand approaches palm up and reaches under the deck to supposedly remove the bottom card. What actually happens is that the second card is removed instead. The tips of the right fingers drag the second card forward, facilitated by the overlap created by the Glide.

tip *The Glide is not seen from the front. It is a secret move that remains hidden under the deck. An alternative method is to approach the deck with the right hand and push the bottom card back a fraction of a second before the second card is pulled forward.*

double lift and turnover

The Double Lift and Turnover is another essential sleight to master if you wish to become a competent cardician. Theoretically the procedure is simple, but to put the theory into effect will take plenty of practice. In theory a "double lift" is the name given to the concept of lifting two cards and displaying them as one. The technique is used to achieve many results, a few of which are explored in the explanations that follow.

There are enough techniques and variations to the turning of two cards as one to fill this entire book. The truth is, every individual finds a technique that is comfortable for them and sticks with it. Further reading will enable you to explore different options, and with time you will find small changes that suit you. As long as your Double Lift is convincing, it does not really matter which technique you choose.

There a few important points to be aware of. The "get-ready" should remain unseen. The turning of the two cards should look natural and arouse no suspicion. In other words, don't say "Here is the top card of the deck", because as soon as you say that people will start to wonder if it really is the top card of the deck. If you just show it, perhaps saying the card's name out loud, people will just assume it is the top card. You must create a reason for placing the card back on to the deck after the first display.

1 The Double Lift requires a "get-ready". It is necessary to separate the top two cards from the rest of the deck. In order to achieve this, hold the deck in left-hand Mechanics' Grip. The left thumb pushes off the top few cards, to the right, in a spread.

secret view

2 While the first finger is curled around the end of the deck furthest from you, the second and third fingers stretch out and begin to pull the cards flush again, but as this happens the fourth finger separates the top two cards of the deck.

secret view

3 The deck should now be held, squared, in the left hand with a Finger Break, as shown, under the top two cards.

4 The view from the front reveals nothing. The cards are simply held in the Mechanics' Grip with a Finger Break below the top two cards.

secret view

5 The right hand approaches the deck in Biddle Grip position. The gap created by the Finger Break enables the top two cards only to be lifted. The right first finger pushes gently on the back of the card(s) to keep them aligned.

6 The right hand turns at the wrist to reveal the face of the card. It is mistaken for the top card of the deck but in reality is the second card from the top.

7 After the display, turn the wrist once again and replace the card(s) back on to the top of the deck. Snap your fingers or make a magical gesture and pick up the real top card of the deck, turning it over to reveal the card has mysteriously changed.

snap change

This is a visually stunning sleight, which takes only a little practice to perfect. With a snap of the fingers one card instantly changes to another. It is recommended that you learn this sleight so that if ever a card trick goes wrong you can simply ask which card was chosen and spread through the deck, cutting the selector's card second from the top. Show the top card as an indifferent card, perform the Snap Change and magically change the indifferent card into the one selected. Magicians call these types of scenarios "outs", that is, they can get the magician out of trouble if a trick goes wrong.

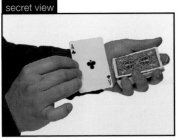

secret view

1 Show the top card of the deck (in this example the Ace of Clubs). Secretly obtain a Finger Break under the top card in the left hand.

secret view

2 Lay the Ace of Clubs face up and square on to the deck.

3 The Finger Break will enable you to pick up the top two cards with ease. The two cards are held together as one between the right thumb and second finger at the extreme end. The first finger is bent on top.

4 Move the card(s) under your elbow and temporarily out of sight.

5 Squeeze the two cards, allowing them to flick off the second finger so that the cards flip over and are pinched at the lower right corner by the thumb and first finger. The cards should still be perfectly aligned.

6 Immediately bring the cards into sight and place them back on to the top of the deck where they can be squared. The card will be seen to have changed.

7 Turn the top card face down to complete the sleight. This is a speedy and highly visual piece of magic.

ribbon spread and turnover

This is a lovely flourish, pretty to watch and a sign of a magician who can handle a deck of cards. The cards are spread and displayed in a neat face-down line, then caused to flip face up "domino-style". You *will find it easier to perform with a deck of cards in good condition and on a soft surface such as a tablecloth or close-up mat. You will also need a clear space to ensure a smooth spread.*

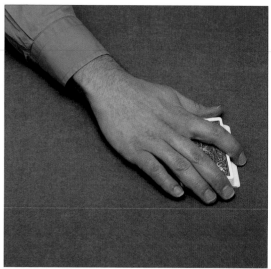

1 Hold the deck face down in the right-hand Biddle Grip. Place the deck flat on the table at your far left.

2 Stretch out your first finger so that it rests on the long edge of the deck and just brushes the surface of the table. Pull the deck to the right a fraction, and the deck will naturally bevel.

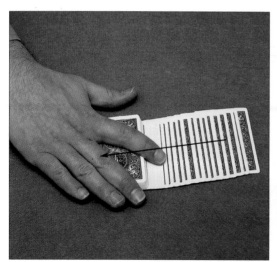

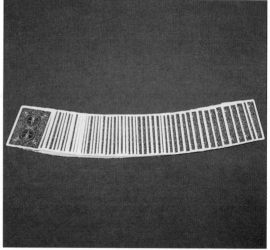

3 Begin moving your hand to the right at an even pace with even pressure. With the first finger, regulate the distance between each card as you continue to spread the deck in a straight line until all the cards are spread out.

4 The result is an even spread of cards in a relatively straight line. With practice you will be able to spread the cards instantly, in under a second, and with absolute precision.

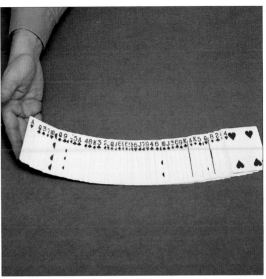

5 To turn the cards face up, lift the edge of the cards at the far left of the spread and run your first finger along the edges so that the spread begins to turn face up "domino-style".

6 When you reach the end of the spread, allow the last cards to drop face up on to your palm in preparation for the final stage. Do not let the cards fall flat on to the table.

7 Now move the right hand to the left, scooping up the deck into one pile. Lift this pile off the table.

8 Finish the sequence by squaring the cards with both hands and continue with your next card trick or flourish.

shuffling cards

Very often you can impress your audience before you even begin a single trick by handling the cards in a way that suggests you have spent considerable time and effort practising. Apart from the Weave Shuffle and Waterfall, these shuffles are not too difficult to master. Indeed, you may be familiar with them already. Often several shuffles are required to thoroughly mix the deck.

overhand shuffle

This is arguably the most commonly used and easiest shuffle. These moves are repeated over and over with varying amounts of cards until you are satisfied the deck has been shuffled.

Due to the fact that the cards are being mixed in small packets, it will take a lot of shuffling to ensure a very thorough disruption of the sequence of cards.

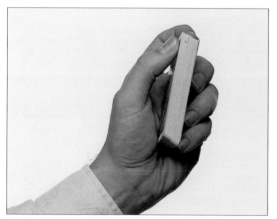

1 Hold the deck with one of its long edges along the crease lines at the base of the left fingers. The thumb naturally rests on the back of the deck, and the fingers do likewise on the front.

2 With the right hand, approach from above and pick up approximately the bottom three-quarters of the deck.

3 In a chopping motion, bring the right hand back to the deck and deposit half the cards on top of the deck. Then bring the right hand away with the other half.

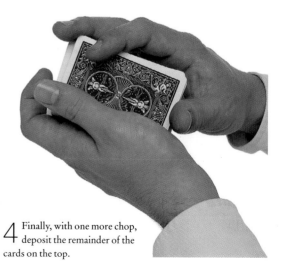

4 Finally, with one more chop, deposit the remainder of the cards on the top.

table riffle shuffle

This is an effective and professional way to shuffle a deck of cards. By controlling the cards as they fall, you can ensure that the last group of cards are "riffled" off the right thumb. Any cards within this group (which was on the top of the deck at the beginning) will be on top of the deck at the end of the shuffle. The Riffle Shuffle can thus be used as a false shuffle, allowing you to retain cards at the top of the deck.

1 The deck should be squared and lying on the table, long side towards you. With the right hand, cut off approximately half of the cards.

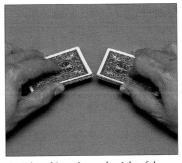

2 Place this packet to the right of the bottom half and mirror your grip with the left hand. With the thumbs of both hands, lift up the back edges. Notice how the corners almost touch. The front edges of the deck rest on the table.

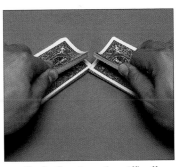

3 Slowly allow the cards to riffle off both thumbs. As this happens, nudge both packets together.

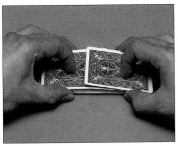

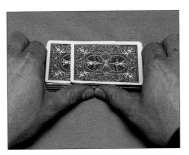

5 Change your grip so that you can push both packets together completely by applying pressure along the short sides of the deck with both first fingers while simultaneously squaring the cards with your thumbs on the long edge nearest you.

4 When this riffle is complete, push each packet into the other to about halfway.

6 The result is a shuffled, squared deck which is then ready for your next miracle.

weave shuffle and waterfall

This shuffle looks fantastic when it is performed smoothly. It creates the impression that you are a master card sharp! You must use a deck of cards in perfect condition because you are relying on the corners of the deck to ensure a good weave. If the edges of the individual cards are split or damaged you will find this shuffle very difficult indeed. With enough practice, you will be able to split the cards into exactly two packets of 26 and shuffle them so accurately that every card will be woven in the opposite direction to its neighbour. Professional magicians know this as the Perfect Faro shuffle. If you can achieve this degree of accuracy every time, you will be able to master almost any card sleight-of-hand trick you may come across in the future. The end result is well worth the effort you need to put in.

1 Make sure the cards are perfectly square. Hold them high up at the tips of the left fingers, as shown here.

2 With the right hand, approach the deck from above. The first finger is held straight out and rests on the short edge of the deck furthest from you.

3 With the right thumb, second and third fingers cut and lift half of the deck up and away from the lower packet.

4 Tap this top half gently against the short edge of the bottom half, to ensure that the edges of both packets are perfectly square.

5 Place the corners nearest you against each other. Notice at this stage how only the corners at the front touch, and how the first finger of the right hand keeps the packets perfectly level with each other.

6 Gently push the corners together, and the cards will begin to weave, as shown here. (You may find that a slight back-and-forth motion will ease the cards into the weave.)

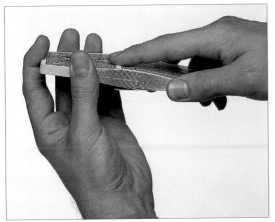

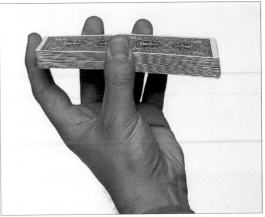

7 Push the packets together so that approximately one-quarter of the cards are overlapped.

8 Adjust the left hand's grip by moving your thumb, third and fourth fingers down to the woven section. This gives you the ability to hold the deck in one hand.

9 Stretch the right hand wide open and approach the deck from above. Your thumb should grip the short edge nearest you, with the fingers on the short edge furthest away.

10 Release the left hand's grip and squeeze the cards into an arc with the right hand. The cards will cascade inwards, producing a lovely waterfall pattern as they fall. Keep the left hand underneath, just in case the cards start to slip. Finish by squaring the deck neatly.

self-working card tricks

It is important to realize that although self-working card tricks are relatively easy to perform, they do require a certain amount of human input and will not work unless the various stages are followed correctly. The advantage of self-working tricks is that you can spend less time learning the mechanics of the trick and more time working on an entertaining presentation.

sense of touch

After performing a few card tricks, state that it is possible to develop super-sensitivity in your fingertips. As a demonstration, shuffle the cards and hold them face down. The top card is held with its back towards the magician, yet by feeling its face it is possible to identify the card every time. Explain that your sensitive fingers allow you to know whether the card is black or red, and how many pips are on it.

secret view

1 From a shuffled deck, deal one card face down into your right hand and hold it in front of you at about neck level. Hold it by the thumb at the bottom edge and the fingers at the top edge, with its back towards you. Your left first finger moves up to touch the face of the card.

2 This shows the view from behind. As the finger touches the face of the card for the first time, gently squeeze your right fingers and thumb. This will begin to bend or bow the card backwards.

3 The left finger is omitted here so that you can clearly see what happens. The card is bowed just enough for you to glimpse the lower left index.

the four burglars

This classic trick is accompanied by a story. Four Jacks are shown to be at the top of the deck, and one by one they are placed separately into different positions. The four Jacks magically return to the top. Read through the steps with your cards in hand until you are familiar with the order of the steps. Then learn the patter and match up the words to the moves. When learnt and performed confidently, this will become a charming addition to your repertoire, and is sure to get a great reaction every time it is performed.

1 Secretly remove any three cards plus the four Jacks.

2 Hold the Jacks in a fan, with the extra three cards squared neatly below the lowest one.

3 Begin by displaying the four Jacks to the audience. (They should be unaware of the extra cards.)

4 Neatly square the cards in the left hand, being careful to hide the extra thickness along the edge of the cards.

5 Turn the packet of cards face down and place them on top of the deck.

6 Take the top card of the deck and, without showing its face, push it into the deck approximately ten cards from the bottom. Leave it protruding half its length.

7 Take the new top card and push it into the deck at the halfway point. Leave it protruding as before.

8 Repeat with the new top card, inserting it about ten cards from the top of the deck.

9 Turn the top card face up to show a Jack, then replace it face down, but protruding from the top of the deck.

10 Slowly push all four cards neatly and squarely into the deck.

11 Dribble the cards from hand to hand, matching your actions to your patter.

12 Deal the top four cards face up to show that the Jacks have returned.

the story *(the numbers correspond to the above steps):*

"There were four burglars named Jack who decided to try to burgle a house (3, 4, 5). The first burglar broke into the basement (6), the second managed to enter the kitchen (7), and the third burglar climbed through an open window in a bedroom (8).

The last burglar stayed on the roof to look out for the police (9). As each of the burglars entered the house (10), the lookout on the roof saw a police car driving towards them. He called his three friends (11), who immediately ran up to the roof, slid down the drainpipe, and made their escape (12)."

hocus pocus

Twenty-one cards are dealt on to the table and one is thought of by the spectator. After a short process of dealing the cards, the magic words "Hocus Pocus" are used to find the selection. This is one of the best-known card tricks, but it still amazes everyone who sees it.

Although the principle and method are mathematical, it requires no skill or mathematics on the part of the magician. Better still, it works every single time as long as the steps are followed in the correct order. Try this out with the cards in hand and you may even amaze yourself!

1 Deal three cards face up from left to right (as if you were dealing a round of cards to three people).

2 Deal another three cards in exactly the same way. Continue until you have three columns of seven cards – 21 cards in total. Ask the spectator to remember any one of the cards. In our example the chosen card is the Queen of Diamonds.

3 Ask the spectator to tell you which column the chosen card is in. (In our example it is in column number three.) Pick up one of the other piles, then pick up the chosen pile and place it on top.

4 Finally pick up the last pile, adding it to the others. Remember the golden rule: the chosen column must be placed in the middle of the other two.

5 Deal three cards from the top of the packet as you did at the beginning, but holding the packet face up.

6 Continue dealing until all the cards have once again been dealt.

7 Ask the spectator to confirm which column their card is in this time. As before, pick up all three columns, ensuring that the chosen column goes between the other two.

8 Re-deal the cards in exactly the same fashion as before. Ask the spectator one final time which column contains their card. Collect the cards as before.

9 Turn the cards face down and explain that to find the selected card you need to use the ancient magic words "Hocus Pocus". Deal the cards on to the table, spelling out loud one letter for each card.

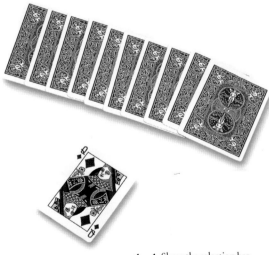

10 The very next card will be the one selected. Ask for the name of the chosen card and turn the top card over.

11 Show the selection has been found and that the magic word has worked.

tip *After the process of dealing has been repeated three times, the mentally selected card will automatically be the eleventh card down from the top of the face-down packet. This means you could use any word with ten or eleven letters to find the selection, so with a little thought you can personalize this trick. You may be able to use your name, your spectator's name or the name of your company.*

reversed

A card is chosen and inserted back into the deck. You explain that you will demonstrate the fastest trick in the world. You then place the cards behind your back for a split second. When they are brought to the front again, you spread the cards and one is seen reversed in the centre. It is the card selected.

This is a typical example of a very simple method used to accomplish what seems like a miracle. Performed well, this effect cannot fail to win over an audience.

1 The set-up is simple and will take one second to accomplish. Secretly reverse the bottom card face up under the face-down deck.

2 Spread the face-down deck between your hands and ask for a card to be selected. Take care that the bottom card is not seen to be reversed.

3 While the card selected is being looked at and remembered by the spectator, secretly turn the deck upside down. To make this easier, you could explain that you will turn your back so that you cannot see the selected card. When your back is turned, reverse the deck.

4 Because of the card reversed earlier, the deck will still appear to be face down. Make sure the deck is perfectly squared, then ask the spectator to push their card somewhere into the middle of the deck.

secret view

5 Announce that you will demonstrate the world's fastest trick. Move the cards behind your back. As soon as they are out of sight, push the top card off the deck and turn the whole deck over on top of this card.

6 Bring the deck to the front again and it will look as if nothing has changed. The deck will still appear face down. Spread the cards between your hands or ribbon-spread them across a table to show that there is one card reversed.

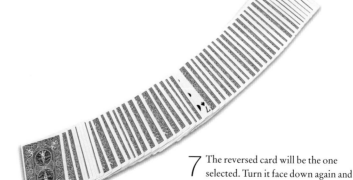

7 The reversed card will be the one selected. Turn it face down again and continue with another trick.

face value

The magician removes a card from the deck and places it to one side as a prediction for later on. A random number of cards are dealt on to the table by a spectator and two piles are made. The top card of each

pile is turned over and the suit of one together with the value of another are combined and found to match the earlier prediction. This is a simple but very baffling card trick.

1 Ask a spectator to shuffle the cards and then hand the deck to you. Fan the cards towards yourself and take note of the top two cards – simply remember the value of the first card and the suit of the second. This combined card will become your prediction. In our example, the prediction would be the Four of Clubs. Remove it and place it to one side, but in full view.

2 Give the deck back to the spectator and ask them to deal the cards on to a table, one on top of the other until they wish to stop dealing. The original top two cards of the deck are now at the bottom of this pile. In order to get them to the top again, the cards must be dealt once more.

3 Discard the rest of the deck and have the pile of cards on the table dealt alternately into two piles. Notice which pile the final card is placed on.

4 Turn over whichever card was dealt last, explaining that you will use the card's value only and ignore the suit. (In our example it is the *Four* of Hearts.)

5 Turn over the top card of the other pile and explain that you will use the suit, but not the value (the Two of *Clubs*).

6 Reveal that your earlier prediction matches the combination of the cards randomly shuffled to the top of the two piles.

tip *On a rare occasion you may find that the first two cards of the deck will not produce a usable prediction. For example, if the Six of Clubs were next to the Six of Spades the prediction should be the*

Six of Spades, but that card cannot be removed from the deck. If this happens, cut the deck, positioning two new cards at the top. Unless you are very unlucky, these new top cards should be usable.

the indicator

A card is chosen and returned to the deck. The deck is spread and one card is found reversed. Although it is not the card selected, it acts as an indicator and helps to find it. This is a good example of how a key card is used to achieve a certain goal, that is, finding the selection.

Once you understand the principle involved, you can use any card as the "indicator" and simply adjust the set-up accordingly. For example, if the Five of Hearts was used, t0he reversed card would need to be set five cards from the bottom.

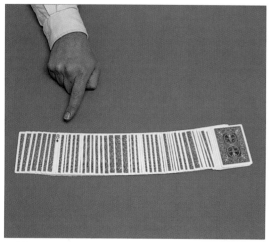

1 The set-up is easy to remember. Reverse any Eight and position it eight cards from the bottom of the deck. This is a secret set-up, so the reversed card should remain hidden.

2 Fan the cards for a selection, but do not spread them too far in case the reversed card is prematurely exposed. With a small amount of practice, the cards can be handled relatively freely.

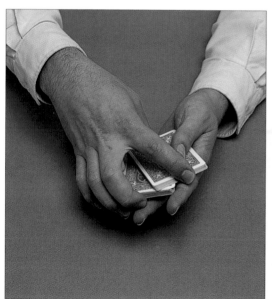

3 While the card is being looked at, swing-cut the top half of the deck into the left hand.

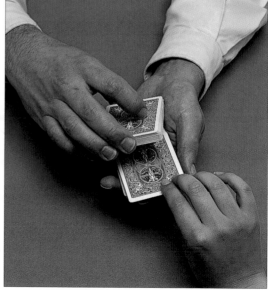

4 Have the selected card replaced on top of the left-hand cards, then place the right-hand cards on top of it.

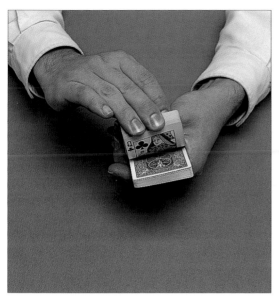

5 Riffle the end of the deck, explaining that one card will reverse itself.

6 Spread the deck and show the Eight reversed in the centre. Cut the deck at this point, bringing the Eight to the top of the deck. The selector will be quick to tell you it is the wrong card.

7 Explain that the Eight is merely an indicator card and indicates to you that the chosen card is in fact eight cards down from the top.

8 Place the Eight to one side and count off seven cards one at a time, out loud. Turn over the eighth card. It will be the card selected.

you find it!

The deck is given to a spectator – the magician never touches it throughout the trick. A card is chosen and returned to the deck, which is then cut a number of times. The magician merely glances at the side of the deck and tells the spectator the exact position of the selected card.

1 To set up the deck, sort all the Hearts into numerical order, Ace through to King. Place this stack on the bottom of the deck, with the Ace lowermost.

2 Set the deck face down in front of a spectator and instruct them to cut off half the cards.

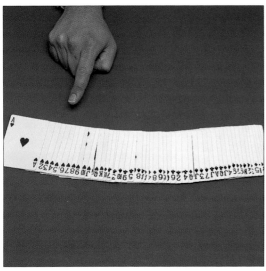

3 Ask them to look at the card they cut to and to remember it.

4 Have the card replaced on the opposite pile (on top of the original top card).

5 Instruct the spectator to complete the cut and square the cards neatly.

6 Now ask the instructor to turn the deck face up.

7 Instruct the spectator to cut and complete the cut. What you need them to do is to cut to one of the cards in the stack which you set up earlier (that is, any Heart). If you are lucky they will do this first time; if not simply ask them to cut the deck again, and again if necessary. Eventually they will cut somewhere into the stack of Hearts. In our example it is the Four of Hearts. Just remember "four".

8 Have the deck turned face down and stare at the edge of the deck as if making some difficult calculations. State that their selection is "four" cards down from the top of the deck. After all the cutting, this seems quite a bold statement to make – even the spectator has lost track of the card. Ask them to deal three cards face down and turn over the fourth. It will be the card selected.

instant card revelation

A card is chosen and returned to the deck in the fairest of manners. Without hesitation, the magician is able to reveal the chosen card. This effect takes advantage of a "glimpsed" card. It should be performed briskly and, as you will see, you do not even need to pull the chosen card out of the deck; you can simply say the name of the card out loud. For some reason it seems more impossible if you just say the name of their card, as opposed to physically finding it. Try both ways and see which method you prefer.

1 Using one of the techniques explained, "glimpse" and remember the bottom card of the deck (in this example, the King of Hearts). This becomes your key card.

2 Spread the cards for a selection, emphasizing the fairness of choice open to the spectator.

3 Ask for the selected card to be remembered (in this example, the Five of Diamonds). Simultaneously square the deck.

4 Swing-cut the top half of the deck into your left hand.

5 Have the card replaced on to your left-hand cards, then place the right hand's cards on top, positioning your key card above the selection.

6 You can make a quick face-up Ribbon Spread along the surface of the table, or alternatively spread the cards between your hands, towards you.

7 Either way, find your key card, and the selected card will be the one directly above it. Remove it from the spread and reveal the selection.

the next card is yours

A card is chosen and returned to the deck. The magician deals the cards one at a time, face up on to the table. While dealing, he states that the next card to be turned over will be the one selected. Even though the spectators are sure the magician has failed, since they have seen that the selected card has already been dealt, much to their amusement and surprise the next card to be turned over is indeed the selected card. This trick is a "sucker" trick – your audience thinks the trick has gone wrong, but it is really part of the presentation.

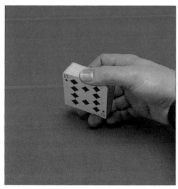

1 Secretly "glimpse" the bottom card of the deck, using one of the methods described earlier. This will be your key card. (In our example it is the Ten of Diamonds.)

2 Using the Two-Handed Spread, offer the cards to a spectator for a selection.

3 Cut half the deck to the table and have the selected card placed on top of this packet. As you place the other half on top to bury their card, you will automatically position your key card directly above their selection. Cut the deck and complete the cut a few times, but do not shuffle!

4 Deal the cards face up, one at a time. When you see your key card, the very next card dealt will be the one selected, but do not pause; carry on dealing about ten more cards. Then say, "I bet you the next card I turn over will be yours". The spectator will immediately accept the bet.

5 Wait a second or two, then watch the spectator's face as you reach for the card immediately next to your key card, which will of course be the one selected.

6 Turn it over and you will win the bet! You will definitely have fun with this one!

do as I do

Two decks of cards are used. Both the magician and the spectator choose a card from their respective decks, then put them back into the centre. The decks are swapped and each looks for their selection. Both cards are placed side by side and, despite the odds against it happening, the cards mysteriously match each other. This is one of the cleverest cards tricks ever invented. Try it and you will amaze everyone who watches it. It simply defies explanation, and has become one of the all-time classic card tricks.

1 Give a deck of cards to the spectator and keep a second deck for yourself. Have both shuffled. As you shuffle your deck, remember the bottom card. This is your key card.

2 Swap decks so that you now know the card on the bottom of the pile in front of the spectator. Explain that they must copy every move you make as closely as possible.

3 Cut approximately half the deck to your right. The spectator will mirror your actions.

4 Pick up the card you cut to and instruct the spectator to remember theirs. Look at your card, although you do not need to remember it. Just pretend to do so.

5 Place the card back on the right-hand pile. Your spectator will copy you.

6 Place the left packet on top of the right. The spectator's card is now directly under your key card. At this stage you can cut the cards as many times as you wish, although it is not necessary to do so.

7 Swap the decks over again and comment to your spectator on the absolute fairness with which you have both chosen a card.

8 Tell the spectator to find their chosen card at the same time as you find yours. Spread through the deck until you see your key card. The card immediately above it will be the one selected.

9 Place your card face down on the table in front of you. The spectator will do likewise.

10 Explain that you both made the same moves at exactly the same time and so in theory you should have arrived at the same result. Turn over the cards to show a perfect match.

invisible traveller

In this deceptive puzzle you cause a single card to travel from one place to another while everything is in the spectator's hands. This is also *known as the Piano Trick. With a bit of thought you could replace the playing cards with other objects that could make a fun presentation.*

1 Begin with a deck of cards positioned in front of you. Ask a volunteer to place their hands flat on the table, palms down, as shown.

2 Pick up two cards from the top of the pile and say, "Two cards are even."

3 Place this pair between the fourth and third fingers of the person's right hand. Now pick up two more cards and say again, "Two cards are even." Place these between the third and second fingers of the right hand.

4 Repeat this again and again on both hands until you reach the final space that is left between the left hand's third and fourth fingers, where you place only one card and say: "One card is odd."

5 Pick up the first pair you dealt and split them, starting two piles on the table. As you lay the pair of cards down on the table say: "Even."

6 Repeat this dealing process, taking each pair and saying "Even" as you lay them on the piles, until you have a single card remaining. Ask the person which pile they would like the odd card to be placed on. Put the last card down on the pile they point to.

7 Make a mystic pass over the two piles and explain that you are invisibly transferring the odd card from one pile to the other. You now count out the piles and it is seen that the pile containing an odd number of cards is the opposite pile to the one chosen for the odd card to be placed on! Really, nothing has happened. The fact is, before the single card was added to a pile in step 6 both piles contained an odd number of cards: because you split the pairs into two piles of seven cards. Your patter has created the impression that both piles are even and that is what makes the trick work.

impossible card location

A deck of cards is split in two and thoroughly shuffled by two spectators. Each chooses and exchanges a card. The cards are shuffled again. Incredibly, and without hesitation, the magician is able to find both cards immediately.

The more your spectators try to figure out how you achieved this, the more impossible it will seem. The secret preparation is actually shown as part of the presentation of the trick, but it is so subtle that it remains absolutely invisible!

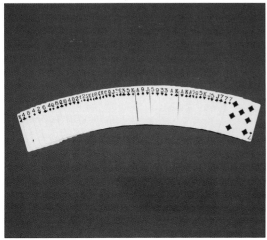

1 Set the deck by dividing all the odd cards from all the even cards. Place one set on top of the other. Spread or fan the deck towards two spectators and explain that although the cards are already mixed, you want to have them mixed some more. A casual glance at the set-up cards will not be enough to see that the deck has been split into odd and even cards.

2 Split the deck at the point where the odd cards meet the even cards. Hand half the deck to each spectator. Ask them to shuffle their cards well. Really stress to the spectators that they can mix the cards as much as they like. This apparent fairness simply increases the overall effect.

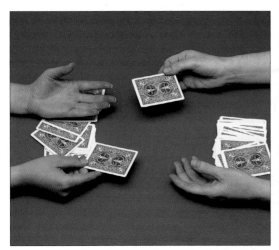

3 Request that the cards are spread out on the table face down and that one from each half be chosen, remembered and swapped with the other person's selection.

4 The selected cards are then placed back somewhere in the middle of the opposite half from where they came.

5 Have both half-decks shuffled well again and reiterate the fairness of the procedure thus far. Ask the spectators to leave the half-decks squared on the table in front of them.

6 Pick up one packet and spread through it with the faces of the cards towards you. It will be easy to find the chosen card as it will be the only even card in the odd packet. Remove it and place it in front of the spectator who chose that card.

7 Repeat the same procedure with the second packet, placing the second selection in front of the other spectator. A little acting ability will go a long way at this point. Make it look as though you are having trouble finding the chosen card, or perhaps you can just start eliminating individual cards, scattering them to the table one at a time until there is only one card remaining in your hand.

8 Ask each spectator to verify the name of their card. Turn each card over and show that you correctly divined the selections. The ease of the method used for this trick allows you to focus on the presentation. Experiment with different styles until you find one that suits you.

magic time

A prediction is made and placed in the centre of the table. A random hour in the day is thought of by a spectator. Twelve cards are laid in the formation of a clock face and a card is chosen to represent the thought-of hour. The magician reveals the thought-of hour and the prediction in the centre of the table is found to match the chosen card.

This trick works on a mathematical principle, and is very clever indeed. Try it with a deck of cards in hand and you will amaze yourself! At the end of the explanation there is a variation of the first method, using a marked card. This has the advantage of being even more deceptive.

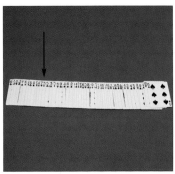

1 The only preparation is to remember which card is thirteenth from the top of the deck. In our example it is the Three of Diamonds.

2 Set the deck face down on the table and write a prediction on a piece of paper, with a question mark on the reverse. Your prediction is the card you remembered. Place it on the table, with the question mark uppermost, not letting the audience see your prediction.

3 Ask someone to think of their favourite hour in the day, and to take that many cards off the top of the deck and put them on the bottom. Turn your back while this happens so that there is no way for you to know what hour it is. Let us assume that they think of 4 o'clock and move four cards from the top to the bottom.

4 Take the deck and deal twelve cards on to the table, reversing their order.

5 Pick up this pile and set the cards out face up in a clock formation around your prediction so that the first card you deal is at 1 o'clock, the second at 2 o'clock, etc. (The 12 o'clock position should be placed so that it is the furthest card from the spectator.)

6 Your prediction card will automatically position itself at their thought-of hour. However, do not reveal it just yet. Build up the suspense by asking the spectator which wrist they wear their watch on. Ask them to hold that wrist over the centre of the circle. Hold their wrist as if trying to pick up a psychic vibe, indicating what hour they chose. Reveal the thought-of hour.

7 Ask the spectator to confirm that you are correct, then call attention to the card at their chosen hour (in this case 4 o'clock). It will be the Three of Diamonds.

8 Turn over your prediction to show a perfect match.

9 If you mark the back of the thirteenth card down (Three of Diamonds), you can lay the cards face down instead of face up. As the cards are dealt, the marked card will indicate the thought-of hour.

secret view

10 This close-up view of the card shows the normal design compared to the subtle mark which is easy to spot if you are aware of it. Part of the design on the back of the card has been filled in with a permanent marker pen which matches the colour of the card.

11 At step 7, after the thought-of hour is revealed and confirmed as being correct, reverse the appropriate card at the thought-of hour.

spectator cuts the aces

A deck of cards is placed in front of the spectator, who cuts it into approximately four equal packets. Although the magician never touches the deck and the spectator mixes the cards some more, the top card of each packet is found to be an Ace.

Four-Ace tricks are very popular with magicians. In fact, four-of-a-kind tricks make up a large percentage of card tricks. This self-working card trick is amazing; the method is simple and the impact on an audience is powerful.

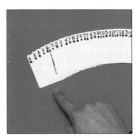

1 To prepare, secretly find the four Aces and move them to the top of the deck.

2 Place the deck on a table and invite a spectator to cut it into two approximately equal halves. Keep track of the original top of the deck at all times (that is, the packet with the four Aces at the top).

3 Ask the spectator to cut one of the packets in half again, and indicate where they are to place the cards.

4 Ask for the other half-deck to be cut in half again in the opposite direction, indicating both verbally and with your hand where the final packet should go. Make sure you still know which pile has the four aces on top.

5 You should have four approximately equal packets in front of you. The four Aces should be on the top of one of the end packets, depending on which way the cards were cut. In our example, the four Aces are on the top of the packet on the far right. Explain that four random points in the deck have been found.

6 Point to the packet at the opposite end to the Aces. Ask the spectator to pick up the deck and to move three cards from the top to the bottom. The fact that the spectator makes all the moves increases the apparent fairness of the whole procedure.

7 Now tell your spectator to deal one card from the top of the packet in their hand to each of the piles on the table, in any order they wish.

8 Having replaced the first packet, the spectator should pick up the second packet and repeat the same procedure; that is, take three cards from the top and place them at the bottom. They should deal one card to the top of each packet on the table.

9 This exact sequence should be repeated with the third packet. Each time explain which moves to make and watch to ensure that the spectator follows your instructions correctly. If any wrong moves are made, it may be because you did not explain the procedure clearly enough.

10 The fourth packet is treated in exactly the same way. This will result in four packets face down on the table, which you have not touched from the very beginning.

11 Explain the randomness of the cuts and that without even touching the cards you have been able to influence the actions taken. Turn over one of the cards on the top of one of the packets. It will be an Ace.

tip *During the sequence of movements what actually happens is that you add three cards on top of the Aces, then move those three added cards to the bottom and deal one Ace to each of the other three piles. All of the other moves are simply a smokescreen to help hide the method!*

12 Turn over the top cards of the remaining three packets, revealing an Ace on each.

four card poker

This is an ideal sequel to Spectator Cuts the Aces. Four groups of four cards are mixed and dealt into four "hands". The spectator chooses a "hand" of cards. Despite the fairness of the selection, the chosen pile is shown to consist of the four Aces!

Although there are several outcomes to this trick, your audience must believe that there is only one. This will only happen if you perform confidently and practise each of the possible scenarios until you are able to do this without hesitation.

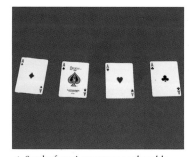

1 Set the four Aces out on to the table next to each other. If you have just performed Spectator Cuts the Aces, you will already be in this position.

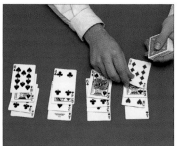

2 Deal three cards on top of each Ace. Place the rest of the deck to one side.

3 Collect each pile, one on top of the other, into one packet. Turn the cards face down and square them neatly.

4 Cut the cards several times, each time ensuring that it is a complete cut. Cutting will not mix the order of the cards; it will merely change the cyclical order. You can even let a spectator do the cutting, which seems to increase the impossibility of any sleight of hand.

5 Re-deal the cards into four piles, side by side. So long as the cards have only been cut and not shuffled, the four Aces will automatically be dealt together in one pile.

6 Square each pile, secretly "glimpsing" the bottom card each time. You must discover which pile the Aces are in, but do so without making your glimpse obvious.

7 There are now several possible outcomes to this trick. Ask a spectator to point to a pile with one hand. If they point to the pile of Aces, simply turn over that pile and show that, despite a completely free choice, they have found all four Aces.

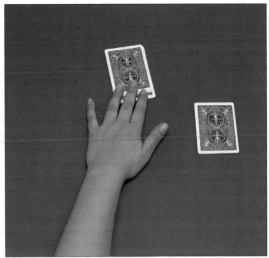

8 If they point to a different pile, ask them to point to another packet with their other hand. If both piles picked do not contain the Aces, remove them, explaining that they are to be discarded. This will leave you with two piles. If, however, the second pile pointed to does contain the Aces, remove the other two piles, leaving two piles on the table.

9 Either way, one of the remaining piles will consist of the four Aces. Explain that you are going to play a very simple game of Four Card Poker and that the spectator must choose a hand for you and a hand for themselves. Ask the spectator to push one pile of cards towards you. Give them an opportunity to change their mind.

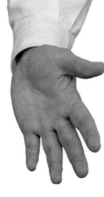

10 If the Aces are pushed towards you, turn both packets face up and display them. Explain that even though they had every chance to change their mind, they gave you the winning hand! If the Aces are kept by the spectator, simply show your cards and ask to see theirs, exclaiming that they are extremely lucky and that you would not want to play cards with them! If you are not 100 per cent confident with the three possible outcomes of this trick, your audience may be confused as to what was meant to have happened. Practise until you can perform this without thinking what to do next.

spell-a-card

A card is selected and replaced in the deck. The magician seems to be in trouble and fails to find the chosen card. It is suggested that maybe the card will answer to its name in the same way that a dog would!

The cards are dealt one at a time on to the table, one card for each letter. The final card proves to be the one selected. This is yet another example of how the use of a key card can create a different effect.

1 Secretly "glimpse" the bottom card of the deck. This will become your key card. In this case it is the Three of Hearts.

2 Using a Two-Handed Spread, offer the cards to a spectator for a selection.

3 Swing-cut the top half of the deck and have the selected card replaced on to the original top card. Place the rest of the deck on top, positioning the key card directly above the selection.

4 You can give the cards a false shuffle at this point, as long as the selected card and key card stay side by side. Spread through the deck face up and explain that you are going to find the selected card. Find your key card. The card above it will be the one selected. In this case the chosen card is the Five of Hearts.

5 Starting from the selected card, begin to mentally spell its name. For every letter, move one card to the left. This is done as the cards are spread and should be practised until you can do it without concentrating too much. When you reach the final letter, ask if you have passed the selected card. The spectator will tell you that you have and will think something has gone wrong. Cut the deck and complete the cut at the card reached on the last letter. It is possible you may reach the top of the deck before you have finished spelling (*see* Tip for this eventuality).

6 Turn the deck face down and ask for the name of the selected card. When it is given to you, start dealing the cards face down to the table one at a time, one card for each letter. The card that is dealt on the final letter will be the one selected.

tip *Occasionally you may run out of cards when spelling the name of the selected card. This is because you cut too deeply when the selected card was replaced. Just continue spelling from the face of the deck, acting as if you need to go through the deck again. Cut the cards as before and continue.*

controlling a card

One of the most important sleights to learn is how to control a chosen card to the top of the deck. It will give you the ability to perform literally hundreds of different card tricks. Discussed here are several ways to control a card. It is always better to learn one really well than to learn several badly. In order to learn how to control a card, it is also important to understand a few other techniques and grips.

finger break

This break is used in a great number of tricks. It is one of the sleights most widely used by professional card magicians, predominantly for keeping control of a desired number of cards and also to aid the shift of the required cards from one position to another. It is an essential sleight that must be mastered if further study of card magic appeals to you. Because it uses the fourth finger, this particular sleight is also known as the Pinkie Break. It is not too difficult to learn, and is worth learning well.

secret view

1 Hold the deck in the left-hand Mechanics' Grip or Dealing Grip. With the right hand, approach from above in the Biddle Grip position and using the right thumb, lift approximately half of the cards about 1cm (⅓in). Release the cards, but allow the pad of the left fourth fingertip to stop the cards from falling flush.

2 The gap between the two packets need not be large – just enough for you to locate at a future point in the particular routine. If pressure is applied from the thumb on top of the deck, the gap will close enough to remain hidden from both the front and sides.

thumb break

The Thumb Break is similar to the Finger Break and is used for the same purposes – to maintain control, or to aid the repositioning of certain cards. It is a vital sleight to learn, but you will be pleased to know that it is not at all difficult and will take no more than one or two trials to understand. It's even easier than the Finger Break!

Hold a Finger Break as described above. With the right hand, approach the left hand from above and pick up the deck in the Biddle Grip position. However, as the thumb grips the back short edge (nearest you), the gap between the two packets is maintained by squeezing lightly between the right thumb and fingers. The cards are held entirely by the right hand, freeing the left hand.

secret view

double cut

The purpose of a Double Cut is to bring a card or block of cards from the middle of the deck to the top. It is a very useful move to master

and, as you will learn, can also be used to control a selected card to the top of the deck.

1 Using the right hand, hold a Thumb Break about halfway down the deck. Drop approximately the bottom quarter of the deck into the left hand.

2 Grip these cards between the thumb and first finger and replace them on top of the right-hand cards.

3 Almost immediately loosen the right thumb's grip, letting the remaining cards (up to the Thumb Break) fall on to the fingers of the left hand.

4 Replace the left hand's packet on to the top of the right-hand cards in exactly the same way. The cards that were immediately below the Thumb Break are now on top of the deck. Square the deck and the Double Cut is complete.

double cut control

The Double Cut is also a neat and effective way to control a selected card to a wanted position in the deck. The same set of moves are seen here to show how the card is controlled to the top. Performed swiftly, it allows you to control the selected card in an unsuspicious and smooth manner. Your audience will assume you are merely cutting

the deck to mix the cards further. No attention should be called to the sequence of cuts. Study and practise this until it becomes second nature. The selected card is marked with a black border so that it can be easily followed throughout the explanation. This is one of the easiest, quickest ways to control a card to the top of the deck.

1 Assume you have had a card selected. Cut off half the deck (in the Biddle Grip) and have the selected card replaced on to the bottom half.

2 As the top half is replaced, hold a Thumb Break between the two packets. You will now perform the Double Cut as explained previously, that is, drop approximately the bottom quarter of the deck into the left hand. The left hand begins to move away with the dropped cards.

3 These cards are gripped between the thumb and first finger and replaced on top of the right-hand cards. Almost immediately, the right thumb loosens its grip, letting the remaining cards (up to the Thumb Break) fall on to the fingers of the left hand. The top card of this dropped packet is the one selected.

4 Replace the left-hand packet on to the top of the right-hand cards in exactly the same way. The selected card is now on top of the deck.

in-jog dribble control

This addition to the Double Cut Control gives a very convincing touch of extra subtlety to the overall look of the sequence. The casualness with which the cards are handled will convince your audience that the selected card is lost in the deck.

1 Have a card selected. Cut off half the deck (in the Biddle Grip) and have the selected card replaced on to the bottom half. Dribble the cards from the right hand on to the selected card, ensuring that the initial few cards are dribbled slightly towards you.

2 This view shows how the remaining cards are dribbled as the right hand moves forward so that the last group of cards fall square with the rest of the deck. The overlap of the cards seen in the above photo is known to magicians as an "in-jog".

3 As the right hand positions itself on to the top of the deck, allow the thumb to lift up the cards above the "in-jog" and secure a Thumb Break between the two packets. From here on, the Double Cut sequence is identical to that explained previously.

4 Drop approximately the bottom quarter of the deck into the left hand.

5 Grip these cards between the thumb and first finger and replace them on top of the right-hand cards. Almost immediately, loosen the right thumb's grip, letting the remaining cards (up to the Thumb Break) fall on to the fingers of the left hand. The top card of this dropped packet is the one selected.

6 Replace the left-hand packet on to the top of the right-hand cards in exactly the same way. The result is that the selected card is now on top of the deck.

run and back control

This is yet another way to control a card, and looks like a legitimate shuffle. You simply shuffle the selected card from the top to the bottom and back to the top again. It is an easy shuffle to master, and is deceptive because it looks so like the shuffle everyone is familiar with. As with any control, do not call attention to what you are doing but simply get on with it, perhaps describing what is going to happen next or asking someone a question. The more casually you handle the cards, the less suspicious people will be. The selected card is shown with a black border so that it can be followed easily during the explanation that follows.

1 Have a card selected and replaced on top of the deck. Begin an Overhand Shuffle by running one card (the card selected) into your left hand.

2 Follow this single card with a regular Overhand Shuffle until all the cards in your right hand are used up.

3 The situation at this stage is that the selected card is now on the bottom, followed by the rest of the deck on top.

4 Start another legitimate Overhand Shuffle.

5 When you are left with a small packet in your right hand, run the cards singly on to the left-hand cards.

6 You will finish with the selected card back on top.

simple overhand control

If you can Overhand-Shuffle a deck of cards, you will not have a problem learning this simple method for keeping track of and controlling a chosen card once it has been replaced in the deck. It can be used in conjunction with other shuffles and controls learnt previously, but is most suitably used with the Run and Back Control, as the motions of the cards match each other and one shuffling sequence will simply become an extension of the other. The selected card is shown with a black border for ease of explanation.

1 Have a card selected and replaced on top of the deck. Begin an Overhand Shuffle by cutting approximately half the deck from the bottom.

2 Toss this packet on to the selected card as you pull up another group of cards. However, when the first packet is tossed it should be "in-jogged" approximately 1cm (⅓in) back from the top of the deck.

3 Throw the second packet on top, flush with the original packet.

4 As your right hand returns to the deck, the right thumb is able to push all the cards above the selected card forward to grip the original top section of the deck. This is made easy thanks to the "in-jog".

5 Throw this final packet on top of everything, and the selected card is back on top.

a false cut

This sleight allows you to create the illusion of mixing the cards even though the order of the deck never changes. Used properly, it is a very useful technique to master. There are many different types of False Cut. Some are flashy and difficult to learn; others, like this one, are simple and invisible because it looks as if you cut the deck when in reality you do nothing!

Success relies on timing the moves so that the cut looks natural. See and feel what it is like to actually cut the cards, then try and match the look and pace of the real cut while executing the False Cut. Performing a real move before attempting a false move is widely practised by professional magicians. Once again, the top card is shown with a black border for ease of explanation.

1 Hold the deck face down high up at the fingertips of the left hand. Your thumb should be on one of the long edges, your second, third and fourth fingers on the other long edge and your first finger at the short edge furthest away from you.

2 With your right hand, approach the deck from above. The right first finger lies across the top card and the thumb and other fingers hold the long edges.

3 With the right thumb, split the cards about halfway down. It is the bottom half of the deck that is held by the right thumb; the top half is held entirely (and only) by the left hand.

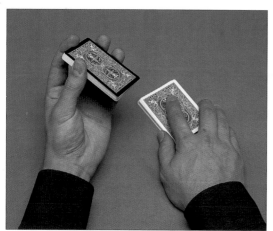

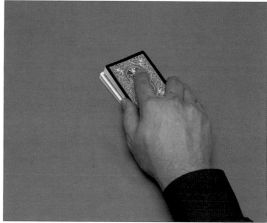

4 With the right hand, pull the bottom half of the deck away from the top half. The right first finger naturally slides over and off the top card and on to the top card of the bottom packet. This half is cut to the table.

5 The right hand returns to the left and completes the cut by placing the remaining half on top of the cards on the table.

card tricks requiring skill

The following card tricks are a little more complicated than the self-working variety taught earlier. Many of the routines use the techniques previously discussed and will require a certain amount of rehearsal, practice and dedication to master. As you will notice, many sleights are interchangeable, and you should aim to experiment in order to find techniques that work well for you.

countdown

A card is selected and shuffled into the deck. A spectator is asked for a number, and that number of cards are dealt to the table. The final card dealt is turned over, but is not the chosen card. The spectator counts the cards again. This time the last card dealt is found to be the one selected. The method to this trick may seem obvious, but people will be amazed because they do not know about controlling cards.

1 Fan the cards for a selection, stressing the spectator's freedom of choice.

2 Have the card returned and prepare to control it to the top of the deck.

3 You can use any control technique. This is the Simple Overhand Control.

4 Ask for a number between 1 and 52. Deal that number of cards to the table, one on top of the other. You will notice that the first card dealt to the table is the one selected. Assume the number chosen was 14. Deal thirteen cards to the table and turn over the fourteenth card. It will not be the one selected.

5 Act surprised by this failure and re-assemble the cards by placing all the dealt cards back on from the top of the deck. As you have just reversed the top fourteen cards, the selected card will now automatically be the fourteenth card down.

6 Give the deck to the spectator and ask them to try. Watch as they deal the chosen number of cards to the table. This time the final card will be the one selected.

tip *If you are able to convince your audience that the selected card has really been shuffled and lost into the deck, the outcome will appear to be a near impossibility. Of course, the best-case scenario occurs if the spectator should happen to choose the number "1". Then you will be able to perform a miracle without having to do anything else – simply turn over the top card. Should this ever happen, stop performing immediately because it is doubtful that anything you do could follow that!*

gliding home

This wonderful trick, based on the Glide, is especially good for a large audience. It is a "sucker" trick, which means that the audience thinks the trick has gone wrong when in reality you are in total control. It never fails to amaze people, but should be performed with a tongue-in-cheek style so as to entertain rather than frustrate or annoy the spectator. Remember, it is alright to fool a spectator, but you should avoid making someone feel or look foolish.

1 Spread the cards for a selection, using either a Ribbon Spread or a Two-Handed Spread.

2 Split the deck in half, pushing off the top two cards of the bottom half and holding a Finger Break beneath them. The selected card is replaced on this pile.

3 Once the selected card has been replaced, square the deck, maintaining the Finger Break.

4 Cut all the cards above the break to the table.

5 Place all the cards remaining in your hand on top of the packet on the table. The selected card has now been controlled to the third card from the bottom of the deck.

6 Explain that you are going to eliminate some cards and that you do not want the audience to give you any clues as to whether you are right or wrong. Hold the deck in the left hand, in preparation for the Glide. Tip the deck backwards to show the bottom card, and explain that you do not think it is the chosen card.

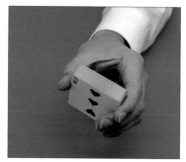

7 Tip the deck down again and slide off the bottom card of the deck. This resembles the Glide, which you will perform soon.

8 Once again, tip up the deck so that the next card can be seen. Remind the audience not to give you any clues.

9 Deal this card to the table next to the first in a similar fashion.

10 Tip the deck up one last time. This time the selected card will be seen, but carry on regardless. Explain that you do not think this is the chosen card.

secret view

11 Start to deal this card to the table next to the first two cards. However, you actually perform the Glide so that the penultimate card is secretly removed instead.

12 Keep the selected card in the Glide position and ask for a number between one and ten. Let us assume that "four" is chosen.

13 Deal three cards off the bottom of the deck, using the Glide. The fourth card you pull off is the selection. Hold it towards you and ask which card was chosen. When you hear the response, act as if there has been some mistake.

14 The spectator will rush for the last card you eliminated and will turn it over. They will be amazed to find it is no longer their card. Turn over the card in your hand and show that you had the correct card all along.

trapped

The two red Queens are placed to one side. A card is chosen and returned to the deck, which is then shuffled. The Queens are cut, face up, into the centre of the face-down deck. In an instant the cards are spread on to the table to reveal one card trapped between them. It is revealed to be the card selected.

This is an involved routine, which will encourage you to become proficient at controlling a card while using the Double Lift and Finger Break. Once you have mastered it, you will have learnt the necessary sleights to perform a whole range of different effects, several of which follow later in this book.

1 Openly remove the two red Queens from the deck and place them face up to one side. Use the Two-Handed Spread to fan the cards for a selection. Ask the spectator to look at and remember their chosen card. Whenever you get a card chosen it is always a good idea for your spectator to show it to at least one other person in case they forget it later in the trick.

2 Control the selected card to the top of the deck, using any of the methods described, or this slight variation of the Double Cut, which is easy to perform and very convincing. Lift half the deck with the right hand and have the selected card replaced on to the left-hand cards. Hold a Finger Break between the two packets as the right hand places its half back on top.

3 Cut approximately one-quarter of the deck to the table.

4 Now cut all the cards above the break on to the packet on the table.

5 Finally, place the last packet on top of everything. The selected card is now on top.

6 Hold the deck face down in the left-hand Mechanics' Grip. Obtain a Finger Break below the top card by pushing the top few cards over to the right with your left thumb. Square the cards with one hand, inserting your fourth finger into the deck one card from the top. Pick up the two Queens and display them in the right-hand Biddle Grip. The bottom Queen should be pulled to the left so that both can be seen clearly.

7 Call attention to the two Queens as you move them to a position just above the deck. Square them together by pushing the left long edge of the bottom Queen against the side of your left thumb. As this happens, secretly add the selected card to the bottom of the two Queens. This is easy because of the Finger Break.

8 The left thumb moves across the face of the top Queen and holds it in place as the right hand moves to the right with the lower two cards (perfectly squared to look like one). This displays one Queen on top of the deck.

9 Place the second Queen (with the hidden card underneath) on top of the first. Essentially what you have done is to display two cards while secretly loading one card in between them.

10 Cut the top half of the deck neatly and squarely to the table with your right hand.

11 Complete the cut by placing the remaining cards on top of those on the table. The deck should now be face down and squared in front of you.

12 Make a magical pass over the cards, then ribbon-spread them across the table to reveal that a face-down card has magically appeared between the two face-up Queens.

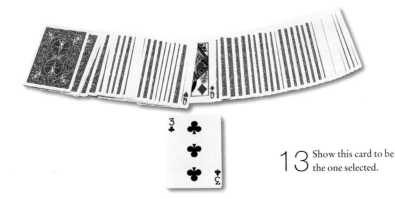

13 Show this card to be the one selected.

card through handkerchief

A card is chosen, then shuffled back into the deck. The deck is wrapped in a handkerchief and held aloft. Slowly but surely the selected card starts to melt through the material until it is completely free of the handkerchief. This routine is a classic of magic and visually *striking to watch. If performed well, the card really looks as though it is melting through the fabric. The best type of handkerchief to use is a medium-sized gentleman's silk handkerchief of the kind that is usually worn in the breast pocket for show.*

1 For this trick, you will need a deck of cards and a handkerchief. Have a card selected and returned to the deck.

2 Using any of the controls taught previously, bring the selected card to the top of the deck. Hold the deck in a left-hand Mechanics' Grip.

3 Cover the deck of cards with a coloured silk handkerchief.

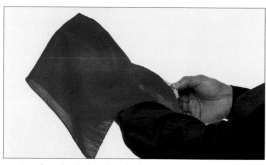

4 Reach under the handkerchief with your right hand and remove all but the top card.

5 Place these 51 cards on top of the handkerchief and square them, with the single card beneath. The deck is still held in the Mechanics' Grip.

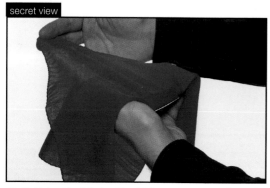

secret view

6 Fold the side of the handkerchief nearest you up and over the deck of cards. The bottom card should remain hidden.

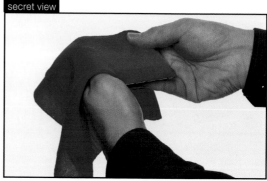

secret view

7 Now fold the material on the right side, underneath the deck. Your left hand will have to alter its grip to accommodate this.

8 Finally fold the material on the left side, under the deck. Hold the loose corners together in your right hand, out to your right-hand side.

9 From behind, you can see that the selected card is trapped on the outside of the handkerchief, within the folds of the material. The folds stop the card from falling out prematurely.

10 Shake your right hand up and down and the card will start to emerge. This is the view that your spectators will see from the front.

11 Continue to shake until just before the card falls out completely. With practice, you will know when the card is about to fall free of the handkerchief.

12 Reach up with the left hand, remove the card and reveal it to be the one selected. The deck can now be unwrapped and you will be ready to perform another card trick.

card on wall

There is a classic magic trick called Card on Ceiling, in which a chosen, signed card is shuffled into a deck. The deck is thrown in the air and the signed card flies out of the pack and sticks to the ceiling.

The problem with this is that it can be difficult to get the card down again and some people object to having a card stuck on their ceiling long after the show is over. So here is a simplified method that looks just as good, which you will be able to use in any venue without ruining the décor. Instead of using the ceiling you stick the card on to a wall or a glass picture frame.

On the other hand, if you have permission or it is your house, you may choose to stick the card to the ceiling. If you throw the card somewhere that can't be reached the result of your trick will last long after you have left. There will be a story to tell every time someone asks, "Why is there a card stuck to the ceiling?".

1 You will need a deck of cards and a piece of adhesive tape. Make the tape into a loop with the sticky side out. The loop should fit loosely around the middle finger of your right hand.

2 Spread a deck of cards in a fan, for a selection to be made.

secret view

3 Take care to keep the tape away from the deck.

4 Ask someone to select a card and remember what it is.

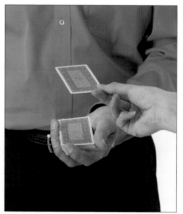

5 Ask them to replace their card on the top of the deck.

secret view

6 Turn the deck over and secretly allow the tape to stick to the back of their card. Slip the loop of tape off your finger.

secret view

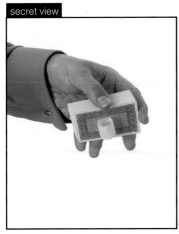

secret view

secret view

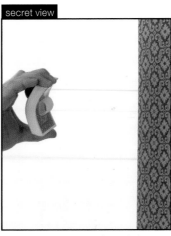

7 Prepare to shuffle the deck of cards. Be sure to keep the tape out of the spectators' view.

8 Notice how this overhand shuffle keeps the chosen card in place at the back of the deck. Squeeze the front and back cards every time you take a batch and the chosen card never moves. From the front this looks like a genuine shuffle.

9 Prepare to "spring" the cards from your hand by bending them as shown, but don't let the audience see the tape. Aim the cards with the tape pointing directly at the wall.

11 The chosen card remains stuck to the wall for a spectacular finish.

tip *You will probably want to use an old deck of cards for this trick, as the cards will end up all over the floor. Try not to let anyone else remove the card from the surface, or they will see how it is stuck: remove it yourself after the show.*

10 Spring the cards at the wall and the selection will stick firmly while all the other cards cascade to the floor.

cards across

*Two packets of ten cards are carefully counted and two spectators
each hold on to one packet tightly. Three cards are caused to fly
invisibly from one packet to the other so that when the cards are
counted again one person has seven and the other thirteen. This is*
*a classic of magic for which there are many methods, most requiring
some form of sleight of hand. The techniques taught here are
relatively simple yet effective. Practise the false counts until you are
super-confident with them. They are the key to the success of this trick.*

1 Hold a deck of cards in your left hand
and openly push off ten cards into the
right hand. Secretly push off another three
cards, obtaining a Finger Break beneath
them. Due to the ten-card spread there is a
huge amount of cover for this "get-ready".

2 Flip the top ten cards face up and
square them on to the top of the deck.
Lift up everything above the Finger Break.
You will now be holding ten face-up cards
with three face-down cards at the bottom
of the packet. Place the rest of the deck off
to one side. It is now necessary to count
these thirteen cards as ten as follows.

3 Hold the packet in the right-hand
Biddle Grip. With your left thumb,
pull off the first card and, using the edge
of the right-hand packet, flip it face down
on to your left hand, counting out loud,
"One". Pull off the second face-up card in
the same manner as you place the first card
back on to the bottom of the packet. Count
"Two". Place this second card to the
bottom, as before, and continue counting
the cards out loud until you reach the end
of the face-up cards. You will have
counted ten face-up cards but will have
secretly added three face-down cards.

4 Give this packet to the spectator on your left, asking them to
hold it tightly between their hands. At this stage they will be
convinced they are holding just ten cards. Now pick up the deck
again and openly spread off another ten cards, counting each card
as you push it off to the right.

5 Lift only seven of the ten cards and immediately square the
edges of these against the cards in your left hand. Don't make
a move out of it; just act casually and nonchalantly.

6 Put the deck to one side so that you can recount the seven cards as ten, as follows. Hold the packet in the right-hand Biddle Grip and use the left thumb to peel off the top card into the left hand, counting out loud, "One". The left hand approaches to take the second card on top of the first, counting "Two". Peel off one more, counting "Three".

7 As the fourth card is taken, place the previous three back on to the bottom of the packet. Do not pause here; just peel off the fourth card, counting "Four". For a second there will only be one card in your hand when there should be four, but your hands do not stop moving and continue to peel off the fifth card as you count "Five". Continue in this fashion until there are no more cards left. You will have counted seven cards as ten. This false count is not easy, but practice will eventually enable you to perform it without hesitation, which is absolutely essential.

8 Give this packet to the spectator on your right and have them hold it securely. Ask each person to confirm how many cards they hold. They should automatically say that they have ten each. Mime sneaking three cards from the spectator on your right and placing them into the hand of the spectator on your left.

9 After this comical byplay, ask the person on your right to count the cards out loud to the table one at a time. There will be only seven cards.

10 The other spectator counts their cards to the table and incredibly they will now have thirteen!

card under glass

Here is a clever little routine that makes use of the Double Lift and Turnover explained earlier. Learning this will make all the hard *work and practice worthwhile! A chosen card is caused to magically change places with an indifferent card isolated under a glass.*

1 Have a wine glass on the table, to your side. Spread a deck for a selection.

2 Hold a Finger Break above the card as it is replaced into the centre of the deck.

3 This photograph shows an exposed view of the Finger Break.

4 Double-cut the cards below the break to the top of the deck. You have controlled the selected card to the top.

5 Perform the Double Lift, showing an indifferent card.

6 Place the double card back on to the deck as your right hand lifts up the glass. Push off the top card of the deck and deal it to the table, putting the glass on top.

7 Dribble the deck on to the top of the glass, holding on to the last card.

8 Turn it over to reveal it was the card just placed under the glass!

9 With a flourish, turn the card under the glass face up to show that it has changed to the one selected.

forcing a card

In many routines it is necessary to make the spectator take a particular card. Using several techniques explained here, even though you "force" a particular card upon the spectator, the selection procedure seems quite fair and above board. A card force properly executed should arouse no suspicion. Several forces are explained here – in most cases you can use whichever you feel most comfortable with.

Hindu Force

This and the Slip Force, which is explained next, are the most practical ways to force a card. The Hindu Force is direct, convincing and relatively easy to execute. A small amount of practice is all that is required to learn how to do this successfully.

1 The card to be forced should be at the bottom of the deck.

2 Hold the deck high up in the fingertips of your left hand. Your left first finger should be at the outer end of the deck.

3 With the right hand, approach from above and take the bottom three-quarters of the deck away. The thumb is on one side, the second, third and fourth fingers on the other, and the first finger bent lightly on top.

4 Allow the cards in your left hand to fall down to the palm as the right hand returns and the left fingers grab a small group of cards from the top of the deck. Allow these to fall on to the cards below.

5 The bottom card in the right hand always remains the same. Ask a spectator to stop you as you Hindu-shuffle the deck. When he or she says "Stop!", show the bottom card of the packet in your right hand. It will always be the force card.

slip force

This card force is simple yet effective. If performed casually and comfortably, it will be successful every single time. The card to be *forced must be on top of the deck at the outset. It is shown with a black border for ease of explanation.*

secret view

1 Hold the deck in the left-hand Mechanics' Grip. Bend the first finger under the deck and run your thumb down the corner of the cards. Ask the spectator to say "Stop!" as you riffle through the cards.

2 The right hand approaches the deck from above and grips all the "riffled off" cards. Lift this packet straight up. Pressure is maintained on the top card of the deck (force card) so that it falls flush with and becomes the top card of the bottom half.

3 Tapping the long edge of the right-hand cards on the top of the left-hand cards to square them will add plenty of cover for the move. Extend your left hand and have the top card (supposedly the card stopped at) looked at and remembered.

cut deeper force

This is an extremely simple way to force a card. However, while this forcing procedure fits some tricks well, it is too laborious to have a *card chosen this way every time. In practice, it is highly advisable that the spectator does the cutting and turning of the cards.*

1 The card to be forced should be at the top of the deck. In our example it is the Three of Hearts.

2 Hold the deck face down in your left hand and cut about a quarter of the cards face up, replacing them on the deck.

3 Now cut about half the deck face up and replace that group of cards on the deck.

4 Explain that you will use the first face-down card you come to. Fan through the cards and cut the deck at the first face-down card. Place all the face-up cards on to the bottom of the deck, turning them face down as you do so.

5 The top face-down card will be the force card.

cross cut force and prediction

This is a very useful force, easy to accomplish and very deceptive, but only if done correctly. It is taught here as part of a simple trick, as its success relies largely on something known as "time misdirection". This is the concept of using time in between a secret move and the result of that secret move, the idea being that when the spectator tries to reconstruct what happened, they cannot recall the exact sequence of events. Even a few seconds is sufficient. As you will soon see, it would look ridiculous to mark the cut and then immediately reveal the card. The spectator would know instinctively that something illogical had happened.

The back of the force card is here marked with a black border for ease of explanation.

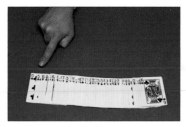

1 When you are ready to start the trick, take a moment to secretly note the top card of the deck. In this example it is the Six of Clubs. This is the card you will be forcing on the spectator.

2 Begin by giving the cards a shuffle or a False Cut that leaves the top card in position. Either way, the cards should be in front of you, face down, with the Six of Clubs on top. Explain that you are going to write a prediction. Draw a question mark on one side of a piece of paper and the Six of Clubs on the other side.

3 Place your prediction off to the side of the table but in full view.

4 Ask a spectator to cut the deck at any point into two packets, side by side. It is important that you keep note of where the original top half is placed.

5 Pick up the bottom half of the deck and place it on the top half of the deck at right angles. As you do this, explain that you are marking the exact position the spectator cut to, for reference later on.

6 Now "time misdirection" is employed by diverting the spectator away from the deck and on to the prediction. Remind your audience that you made a prediction before the cards were cut and that the cards were cut at a completely random location. Reveal your prediction to be the Six of Clubs.

7 The true orientation and order of the deck will have been forgotten by the time the audience's attention returns. Lift up the top packet and explain that you are finding the exact point in the deck marked earlier. In reality you are about to turn over the original top card of the deck.

8 Turn over the supposed cut-to card and reveal that it matches your earlier prediction.

special gimmicks

There are a variety of specially made playing cards, available from magic shops, which will enable you to perform some amazing tricks. These cards look normal but are specially faked in some way.

Explained here are several special gimmicks you can construct yourself. They are not difficult to make and they give you the ability to show people tricks that they will have never seen before.

pips away

The Two of Diamonds is picked by a spectator. The card is placed into the centre of the deck and the magician explains that it will magically appear at the top of the deck again. The top card is turned over but it is the Three of Diamonds. With a flick of the fingers one of the pips flies off the card, leaving the magician holding the Two of Diamonds!

1 Using a scalpel, carefully cut out one of the diamond pips from a spare card.

2 Attach a tiny piece of reusable adhesive to the underside of the diamond pip.

3 Stick the diamond pip in the centre of a duplicate Two of Diamonds so that at a glance it resembles the Three of Diamonds.

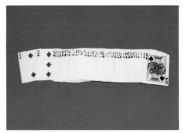

4 Set up a deck so that the real Two of Diamonds is on top and the special Two of Diamonds is second from the top.

5 You will need to force the Two of Diamonds using the Cut Deeper Force. Hold the deck face down on your left hand and ask a spectator to cut off about a quarter of the cards and to turn them face up on top of the deck.

6 Now ask them to cut about half the cards and to turn them face up on top of the deck. Explain that you will use the first face-down card you come to.

7 Spread the deck until you come to the first face-down card. That is the force card. Remove all the face-up cards and place them face down on the bottom of the deck.

8 Lift the top card and show that it is the Two of Diamonds. Do not look at the face of the card yourself.

9 Push the Two of Diamonds clearly into the centre of the deck, then slowly square the cards.

10 Riffle up the end of the deck and explain that the chosen card will pass through all the cards and return to the top again.

11 Hold the cards in the left-hand Dealing Grip and push the top card to the right with your thumb. With your right hand, grip the card at the top right-hand corner so that as the card turns face up, your fingers are automatically covering the corner pip, which should show "3" but actually shows "2".

12 Turn the card face up, hiding the far corner pip under your left thumb. Display the special "Three" of Diamonds and ask whether it is the chosen card.

13 When the spectator tells you that the chosen card was the Two of Diamonds, say "Watch!" and prepare to flick the centre pip with your right finger and thumb.

14 As you flick the pip, it will fly off so fast it seems to disappear, leaving you with the chosen card, the Two of Diamonds.

tip *Remember that there is a duplicate Two of Diamonds in the deck, so be sure to remove one of them before giving the deck out for examination.*

changing card

A card is selected and shuffled back into the deck. You remove one card from your pocket. It is seen to be incorrect. With a shake of the hand, the card changes into the correct card.

As a variation, you could force two cards, in this example the Six of Clubs followed by the Jack of Spades. Then you can show the first prediction and magically change it to the second.

1 Choose two different cards (in this example they are the Six of Clubs and the Jack of Spades), plus a spare third card. Fold both of the chosen cards inwards with a sharp crease across the centre.

2 Glue one half of the folded cards back to back, ensuring perfect alignment.

3 This will create a card that can be shown as either a Jack or a Six.

4 Apply glue to the remaining area of the back.

5 Glue it to the face of the third card. This will strengthen the gimmick.

6 Fold the flap into the "up" position, with the Six of Clubs facing outwards. Place this card face down into your breast pocket.

7 Take a deck of cards and place the Jack of Spades on the bottom in preparation for a card force.

8 Shown here is the Hindu Force, but you can use any force that you feel confident performing.

9 Ask a spectator to say "Stop!", then show the bottom card. It will be the Jack of Spades. Shuffle it into the deck and put the cards to one side.

10 Reach into your pocket and remove the fake card, displaying it in your left fingers. Hold it tightly so that the double thickness remains hidden. Ask if you have the correct card. The spectator will tell you it is wrong. Ask which card was chosen.

11 Bring your right hand in front of your left and let the top of the fake card spring forward.

12 As your right hand moves down, allow the flap to open completely so that the card appears to change.

13 Re-grip the card so that the entire surface can be displayed. Try to keep the flap aligned.

find the lady

This trick is a famous illegal swindle, often seen played on the streets of cities worldwide, in which people lose their money by betting on the card they believe to be the odd one out. It has many other names, including Three Card Monte and Chase the Ace. Show your friends why they should never play this game.

Three cards are displayed – two Eights and a Queen. Even though your spectator is sure they know where the Queen is, when they turn over the card they find the Queen has changed into a Joker. With some thought, the Joker can be made to change into many other things, including your business card!

1 Using scissors, cut a piece off a Queen card. The exact size does not matter, but try to cut about a third of the card. It should taper towards one end, as shown here.

2 Trim about 5mm (¼in) off the tapered end. This is so that the gimmicked card will work more smoothly, as you will see.

3 Attach a piece of adhesive tape along the back of the long outer edge of the Queen, and stick it to one of the Eights in a slightly fanned position. The tape acts as a hinge. Experimentation will make this clear.

4 This is how the completed fake card should look.

5 Insert a Joker behind the flap on the fake card and align the edges.

6 Lay another Eight on top so that it looks like a fan of three cards. The Joker will be completely hidden, and it looks as if you are holding two Eights with a Queen in the middle.

7 Display this fan of cards and explain that the spectator simply has to keep their eye on the Queen and remember where it is.

8 Turn the fan of cards face down by turning your wrist, then ask them where they think the Queen is. They will tell you it is in the middle. Ask them to remove the middle card.

9 When they turn it over, they will be amazed to find it is a Joker. Close the fan of cards slightly so that you can turn the cards face up again to flash the two Eights.

card through tablecloth

This effect is simple. A chosen card vanishes from the deck and reappears under the tablecloth, or indeed anywhere you wish to make it appear – your pocket, under a plate, under a spectator's chair or in their pocket. Wherever you decide, make sure you plant it there a long time before you begin the trick. If you were to be seen setting up the trick, the ending would be spoilt.

This is the perfect example of a method that is so simple yet so very baffling. When performed well it should look like a miracle and would probably even fool knowledgeable magicians! After reading through the method, think about other ways in which the vanish of the card could be used.

1 There are two stages to this routine: the disappearance of the chosen card and its reappearance at the end. The card that vanishes is forced. Begin by taking any card from the deck (in our example, the Ace of Clubs) and, using scissors, trim off about 1mm (¹⁄₁₆in) from one short end.

2 Take any card from a spare deck (in our example, the Eight of Hearts). This will be the card that vanishes. Apply glue (here marked black) to the bottom third, and glue it to the Ace of Clubs along the untrimmed end, so that the glued edges align perfectly.

3 Leave the glue to dry. This is how the faked double card should look. Notice how the Eight of Hearts is easy to lift away because of the strip you trimmed off the Ace earlier. (This trimmed card is known as a "short card".)

4 Insert this double card into the middle of the deck, remembering the orientation so that you know which is the unglued end.

5 The second stage to this trick is the reappearance of the card. From the deck, take the card that matches your duplicate card (the Eight of Hearts) and place it secretly under the tablecloth. (This should be done before the audience arrives.)

6 The preparation is now complete. Hold the deck of cards face down in the left-hand Dealing Grip. (The open side of the short card should be facing away from you.)

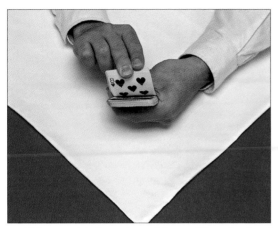

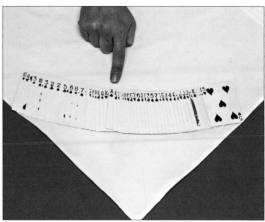

7 Using your right first and second fingers, riffle up the edge of the deck. The cards will automatically stop at the duplicate Eight of Hearts because of the short card. If you listen carefully you will hear a click. With practice, you will be able to stop at the short card every single time. In performance explain that as you riffle the deck of cards you want the spectator to say "Stop!" at any time. Begin the riffle and watch their lips. You must time the riffle so that when they say "Stop!" you are able to let all of the cards below the short card fall. This will take a little practice but is not too difficult, especially if you start the riffle slowly. If you start too fast, you may pass the short card before the spectator has a chance to say "Stop!" Ask the spectator to remember the card they stopped at, then allow the remainder of the deck to riffle off your fingers.

8 You have several options here to show that the card has vanished from the deck. You could spread the cards neatly along the table in a Ribbon Spread (as seen here). In our example, the Ace of Clubs is actually a double card with the Eight of Hearts hiding secretly behind it. Nobody will ever suspect this. Ask the spectator to find their card and they will have to admit that it is no longer there. Another way to do this is to give the deck to the spectator and ask them to deal the cards one at a time on to the table until they find their card. Nobody ever notices the difference in thickness of one card. This is perhaps the most convincing way of proving that the card has actually vanished from the deck.

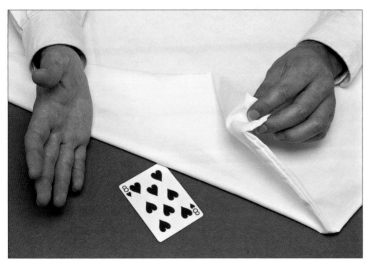

9 Slowly reveal the card under the tablecloth. Do not underestimate how effective this routine is. This is one of the cleverest ways to vanish a card from a deck, and there seems to be no explanation for its disappearance. As mentioned in the introduction, with a little thought the card can be made to reappear just about anywhere. You are limited only by your imagination.

rising card from box (version 1)

A chosen card is shuffled into the deck, which is then placed inside the card box. The box is held at the fingertips and one card rises up into view. It is the card selected.

The best thing about this simple trick is that it does not require a special deck, so as long as you keep the cards in the special box you will be ready to perform it at any time. It is the perfect "end" trick to your act, as you finish with the cards back in the box, ready to put away in your pocket.

The special box is very simple to make and will only take a few minutes of your time, yet the result is a trick that will truly mystify your audience.

1 Remove a deck of cards from the box. Using a scalpel, cut a section from the flap side of the box approximately 1.5cm (⅝in) wide x 5cm (2in) long.

2 Place the box to one side so that the cut-out section remains unseen throughout the trick. Spread the cards for a selection.

3 Control the selected card to the top. Shown here is a Double Cut to the table. With the right hand, lift the top half off the deck and have the selected card replaced.

secret view

4 Replace the top half of the deck, holding a Finger Break between the two packets.

5 Cut approximately a quarter of the deck to the table.

6 Now cut all the cards above the break on top of those on the table. The cuts should be made briskly.

7 Finally, place the remaining cards on top. The selected card has now been secretly controlled to the top. You can follow this with a false shuffle and False Cut if you feel confident enough.

8 Place the deck in the box so that the faces are pointing outwards. Make sure the cut-out section at the back of the box remains hidden.

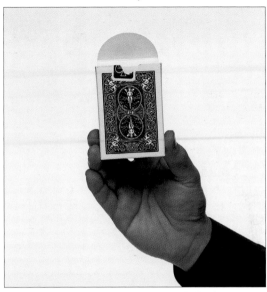

9 Hold the box in the fingertips of your right hand. Notice how the box is held in such a way that the right first finger cannot be seen.

secret view

10 Insert your first finger into the back of the box through the hole and slowly push up the top card of the deck.

11 From the front, the selected card is seen to rise mysteriously from the box.

rising card from box (version 2)

The idea of a chosen card rising from a deck is an old one, and believe it or not there are literally dozens of methods for accomplishing this effect. This is a clever version that is easy to master.

In this version a card is freely chosen and returned to the centre of the deck. The deck is placed in the card box and a small "handle" is inserted through a hole in the side of the box. The handle is "cranked" and the chosen card comically begins to rise out of the deck.

It is best to use a new deck of cards for this trick, and the preparation is a little more elaborate than most tricks require, but you will find the reaction you receive from your spectators more than worth the extra time and effort.

1 Perfectly square a new deck of cards. Using a pencil, mark a very light, straight line along the edge of the deck approximately 1.5cm (⅝in) from the top. This line should not be obvious at a casual glance, but clear enough for you to see. The line shown here is thick for clarity.

2 Using a scalpel, cut a small square hole in the side of the card box so that it matches up with the pencil line.

3 Test the position of your cut-out by placing the cards into the box and viewing the line through the hole.

4 Attach a small piece of double-sided adhesive tape to the end of a toothpick. It may help to roll the tape between your fingers so that your natural skin oils reduce the stickiness of the tape slightly. Experimentation will make this clear.

5 Begin by having a card selected. While the spectator is looking at the card, secretly turn the deck end to end.

6 Ask the spectator to replace their selected card anywhere into the centre of the deck.

7 Replace the deck in the card box, positioning the secret pencil line on the opposite side to the cut-out.

8 Produce the toothpick. Insert the end that has the adhesive tape attached to it into the deck through the cut-out and exactly next to the chosen card. This can be found because it will have a tiny pencil dot on the edge. (That is the reason for using a new deck; the whiter the edge of the cards, the easier it is to see the pencil mark.)

9 Push the toothpick into the deck about halfway. The adhesive tape should be touching the chosen card.

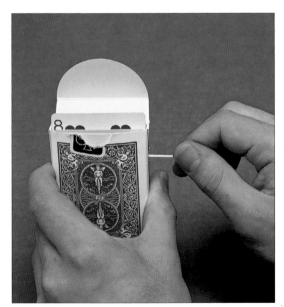 

10 Begin twisting the toothpick in a clockwise direction. The tape will adhere to the chosen card and start to "crank" it upwards from the box.

11 Continue twisting the toothpick until the card is completely exposed and has risen almost all the way out of the deck.

card to matchbox

A spectator chooses a card. You remove a card
from your pocket and ask if it is correct. It is
not. With a wave of your hand, the card
instantly changes into a matchbox. This is
opened and a folded card is discovered inside.
It matches the selected card!

In order to make this gimmick, you will
need a matchbox, a second matchbox cover
(top and side required only), glue, a scalpel
and duplicate cards. It may take some time
for you to make up this particular gimmick,
and you may need several trials before you
make one that works perfectly. Experiment
with different sized matchboxes to find one
that works well.

1 Place a duplicate Queen of Hearts
face down in front of you. Glue a
complete matchbox on to the card at the
top left-hand corner.

2 Using a scalpel, carefully score the
point where the card meets the box.
Fold the card inwards.

3 Score the card once again, this time where the card meets the
edge of the box. Fold this side down so that it lies against the
striking edge of the box.

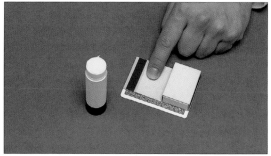

4 Unfold the card. Glue the top and side from the second
matchbox cover to it as shown. The folds in the cover should
match up with the scored sections in the playing card.

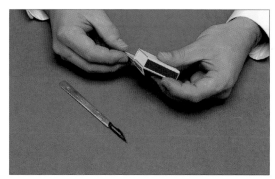

5 The card overhangs along one edge. Score along the length of
the overhang so that it folds inwards.

6 When the box is now folded along the creases, the card will
fold face inwards and be hidden. You may need to trim the
playing card slightly in order to ensure a perfect fit.

7 Take another duplicate card (in this example, the Six of Diamonds) and fold it into quarters.

8 Place the folded Six of Diamonds in the drawer of the matchbox. Hold the matchbox with the Queen of Hearts in the open position. Place it in your left jacket pocket, in readiness for the routine.

9 Force the Six of Diamonds in the deck, using any of the force techniques described. Shown here is the Hindu Force. Start with the Six of Diamonds on the bottom of the deck.

10 Begin the Hindu Force, asking a spectator to say "Stop!" at any time.

11 Show the force card, then shuffle it legitimately into the deck again. ▶

12 Reach into your left jacket pocket and remove the card in the open position. The hidden matchbox should rest against the palm of your hand. Ask "Is this your card?" The answer will of course be "No".

13 Say "Watch!" Gently shake your left arm up and down. Simultaneously with the fourth finger of the left hand bend the overhang upwards along the crease.

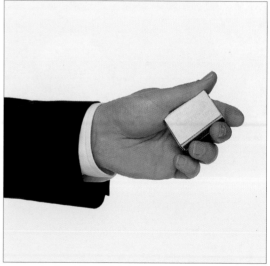

14 Now bend the fingers inwards, folding the card in half along the centre crease you made earlier.

15 Finally, with your left thumb, fold the remaining section along the edge of the box. You can now stop shaking your hand and show that the card has changed into a matchbox.

16 Explain, "Inside the box is one card." Slowly push open the drawer of the matchbox. The duplicate of the forced card that you placed inside the box will become visible.

17 Tip out the contents – a folded card. Remember to keep the gimmick held firmly so as not to expose the secret of the card stuck to the outside of the box, but try to look as though you are handling it casually.

18 Unfold the card and have the spectator confirm that it was the card they selected at the start of the trick.

kiss me quick

A card is chosen by a spectator and shuffled back into the deck, which is then placed back in the box. The spectator blows a kiss at the deck of cards and when the cards are removed one card is seen reversed in the middle, with a big lipstick mark on its face. It is the chosen card.

1 Prepare the trick by putting a lipstick kiss on the face of a card. You will need a duplicate of this card, which should be placed at the top of the deck.

2 Place the deck in the box, with the "kiss" card at one end.

3 To perform the trick, remove the deck of cards from the box leaving the "kiss" card secretly within.

4 You will now force the duplicate card on to the spectator. (It should be the top face-down card.) Hold the deck on the palm of your hand and ask the spectator to cut a small number of cards off the deck and turn them face-up, returning them to the deck.

5 Now ask the spectator to cut a bigger batch of cards from the deck, turning those face-up too and replacing the pile once again.

6 Explain that the first face-down card you come to will be theirs. Spread through the deck and the very first face-down card will be your duplicate. (This technique is known to magicians as the "cut deeper force").

7 Ask your spectator to remember the card and then return it to the deck. Give the deck a shuffle.

8 Return the deck to the box. As you insert the cards be sure that the deck is oriented the opposite way around to the "kiss" card, which should be positioned somewhere in the middle of the deck.

9 Ask a female spectator who is wearing red lipstick to blow a kiss at the deck of cards.

10 Remove the deck from the box and spread out the cards face down. One card will be reversed and it will be the chosen card, with a great big kiss on it.

advanced flourishes

The irony with sleight of hand is that one spends a great deal of time learning a "move" that usually remains secret! Of course, spectators are impressed by magic tricks when they cannot see how

they are done, but you can impress them in a different way by fancy flourishes such as the ones that follow – you are demonstrating, in a dramatic fashion, that you can make the cards do whatever you want.

thumb fan

This is a neat fan, produced with two hands. You will need a deck of cards in good condition. Once learnt, this fan can be used whenever

you need to have a card selected. It is a prettier spread than the Two-Handed Spread taught earlier on.

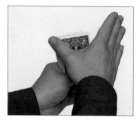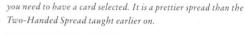

1 Hold the deck in your left hand. The base of the deck should align with the top of your third finger. The thumb grips the deck tightly along the bottom third.

2 With the right hand, approach the deck. The right thumb stretches out and reaches a position at the top left corner of the deck.

3 The right thumb moves in a small semicircle while the left thumb grips the deck tightly. The cards will automatically pivot under the ball of the left thumb. If the fan looks messy, you may need to reposition your left thumb.

4 From the front, a beautiful display of cards is seen.

pressure fan

This is perhaps the neatest fan of all. A good-quality deck of cards is essential. While similar to the Thumb Fan, this fan is even more

attractive to watch being formed because the semicircle of cards just seems to pop into shape by itself.

1 Hold the cards in the right-hand Biddle Grip and bend them by squeezing the fingers and thumb together. Place the bowed cards into the left hand, between the thumb, second finger and third finger. The bottom edge of the deck should be level with the third finger.

2 The left hand stays perfectly still as the right hand turns, allowing the cards to riffle off one at a time, describing a semicircle. Pressure must be maintained correctly for the cards to fan smoothly.

3 This view shows how the pressure created bends the cards into a flower-like display.

4 Viewed from the front, the fan looks symmetrical, neat and very professional.

one-handed fan

In this flourish, the cards are fanned neatly and quickly with one hand. A little practice will enable you to produce a beautifully *aligned fan every time. A good-quality deck of cards in perfect condition will increase your chances of success.*

1 Hold the deck in your right hand. The edge of the deck sits halfway between the first and second joints of the fingers. The thumb grips the deck at the bottom corner.

2 This view shows the position of the hand without the cards.

3 Close your hand up into a fist. This view shows the finishing position of the hand without the cards.

4 As you close your fingers, the result is a fan of cards.

one-handed reverse fan

This fan results in a deck that looks blank because the indices of the cards remain hidden. As with all card work involving fans, you need a deck of cards in good condition. If you wish to create the illusion of *a blank deck, you will also need to use a deck with only two indices as opposed to four, and you will require a blank card which should be positioned at the face of the deck at the start.*

1 Hold the deck in a grip similar to the finishing position of the One-Handed Fan. However, the cards are not yet spread.

2 This reverse view shows how the fingers are all closed in a fist.

3 Open your fingers to spread the fan. Practise the move slowly at first, and experiment with different positions – you may find that it helps if your first and second fingers pull back slightly as they open. You should be able to make an impressive flourish.

4 The front view shows how the deck looks blank, with the indices hidden from view. If you place a blank card on the face of the deck before you begin, the illusion of a blank deck will be perfect.

giant fan

This is a nice quick flourish. A deck of cards is split in two and woven together, then the cards are fanned. The result is a fan of cards that looks like it has been made with a jumbo-sized deck! You may be able *to think of a line of patter to accompany the flourish, for example, "For those of you who can't see at the back of the room, here is a trick for you!" or "Look, a giant deck of cards…or maybe we are shrinking!"*

3 Push the cards together until they protrude about half their length.

1 The initial sequence of moves is similar to that of the Weave Shuffle. Hold the cards high up in the fingertips of the left hand. Your thumb should be on one of the long edges and your second, third and fourth fingers on the other. Your first finger rests on the short end.

2 With your right hand, lift approximately half the deck and weave the two halves together as neatly as possible. Ensure the first and last cards of the right-hand packet become the bottom and top cards of the deck. (*See* Weave Shuffle and Waterfall for more details on weaving cards.)

4 Spread the deck between both hands and you will have a magnificent Giant Fan.

comedy card force

It is always fun to make people laugh, and it shows you do not take yourself or your magic too seriously. In this flourish, you fan a deck of cards for a selection and stress how fair the choice is. As you talk, one *card sprouts out of the deck and moves backwards and forwards as if to say "Choose me!" Your spectators will laugh at the irony of this supposedly fair selection procedure!*

 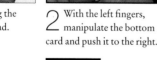

secret view

1 Fan the cards, using the Two-Handed Spread.

2 With the left fingers, manipulate the bottom card and push it to the right.

secret view

3 Take this card with the right fingertips and thrust it forwards.

4 From the top, it looks as if the card has a life of its own. You can make the card run around the perimeter of the fan by swivelling the card with the third finger, using the second finger as a pivot point. Play with this move with the cards in your hands until you develop the knack.

card spring

Picture a magician with a deck in their hand and you will visualize the cards being juggled and shuffled with dexterity and precision. In this spectacular display of skill, the hands are held wide apart yet the cards seem to take on a life of their own, springing with perfect direction out of one hand through the air and into the other hand.

Be prepared to spend most of your practice time picking cards up off the floor! The best place to practise is over a bed so that when (not if) you drop the cards, you won't have to reach so far to pick them up.

You may find it easier to start with your hands very close together until the cards start springing, then move your hands further apart, and as the spring finishes, bring both hands back together again. Trial and error is the only real way to learn how to spring cards properly. With practice, you should be able to get your hands as far as 30cm (12in) from each other – maybe even further. This is a fun flourish that you will enjoy performing. Use a good-quality deck of cards, otherwise they may become ruined when the cards are bowed.

1 Hold the deck in the right-hand Biddle Grip, at about chest level. It is important that the deck is held firmly.

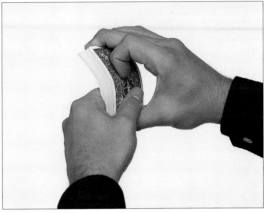

2 Push the middle of the cards up with your left hand, squeezing them with your right hand to bend them.

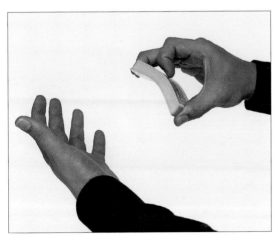

3 Hold your left hand about 10cm (4in) under the deck. (With practice, you will be able to increase this distance dramatically.) Your fingers should be outstretched, ready to catch the cards as they hit your hand.

4 Continue to bend the cards until they start to slip off the fingers. The key to success is ensuring that the cards slip off the fingers and not the thumb. (If you experience this problem, try holding the cards further up the thumb. The ideal position is usually in the middle of the first joint.) As the cards hit the left hand, begin to tighten your fingers to hold the cards in place.

back palm

If you have ever seen a magician pluck cards from the air, you will know how wonderful this illusion is. It is not easy to perform well and requires plenty of practice but, like riding a bicycle, once you have learnt the basics you will never forget how to do it. This type of magic is best suited to stage acts and performances where there is some distance between you and the audience.

If you go on to learn more about magic, you will discover moves and sleights that enable you to produce a constant fan of cards at your fingertips, and even moves that allow you to show that the back and front of the hand is empty before producing a card. Some magicians make a very successful living from acts that contain nothing but card manipulations such as this.

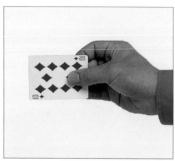  

1 Hold a card in the fingertips of the right hand, with the fingers on the back and the thumb on the front.

2 Bend your middle two fingers inwards and push with your thumb while straightening your first and fourth fingers. The view seen here is from above.

3 Bring your first and fourth fingers around to grip the card from the front at either side. Curl the fingers until they are level with your middle two fingers, making sure that the top of the card is below the ends of your fingers.

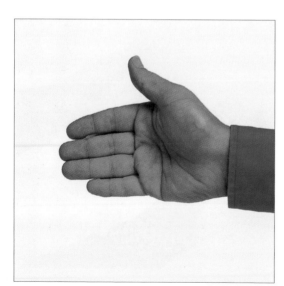

secret view

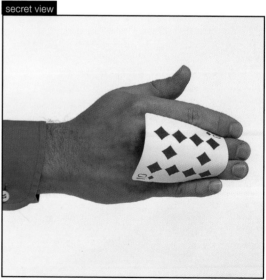

4 Close the gaps between your fingers (these gaps are known to magicians as "windows") and straighten them out so that the card is carried around to the back of the hand. The cards are gripped by the first and fourth fingers only. From the front, the hand should look completely empty.

5 This back view shows the true situation – the card is pinned to the back of your hand. The moves should happen one after the other, very quickly. Added "misdirection" can be created by gently waving the hand up and down.

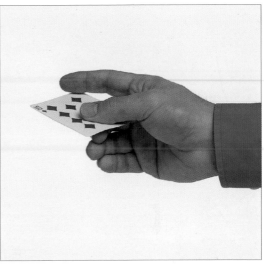

6   To make the card reappear, reverse the sequence above, but with some subtle differences. Close your hand into a fist, bringing the card to the front of the hand. The thumb is positioned on the front and pinches the card against the middle two fingers as before.

7   With the thumb, drag the card between and through the first and second fingers. As the card is pulled, open the fingers.

8   The card pivots until it is completely straight. The first finger moves behind the card, so that you finish with the card held between the tips of the thumb and fingers.

9   Try experimenting with other similar-sized objects. For example, hand out your business card with a magical flourish! Magic always works best when it occurs unexpectedly.

money
magic

Money is the one thing that most people carry with them at all times. The following pages reveal some wonderful magic tricks for you to perform. Have you ever dreamed of making money appear from nowhere at your fingertips, or of being able to change a blank piece of paper into a banknote? If so, your dreams are about to come true – or so your audience will believe!

a good run for your money

Rightly or wrongly, the one thing most people desire in their lives, along with health and happiness, is money. If we could really perform magic, we would make money appear so that we could live the life of our dreams and help others live theirs. The idea of producing money out of thin air was born a long time ago. There cannot be many children who have never had a coin pulled from behind their ear.

Towards the end of the nineteenth century, one of the most skilled coin manipulators of all time created an act entitled "The Miser's Dream". His name was Thomas Nelson Downs and he billed himself as the "King of Koins". The act is said to have lasted about 30 minutes and contained only coin magic. His act was so popular that he left his American homeland in 1899 and travelled throughout Europe, where he found further fame and success. Part of his act involved showing his hands completely empty, removing his hat, showing that empty too, then producing coin after coin after coin. Each coin was thrown into the hat until it was full of money. "The Ariel Treasury", as it was then called, is now better known by magicians as "The Miser's Dream", in remembrance of the late, great T. Nelson Downs. It is still being performed regularly today, and is received as well now as it was then.

For general coin tricks and coin manipulation you can use any coins that may be to hand, but magicians favour the American half-dollar for its size, weight and

Above: You too can learn how to produce money at your fingertips from out of thin air!

Left: An early poster publicizing the master coin manipulator Thomas Nelson Downs (1867–1938), also known as the "King of Koins". Many theatres and agents were dubious about booking an act comprising only coin tricks, thinking that it would be too monotonous and that the coins would not be seen easily in a large theatre. However, Downs proved the sceptics wrong when his performances caused a sensation wherever he worked.

Above: Magicians all over the world have been performing magic with coins for centuries. Coins are available in all shapes, sizes and colours, and they are easy to find at any time.

Above: No matter where you are in the world, you will always be prepared to amaze and amuse with a few banknotes and a little knowledge of the secrets in this book.

gripping qualities. The milled edge makes it relatively easy to palm and manipulate. Try to choose shiny coins to maximize their visibility. Old coin shops are often a great source for a variety of different coins in all manner of shapes, sizes and colours. Introducing such items to your audiences will cause interest. You may even be able to build a presentation around the existence of the coin. Where does it originate from? How did you come to possess it?

The following pages reveal how to make banknotes and coins appear and disappear (Appearing Money, Handkerchief Coin Vanish), how to cause coins to change places (Switcheroo) and bend (Bending Coin, Versions 1 and 2), and even how to turn a piece of blank paper into a banknote (Paper to Money). Basic sleight of hand is explained, and with the knowledge of a few of these routines you will always be able to perform a trick or two.

Above: Make a coin melt through the centre of a silk handkerchief without any damage whatsoever.

Above: Challenge your friends to balance a coin on the edge of a banknote.

Above: Make a banknote defy gravity by floating it above your hand. No strings attached!

easy money tricks

All of the tricks described in this chapter require money. Thankfully, the only thing you will actually have to invest is your time in order to learn the tricks described. The first few tricks are easy to learn and

perform. They fall into the area of impromptu magic, since they require no special set-up or gimmicks. You can perform these easy money tricks at the drop of a hat.

linking paper clips

Two paperclips and a rubber band are hooked on to a banknote. The three separate objects instantly link together! This is an old classic of

magic and only requires everyday objects, so is ideal for those occasions when you are suddenly asked to perform unprepared.

1 Fold one-third of a banknote under itself and attach a paperclip at the edge.

2 Place a rubber band over the note, at approximately the centre, as shown here.

3 Fold the other side of the note in the opposite direction to the first fold. Using a second paperclip, clip this edge to the top layer of the fold made earlier.

4 Grip both sides of the banknote and gently pull your hands apart until the banknote is stretched out flat.

5 The result is a rubber band with two paperclips linked together, hanging from a banknote. It seems impossible. The three items link so quickly that it will take your spectators completely by surprise.

double your money

This clever feat of origami makes a single banknote look like two. It is an ideal trick to perform impromptu if you carry the folded note around with you, and is sure to convince your audience. Just don't let them handle the note or they will discover the truth!

1 To prepare the trick, fold a banknote in half crossways.

2 Open the note and fold it in half again, lengthwise.

3 Pinch the note between each crease with your fingers and thumbs.

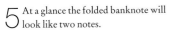

4 Flatten the folds on both sides so that the edges all line up.

5 At a glance the folded banknote will look like two notes.

suspension bridge

The challenge here is to find a way to suspend the middle glass between the outer two, using only the banknote for support. The two outer glasses must not move. The solution involves a little origami in order to increase the strength of the paper.

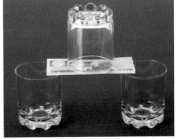

1 Gather together a crisp banknote and three glasses. Position the glasses close together in a row.

2 Pleat the note horizontally, using as many small folds as possible, making sure each crease is as firm as possible.

3 Place the note between the two glasses. Turn over the third glass, so the weight is distributed over a larger area, and put on top.

bending coin (version 1)

A coin is examined and then held in the fingertips. The magician creates an optical illusion which makes the coin look as if it is bending like rubber. This effect can be followed by Version 2, which appears later in this chapter. To accompany the trick, you could explain that although a coin is made of metal and therefore solid, the magical warmth of your hands can cause it to melt!

1 Hold a coin with both hands, thumbs on the back of the coin, first and second fingers on the front. Allow as much of the coin's surface as possible to be seen by pushing the thumbs forward and pulling the edges of the coin back.

2 This is the view from above, and it can be seen that a good deal of the front surface of the coin is visible.

3 Move both hands inwards so that the backs of your hands move towards each other. The thumbs maintain contact with the coin at all times. Move your hands back to the position shown in step 2 and repeat the motion five or six times.

heads I win!

A pocket full of change is emptied on to the table and a small selection of coins chosen. While the magician looks away (or leaves the room) the spectator is instructed to turn over two coins at a time, as many times as desired. Finally they are asked to hide one of the coins under their hand before the magician returns. The magician is able to reveal, with absolute accuracy, whether the hidden coin is heads up or tails up!

1 Throw some change on to a table. You can use any number of coins, but six or seven is perfect. Note whether there are an even or odd number of coins facing heads up. In our example, there are three heads up so we simply remember "Heads are odd".

2 Turn your back and instruct the spectator to turn over two coins at a time, as many times as desired. All the while, keep remembering "Heads are odd". Ask for any one of the coins to be covered before you turn around.

3 Glance at the uncovered coins on the table to see how many coins are now heads up. In our example, there are three. Remember "Heads are odd"? If there are an odd number left, then the hidden coin must be tails up. If there were an even number remaining heads up, then the hidden coin would also be heads up.

4 Assume a hypnotic state, or pretend to receive psychic vibes, then reveal the orientation of the hidden coin. If your instructions have been followed correctly, Heads I Win! will work every single time. Most people carry small change with them, so you can perform this trick at a moment's notice.

explanation
The reason this trick works is because the coins are turned over two at a time, so if there are an odd number of heads facing up at the beginning there will be an odd number of heads facing up at the end, and vice versa.

the pyramid game

Can you turn the pyramid upside down by moving only three coins? Many people have access to enough coins for this puzzle, whether ones that they happen to have in their pocket or that are borrowed from friends, making this a great impromptu trick. Pose the problem and leave your friend to try and puzzle it out for a few minutes before revealing the solution.

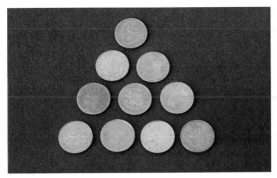

1 Lay ten coins, preferably of the same denomination, on a table in a pyramid shape.

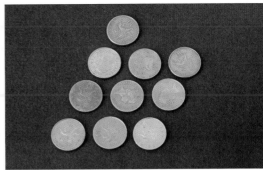

2 Pick up the coin at the bottom right of the triangle and position as shown here.

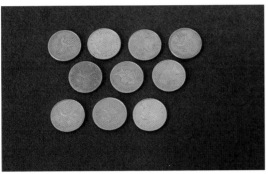

3 Move the coin at the top of the triangle and put it at the end left of the top row.

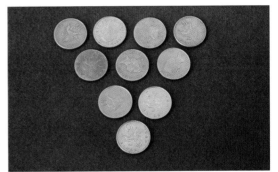

4 Move the bottom left coin and position so that it completes the upside down triangle.

coin con

In this stunt you have to remove the paper the coins are resting on, but leave the coins in place balanced on the rims of the glasses.

This stunt uses the same method as that which was used for Card Flick and may require a few goes in order for it to work properly.

1 Place two coins on a slip of paper resting on two glasses.

2 Now simply strike the paper firmly with your finger, in the centre and straight down towards the table. The speed of the downward movement will free the paper, so it will drop down to the table , leaving both coins sitting on the edge of the glasses, undisturbed.

impossible coin balance

This is a perfect way to win a drink! Challenge your friends to balance a coin on the edge of a banknote. The chances are, no matter *how hard they try or how many different ways they attempt to tackle the problem, they will not succeed unless they know the secret.*

1 The success of this stunt relies on the use of a crisp banknote. Fold and sharply crease the note in half, along its length.

2 Fold the note in half again, this time along the width. Ensure that the creases are sharp and neat.

3 Place the note on a table so that the folded edge is pointing upwards. Position a coin on top of the "V" shape.

4 Slowly and gently pull both edges of the note away from each other, straightening the paper. The coin will always find its centre of balance and will remain on the folded edge of the note, in an apparently impossible position.

explanation *In reality, the short crease is never pulled completely flat and the tiny kink in the paper is enough to stop the coin from falling off. Once the banknote is stretched flat, a steady hand is vital for the success of this trick.*

what a mug!

This is a very easy and fun practical joke to play on your friends, and requires just a coin and a mug. Although this trick is a simple "gag", *it is the perfect prelude to Mugged Again and will add an element of humour to the routine.*

1 Place a coin on a table and cover it with a mug. Tell the spectators that it is possible for you to pick up the coin without even touching the mug. When they say they don't believe you, ask them if they want to make a small bet.

2 Say, "It's easy because I never really put the coin under the mug in the first place." When someone lifts the mug to check if it's still there, simply pick up the coin from the table and demand your winnings.

mugged again!

This is a perfect follow-up trick to What a Mug! This time you tell the spectators that you will get a from coin under a mug while they hold the mug pinned to the table. You will need to use a little sleight-of-hand but it is not too difficult.

1 Hold a coin secretly in the fingers of your right hand. Show a similar coin at your fingertips and place it on the table, then cover it with a mug.

2 Explain and demonstrate that you are going to get a coin under the mug while they hold their finger on the top of the mug. Keep the other coin secreted in your right hand. This is a view from your angle.

3 From the front the coin remains hidden and your right hand looks relaxed and normal.

4 Now comes the fun part. Tilt the mug away from you and reach inside as if you are removing the coin from the table. Actually you leave the coin where it is and push the hidden coin to your fingertips under the mug. It is the hidden coin that you bring into view.

5 From the front it looks just as though you have removed the coin.

6 Now a spectator pins the mug to the table with their finger and you ask them to close their eyes so they can't see how it is done. When their eyes are closed tap the coin in your hand against the mug to make it sound as if you are doing something, then put the coin in your pocket.

7 Tell the spectator to open their eyes and have a look under the mug – the coin will still be there!

tip *At step 4 do the move without saying anything at all. It should simply look as though you picked the coin up from the table. Try not to call attention to the move.*

penetrating banknote

A folded banknote penetrates a strand of rubber band in a most visual way. This trick is similar to another trick called Bandit Bill,

although the method is slightly different. If you keep the prepared note with you at all times you can perform this trick at any time.

1 Prepare a banknote by carefully folding it in half along its length to make a sharp crease.

2 Unfold the note and then fold one half into the middle.

3 Repeat with the other side. The crease must be sharp for the trick to work.

4 Refold the note along the first crease as shown.

5 Fold the banknote in half at an angle and crease it well so that it holds its shape after you let go.

6 Using a sharp craft knife cut a "V"-shaped notch near the fold, as shown. The cut should go through only one layer of the banknote. You are now ready to perform the trick.

7 Open the banknote and display it, holding it by your fingertips. You can use your index finger to hide the secret cut, although it is unlikely that anyone will see it. Refold the note.

8 Hold a rubber band between your left thumb and first finger. Hold the folded banknote under the bottom strand of the band and make sure the "V" cut is at the back.

9 Raise the banknote to the band and allow the "V" to hook over the bottom strand. Let go and the banknote will hang as if it is actually folded over the band.

10 The illusion is perfect from the front but from the back you can see how the cut in the paper holds it against the band.

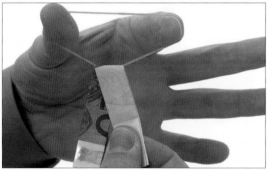

11 Gently pull the banknote downwards. This flexes the band and adds to the illusion greatly.

12 Slowly rub the banknote on the band and disengage the "V". Pull off the note very slowly and it will look as though it is melting through the rubber band.

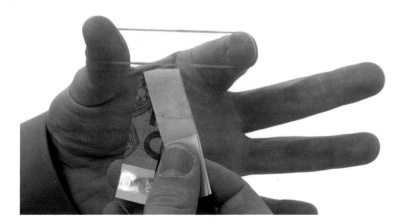

13 Finally move the banknote away from the band and, if you wish, unfold it, smoothing down the "V" so that it can't be seen, and put it in your pocket.

tip *You could keep a duplicate folded banknote in your pocket, so that if anyone asks to examine it closely you can remove the uncut note and show them.*

magnetic money

This is a very quick trick that can be performed at a moment's notice. Two banknotes are shown on both sides, then laid together on the table in a criss-cross fashion and rubbed on the tablecloth as if to *create "static electricity". The top note is lifted up and, incredibly, the lower note seems to adhere to it as if magnetized. The notes are then separated and given out for examination.*

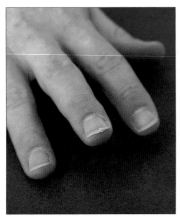

secret view

1 You will need a tiny piece of reusable putty adhesive, which you stick on the tip of your middle finger. Display two banknotes or borrow them from a spectator. This trick works best with fairly new, crisp notes. They should have a design with some colouring similar to the putty somewhere in the middle.

2 As you take the banknotes, stick the putty to the centre of one of them. It will be almost invisible, and will certainly not be noticed by the spectators if the note is glanced at casually.

3 Lay the note with the putty on the table and place the other note crossways on top of it. The piece of putty will be sandwiched in the middle.

4 Secretly squeeze the notes together so they stick to one another as you rub them over the surface of the table, supposedly to create the static electricity.

5 Bring the notes back to the centre of the table and slowly lift the upper note by the ends.

6 As you slowly raise the upper note the lower note will adhere to it and lift off the table.

7 Release both notes and allow them to drop back to the surface of the table.

8 Separate the notes and rub them on the table again, apparently to discharge the static.

9 As you pick up the notes from the table, secretly scrape off the putty with your right middle finger.

10 Finally, hand out the banknotes to the spectators for examination. There will be nothing to find.

basic coin techniques

Now that you have learnt some easy money tricks, it is time to learn a few sleight-of-hand techniques that will enable you to perform some even more amazing magic. Many of these techniques will take time and practice to master, but the outcome is most rewarding. As suggested earlier in the book, practising in a mirror will make it much easier for you to correct your own mistakes.

finger palm and production

The Finger Palm is an essential grip in coin magic, allowing you to secretly hold and therefore hide a coin (or any small object) in your hand. The coin can then be made to appear from anywhere, using the Finger Palm Production (for example, from behind a child's ear).

1 Position the coin at the base of your right second and third fingers. It is held in place by the creases in your skin and by your fingers curling in to hold it. Try to forget that you are holding a coin – look in a mirror to see if you can hold your hand naturally by your side. Your hand should not look as though it were holding anything.

2 You can produce the coin in many different ways. One way is to pretend that you have spotted something floating in the air in front of you. Point it out with the hand that is secretly holding the coin.

3 As you reach for the invisible "something", use your thumb to push the coin from its position at the base of your fingers to the fingertips.

4 Try to allow as much of the coin to be seen as possible. The coin seems to appear during the movement between pointing at the floating object and you reaching for it.

5 From the front, it looks just as if you have plucked a coin from thin air.

thumb clip

This is another technique for gripping a coin secretly in your hand. It can also be used to "vanish" a coin. The beauty of this grip is that it allows wide movement of the fingers, while convincingly keeping the coin out of sight.

1 Begin by resting the coin on the right fingers. It should lie flat, in the middle of the first and second fingers.

2 Close the fingers into a fist. The coin almost automatically ends in a position which can be clipped by the thumb.

3 With the hand open, the coin remains hidden from the front. This exposed view shows the Thumb-Clipped coin.

classic palm

This is one of the most useful sleights to learn. It enables the performer to hide any small object (in this case a coin) in the palm of the hand, without its presence being detected. The most important aspect of any Palm is that the hand must appear natural, so do not hold your hand in an awkward position or move in a way which attracts attention. A common problem is that both the thumb and fourth finger will try to flare out at an unnatural angle, but this will happen less as you learn to relax your hand. After enough practice, your hand will develop tiny muscles that will help you to palm. A palmed object should not be gripped tightly; a gentle touch is all that is required.

1 Place a coin on your outstretched hand. It should lie flat on the tips of the second and third fingers.

2 Keep the fingers parallel to the ground as you turn your hand palm down. The coin should be directly below the palm of your hand.

3 Push the coin into your palm with your second and third fingertips. The exact position of the coin is crucial to success. You may have to move it about a few times and try the coin in slightly different areas of the palm until you feel comfortable.

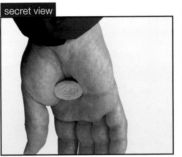

secret view

4 Remove the second and third fingers from the coin, trapping the coin in the palm by gently squeezing the edges between the fleshy pad of the thumb and the area of skin at the opposite edge of the coin.

secret view

5 This view shows the correct position of the coin. The coin need not be pinched hard. Only a gentle pressure is needed to stop the coin from falling.

6 The coin can be held in the Classic Palm without detection, however it must look natural.

7 In this example, the distortion of the hand is totally unnatural and therefore a clear sign that it hides something.

secret view

8 Continue your everyday activities (such as writing, typing and eating) with a coin palmed, and you will soon learn to forget it is there.

Downs Palm

The Downs Palm is named after the nineteenth-century American magician Thomas Nelson Downs, who is still recognized as one of the finest manipulators of coins ever. This grip is very deceptive as you can show both the front and back of the hand empty before producing a coin. There are angle problems, however, and anyone viewing from too high or too low may glimpse the hidden coin. Practise and check your movements in the mirror – before long you will develop an instinct as to whether or not the coin can be seen.

Performed well, this creates a beautiful effect. The coin can be plucked from the air or from any suitable location.

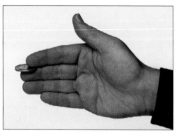

1 Grip the coin between the tips of the right first and second fingers.

2 As the hand closes, the coin should naturally position itself in the crotch of the thumb.

secret view

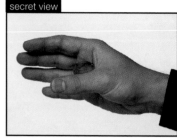

3 Open the fingers, leaving the coin gripped in the web between the thumb and the first finger.

4 You can show your hand from both front and back without the coin being seen, as long as you keep the correct angle in relation to the audience.

Downs Palm production

1 To produce the coin, reverse the above moves. Close your hand, ensuring that the edge of the coin becomes gripped between the tips of the first and second fingers, as seen here.

2 Open your hand, bringing the tip of your thumb on to the edge of the coin and keeping this contact as your hand continues to open.

3 Finally, pinch the coin between your thumb and second finger. Steps 1, 2 and 3 should happen together in one seamless movement.

Bobo Switch

This is a method of switching one coin for another. It was invented by French magician J.B. Bobo in about 1900, and is still used widely today. The switch is not used as a trick by itself, but being able to switch your coin for a spectator's is an invaluable tool. Bending Coin (Version 2) is an example of the use of the Bobo Switch. Study the following explanation carefully and it will not take too long to learn.

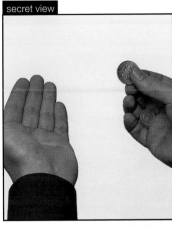

1 Hold the coin to be switched in the right-hand Finger Palm position. Borrow a coin from a spectator and hold it clearly displayed in the right fingertips. Hold the left hand out flat.

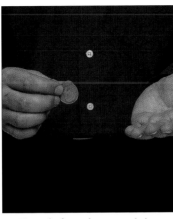

2 From the front, the secret coin is completely hidden in the right palm.

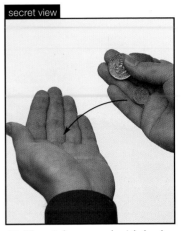

3 The switch occurs as the right hand tosses the borrowed coin into the left hand. It goes unnoticed because the coin is in motion the entire time. The right second and third fingers extend to cover the coin and the secret coin is allowed to fall from the Finger Palm position to the outstretched left hand.

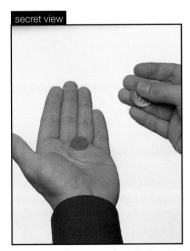

4 Without hesitation, the right thumb pulls the borrowed coin into the Finger Palm position, and the left hand closes around the switched coin.

5 From the front, the action of tossing the coin from one hand to the other looks very natural and should not arouse any suspicion from your audience.

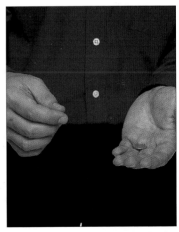

6 Slowly open your left hand to show that the coin has been switched.

coin roll

This flourish is a well-known favourite with audiences worldwide. A coin is rolled across the knuckles in a flourish which looks as magical as it is beautiful. The Coin Roll is a wonderful example of digital dexterity; it is also one of the most difficult things you will *learn in this book. You can practise it while you are watching television. Once you have mastered it, try learning it with the other hand and perform two Coin Rolls simultaneously! It is possible to perform the Coin Roll with four coins, each coin rotating ahead of the next.*

1 Close your hand into a loose fist. Your knuckles should be parallel with the floor. Begin by balancing a coin on the tip of your thumb.

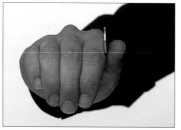

2 Pinch your thumb against the side of your first finger so that the coin flips on to its edge.

3 Loosen your thumb's grip on the coin so that it balances on the back of the first finger. At the same time, raise your second, third and fourth fingers just enough to clip the coin's edge between the first and second fingers.

4 Raise your first and third fingers while lowering the second finger. This allows you to roll the coin across the back of the second finger.

5 Lower the third finger and raise the second and fourth fingers. The coin will roll across the back of the third finger. Allow the coin to flip over and rest on the side of your fourth finger.

6 Move your thumb under your hand, towards the coin.

7 The coin is transferred to the tip of the thumb, which carries it back under the hand to the start position.

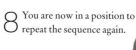

8 You are now in a position to repeat the sequence again.

coin vanishes

There are countless ways to make a coin vanish. The French Drop, Fake Take and Thumb Clip Vanish are all sleight-of-hand methods and generally should not be used as tricks in their own right. As you become more experienced, you will find that you can incorporate the coin's disappearance into a longer sequence, which can be extra mystifying and a lot of fun.

french drop

This is one of the oldest and best-known techniques used to "vanish" a coin or any other small object. The coin is held in the fingertips of the left hand and supposedly taken by the right hand. In reality, the coin is secretly retained in the left hand. This move should not be shown as a trick on its own, but as a way of "vanishing" a coin within another trick.

1 Display a coin by holding it high in the left fingertips. As much as possible of the surface of the coin should be seen.

2 The right hand approaches the left to supposedly take the coin. The thumb goes under it while the fingers go over it.

3 As soon as the fingers close around the coin and it is out of view, let the coin fall into the left hand.

secret view

4 The coin falls between the right thumb and the back of the left fingers, almost in Finger Palm position.

5 From the front, it looks as though you pinch the coin with your right fingers and thumb. Watch the coin yourself and actually believe that you are taking the coin.

6 Move the right hand up and to your right, at the same time allowing the left hand (with the coin) to drop naturally to your side. Follow your right hand with your eyes. Your hand should look as though it is actually holding a coin.

7 Squeeze your right hand slowly, supposedly shrinking the coin. Open the fingers wide and show the coin is no longer there.

tip *To make the move more convincing, place a pencil on a table, off to your left-hand side. Hold the coin in the start position. Execute the French Drop, then immediately use your left hand to pick up the pencil. Tap your right hand with the pencil, then show that the coin has vanished. Using the pencil like a wand provides a reason for taking the coin with your right hand – it is more natural to pick up the pencil using your left hand than to reach across your body with your right hand. When executing a sleight, it is very important to justify moves which may look strange if made without a reason.*

thumb clip vanish

This creates the illusion of placing a coin in your left hand while you secretly retain it in your right hand. It makes use of the technique in magic known as "time misdirection". If you leave enough time between secretly retaining the coin and showing that it has

"vanished", the audience will not be able to remember the last time they actually saw the coin or in which hand they saw it. This makes it very difficult for them to reconstruct the method. "Time misdirection" can be applied to many other secret moves and routines.

1 Display a coin on your right fingertips in preparation for the Thumb Clip.

2 Display your open left hand at waist level. Move the left hand up. At the same time begin to close the right hand, placing the coin into the Thumb Clip.

3 Supposedly place the coin on to the fingertips of the left hand, but secretly retain the coin in your right hand.

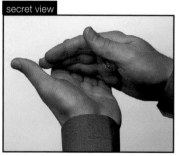

secret view

4 This view from behind shows what is happening.

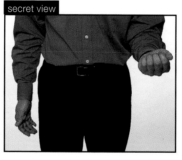

secret view

5 As the right hand moves away from the left and drops to your side, the left fingers close around the "coin". Your eyes must follow your left hand and your body language should suggest that the coin really is in this hand. This exposed view shows the coin in the right hand; in performance it would be hidden in the Thumb Clip or would be allowed to drop into the Finger Palm position.

6 The left hand moves away from your body, to the left. Open the hand and show that the coin has disappeared.

7 To make the move look more natural, give your right hand something to do after it leaves the left hand. Pick up a pencil with the coin in the Thumb Clip. Tap your left hand with the pencil, then show that the coin has gone. Even better, have the pencil in your right pocket and, as you take out the pencil, leave the coin in your pocket.

fake take

Like the French Drop and the Thumb Clip Vanish, the Fake Take enables you to secretly retain an object in one hand while supposedly taking it in the other hand. Try to provide a reason for taking the coin in the right hand – for example, to pick something up with the other hand. This type of sleight should not be used as a trick in its own right, but as part of a longer routine. In some routines the French Drop or Thumb Clip Vanish will be more suitable than the Fake Take. However, it is important to learn several ways to achieve a similar result so that you can choose which looks best. It will not necessarily be the same technique every time.

1 Display a coin on the outstretched fingers of your left hand at about waist height. The coin should be in a position ready for a Finger Palm.

2 The right hand approaches the left hand, supposedly to take the coin. The right fingers lie flat on top of the coin.

secret view

3 The left hand begins to close as the right hand feigns pinching the coin with the thumb against the fingers. This view from behind shows that in reality the coin remains in exactly the same position, ready to be finger-palmed by the left hand.

4 The right hand swings to the right (with the back towards the audience) as the left hand drops to your left side, supposedly empty, holding the coin in a Finger Palm.

5 As the right hand moves across your body, watch it as you would if the coin was really there. Your body language should suggest that the coin really is in your right hand.

6 Slowly open your right hand to show that the coin has vanished.

sleeving a coin

Magicians are always accused of using their sleeves to secretly hide objects. In fact very few tricks rely on this method, known as "sleeving". There are many different sleeving techniques. If you perfect this method, you will be able to make a coin disappear instantly without the need for any gimmicks. The only requirement is that you wear a jacket with loose-fitting sleeves. The trick will take lots of practice to perfect, and many people give up too soon. If you persevere, you will be rewarded handsomely with a baffling quick trick which will amaze all who see it. Sometimes, even when you know how a trick is done, it still looks magical. Such is the case here.

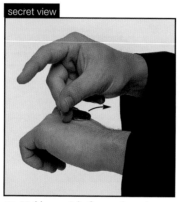
secret view

1 Close your left fingers into a fist. Place a coin on the back of your hand. The coin must be parallel with the ground, otherwise it may fall off.

2 Hold your right fingers above the coin. Snap your fingers. As your right second finger snaps off the thumb, it strikes the coin. With practice, if you strike the coin correctly it will automatically sail through the air and up your right sleeve.

3 As soon as the sound of the snap is heard, the coin seems to melt away. Try to keep your left hand perfectly still and as soon as the coin disappears, freeze, so that your spectator doesn't think you tried to sneak the coin away with your right hand.

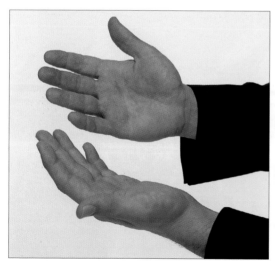

secret view

4 Show both hands back and front. They are unmistakably empty. Keep the right arm slightly bent and be careful not to let the coin fall out of your sleeve.

5 You can retrieve the coin by allowing your right arm to hang by your side. The coin will fall from your sleeve and you can catch it in the Finger Palm position.

coin in elbow

You hold a coin in your fingertips and rub it against your elbow. After several apparently unsuccessful attempts the coin seems to *dissolve into your elbow, disappearing completely. This is another good example of how "misdirection" works.*

1 This is best performed sitting at a table, although you could perform it standing if you alter the handling slightly. Hold a coin in your right fingertips and bend your left arm. (Your left hand should be in a position next to your left ear.) Rub the coin against your elbow. After a few seconds, let the coin fall to the table.

2 Pick up the coin with your left hand and display it on the fingers as you explain that you will try again. Pick up the coin from the left fingers with the right hand. This should be done to look identical to the Fake Take described earlier, which is the move you will be performing later in the trick.

3 Once again repeat the rubbing sequence, only to let the coin fall to the table again. Your audience will become accustomed to these moves, which will help you to accomplish what happens next.

4 Just as before, go to pick up the coin with your left hand and display it in the left fingertips. However, as the right hand approaches to take the coin from the left, execute a Fake Take. Briefly the right fingers mime taking the coin while the left hand returns to a position near the left ear. ▶

5 This view shows the coin in the left hand. Secretly slip it under the back of your collar to dispose of it. Using your right hand, rubs the supposed coin into the elbow.

6 After a few more seconds of rubbing, show that the right hand is empty. The coin has apparently been absorbed into your arm.

7 Display both hands to complete the "vanish". The coin can be recovered later. Make sure your shirt is tucked in, or the coin may fall out!

universal vanish

This simple sleight-of-hand trick is handy to know as you can make practically anything disappear with a wave of your hand. As with all tricks, practice is essential to make it really work well. This works best if your spectators are seated opposite you.

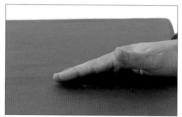

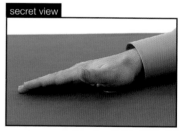

1 You need to be seated at a table. Have the object that is to vanish in front of you. In this case it is a coin.

2 Turn your hand palm down so that it covers the coin and is almost flat on the table.

3 Move your hand forward until the coin touches the heel of your hand. Make small circular motions so the coin continues to slide beneath the heel of your hand.

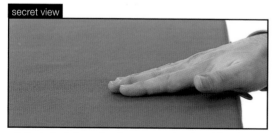

4 As the heel of your hand moves over the edge of the table the coin drops secretly into your lap.

5 The hand continues to "rub" the coin, moving forward and away from the table's edge. Finally, flip your hand over to show the coin has vanished.

gravity vanish

This technique is another great way to make many types of small objects seemingly disappear into thin air. Its success depends largely on timing and the use of angles. It must be seen just from the front, so do not attempt to perform this trick if there is any possibility that the audience will have a view from the side, or you will give away the secret of how it is done.

1 Hold a small object (in this case a coin) in your left hand. Notice how the object is held and displayed.

2 Rotate your hand at the wrist so that the back of your hand blocks the spectators' view of the coin.

3 Count to three, each time raising a finger. Notice how the right hand comes right in front of the left hand so that it is concealed from view.

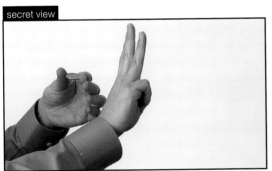

secret view

4 This view shows how things look from the side. The coin is hidden from the audience both by the angle at which it is being held and by the right hand.

secret view

5 As you say "Three", drop your right hand to the table and simultaneously let the coin fall from your fingers. The left hand must not open its fingers but simply loosen its grip.

6 From the front, the coin's journey remains hidden behind your right hand.

7 Finish by rubbing your left fingers together and then opening the hand wide to show that the coin has gone.

disappearing coin in handkerchief

A coin is clearly seen wrapped in the centre of a handkerchief. With a magical gesture the handkerchief is pulled open to reveal that the coin has completely vanished. This simple and impromptu trick is one of the very best you could ever learn. Try it now and you will amaze yourself, as the coin seems to disappear into thin air! It is one of the few tricks where the secret is almost as amazing as the trick itself.

1 Lay a handkerchief in front of you in the shape of a diamond. Place a coin just a tiny bit to the left of the centre.

2 Fold the bottom half up to meet the top and pick up the right hand corner of the triangle that is formed.

3 Now fold the right side over to meet the left. The coin should not move during either of these folds.

4 Pinch the coin inside the handkerchief with your right hand and slowly turn the coin over and over, rolling up the handkerchief as you do so.

5 Continue rolling up the handkerchief until you reach the top.

6 Grip the two pointed ends, one in each hand, and slowly pull them apart.

7 The coin has vanished! Actually it is inside a secret fold, but no one would ever guess.

8 Tilt the left side of the handkerchief up so that the coin secretly runs down into your right fingers.

9 This is an exposed view of the coin once it has landed. Notice how it sits on the fingertips.

10 Bunch the handkerchief into your right hand, covering the coin. You can finish by placing the handkerchief and coin in your pocket.

handkerchief coin vanish

A coin is placed under a handkerchief and held by a spectator. The handkerchief is shaken out and the coin seems to melt away. A specially prepared handkerchief is required. Cut a corner from a duplicate handkerchief. Stitch it neatly into one of the corners of the handkerchief along three sides. Before stitching the final side, drop a coin into the secret pocket.

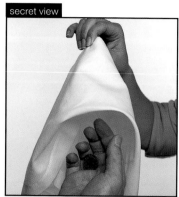

1 Show the coin held in the right fingertips. The handkerchief is opened and held by both hands. The special corner is held in the right hand together with the coin. Your right fingers hide the secret pocket.

2 As you move the coin under the handkerchief (aim for the centre), take the hidden coin with it. Ask a spectator to hold the coin through the fabric. They will assume they are holding the one shown originally, but it is really the duplicate coin sewn into the corner.

3 Allow the loose coin to fall into the Finger Palm position, then remove your hand from the handkerchief in a natural manner.

4 Hold one corner of the handkerchief in each hand and ask the spectator to drop the coin on your command. Count to three and say "Let go!"

5 As they do so, the coin seems to melt away and the handkerchief can be displayed completely empty. You can finish by folding it up and putting it back in your pocket.

clever coin vanish

A coin is placed under a handkerchief and held by a spectator. When the handkerchief is shaken out, the coin melts away. The effect is the same as in Handkerchief Coin Vanish, but the method is very different. This is true of many tricks: there are, for example, dozens of ways of sawing a woman in half! Next time you think you know how a trick is done, take a closer look and see if you really do.

1 To prepare, secretly place a coin into the lining of your tie so that it lies down by the tip.

2 To begin the performance, show another coin in your right hand and an opaque handkerchief in your left.

3 Place this coin under the handkerchief, taking the tip of your tie with it. Practise this in front of a mirror.

4 Hold the handkerchief at approximately waist height and close to your body so that your tie continues to hang naturally. If you lift your tie too high, your audience will see what you are doing.

5 Ask a spectator to hold the coin, which is really the one in the tie. As in Handkerchief Coin Vanish, allow the other coin to fall into the Finger Palm position, then casually remove your hand.

6 Hold one corner of the handkerchief in each hand and ask the spectator to let go. Display the handkerchief completely empty and hand it to the spectator for examination. They will find nothing.

tip For a complete "vanish", simply hide the coin in the lining of your tie as you place it under the handkerchief. This way you will not have to palm anything. The use of your tie is so subtle that the method will never be guessed by your spectators.

dissolving coin (version 1)

A borrowed, marked coin is covered with a handkerchief and dropped inside a glass of water. The spectators can hear the coin plop as it enters the water, yet when the handkerchief is removed, the coin has gone. The marked coin can then be discovered in a variety of ways.

1 Hold a handkerchief by one corner with your left hand, with a glass disc secretly hidden under the fingertips behind the handkerchief.

secret view

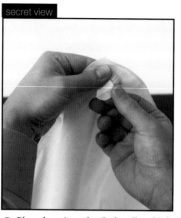

2 Place the coin under the handkerchief, and as your right hand comes close to the left one allow the coin to fall into your fingers as shown, while simultaneously positioning the glass disc in the coin's place.

3 Hold the glass disc up under the handkerchief so that its outline can be seen through the material. Everyone will think this is the coin.

4 Take hold of the handkerchief with your left hand and position it over the glass of water. The coin is still held secretly in the right hand. Let the disc drop into the water with a plop.

5 Pull the handkerchief away using your right hand, making sure that the coin is adequately covered by the handkerchief.

6 The coin has vanished. You can even let the spectators look straight down into the glass and they will see nothing.

tip *To reproduce the marked coin at the start of the trick (which will then be hidden in your right hand) you can reach into a spectator's pocket and reveal the coin, creating the illusion that it somehow travelled across time and space invisibly, or you may want to use it to perform Marked Coin in Ball of Wool.*

dissolving coin (version 2)

Here is a different method for what is essentially the same trick. A coin (marked if desired) is dropped into a glass of acid, which *instantly dissolves it. Do not perform both versions of this trick in the same act. Try out both, and then perform the one you prefer.*

1 You will need a tall glass, a coin, a handkerchief and a bottle of water with a label that suggests that the contents are dangerous.

2 Pour some of the liquid from the bottle into the glass, explaining that it is a very strong acid that will dissolve anything it touches (except for glass, of course!).

3 Show the coin to the audience and hold it in the centre of the handkerchief with your right hand. Pick up the glass with your left hand. Notice how the glass is held.

4 Move the handkerchief over the glass and position the coin above it.

5 This secret view shows how the glass is tipped forwards and how the coin is actually positioned behind it. Let the coin fall in the direction of the arrow.

6 As the coin falls it will hit the side of the glass before resting in your left hand. The spectators will hear the coin hit the glass and assume it went inside.

7 As this shot from the front shows, the spectators cannot see that the coin is now in your left hand.

8 As you pick up the edge of the handkerchief to remove it from the glass, secretly pick up the coin from the palm of your left hand using the fingertips of your right hand.

9 With the coin now hidden under the handkerchief you can remove the handkerchief from the glass completely to show that the coin has vanished, and explain that the acid has dissolved it.

escaping coin

A conical glass has a small coin at the bottom of the glass covered by a large coin on top of it. How do you remove the small coin without touching either the glass or the coins? This may require several attempts, but you will be able to do it in the end.

1 You will need a conical glass, a large coin and a tiny coin. Drop the small coin into the conical glass.

2 Drop the larger coin on top of it, so that it completely covers the smaller coin.

3 Blow sharply into the near side of the glass, in the direction shown by the arrow.

4 Believe it or not the larger coin will flip out of the way and the small coin will fly out of the glass.

coin through hole

The challenge is to push a large coin through a hole only half its size. The paper can be folded but not torn. Allow spectators to have a go at doing it themselves before you show them how it is done. Unless they have seen the stunt before, they won't be able to do it.

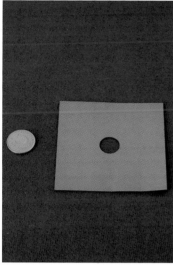

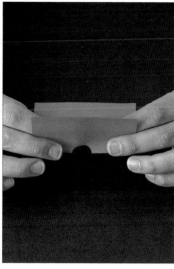

1 Carefully cut a hole about 1.5cm (⅝in) in diameter in a piece of paper. You will also need a coin that is clearly considerably larger than the hole.

2 Fold the piece of paper in half, as shown, with the hole facing down, towards the table.

3 Drop the coin into the folded piece of paper so that it rests in the hole.

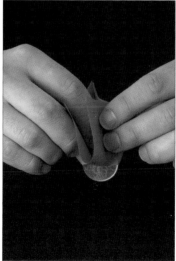

4 Now bend the paper upwards as shown. This action will stretch the hole slightly.

5 This allows you to push the coin carefully through the hole without damaging the paper.

6 You may need to experiment with holes and coins of different sizes in order to create the very best-looking illusion possible.

coin through ring

*A coin is placed under a thick handkerchief. The corners of the
handkerchief are gathered together and threaded through a finger*
*ring smaller than the coin, securing the coin inside. The magician
causes the coin to pass through the handkerchief, freeing the ring.*

1 Hold a handkerchief by one corner
in your left hand and a coin in the
fingertips of your right hand.

2 Cover your right hand and the coin
with the handkerchief, and remove
your left hand.

3 Secretly gather a pinch of material at
the back of the coin. This pinch is held
with the thumb of your right hand.

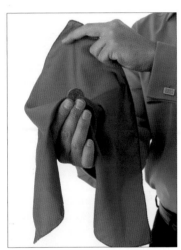

4 Raise the front of the handkerchief
with your left hand to show the coin
underneath. At the same time secretly grip
the back of the handkerchief between the
thumb and forefinger of your left hand.

5 Cover the coin again with the
handkerchief, but secretly carry both
layers of the handkerchief forward.

6 This close-up view shows that the
coin is now really on the outside of
the handkerchief.

7 Twist the handkerchief several times under the coin. The fabric will twist around, hiding the ring.

8 Ask someone to hold on to the coin through the handkerchief. If you keep the "open" side downwards no one will suspect the coin is actually on the outside. Gather the four corners of the handkerchief and thread them through a finger ring, pushing it up to the coin.

9 Take back the covered coin from the first person and ask two people to hold two corners each and stretch out the handkerchief, as shown.

secret view

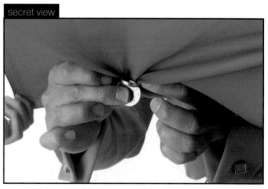

10 Reach underneath the handkerchief and remove the coin from within the folds.

11 This picture shows from underneath how the coin is removed from the folds of the handkerchief.

12 Release the coin and the ring so that the two people are left holding only the empty handkerchief.

13 Finish the trick by tossing both the ring and the coin on to the stretched-out handkerchief.

coin through coaster

A glass is covered with a drinks coaster and a coin is visibly caused to pass through the coaster and into the glass. Performed properly, the illusion of the coin melting through the coaster is perfect. This is perhaps one of the most challenging tricks in this book, but the effect is worth the effort. You will need a glass, a coaster, two identical coins and several hours to practise and make the moves flow smoothly.

secret view

1 Secretly hold a coin on the fingertips of your right hand and pick up the coaster with your left hand.

2 Cover the coin with the coaster so that you are holding both the coin and the coaster in your right hand.

3 Now you need to learn a move that enables you to show both sides of the coaster without revealing the coin. As you turn your hand over to show the reverse side of the coaster, bend the fingers in, sliding the coin back so that as much of the coaster as possible is visible. Then turn your hand back, reversing the sliding motion.

secret view

4 Display the second coin in the fingertips of your left hand and simultaneously move the coaster towards the top of the glass. The coin under the coaster is shown here, but it must remain hidden when you perform the trick.

5 Tap the visible coin against the side of the glass as you lay the coaster on top, secretly trapping the hidden coin between the rim of the glass and the coaster. The noise from the tapping will cover any noise the hidden coin makes as it touches the rim.

6 Show the visible coin being held between the finger and thumb of your right hand, while your left hand holds the coaster in place on the glass.

7 With the coin between the finger and thumb of your right hand, tap it against the coaster three times. After the third tap, squeeze the coin, flipping it sideways and pinching it so that it is hidden behind the right fingers. (This is called a "pinch vanish".) At the same moment, lift the coaster at the back with your left thumb to disengage the coin, which is then seen and heard to clink into the glass.

8 This picture shows how things look from your side at the moment when the coin apparently penetrates the coaster.

9 As soon as you hear the coin clink into the glass lift the coaster off the glass with your left hand.

10 Transfer the coaster to your right hand, placing it over the hidden coin, and tip the visible coin out of the glass on to the table.

11 Finally, place the coaster on the table (leaving the hidden coin underneath) and display both hands to show that they are empty.

coin wrap

A coin is wrapped in a piece of paper. It can be seen and even felt until the final moment when the paper is torn into pieces and the coin seems to have vanished without a trace. This is an ideal way to "vanish" a *marked, borrowed coin, which can then be made to appear in another trick later on in your act (for example, Coin in Egg and Coin in Bread Roll). This is a baffling "any time" coin trick worth learning.*

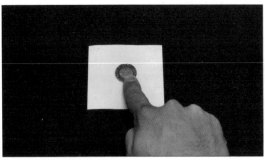

1 You will require an opaque piece of paper approximately 9cm (3½in) square. Place a coin into the centre of the paper.

2 Fold the paper upwards against the bottom of the coin with a sharp crease.

3 Fold the paper to the right and back, behind the coin. Make the creases as sharp as possible.

4 Repeat with the left side of the paper. Be careful not to wrap the coin too tightly, as this will hinder the secret move.

5 Fold the top flap back, at the edge of the paper. It seems as if the coin is trapped, but in reality it can escape from the top of the paper where a gap has been left.

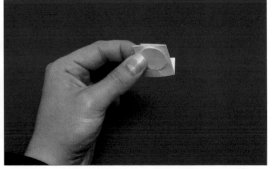

6 Press the coin against the paper with your thumbs, turning the package end over end as you do so. This will position the opening of the packet towards the bottom, while creating an impression of the coin on the paper, proving its presence.

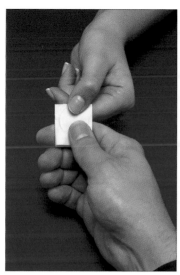

7 Have a spectator verify that the coin is still there. Carefully note the position of the paper at this point.

8 Release your thumb's grip, allowing the coin to fall from the paper. The back of your right hand provides a good deal of cover.

9 The coin lands in the right-hand Finger Palm position. It should fall easily from the paper. If not, your folds at steps 3 and 4 may have been too tight.

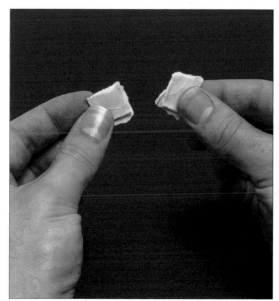

10 Tear the paper in half, then into quarters. The coin remains hidden in the Finger Palm.

11 Toss the pieces of paper on to the table to complete the "vanish". Make the coin reappear in a place of your choice (see More Money Tricks for ideas).

magic papers

A piece of folded coloured paper is opened to reveal inside it another folded paper of a different colour; this too is opened to reveal another folded paper, and this in turn is found to contain a last folded paper. When the smallest piece of paper is unfolded fully, a small coin is placed inside. The coloured papers are re-folded, a magic spell is cast and when the papers are opened once again, the contents have changed into a coin of a much larger denomination. This is handed back to the surprised and very happy donor. You will need several different-coloured sheets of paper for this trick. A pair of scissors or a guillotine is also required to cut the paper to size. Using the magic papers you can also make coins appear and vanish, as well as change their denomination.

1 Using scissors, cut out a 20cm (8in) square of red paper. Cut out two 18cm (7in) squares of blue paper, two 16cm (6¼in) squares of yellow paper and two 14cm (5½in) squares of green paper.

2 Starting with a green square, fold the paper twice, to create three equal sections, as shown.

3 Fold this strip into three equal sections. Repeat these folds with each of the other papers. Make sure that the folds are neatly done and that the creases are sharp. When each paper is unfolded it should be divided into nine equal squares.

4 Carefully glue the two blue papers back to back so that they are joined at their centres, as shown.

tip *The best way to end the trick is to give the larger value coin to the person who lent you the small one.*

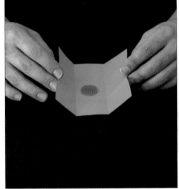

5 Place a coin of high denomination in the centre of a green square and wrap it up inside the paper, along the folds you made earlier. Place this green packet in the centre of a yellow paper and fold it inside. Finally, place the yellow paper inside the blue and fold the blue paper around it.

6 Now assemble the other papers by laying the red paper down first, followed by the (double) blue paper, with the hidden packet containing the coin of high denomination underneath, as shown.

7 Now place the yellow paper on top of the blue and the last green paper on top of the yellow. Fold each one inside the other to complete the set-up.

8 To perform the trick, show the packet of folded paper and a coin of low denomination. (Borrow this coin from a spectator if possible.)

9 Open the nest of papers (being careful not to reveal the underside of the prepared blue sheet) and place the low-value coin in the centre of the green paper. Wrap the coin up in the green paper, then wrap this in each of the other papers in turn.

10 Secretly turn the blue paper over as you make the final fold in it.

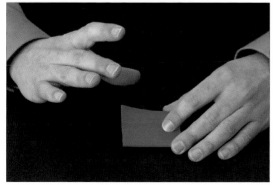

11 Wrap the blue paper up in the red paper, and cast a "mystic shadow" over the packet.

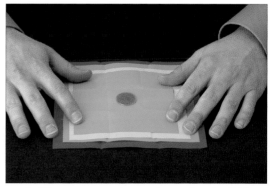

12 When you re-open the nest of papers the coin of high denomination will be revealed.

coin vanish from matchbox

A coin is placed inside an empty matchbox. The box is shaken to prove the contents are still there, but moments later the box is shown empty. You can then choose any method you like to make the coin reappear.

You could also adapt the method used in Vanishing Box of Matches (see Match Magic) to add to this routine, enhancing the illusion of the coin being in the box even after it has gone.

1 Open the drawer of an empty matchbox. Insert a coin and display it clearly.

2 Hold the matchbox in your left hand and close the drawer, trapping the coin.

3 Transfer the box to your palm-down right hand.

4 Shake the box by turning your right hand over and back several times. The coin will rattle, proving its presence.

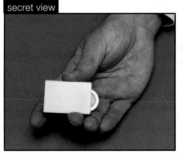
secret view

5 Rattle the box again, but as the hand turns palm up, squeeze the sides of the box so that the top of the box bows open just enough to let the coin slip out into your right hand. This secret move can be disguised by tilting the hand upwards and towards you slightly.

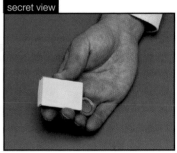
secret view

6 The coin is secretly retained in the Finger Palm position.

7 As the wrist is turned over again, the box is transferred back into the left hand. The left hand holds the box between the thumb and second finger.

8 The left first finger pushes open the drawer to show that the coin has vanished. The box can be dismantled and checked by the audience. There will be nothing to find.

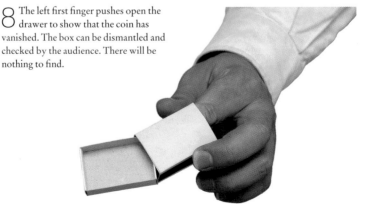

pencil and coin vanish

A coin is held in the fingertips and tapped three times with a pencil. Unexpectedly, the pencil disappears and is found behind the magician's ear! The coin is tapped again and vanishes completely. This routine can be performed at any time, anywhere. Instead of a coin, you can use anything small enough to hide in your hand. This routine is a practical example of how "misdirection" works. It is also a "sucker" trick in that your audience thinks they are let into the secret when in reality you still manage to amaze them.

1 Hold a coin on the outstretched palm of your left hand. Hold a pencil in your right hand. Stand with the left side of your body towards the audience.

2 Tell everyone to watch carefully. Tap the coin three times, each time bringing the pencil up towards your right ear.

secret view

3 On the third tap, without any hesitation, leave the pencil behind your ear. The first two taps are made to build the expectation that the coin is going to vanish.

4 As your hand descends to tap the coin, open it wide and look amazed as you seem to realize at the same time as your audience that the pencil is no longer there.

5 Explain that you should never reveal the secret to a magic trick, but that you are going to break that rule. Turn your body so that your right side is now towards your audience. Point out the pencil behind your ear.

secret view

6 As you do this, secretly place the coin into your left trouser pocket.

7 Explain that you will do the trick again. Return to the position you were in before, with your left side to the audience. Your left hand should be closed as if it holds the coin. Tap your hand three times with the pencil, then open it to show that this time the coin really has gone.

tip *The success of this trick relies on the spectators convincing themselves that the coin is going to vanish. They will be so focused on watching the coin that they will fail to watch the pencil!*

more money tricks

This section explains the methods to various tricks that require some of the knowledge learned so far. Coin in Egg uses the Coin Wrap vanish and Bending Coin (Version 2) utilizes the Bobo Switch, while

several use palming techniques. The final magic trick in this chapter, Paper to Money, does not require difficult sleight of hand, but is a very strong, visual illusion which you can perform at any time.

switcheroo

In this trick you introduce a game of hand-eye co-ordination. A coin is held on the outstretched palm of a spectator. You explain that you are going to try to grab it before the spectator can close their hand.

You manage to grab the coin twice, but fail on the third attempt. When the spectator opens their hand, they see you have not only removed the coin, but have replaced it with a different coin!

1 For this trick, you will need two different coins. Place one coin on the palm of a spectator's hand.

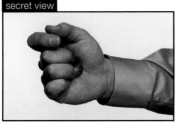

secret view

2 Hold the second coin classic-palmed in your right hand. Details regarding the Classic Palm can be found in Basic Coin Techniques.

3 Explain that you will try to grab the coin before the spectator closes their hand, and that they are not allowed to move until you do. Your fingers should be curled in except for your thumb and first finger, which will act like a pair of pincers.

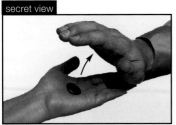

secret view

4 As the right hand descends, open it fully so that the hidden coin is brought down on to the spectator's fingertips. The force of this motion will bounce the coin in their palm up in the air.

5 Grab the coin as it bounces, and the spectator will close their hand around the second coin. This occurs so fast it that is impossible for them to feel or see what has happened.

6 The spectator will think you failed, but when they open their hand, they will see that you have switched the coin!

tip *This is a genuine act of sleight of hand, which relies on fast movement and precision timing. With practice you will be able to perform it successfully nearly every time, but it doesn't matter if it takes more than one attempt, because it is not a trick but an example* *of your dexterity. In order to build a little routine, begin by simply taking the spectator's coin, without performing the switch. It is not as difficult as you might think. Explain that you want to try again and repeat it. The third time, execute the switch.*

coin through table

This quick trick will catch people off guard. A coin is made to pass straight through the centre of a table. Once you understand the workings of the trick, try using three or four coins and making each coin pass through the table using a different method.

1 With your left hand, tap a coin on the surface of a table at random points, explaining that every table has a particular "soft spot". Display the coin in your left hand in readiness for a Fake Take.

2 Now execute the Fake Take. With your right hand, pretend to pick up the coin. In reality the coin never moves from the left hand.

3 The right hand moves away, pretending to hold the coin in the fingertips. At the same time, the left hand drops below the table to a position directly under the right hand.

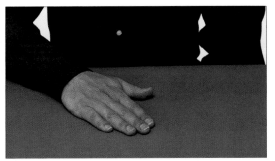

4 Slap the right hand flat on the table, and just at the same moment slap the coin on the underside of the table with your left hand. The result will be a sound which will make the spectators believe that the coin is under your right hand.

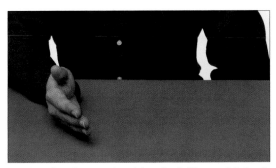

5 Pause for a few seconds and then slowly lift your right hand to show that the coin is no longer there.

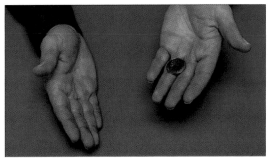

6 Bring the coin out from below the table on the outstretched palm of your left hand.

coin through handkerchief

A coin is placed under the centre of a silk handkerchief. A layer of silk is lifted to confirm to the audience that the coin really is *underneath. Very slowly the coin begins to melt visibly through the fabric. The silk is unfolded to show the absence of any holes.*

1 Hold a silk handkerchief by its edge in the left hand and display a coin in the fingertips of the right hand.

2 Drape the silk over the coin, positioning it directly in the centre, as shown here.

3 With the aid of your left hand, obtain a pinch of cloth between the back of the coin and your right thumb.

4 Lift the silk with your left hand to display the coin still held by the fingertips. Note how it is lifted back directly over the arm and above the other half of the silk.

5 Let go with your left hand and flick your wrist down so that both layers of the silk fall forward over the coin. The coin is now outside the silk, hidden under the pinch held by your thumb.

6 Wrap and twist the silk so that the shape of the coin is clearly visible through the fabric. Be careful not to expose the coin accidentally.

7 In this view from behind, you can see that the coin is being held by the fingers and the fabric that surrounds it. Begin to pull the coin up and into view.

8 From the front, the coin appears to be slowly melting through the silk. With practice, you will be able to make the coin look as if it penetrates on its own by simply pinching your left fingers together and using your right hand to support the coin as it emerges.

9 Remove the coin completely. Display both the coin and the silk – you can safely hand them to the audience for examination.

marked coin in ball of wool

A borrowed, marked coin vanishes, only to be discovered inside a small cloth bag in the centre of a ball of wool! This is a great trick – because it takes so long to reach the centre of the ball of wool, and the pouch is so well sealed up, it seems impossible that a borrowed coin could be inside. The preparation takes some time, so start getting it ready well in advance.

1 Take a piece of thick card (stock) about 10cm (4in) wide and 12cm (4¾in) long. Place a large coin in the middle of the card and mark its width on the card with a pencil. Draw straight lines this distance apart along the length of the card. Draw two more lines 3mm (⅛in) outside the existing lines.

2 Score along the marked lines and fold to create a long, flat tube. Use glue to stick the two sides together. Press together firmly between your thumb and fingers and allow it to dry completely before you release it.

3 When it is finished, the tube should be just big enough to allow a coin to slide along it with ease.

4 Insert one end of the coin slide into a small pouch and hold it in place with a tightly twisted rubber band around the neck of the pouch.

5 Wrap a ball of wool around the pouch and some of the cardboard tube.

6 Place the finished article inside a paper bag, making sure that the coin slide faces upwards but cannot be seen.

7 To perform the trick, borrow a coin, have it marked with a pen and make it vanish using any of the methods explained in this book. Vanishing Coin in Handkerchief is ideal. Reach into the paper bag with the coin secreted in your right hand.

8 Secretly drop the coin into the prepared slide so that it is inserted in the bag in the centre of the ball of wool.

9 Pull the coin slide out of the ball of wool and leave it at the bottom of the bag as you take out the ball of wool. You may find you need to grip the wool through the bag with your left hand to assist in pulling out the slide.

10 Display the ball of wool to the spectators. Squeeze it slightly as you do so, to close-up the gap left by the coin slide.

11 Ask a volunteer from the audience to unwrap the ball of wool.

12 When they eventually finish unravelling the wool, which will take some time, they will discover the little pouch.

13 Ask them to verify that it is securely closed with the rubber band.

14 Ask them to open the pouch and remove the coin, and to verify that it is indeed the same coin that they marked earlier.

coin in egg

This is one of the many methods that exist for producing a coin from nowhere. These can either be used independently, perhaps to introduce a coin that you will proceed to use in another trick, or can follow on from a "disappearing" trick, to make a coin reappear.

In this trick, the mystery is increased by vanishing a marked coin borrowed from a spectator. The marked coin is then found inside an egg chosen at random by the spectator. With a little thought, there are many other places that you can make the coin appear from.

1 Borrow a coin from a spectator and ask for it to be marked with a permanent marker pen for later identification.

2 Vanish the coin using any of the methods described earlier. The coin should end up in Finger Palm position. The Coin Wrap would work well here.

3 Display a box of eggs and ask someone to point to any one at random. Lift and display the egg with your left hand.

4 Transfer the egg to the right hand, placing it directly on top of the finger-palmed coin. The coin should remain completely hidden from view.

5 The left hand brings a glass to the centre of the table and the right hand taps the egg on the side of the glass, breaking the shell. The eggshell is opened with one hand so that the contents of the egg fall into the glass. Simultaneously allow the finger-palmed coin to drop into the glass with the egg. If timed correctly, it looks just as if the coin falls from the centre of the egg.

6 Scoop the coin from the glass with a spoon and have the mark verified as that which the spectator made a few minutes before. Have a napkin ready to wipe the coin dry. Using a similar method, you could also make the coin appear inside other impossible places, such an unopened can of food held by a spectator throughout the trick. The possibilities are endless.

coin in bread roll

In this trick, after "vanishing" a coin, you find it seconds later inside a bread roll that has been sitting on the table the entire time! To make this effect more astonishing, ask someone to mark the coin with a pen so that when they see it again they can be sure that it is the same coin. You could also ask them to choose from a selection of rolls, adding an extra dimension of mystery to the presentation.

secret view

1 Make a coin disappear, using one of the methods described earlier. Finish with the coin secretly hidden in your right hand. Ask someone to pass you a bread roll. Hold it with both hands so that the coin is hidden on the bottom. This view shows the right hand a split second before the roll is placed on top of the coin.

2 Bend both sides of the roll up so that the bottom splits open. With your fingers, begin to push the coin into the split. This exposed view shows the coin entering the roll. In performance, the bottom of the roll must be pointing down towards the table to hide these actions.

3 Bend the roll in the opposite direction with both hands so that the top cracks open. As it does so, the split at the bottom closes up and the coin appears to come from the centre! Ask the spectator to remove the marked coin and verify that it was the one they marked a few moments earlier.

coin through pocket

A coin is held against the outside of the trouser pocket and caused to pass through the fabric into the pocket! This quick routine makes use of the Finger Palm. It is quite easy to perfect and makes a good

impromptu trick to remember for those times when you are stuck without props. Try to enhance the illusion by using the biggest, shiniest coin you can find.

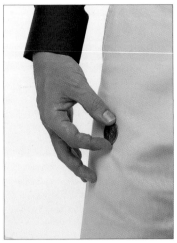

1 Display a coin held against your right thigh, in line with the bottom of your pocket.

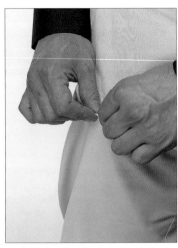

2 With both hands, pinch the fabric underneath the coin. Turn over the coin, simultaneously covering it from view with the fabric.

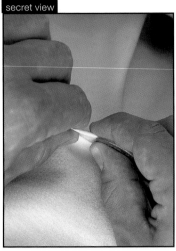

secret view

3 Secretly slip the coin into the right-hand Finger Palm position, using your thumb. This is unseen from the front. The photograph here shows your view.

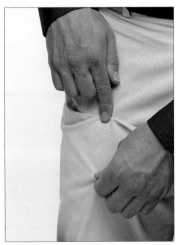

4 With the coin still hidden in the Finger Palm, hold on to the top of the fold with your right first finger. Position your left first finger and thumb under the right and pinch a small piece of fabric.

5 Pull the fabric flat and show that the coin has vanished.

6 Reach into your right trouser pocket. Remove your hand with the coin displayed clearly at its fingertips.

bending coin (version 2)

Earlier in the book, Bending Coin (Version 1) showed how to create the illusion of a coin bending. You will now have learnt the necessary skill to perform a similar type of illusion, which is the perfect follow-up. The amazing thing about this trick is that at the end you give the lender their coin back in its bent condition – a souvenir they can keep forever!

secret view

1 To prepare, you need to bend a coin. First cover it with a cloth so that you do not mark it. Use a pair of pliers to hold the coin, then bend it with another pair of pliers. The result will be a coin that looks like the one shown here.

2 Before you begin, hide the bent coin in the right-hand Finger Palm position. Begin the performance by borrowing a coin which matches yours, and hold it in your fingertips as shown. Perform Bending Coin (Version 1) as described earlier.

3 At the end, hold your left hand out flat with the coin held in the right fingertips. You now apparently toss the coin from your right hand into the left. In reality, you perform the Bobo Switch, as described earlier.

secret view

4 This exposed view shows the bent coin lying on your left hand and the right coin about to be placed in the Finger Palm position. There should be no hesitation in your actions.

5 As the coin touches the left hand, it closes immediately into a fist so that the bend remains hidden. Squeeze the coin hard as if you are squashing it.

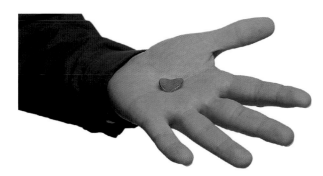

6 Open your left fingers wide to show that the coin really does have a bend in it. Give it back to the spectator, who will treasure the curiosity and think about it long after the event. As mentioned earlier, Bending Coin (Version 1) is a great prelude to this trick, and together they make a nice, memorable routine.

coin cascade

Ten coins are counted out loud and held by a spectator. Three invisible coins are tossed towards the spectator and when they open their hand and count the coins again they now have thirteen coins!

This is a great impromptu trick that can be performed almost anywhere. You can also substitute the coins for other small objects such as peanuts or sweets (candies).

1 You will need a hardback book and thirteen coins.

2 Insert three coins into the spine of the book. You will notice that when the book is closed the coins remain hidden and are held securely within the spine.

3 Display the remaining ten coins on the palm of your hand and hold the book in the other hand.

4 Give the coins in your hand to a volunteer. Open the book somewhere in the middle and ask the volunteer to count out loud as they place each of the coins on the book.

5 When they reach the last coin and say "ten", tip the coins into their cupped hands. The hidden coins will tip out with the other ten coins, completely unnoticed by your volunteer.

6 Mime throwing three invisible coins towards the volunteer, and ask them how many they would have if the coins were real. They will answer "thirteen".

7 Ask the person to count out the coins on to the book once again, and to their astonishment they will indeed have thirteen coins!

tip *A nice idea is to find a book on the subject of making money. Then when you do the trick you can mention that the information in the book works really fast!*

concorde coin (version 1)

In this simple yet incredibly effective trick, a coin is shown to have travelled invisibly from the right hand to the left. This is another of those rare tricks where the method is almost as impossible as the *effect. The coin really does travel invisibly from one hand to the other. For best results, perform the trick on a soft surface, such as a carpet or a tablecloth.*

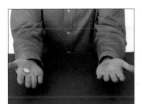   

1 Hold a small coin in the palm of your right hand. Notice how it is positioned, just below the base of the first and second fingers. Hold your left hand palm up as well, about 25cm (10in) from the right hand. The backs of your hands should be close to the floor or table.

2 Now turn both hands palm down very quickly. The right hand should move a fraction of a second before the left. With practice the coin will be flicked from the right hand to the left as they turn over. The coin moves so fast that the eye cannot see it. Fortunately, the camera can.

3 Take a few moments to explain that you are going to make the coin travel from your right hand to your left hand using magic. (Of course it is all done now, but as far as the spectators are concerned nothing has happened yet.)

4 Slowly raise your hands to show that the coin has indeed travelled across to the left hand. This really is a case of the hand being quicker than the eye.

concorde coin (version 2)

Here is an impressive variation of the trick above. Instead of using the surface of a table or the floor, this version can be performed *standing up. The moves are identical, apart from the fact that as the hands turn over they close into fists.*

1 Hold the coin in the palm of your right hand as before, and hold your left palm 25cm (10in) from your right hand.

2 Quickly flip your hands over, throwing the coin across to the left hand as you do so.

3 Having caught the coin, ball your hands into fists.

4 Open your hands to show the coin has travelled across.

tip *You can add a little misdirection to improve the trick still further. Start by showing the coin in your right hand then turn both hands over without throwing the coin. Say: "I am going to make the coin travel from my right hand to my left hand. In fact, it has already happened. But the hard thing is to make the coin travel back again ... look, it's back." Open your hands and show the coin in your right hand where it has been all along. Of course this is a silly joke, but as soon as the spectators laugh you turn your hands over again (this time doing the secret move) and say: "No seriously, I can do it – watch." Performing it like this means that no one will see the move when you actually throw the coin because they think the trick is over. You do the move when they are least expecting it to happen.*

appearing money

Imagine reaching up into the air and producing real money. You would never have to work again! Your audience doesn't have to know the money was yours to start with. This is one of the best *impromptu tricks you can perform. If you set up the trick prior to receiving your bill or check at the end of a meal, you can magically produce a tip for your waiter.*

secret view

1 To perform this trick, you will need to wear a long-sleeved shirt. Take a banknote and fold it in half, widthways, down the middle.

2 Carefully roll the note tightly into a cigarette shape, starting at the fold, as shown here.

3 Place the rolled-up note into the crook of your left elbow. Fold over the fabric to hide the note and to keep it in place. Keep your arm bent to prevent the note from falling out.

4 Show your right hand empty, simultaneously pulling your sleeve up with your left hand. This should look very natural, and will make your audience less suspicious when you repeat it.

5 Repeat the motion with your left hand. However, as the right hand tugs the sleeve, it secretly grasps the rolled-up note from the crook of your elbow.

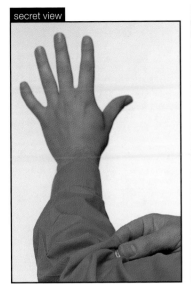

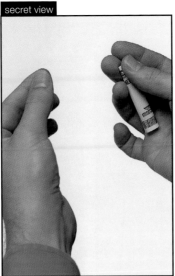

6 The exposed view shows how the left hand creates enough misdirection for this to happen. The right hand secretly retrieves the note, while the audience are focused on making sure that your left hand is empty.

7 Bring both hands to a position in front of you, at about chest level. The rolled-up note is held hidden in the right hand. The top end is pinched between the thumb, first and second fingers. These fingers pull the rest of the note back and out of sight.

8 From the front, both hands still look completely empty. This is a very convincing illusion.

10 Snap open the note.

9 Bring your fingers together and, without pausing, use your right thumb to pivot the note into a position that allows both hands to grip an edge each.

paper to money

A piece of blank, white paper is shown on both sides. It is folded several times and then unfolded again. It instantly changes into a banknote! The larger the value of the note, the more impressive

the effect is. Try this out and you won't be disappointed. The success of the trick depends on the gimmick being made perfectly so that it operates easily and smoothly.

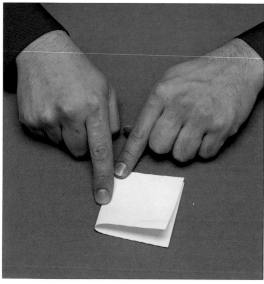

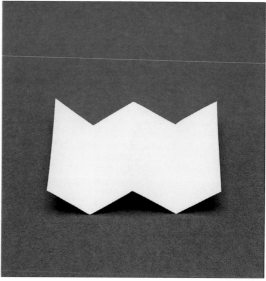

1 To prepare, cut a piece of paper exactly the same size as the banknote. Fold it neatly in half precisely down the middle.

2 Unfold the paper, turn it over and fold each side in half again, creasing the paper sharply and neatly.

3 Fold the paper along the creases, concertina-style, ensuring that the ends of the paper are to your right. Fold it up and towards you, making one final sharp crease directly down the centre.

4 Unfold the paper and repeat exactly the same procedure with the banknote. It is vital to the success of this trick that the creasing and folding is as neat and accurate as possible.

5 Apply glue to the upper right corner of the paper. (This section is marked in black for ease of explanation.)

6 Attach the glued corner of the paper behind the lower right corner of the banknote. Check that the edges match up exactly and that both pieces are perfectly aligned. Check the photograph here to ensure that you have orientated the papers correctly.

7 Fold the banknote along its creases so that you finish with it folded neatly at the top right corner of the white paper. If the edges of the banknote extend beyond the edges of the paper, the handling will be hindered.

8 Turn over the paper and hold it so that your right fingers cover the banknote, which is now positioned under the bottom right corner of the paper. This is how you should hold the paper when you begin the performance. The gimmick can be kept in a wallet or pocket until needed.

 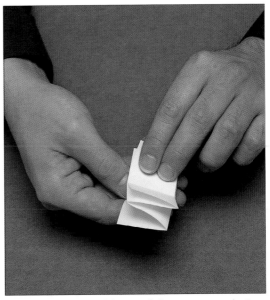

9 In performance, hold the paper with both hands, thumbs on top, fingers below. Quickly display the paper front and back by turning both wrists. When the back is seen, the banknote is hidden under the right fingers. Explain that money is printed on very special paper and that you have managed to find a piece.

10 With the front of the paper facing up once more, begin to fold the paper from left to right concertina-style, along the creases, with your left fingers. ▶

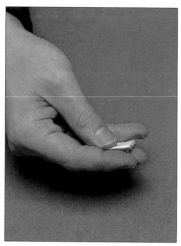

11 Fold the paper back towards you, still using the creases made previously. (Notice how the right hand stays in the same position throughout.)

12 Lift the right thumb and clip the package between the thumb and first finger. Then quickly lift the right third finger, clipping the paper between the right third and second fingers.

13 Squeeze these fingers together, flipping the package up at right angles to the fingers.

14 Your right thumb helps to turn the paper end over end. These steps are all done in one quick movement with a shake of the wrist, and take only a second.

15 The crease in the banknote will open slightly under its own tension. This enables the right thumb to push open the first fold without fumbling.

16 Immediately, the left fingers open the banknote out completely flat.

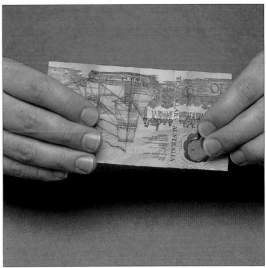

17 Turn your wrists, showing the back of the note exactly as you did at the start of the routine. This time it is the paper that is hidden under the right fingers.

18 Finish by displaying the front of the banknote again, then quickly put it away in your pocket or wallet.

tip *Make sure that you have a duplicate banknote (with similar crease lines) in your pocket or wallet so that if somebody asks to examine it, you can give them the duplicate note instead.*

match
magic

Matches can be found almost anywhere. Their very existence is a reminder of our ability to perform real magic and create fire at will. The shape and size of ordinary matches, together with the matchbox or matchbook they are housed in, create opportunities for optical illusions and simple magic tricks. With a box of matches in your pocket, you can be ready to perform an entire magic show!

mix and match

One of humanity's greatest achievements was discovering how to create fire. Perhaps this was the first magic trick ever performed – it certainly must have felt like magic at the time. Our desire for "instant" fire was not satisfied until approximately 1.5 million years later, in about 1680, when a match similar to our modern ones was invented. The phosphorus used was deadly, and despite several attempts to create non-toxic alternatives, it wasn't until around 1910 that matches were made with harmless chemicals. They were then sold throughout the world. Well over 500 billion matches are now used each year – that's a lot of matches!

As a result, matches can be found everywhere. Most people have a box or two at home, and restaurants, bars and clubs will certainly have them.

There are magicians who use fire as a major theme in their act, and build a reputation on effects of this nature. Most of the following tricks do not require you to actually light a match, so they can also be performed with cocktail sticks. As has been mentioned throughout the book, always try to be adaptable to whatever props are around you. It is advisable to learn several stunts and tricks that you can perform "impromptu" –

Above: British magician Colin Rose is well known for his fire-themed acts. One of these acts – "Fantasy in Flame" – thrilled audiences on television and in casinos and nightclubs the world over. In the 1970s his superb and dramatic manipulations of fire were enjoyed by hundreds of thousands when he toured with the legendary Richiardi Jnr.

Left: An artist's impression of the discovery of fire. Such an event would have been incredibly magical and wondrous to watch, but would probably have been met with severe apprehension.

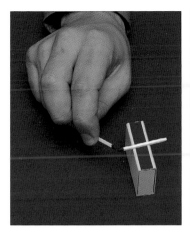

Above: Can matches really conduct static electricity? Your friends will believe so when you show them the Static Match!

Above: The next time you need to light a candle, cigarette or cigar, magically produce a lit match from behind your lapel – Lit Match Production.

Above: A match is torn from a matchbook and lit. Seconds later it disappears, only to be found reattached inside the book – Burnt Match in Matchbook.

such tricks can often be more impressive than a fully prepared show. Performing impromptu magic should not mean that your tricks are unrehearsed; it simply means that you are able to do an off-the-cuff routine.

If you learn some of the simple stunts in the following pages, you will be able to amaze your friends by making a lit match appear before using it to light a cigarette or candle (Lit Match Production). Then you will learn how to "vanish" it using a relatively unknown method (Vanishing Match). To demonstrate

the idea that wood can channel static electricity, you can make matches move and jump (Static Match and Jumping Match).

You will also learn how to make two solid matches pass through each other several times under impossible conditions (Match through Match), and how to rip a match from a matchbook, light and "vanish" it only to show the burnt match re-attached back inside the matchbook (Burnt Match in Matchbook). These are two of the best impromptu tricks in magic.

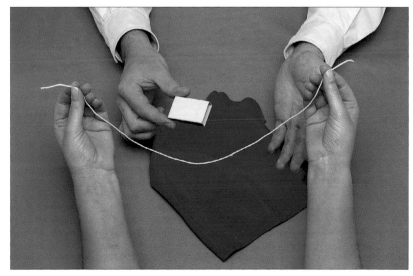

Right: Matchbox off String is the impossible penetration of one solid object through the other. The concept of penetration forms the basis for many "effects" in magic.

match through safety pin

The illusion created by this little stunt is that of a match passing through the bar of a safety pin. Although not a particularly difficult magic trick, it is a good example of how speed can deceive the eye.

It is a small party trick which can be made up quickly and cheaply with objects that most people would be able to find in their houses or place of work.

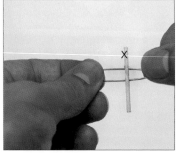

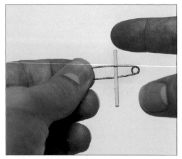

1 Using a scalpel, carefully cut the head off a match and push the sharp point of a safety pin through the centre. Close the safety pin and the set-up is completed. You may find that the match splits when you insert the pin. If this is the case, try first soaking a match for a few minutes in water in order to soften the wood.

2 Hold the safety pin with the left hand and position the match so that the top half is against the top bar of the pin. Flick the match, striking the point marked "X".

3 If you strike the match correctly, it appears as if the match passes straight through the top bar of the pin and on to the other side. In reality, what happens is that the match bounces off the top bar and rotates backwards in a complete revolution so quickly that it is virtually impossible for the human eye to see.

self-extinguishing match

You light a match and hold it in your right fingertips. You then extinguish the flame by blowing up your left sleeve! Often the best time to perform magic is when nobody is expecting anything to happen – if you catch people off guard, you can really amaze them.

Try this trick the next time you light a match. Don't call attention to your actions; just do it as if it is the most natural thing in the world. The match extinguishing itself looks very magical. Sometimes these little magic tricks can be as enjoyable as the more involved routines.

secret view

secret view

1 Strike a match and hold it up in the air away from your body.

2 Hold the match in between your right first and second fingers, so that your thumbnail is in a position to flick the match as you blow up your left sleeve.

3 Blow up your left sleeve and at the same time allow the end of the match to flick off your thumbnail.

4 The sudden movement of the match causes the flame to extinguish itself.

broken and restored match

A match is wrapped in the centre of a handkerchief. A spectator breaks the match into two pieces through the fabric, but when the match is unwrapped, it has magically restored itself. This trick is very old, but rarely seen. It is easily prepared and simple to execute, so is ideal for those times when you are asked to perform "at the drop of a hat". It also works with cocktail sticks.

1 Push a match into the seam of a handkerchief. The material of the handkerchief should hide the secret match perfectly – if it does not, then try using a thicker handkerchief.

2 When you are ready to perform, set the handkerchief on the table with a corner at the top and the hidden match in the corner nearest you. Openly place another match in the centre. With your right hand, bring the corner with the hidden match up into the centre.

3 Immediately fold the left corner into the middle, then the right corner, and finally the top.

4 Lift the secretly hidden match through the cloth. Hand it to a spectator and ask them to break it in half. The spectator will assume this is the same match they saw just a few moments ago.

5 Unfold the handkerchief one corner at a time. With the right hand, grip the last corner to cover the hidden match.

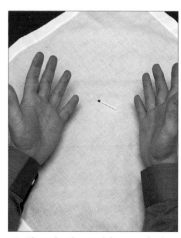

6 Show that the match has completely restored itself. Finish by folding up the handkerchief and pocketing the evidence of the hidden, broken match in the corner!

vanishing match

A match is held at the extreme fingertips and magically dissolved into thin air. In order to perform this amazing trick, you need to be wearing a ring on your right third finger.

This is another simple trick which is ideal for a spur-of-the-moment performance. You could also vanish a cocktail stick, but you must be careful not to stab yourself with it!

1 Hold a match between the tips of your thumb and first finger.

2 Curl your third and fourth fingers in, so that your second finger can angle the match towards the ring.

3 Use your thumb to push the match behind the back of your third finger and underneath the back of the ring.

`secret view`

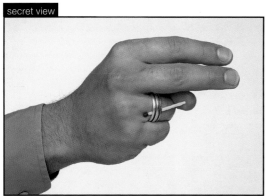

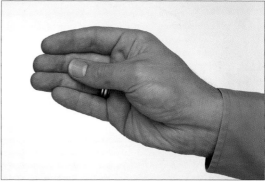

4 This is what the move looks like from the other side. You must make sure that nobody is watching you from behind.

5 Straighten out your fingers and rub your thumb as if dissolving the match.

6 Hold your hand out flat, but with your fingers closed together.

7 Finally spread your fingers wide to show that the match has completely gone.

vanishing box of matches

A box of matches is shaken and a spectator is asked to guess from the sound alone how many matches are inside. Whatever their answer, they are proven to be wrong when the box is opened and the matches have vanished! The effect of sound is strong and can be used in many different ways. For instance, once you are familiar with the workings of the principle described below, it is possible to

demonstrate a similar game to the old street swindle Three Card Monte. Three empty matchboxes are placed next to each other; one supposedly contains matches. The spectator has to keep their eye on the "full" box of matches as you move them and mix them around. You can prove that any of the boxes are empty or full at any time, depending on which hand you shake the box with.

1 To prepare, half fill a matchbox with matches and close the box. Do not overfill the box, otherwise the sound the matches make when shaken will become muffled.

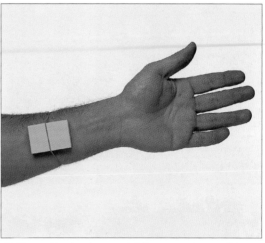

2 Put a rubber band on your left forearm, under your shirt sleeve. Place the box under the rubber band. You are now ready to perform the trick.

3 Shake an empty matchbox with your left hand. The rattling sound that is emitted comes from the hidden box up your sleeve. Ask the spectator to guess how many matches are inside the box. It doesn't really matter what their answer is.

4 Open the box and show that it is completely empty. You can hand it out for examination and allow your spectator to dismantle it if you wish.

take cover

A matchbox is shaken and heard to contain matches. The box is opened and the matches are definitely there, but the matchbox cover *vanishes into thin air! It reappears inside the magician's pocket. This clever prop should only take about 10 minutes to construct.*

1 You will require two matchboxes, some glue and a pair of scissors to make this trick.

2 First separate the cover and the drawer of one matchbox. Cut the side and front off the cover.

3 Glue this to the base and side of the drawer, as marked in the picture.

4 Make sure the edges do not overlap by trimming any excess card away. Remove and discard the drawer from the other matchbox, and put the cover in your pocket. Put some matches in the prepared drawer and you are ready to perform the trick.

5 To perform, hold the fake matchbox upside down so that the top and side face the audience. The matches will be loose so be careful they don't fall out of the inverted box. Shake the box and say: "Watch carefully."

6 Close your fingers around the box and turn your hand over. You must now turn your body so your left side is facing the spectators.

7 Use your left thumb to push the drawer out from your hand and take it with your right hand. The illusion is perfect. The gimmicked top and side will be hidden.

8 This is the view of how the box is held from beneath.

9 Wait a few seconds in the position shown. Your friends will believe you have the match box cover in your left hand.

10 Crumple the fingers of your left hand and open them to show that the box has gone.

11 Transfer the drawer to your left hand, and reach into your pocket with your right hand to remove the duplicate cover.

12 Slide the duplicate cover over your gimmicked box to finish the trick.

static match

This is similar to the Jumping Match which follows, but is slightly easier to perform. One match is balanced on the edge of a matchbox and the other match rubbed against your arm to create "static electricity". As the two match heads touch, the "static" is transferred and the match on the box shoots off like a rocket. In fact static has nothing to do with the method but it makes an interesting presentation.

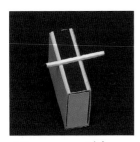

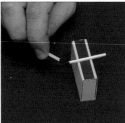

1 Remove one match from a matchbox. Stand the matchbox on its side and carefully balance the match on top at right angles, as shown here.

2 Rub the second match on your sleeve, supposedly to generate static electricity. Rub your foot on the floor at the same time, as if trying to harness as much electricity as possible. Hold the match between your thumb, first and second fingers. Its tip should sit under the second finger's nail.

3 Slowly approach the balanced match until the heads touch each other. You should act as if you might be about to receive an electric shock so that your actions interest the spectator.

4 As soon as the heads touch, allow the match to snap out from behind your fingernail. The force of the resulting jerk will be transferred through the first match and into the second. The second match will fly away at speed.

jumping match

Two matches are held at the extreme fingertips. One is rubbed on the sleeve and is held underneath the other. A few seconds later one of the matches flies away as if charged with electricity. The secret to the trick is the vibrations that are caused by rubbing a match against your fingernail. These vibrations make the match jump. They travel along one match and through the other, making it move without any apparent cause. If you practise enough, you can make the match jump completely off your finger and on to the table.

This effect will also work with toothpicks and even chopsticks. Try linking this trick with the Static Match explained above.

1 Rub a match against your sleeve, saying that you are charging it with static electricity. Then hold its edge between your right thumb and first finger. Position your second finger so that the match is pulled against the base of the fingernail.

2 Balance the second match on the first match, using your left first finger.

3 Pull the right hand's match back against your fingernail and scrape it against the nail. This is a tiny movement, which is completely unseen. The balanced match will begin to jump as the vibrations travel along.

lit match production

The next time you need to light a cigarette or a candle, simply reach behind your lapel and produce a lit match! As with all effects using matches and fire, you must be extremely cautious.

This is not really a trick in itself, but it does provide a small, visual magical moment. It is nice to be able to make things happen magically; after all, if you are a magician it is only right that you can produce fire at will – why would a magician need a lighter or a box of matches?

1 To prepare, fold the striking panel from a matchbox in half.

2 Thread the striking panel through the bars of a safety pin, as shown above.

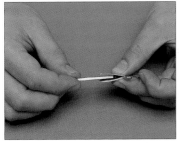

3 Carefully position a match with its head between the two surfaces of the striking panel.

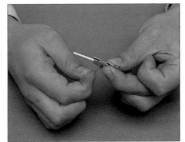

4 Wrap a rubber band tightly around the match and panel to keep everything locked in place.

5 Attach this "gimmick" under your right lapel. You can leave it in position for as long as you like.

6 When you are ready to perform, reach behind your lapel and grip the match tightly with your right hand.

7 Quickly pull the match downwards and outwards. The match will strike against the panel and ignite as it leaves the gimmick.

match through match

The idea of one solid object passing through another is a wonderful concept. It is simple to understand and everyone knows that it is impossible. This superb effect can be performed at any time as long as you can find two matches (or toothpicks). Two solid objects are caused to pass through each other not once but twice!

Most magic tricks should never be repeated, but if you perform this one well you can repeat it many times without fear of the method being detected. You will need to practise this effect until you can perform the secret moves without thinking. Just a little practice is all it will take to become confident.

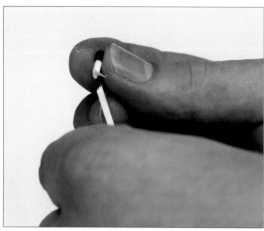

1 Break the heads off two matches and discard them. They are no longer needed.

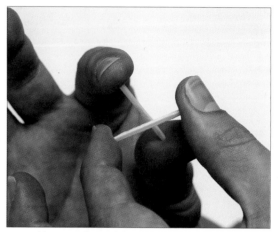

2 Hold one match in each hand between the tips of your thumb and first finger. Your right first finger should be holding a rough, broken-off end. Squeeze it tightly so that the rough end sticks into the skin of your finger.

secret view

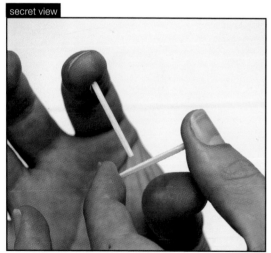

3 Tap the matches together three times. On the third tap, lower the right thumb. Because the match is wedged into your skin, it will remain suspended in the air for a fraction of a second as your thumb passes under the other match.

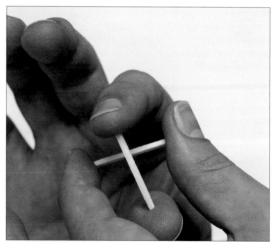

4 As soon as your right thumb is on the other side, re-grip the match again. The action takes place in under a second and the illusion created is of one match passing though the other. You can now reverse the above actions and remove the matches from each other. This is a great close-up magic trick.

matchbox off string

The cover of a matchbox is threaded on to a length of string. Both ends are held by a spectator and a handkerchief is placed over the centre. The magician reaches under the handkerchief and without any tearing or cutting is able to remove the box from the string.

To make the trick self-contained, find an opaque silk handkerchief that is thin enough to fold up and place inside the box together with the string. This way you can carry the whole trick around in one box.

1 Carefully prise open the glued joint of a matchbox cover, using a scalpel. Try to keep the card as flat as possible. It may take several attempts with different covers to split the box open without damaging the card.

2 Apply some reusable adhesive to a couple of points along the joint so that you can open and close the box repeatedly. When closed, the matchbox cover should look normal and arouse no suspicion. You are now ready to perform the trick.

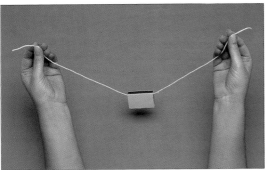

3 Thread the matchbox cover on to a piece of string. Ask a spectator to hold one end of the string in each hand.

4 Cover the box with a handkerchief, explaining that the magic has to happen under the cover of darkness.

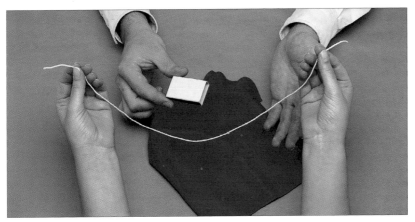

5 Reach under the handkerchief and unstick the prepared cover. Remove it from the string, then re-stick the join, making sure that you line up the sides of the box as evenly as possible. Display the box and remove the handkerchief. Try linking this trick with another that utilizes a piece of string, silk or a matchbox. There are many suitable effects in this book.

burnt match in matchbook

A match is torn out of a matchbook and lit. The burnt match vanishes and is found re-attached back inside the book. If you *learn this trick well, you will have a very strong piece of magic at your disposal wherever there is a book of matches around.*

1 Before you begin the performance, open a matchbook and tear out a match.

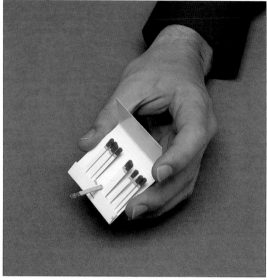

2 Bend another match forward and set it alight using the first match. Be very careful not to set alight the other matches. Blow out the flame and wait a few seconds for the match to cool.

3 Hold the burnt match under your left thumb so that it is hidden from view. The preparation is now complete.

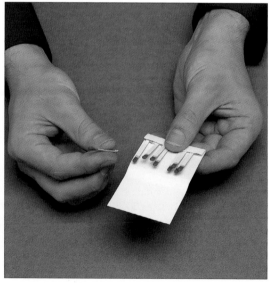

4 Show the matchbook and openly tear out one match, making sure the bent match remains hidden underneath your thumb.

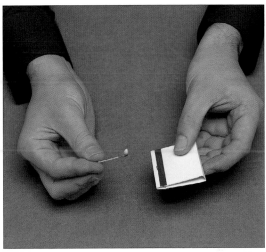

5 Close the matchbook by folding it backwards in order to keep the burnt match hidden. As the cover is closed, the burnt match is unbent and goes back into position next to the others.

6 Light the torn match and place the matchbook on the table, in view. Extinguish the flame.

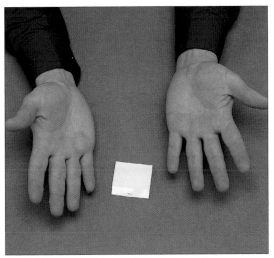

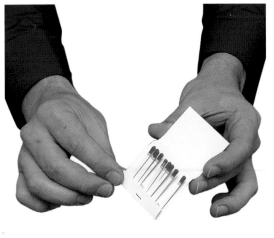

7 You must now "vanish" the match using any method you feel comfortable with, such as Vanishing Match or Fake Take (see Money Magic chapter). Another simple vanish can be accomplished while shaking the lit match to extinguish the flame. In a continuing motion, throw it over your shoulder and across the room. (Make sure the match is extinguished before you let go!) Continue to shake your hand up and down as if the match were still there. Give a few more shakes, then slow down to a halt and show that the match is gone.

8 Open the matchbook and show that the burnt match has miraculously re-attached itself inside!

box it

Match puzzles have been in existence for almost as long as matches themselves, and they are particularly good since they can be performed anywhere. This puzzle is a classic and is not too difficult. The challenge is to move just two matches to make six squares.

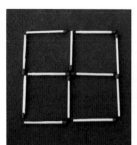

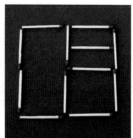

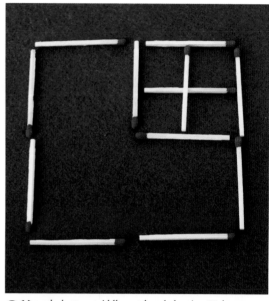

1 Lay 12 matches on the table to form four squares.

2 Pick up the middle left match and position to bisect the top left square.

tip *You could also use pencils, chopsticks, toothpicks or any other straight objects that you have to hand to perform these simple match puzzles.*

3 Move the bottom middle match and place it at 90 degrees to the other match to form a square within a square.

numbers up

You are not allowed to break any matches to solve this puzzle. The secret to finding the answer is to think laterally. You may need to drop hints for those of your friends who are finding it hard to solve the puzzle for themselves.

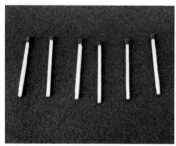

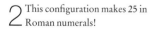

1 Rearrange these six matches to make the number twenty-five.

2 This configuration makes 25 in Roman numerals!

fish!

Can you make this fish swim in the opposite direction in just three moves? Even when you know the solution to this puzzle, it is quite difficult to get right. It is worth trying it yourself and practising if necessary before challenging someone else to do it.

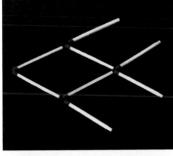

1 Use eight matches to make the image of a fish.

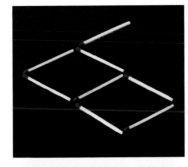

2 Move the top far right match and position as shown here.

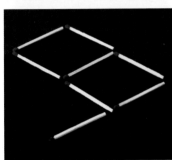

3 Move the top right match and place it at the bottom on the left, as shown.

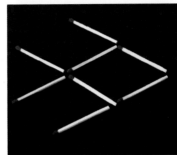

4 Finally, move the top left match and position as shown.

cocktail glass

Can you work out how to remove the cherry from the glass by moving just two matches? The glass must not change shape.

The reason that this puzzle is so hard to solve is due to the fact that the glass ends up at a different angle from that at which it started.

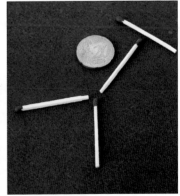

1 Lay four matches in the shape of a cocktail glass and put a coin in the glass to represent a cherry.

2 Move the bottom match and position as shown.

3 Move the match to the left of the coin as shown. The glass has rotated but did not change shape!

string and rope magic

There is a well-known saying, "Give a man enough rope and he will hang himself." There is another, less well-known saying, "Give a magician enough rope and he will show you a trick!" The following pages explain a variety of tricks using string, cord and rope. You will soon be able to cut and restore them, make them pass through human flesh and make knots mysteriously disappear at will.

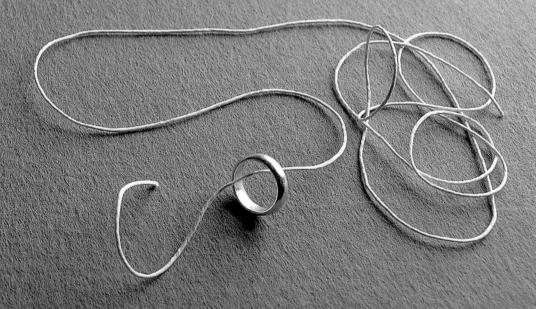

learn the ropes

One of the most famous stories in magic is that of the legendary Indian Rope Trick. There are many versions of this trick. In one version a fakir caused one end of a long piece of rope to rise slowly into the air, where it would disappear through the clouds and remain perfectly rigid. A small boy would then climb the rope until he too vanished into the mist. In a rather gruesome moment the boy would fall from the sky limb by limb. His limbs were placed inside a basket and the rope would fall to the ground. From the basket would then rise the boy, who was found to be in perfect condition. In some stories the boy was chased up the rope by the fakir, and in others the boy simply vanished when he reached the top. The variations seem to be endless.

It is hard to pinpoint exactly when this illusion first came into existence because accounts vary and most, if not all, of those who wrote these accounts did not experience the illusion first-hand. It is believed that the first reported sightings were around 1350. Centuries later, in the early 1900s, many well-known illusionists, such as Thurston, Goldin, Hertz, Kellar and Kalanag,

Above: A typical nineteenth-century depiction of a suspension/levitation which would have been performed by fakirs trying to convince the public of their special powers. Such illusions were easily duplicated by magicians of the time.
Left: This drawing of a magic trick was published in *The Discoverie of Witchcraft* (1584) and suggests that string, cord and rope have been used by conjurors for centuries.

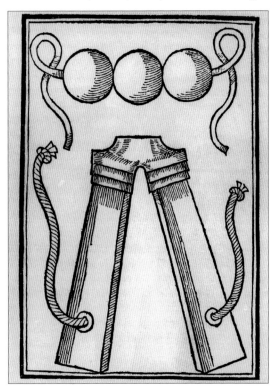

began performing elaborate versions of the trick in theatres across the world, much to the delight of their audiences. The addition of the famous Indian Rope Trick to their repertoire and the legend that surrounded it guaranteed valuable publicity.

Even though many of the principles of rope magic are old, there are still many new techniques being developed and invented. The French magician Tabary is currently one of the freshest innovators in rope magic. His performances have astonished magicians and non-magicians across the world and won him a coveted first place at the FISM international magic convention in 1991, making him a close-up world champion.

Magic shops sell "magicians' rope" in hanks. This is relatively inexpensive and available in a wide range of colours. You can use any type of rope, but try to find one with a high cotton content which is soft and flexible. You may find the rope needs to be cored – some ropes are made up of an outer layer and an inner core. The core can often be removed by pulling it from one end. You will be left with the sleeve of soft cotton, which makes perfect rope for manipulating and cutting.

The ends of the rope may begin to fray, and there are several ways to avoid this happening. The easiest is to stitch the ends with a thread of similar colour. Alternatively you can paint clear glue on to each end to seal the ends completely.

A staple of many magicians' repertoire is the Cut and Restored Rope effect. A length of rope is cut into two – sometimes three – pieces and caused to restore itself. There are dozens of methods in existence, and several are explained in this book. With a little thought, you can link several of these routines together to create a small performance that can be used as an act on its own or as part of a larger programme.

Above right: Seen here is a demonstration of a version of the Indian Rope Trick being performed in England, 1935.

Right: A publicity poster for nineteenth- and twentieth-century magician Carl Hertz, who regularly featured a version of the Indian Rope Trick in his illusion show.

Below: A popular rope trick wherein several silk handkerchiefs magically pass through a length of rope to which they are securely tied.

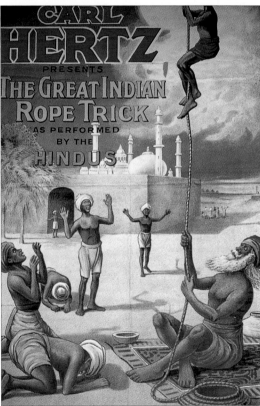

cut and re-strawed

A long piece of cord is threaded through a straw, which is then bent in half. The straw and cord are cut through the middle and displayed in two pieces, but when the cord is removed from the straw, it has *magically restored itself! The best straws to use are those found in fast food restaurants. The only preparation required is a slit which must be cut and which will remain hidden by the stripes on the straw.*

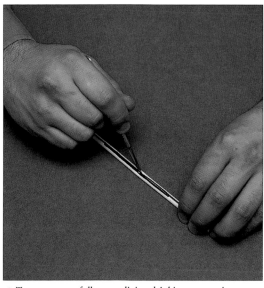

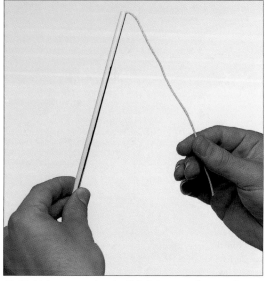

1 To prepare, carefully cut a slit in a drinking straw, using a scalpel. The slit should not go all the way to the ends. It is seen as a black line here for ease of explanation.

2 Hold the straw so that the slit is facing towards you and therefore hidden from anyone viewing from the front. Thread a cord through the straw so that a piece hangs from each end.

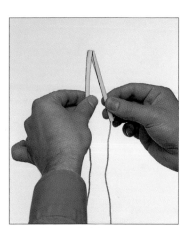

secret view

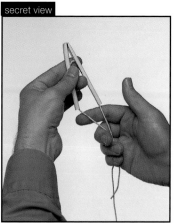

3 Hold one end of the straw in each hand and bend it in half so that the slit is on the inside.

4 Hold the straw in the left fingertips and pull the ends so that the middle of the cord slips out of the slit and behind the left first finger. Pinch the cord together with the straw between the left first finger and the thumb.

5 Cut the straw neatly in two. The middle of the cord remains hidden but the illusion created is that both the cord and the straw have been cut.

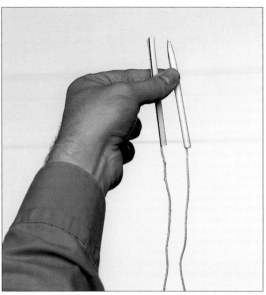

6 From the front, it can be seen that the cord is hidden behind the left forefinger, which looks very natural holding the straw in two pieces.

7 The view from your side is almost as convincing! Begin to pull one end of the cord downwards.

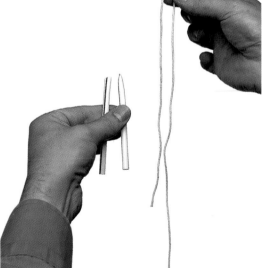

8 Continue pulling until the cord is removed completely. Pause to let the effect register with your audience.

9 Show that the cord is completely restored. If you wish, you can immediately hand the cord out for examination, but be sure to discard the straw in case the slit is discovered.

indestructible string

A length of string is wrapped in a piece of paper. The paper is clearly cut into two pieces and yet the string is somehow completely unharmed. "Cut and Restored" is a classic theme in magic; the impossibility of tearing, cutting or sawing something or someone in two and restoring it or them has fascinated audiences worldwide for hundreds of years.

1 You will need a piece of string approximately 50cm (20in) long, a pair of scissors and a piece of paper about 10 x 7.5cm (4 x 3in).

2 Make a fold about 2.5cm (1in) up from the bottom of the paper. Now fold the top piece down so that it just overlaps the bottom edge of the paper. This completes the preparation.

secret view

3 To perform the trick, hold the folded paper open, towards you, and lay the string along the lower crease. Notice how the thumbs of each hand pinch the string and paper to hold it all in place.

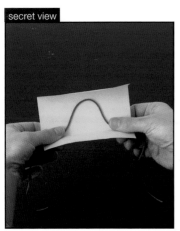

secret view

4 Now lift the bottom flap of the paper upwards, towards you, with your middle fingers and at the same time slide your thumbs inwards so that the middle of the string becomes a loop.

5 This action is completely unseen from the front.

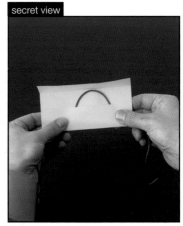

secret view

6 Continue to fold up the flap and grip the string through the paper with your thumbs, as shown here.

secret view

7 Keeping your thumbs still, use your left index finger to pull the loop of string down.

8 Now fold over the top flap of the paper using your right forefinger.

9 Grip the paper and string with your left hand as shown. Pinch the loop of string inside the paper with your thumb to make sure it stays still. Remove your right hand.

10 As you prepare to cut the paper, insert the top blade of the scissors through the loop and adjust the position of your grip so your fingers straddle the blades and hold on to both sides of the paper. Mind your fingers!

11 From the front it looks as though you are going to cut through both the paper and the string.

12 With one snip, cut the paper in two. Ensure that the half of the paper in front overlaps the half at the back to hide the intact string and maintain the illusion.

13 Slide the two pieces of paper apart, showing the string intact in the middle.

tip *If you are left handed, simply reverse the hand positions so that you can cut using your left hand.*

jumping rubber band

A rubber band is placed over the first and second fingers, then magically caused to jump to the third and fourth fingers. This is a very simple trick which you will have no trouble in mastering. You could perform this before another trick such as Linking Paper Clips.

secret view

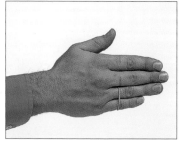

1 Place a rubber band over the first and second fingers. The back of your hand should be towards the audience. Pull the band away from your hand.

2 Close your hand, inserting all the fingers into the rubber band. Let the band snap over the fingertips. From the front, it will simply look as though the band is on the first and second fingers.

3 Quickly open your hand. The band will automatically jump over to the third and fourth fingers.

secret view

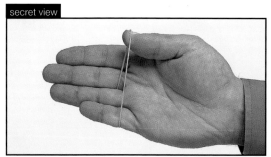

secret view

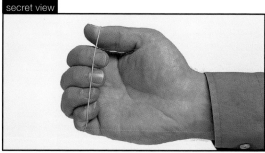

4 It is possible to make the band jump back again. The move can also be accomplished with one hand. Hook your thumb under the band and stretch it up so that you create a gap, as before.

5 Close the fingers again, inserting them into the gap created. Release your thumb from the band.

6 Open the hand again and the band will jump back to its former position.

string through arm (version 1)

A piece of string is tied into a continuous loop. It is wrapped around a spectator's arm and magically penetrates the flesh and bone without any damage whatsoever! The principle relies on your moves being

quick and smooth. The secret move is covered by the speed of the hand which, in this case, really does deceive the eye. A piece of string is a simple, compact prop to carry around.

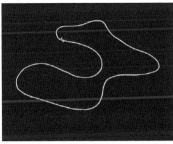

1 Tie a piece of string, approximately 90cm (3ft) long, into a loop with a strong knot.

2 Hold the loop under a spectator's arm and ask them to create an impenetrable barrier by gripping their hands firmly together, as seen here.

3 Bring both ends of the string up to meet each other, then pass one loop through the other. Grip the string and tug it gently to show that it is unquestionably trapped on the arm.

4 Move both hands up to each other again, then hook the left first finger around the top strand of the right hand's string.

5 Maintain the first finger's grip, but release the other portion of string from the left hand.

6 Pull both hands apart until the string is held taut. It will now be above the spectator's arm. It is important that steps 4, 5 and 6 happen together in one smooth motion in order for the illusion to look its best.

string through arm (version 2)

A spectator holds out their arm and a piece of string is held underneath. A few tugs and the string passes straight through their arm to the other side! Or does it?

To prepare for this trick you need to thread two small beads on a piece of string, approximately 45cm (18in) long, tying a knot at each end. The beads should be loose and free to slide from one end to the other. These beads are not meant to be a secret but neither should you call attention to them. When you pinch your finger and thumb around them, you should hardly be able to see them. Try to ensure that the knots at the ends of the string are tied as tightly as possible so that they do not come undone while performing.

1 Starting with both beads at the left end of the string, place the string under the outstretched arm of a spectator. The string should be held taut and at the fingertips.

2 Bring both ends of the string together. Grip one of the beads tightly with your right fingers, keeping the end bead gripped in your left hand.

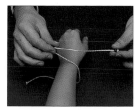

3 Allow the end of the string held by the right hand to drop, then quickly pull both beads taut. What really happens is that the string passes under the arm.

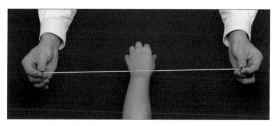

4 At full speed the eye cannot detect the route the string takes. The illusion of the string passing through the arm to get to the other side is very convincing!

string through ring

You can make a piece of string pass through many other solid objects. Here the same trick is performed using a spectator's finger ring.

As before, you need to attach two small beads to a piece of string. Then ask a spectator to lend you a ring. The best type of ring to use is a plain wedding band. In any event, you should avoid borrowing rings that have precious stones, in case one of them should fall out.

1 Ask a spectator to pinch a ring tightly between their finger and thumb. Thread the string through the ring. Both beads must be to the left.

2 Bring both hands together, pinching a bead between finger and thumb of each hand.

3 Drop the end held in your right hand and pull the beads apart.

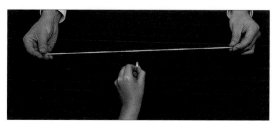

4 The string appears to have melted through the band of metal. A little thought will reveal many other objects which could be used instead of a spectator's arm or a finger ring – the handle of a mug, for example.

rope through neck

The two ends of a piece of rope are seen hanging over both shoulders. Despite the fact that the rope clearly passes around the back of the head, with a sharp tug it visibly penetrates the neck. This trick also works very well with a tie, which is perhaps a more appropriate item to have hanging around your neck! Please note that care should be taken when wrapping any sort of cord around your neck.

1 To prepare, run the rope across the front of your neck, and tuck it just under the edge of your shirt collar.

2 Once this secret preparation has been accomplished, you are ready to perform. Viewed from the front, it looks as if you have a piece of rope hanging around your neck and over your shoulders.

3 Hold both ends of the rope and pull gently until the line becomes taut.

4 With one quick action, pull the rope hard with both hands. As the rope stretches out, it is pulled from under your collar so quickly that the eye will be unable to detect the secret.

rope through neck again!

The general rule is "Never repeat a trick" but there are exceptions, for example when you have several methods for achieving the same effect. This is the ideal follow-up to Rope through Neck because the *method is completely different, even though the two tricks look very similar. Once again, a tie will work just as well, and as mentioned before you should take care whenever looping cord around your neck.*

1 Hang a piece of rope, approximately 1.8m (6ft) long, around your neck so that the left side hangs lower than the right. Experimentation will make it clear exactly how much rope should be hanging from either side.

2 With the right hand, grasp the left side of the rope between your thumb and first finger about a quarter of the way down. Now reach over with the left hand and pinch the right side of the rope about a quarter of the way up from the bottom.

3 Lift the right hand, with the rope, across the front of your neck and around to the middle of the back of your neck.

4 A split second after the right hand has started moving, the left hand begins its journey. It takes its piece of rope and wraps it around the back of your neck from right to left (the same way as the first piece). Your left arm moves over your head to achieve this.

secret view

5 The result is a bight or loop of rope, which is trapped by the loop made by the shorter piece.

6 From the front, it looks as if you have wrapped the rope around your neck. Hold one end in each hand and pull the rope taut.

7 Pull sharply with both hands. The bight of rope will slip out of the other loop and the rope will fall away from your neck. Make sure the rope is pulled completely taut.

hunter bow knot

In this trick, a slip knot is tied into a length of rope with a pretty flourish. This method of tying a slip knot is quite tricky to learn, but once you understand the moves you will never forget them.

The beauty of this particular tie is that the knots created look completely tangled until they all dissolve into thin air! You can incorporate the Hunter Bow Knot into other rope tricks and routines.

1 Extend the first and second fingers of your left hand and hang the centre of a piece of rope over them. Position your right first and second fingers about 2.5–5cm (1–2in) down the rope, below the left second finger.

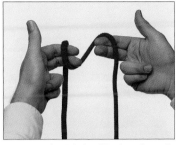

2 Move the right hand back, under and up, curling your fingers enough to pull the rope back, and loop it around the tips of your left fingers.

3 With both hands, grip a portion of the rope between your first and second fingers, as shown here.

4 Gripping tightly, pull the right hand to the right and the left hand to the left. The result will be a bow.

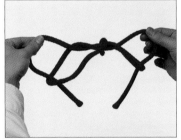

5 Reach into the tops of both loops and pull the ends through.

6 Slowly pull both ends of the rope, tightening the knot.

7 Give one final tug and the knot will disappear! If you find that the knot does not dissolve, you may need to experiment at step 5 by pulling the ends of the rope through the opposite sides of the loops.

impossible knot

Challenge a spectator to tie a knot in the centre of a piece of rope without letting go of the ends. Although you may find this difficult to *learn initially, once you understand which hand goes where you will be able to make the Impossible Knot in an instant, without thinking.*

1 Hold one end of a piece of rope tightly in each hand.

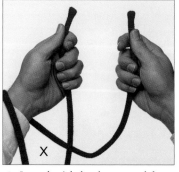

2 Loop the right hand over your left arm and behind the rope held in your left hand. Bring it back to a position similar to that at the start. Now move your right hand through the loop marked "X".

3 Once your hand has passed through the loop, pass it through the second loop marked "X".

4 Stretch both hands out. You should now be in this position.

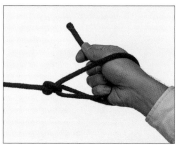

5 Allow the rope to slip off your left wrist, then pull the rope taut.

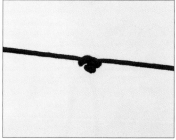

6 Repeat this with the right loop. You will be left with a knot in the centre of the rope.

7 Tug both ends and the knot will disappear before your eyes!

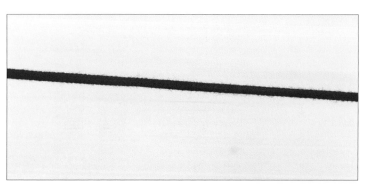

slip knot

A knot is tied without letting go of the ends of the rope. The knot is then plucked off the rope and thrown into the audience! This is a great *"bit of business" to add to a longer rope routine because it always receives a laugh from the audience.*

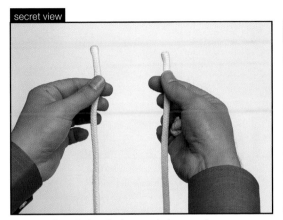

secret view

1 You will need a length of rope and a knot cut from a spare piece of rope. To prepare, hide the extra knot in your right-hand Finger Palm position (*see* Money Magic chapter). Hold one end of the main piece of rope in each hand.

2 Tie a knot without letting go of the ends of the rope, as described in Impossible Knot. Hold one end of the rope in the left hand.

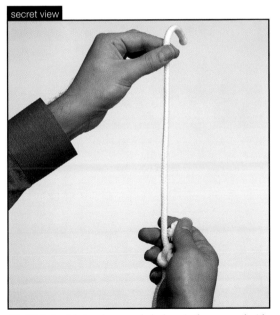

secret view

3 With the right hand, approach the knot in the rope, and with the little finger, grip the rope just under the knot. The fourth finger tugs the rope, undoing the knot as you simultaneously pluck the knot off the rope, bringing the hidden knot into view in the fingertips.

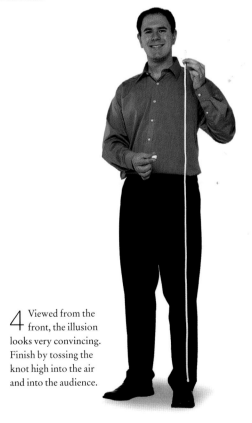

4 Viewed from the front, the illusion looks very convincing. Finish by tossing the knot high into the air and into the audience.

cut and restored rope (version 1)

A length of rope is unmistakably cut in half, yet is magically restored to its former condition. This is an absolute classic of magic and is still *performed today by many magicians. You can follow this version with the next. They work perfectly together.*

1 To prepare, place a pair of scissors in your right pocket. Bend an offcut of rope, approximately 10cm (4in) long, in half and hold it secretly in the left hand between the thumb and first finger. This piece must remain hidden at all times.

secret view

2 To begin your performance, hold a longer piece of rope, approximately 1.8m (6ft) long, next to the short piece, as shown. From the front, it looks as though you have only one piece of rope.

secret view

3 With the right hand, grab the centre of the rope and bring it up to the hidden short piece. It will look as though you are simply repositioning the middle of the rope so that it can be displayed. In reality you are going to switch the ropes.

secret view

4 Clip the "real" centre between your left thumb and first finger while extending the short piece up into view. The move should take seconds and should arouse no suspicion.

5 Remove the scissors from your pocket. From the front, the image is very clear. You have simply found the centre of a piece of rope and are holding it before cutting it in half.

6 Cleanly cut the rope in half. Of course you are actually cutting through the centre of the short piece.

7 Trim the ends of the rope, allowing the pieces to drop on to the floor. Continue trimming until all of the short piece of rope has been cut and dropped so that you destroy the evidence in front of the audience! Make a magical gesture, then stretch out the rope between both hands to show that it is completely restored.

cut and restored rope (version 2)

This version of this famous trick follows very well after the first. Try it out and you will fool yourself! As you will see, with the extra knot in your right hand, you can follow this with the Slip Knot trick. This

illusion works because it becomes difficult to follow exactly which section of the rope is being cut and, while it looks like the centre, it is actually a piece just a very short distance from one of the ends.

1 Hold the centre of a piece of rope, approximately 1.5–1.8m (5–6ft) long, with your left hand and bring the right end of the rope up to meet it. With your left thumb and fingers, grip the rope about 7.5cm (3in) from the end.

2 Loop the short end of the rope away from you and over the top of the centre. Bring it back underneath, as shown. Thread the end through the gap marked "X".

3 Pull the short end of the rope and the part that emerges below the knot, to tighten the knot.

4 Cut the left-hand side of the loop just under the knot.

5 Clearly display what looks like a piece of rope cut in two and held together with a knot. Actually the rope is in one piece and the knot is simply a tiny section of rope tied around the centre.

secret view

6 Begin to wind the rope around the fingers of your left hand. As you reach the knot, allow it to slip along, hidden in the fingers of your right hand.

secret view

7 Continue to wind the rope until the knot falls off the end. Keep the knot hidden in the Finger Palm position.

8 Stretch out the rope between both hands to show that it has restored itself. You are now in a perfect position to continue with another rope trick of your choice.

rope through apple

An apple is cored and two long pieces of rope are threaded through. To further secure the apple to the ropes, a knot is made. Despite the impossibility of the situation, the apple is pulled free of the ropes without any harm to either.

This routine is ideal for a large crowd as well as a more intimate gathering. Although only small props are used, they can be made to fill a large stage with a spectator either side of you. It is an effect that, as magic advertisements would say, "Packs Flat, Plays Big".

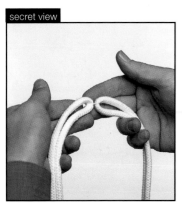

1 Prepare two pieces of rope, each about 1.8m (6ft) long, by folding them in half. Loosely stitch the centres together. The stitches should not be too tight because they must be snapped at a later stage.

2 In performance, unfold the ropes so that they run parallel to each other. Invite two people to help you, and give them two ends each. Ask them to tug on the ropes to prove that they are exactly what they appear to be.

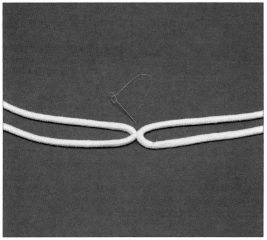

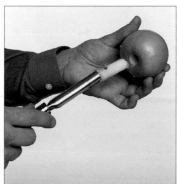

3 Hold on to the centre of the ropes and ask your helpers to let go. As the ends drop, grip the centre of the ropes with both hands and switch one of the ropes around, arranging them so that they are held together by the stitches. The thread is hidden from the front by your fingers, and the repositioning happens as you raise the ropes to temporarily place them over your shoulders.

4 With the ropes now safely resting around your shoulders, your hands are free to pick up an apple corer and remove the core from the apple.

5 Remove the rope from around your neck, hiding the centre in your left hand. Thread the ends of the ropes through the apple. (The two ends that go into the apple belong to the same piece of rope.)

6 The left hand provides enough cover to prevent the centre section of the rope being seen. Continue to pull the ropes through the apple until the join is hidden inside it.

7 Ask the spectators to hold the ends of the ropes. To secure the apple further, suggest tying a knot in the ropes. Take one end from each side (it doesn't matter which) and tie a simple overhand knot. Give the ends back to the spectators.

8 Cover the apple with a handkerchief, explaining that the magic has to happen under the cover of darkness!

9 Reach underneath and ask the spectators to pull the ropes taut. The thread will snap and the ropes will automatically fall away from the apple. You may find it helpful to slide the apple back and forth along the ropes as they are pulled taut.

10 Display the apple and remove the handkerchief. Give the apple to one spectator and the ropes to the other to be examined. The secret to the trick was destroyed by the spectators themselves!

ring on a string

A ring penetrates a piece of string, the ends of which are both in view throughout the manoeuvre. This trick requires a ring, a safety pin *and a handkerchief. It has its roots in an effect called "Sefalaljia", which was created by Stewart James.*

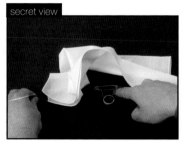

1 Show a length of string approximately 45cm (18in) long and lay it on the table. Borrow a ring or use your own. Lay it next to the centre of the string. Then explain that by using a safety pin you can make it look as if the ring is actually threaded on the string.

2 Cover the middle of the string with a handkerchief. Make sure both ends are clearly in view.

3 Under the handkerchief, push a small loop of the string through the ring.

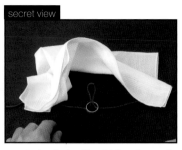

4 Push the safety pin through the string and pin the left side of the loop to the string to the left of the ring, as shown. This will leave you with the loop marked with an "x" above.

5 Put the first finger of your right hand into the loop and hold the left end of the string with your left hand.

6 This is what it looks like from the front. Explain that the ring can't really be on the string, as the ends have not been out of sight.

7 Pull the string to the left while keeping your right finger pinned to the table. The string will be pulled through the ring. This is covered by the handkerchief.

8 Finally, remove the handkerchief, undo the pin and show that the ring really is on the string.

Chinese coin off string

A Chinese coin with a hole in it is threaded on to a length of string. A spectator holds both ends of the string, and yet you are able to remove the coin. This is a perfect follow-up to Ring on a String. You will see that the two tricks can easily be incorporated into a routine.

secret view

1 You need a piece of string, a handkerchief and two identical Chinese coins with holes in the middle (or you can use two matching rings instead). Hide one of the coins in your right hand: your audience must be aware of only one coin throughout the trick.

2 Thread the visible coin on to the string and have a spectator hold both ends.

3 Cover the coin on the string with a handkerchief. This view shows the hidden duplicate coin concealed in your right hand.

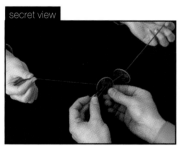
secret view

secret view

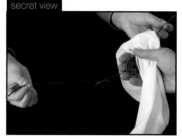
secret view

4 Under cover of the handkerchief (which has been removed here for clarity) pull the centre of the cord through the hole in the middle of the loose coin.

5 Now pass this loop over the coin so that the coin hangs as shown.

6 Hide the original, threaded coin in your hand and slide it to the right, pulling the handkerchief over as you do so.

7 Slide both hands to the ends of the string: your spectator will let go. Allow the coin hidden in your right hand to slip off the cord, as you say, "Don't let go of the ends!"

8 The spectator will take hold of the ends again, but the original threaded coin is now off the string and hidden under the handkerchief. ▶

tip *The success of this trick relies on the spectator letting go of the cord at stage 7 looking like an error on their part. Don't ask them to let go, simply make it happen by moving your hands. As soon as it occurs (allowing the hidden coin to slip off), make a big deal of the fact that they mustn't let go and get them to hold on again. If you can make this moment look natural and keep the second coin hidden, this is a very baffling trick.*

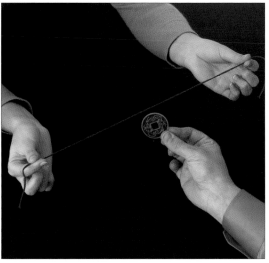

9 Put the handkerchief and the hidden coin in your pocket or to one side, keeping the coin concealed, then slowly untie the simple knot that holds the coin on the string.

10 Finish by showing that the coin has magically passed through the string.

beads of mystery

Three beads magically escape from two pieces of cord on to which they are tied. This trick is interesting as the method can be adapted for all kinds of tricks, large and small. You will find other tricks in this book that use a similar principle.

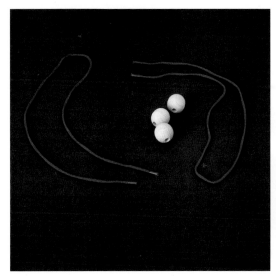

1 You will need three large beads and two pieces of thin cord, each approximately 30cm (12in) long.

2 Prepare by folding both cords in half and then looping the centre of one through the other.

3 Thread a bead on to the right-hand cord and slip the looped centres inside the bead so that the preparation is hidden.

4 Thread the other two beads on to the cords, one on each side. From all angles it looks as though you have three beads threaded on two lengths of cord. Only you know that the cords are looped.

5 Display the beads on the cord to your audience and explain that you are tying a knot to make sure they are secure.

6 Hold the cords at either end and place the beads on the palm of a spectator's outstretched hand.

7 Ask the spectator to close their hand tightly over the beads.

8 Pull on the cords and the beads will be released into the spectator's hand.

9 After the spectator has opened their hand you can give everything out for closer examination.

enchanted ball

A golf ball is placed on a table and with the apparent use of telekinetic powers is caused to move on its own. This trick takes a lot of careful preparation, so rig the table before your dinner guests arrive.

You will need a golf ball, a key ring, a needle, some fishing line and a small bead. A large bead and bright thread have been used here for clarity, but you should use thin fishing line and a small bead.

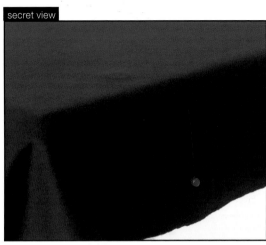
secret view

1 Attach a long length of fishing line to the key ring. Set this on a table and run the line off the far end.

2 Cover with a tablecloth and run the line under the table and back to your side. Using a needle, thread the line through the tablecloth and secure the end of the thread to a small bead.

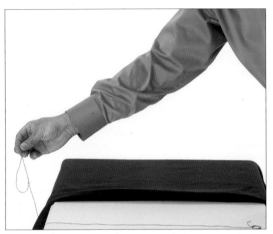
secret view

3 Show a golf ball to the spectators, handing it out for examination. Take back the ball and put it on the table, on top of the key ring, which should be invisible under the tablecloth. Engage the bead in between your fingers and strike a pose.

4 Wave your hands over the ball and slowly move them backwards. The ball will start to move away from you. When it reaches the far side lift it up in the air and toss it out to be examined as you covertly drop the bead behind the table.

ping-pong balance

A piece of rope and a ping-pong ball are shown to the spectators. The ball is then magically balanced on the rope and even made to roll backwards and forwards without falling. Defying gravity is a

favourite theme for magicians, and is used in almost all types of magic. If you can perform this smoothly, it is almost as if the ball is under your complete control.

1 Prepare a piece of rope by stitching a length of fine thread of a similar colour to it at both ends.

2 Place the ping-pong ball on a stand made from a rolled-up piece of card (stock). Stretch the rope out between your hands. The rope and thread should be held as in the previous picture.

3 Lower the rope so that it goes in front of the ball while the thread goes behind it.

4 Slowly lift the rope and the ball will look as though it is balanced on it.

5 Tilt the rope gently to one side and the ball will roll along it without falling off.

6 Slowly lower your hands to return the ball to its stand and release the ends of the rope.

rising tube mystery

A paper tube held together with paperclips is seen threaded on to two lengths of cord. Defying gravity, the tube not only remains suspended *when held upright, but rises up the cords in an uncanny fashion. Everything is handed out for examination.*

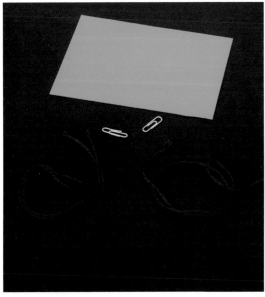

1 You will need a sheet of paper, two paperclips and two identical, long pieces of cord.

2 Fold both lengths of cord in half and insert the centre of one through the other to create a small loop.

3 Attach a paperclip to the loop and clip this on to the edge of the paper.

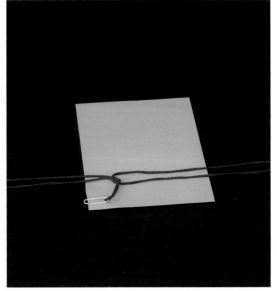

4 If you have attached it properly, the set-up should now look like this, and everything should be secure.

5 Now roll up the paper into a tight tube so that the cord is on the inside.

6 Once the whole sheet is rolled, reposition the paperclip so that it holds the roll together.

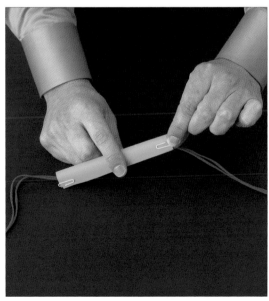

7 Use a second paperclip to hold the roll at the other end. This one should be clipped only to the paper and not to the cords.

8 To complete the set-up, pull on the cords until the loop is just at the top of the tube. ▶

9 Hold the cords up by the end and show that the tube is defying gravity.

10 Grip the bottom cords and pull very gently.

11 The tube will slowly travel up the cords!

12 When the tube reaches the top, hold both ends of the cords together and begin to disassemble the cords from the paper.

13 Remove both paperclips and show them to the audience.

14 Unroll the paper and hand everything out to the audience for examination. You could even challenge them to try to do it themselves!

interlocked

Two people have their wrists tied together with rope. The ropes are interlocked and the challenge is for the two to separate without *untying the knots. Unless they know the secret, this problem can take a long time to solve.*

1 Tie a length of rope around both wrists of each of two people. Before you make the last knot, link the two ropes as shown.

2 To get free, one person must thread the centre of their rope under the loop around one of the other person's wrists.

3 This loop is then slipped over the top of their hand.

4 The back view shows how the ropes are being untangled.

5 The result is that the two people have released one another without untying the knots.

impossible link

A pencil on a loop of string is attached to someone's buttonhole. While you seemed to put it on easily they will have a tough time getting the *pencil off again unless they know the secret. This is a fantastic stunt to play on people, and is guaranteed to frustrate them.*

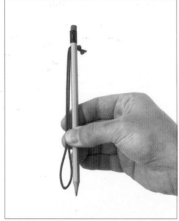

1 Pencils with string attached can sometimes be found in novelty and souvenir shops but are hard to find. It is easy to make your own by drilling a small hole in the top of a pencil and then tying a loop of string through the hole.

2 The loop of string must be a little shorter than the pencil (even when stretched to its full extent).

3 Pull a large section of the coat near a buttonhole through the loop of the string. You need to pull as much material through the loop as possible.

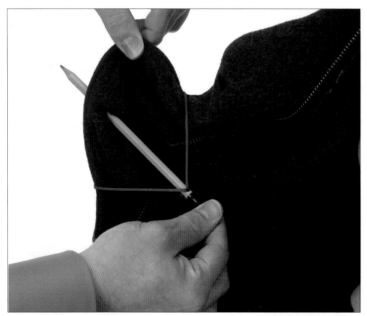

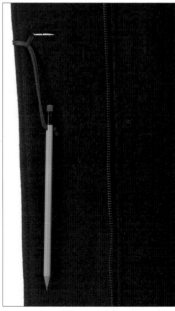

4 Carefully guide the tip of the pencil through the buttonhole of the coat. You may need to use a bit of force to get the angle right.

5 Gently pull the pencil through to complete the set-up.

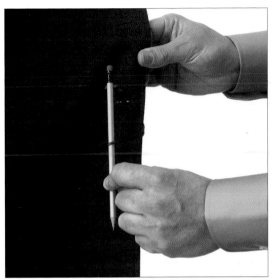

6 When your victim demands that you remove the pencil after failing miserably, do the following. Lift the pencil through the loop as far as it will go.

7 Pull the pencil out so that it is at right angles to the buttonhole, then push the top back through the buttonhole.

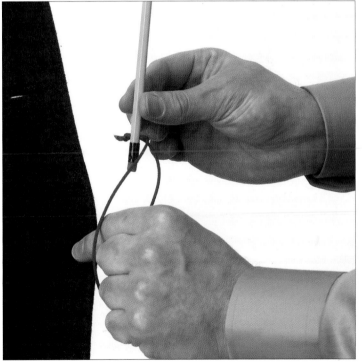

8 Hold on to the pencil and once again pull as much fabric as you can through the loop of string.

9 You will now be able to remove the pencil completely.

escapologist

Despite your hands being tied together with a handkerchief, you are able to escape from a rope that secures you. This is a great trick but you must practise it a lot if you are to make it deceptive. The method is similar to the one used in Interlocked.

1 Ask a spectator to tie your wrists together with a handkerchief or silk.

2 Now ask them to thread a length of rope between your arms.

3 They hold on to the ends and pull to confirm that you cannot escape.

secret view

4 Just before they pull, you must work a little piece of the rope between the heels of your palms, as shown.

5 Move your hands to the left and right to show you can't escape but as you move, work the rope further into your hands.

secret view

6 This is clearly shown in this close-up view.

7 The movement of your arms hides the fact that you are now slipping the rope over your left hand.

secret view

8 Again, this close-up shows exactly what is happening.

secret view

9 Once the rope is over your hand, pull back sharply: the rope will work its way under the handkerchief on the side of your hand.

10 You will be released from the rope, but you can show that your wrists are still genuinely tied together.

lord of the rings

A solid ring links on to a length of rope whose ends are firmly tied to your wrists. Here, the ring was made of rope but you could use a *bangle or any other object that fits over your wrist. Avoid performing both this trick and Escapologist in the same show.*

1 You will need two identical rings and a length of rope.

secret view

2 Prepare by placing one of the rings over your wrist and hiding it up your right sleeve.

3 In performance have someone tie one end of the rope around each of your wrists. Show the ring and explain that you will get it on to the rope. Of course, this sounds impossible.

4 Ask someone to cover your hands with a large cloth.

secret view

5 Under cover of the cloth (removed here for clarity) secretly hide the loose ring inside your shirt.

secret view

6 Pull the duplicate ring out of your sleeve, over your wrist and on to the length of rope.

7 Remove the cloth to show you have caused one solid object to penetrate another.

silk, thimble and paper magic

Magic tricks using simple everyday objects such as handkerchiefs, thimbles and paper have always been popular. The following pages introduce you to many sleights using these objects.

make something of it

Many areas within the art of magic are relatively small when compared to, for example, card tricks. However it is important to offer your audience a variety of magical effects, and so in this chapter we have grouped together three smaller areas of conjuring: magic with handkerchiefs or "silks", magic with thimbles, and magic with paper.

Handkerchiefs are frequently used in magic. Some of them are ordinary, the kind you might find in a department store, but most are extremely thin and made of silk. These can be purchased from magic shops and are ideal – they can be displayed as a large piece of fabric, but it is also possible to squash them down into a very small bundle which can be handled and hidden easily. Magicians call these handkerchiefs "silks". Silks can be purchased in a number of different sizes, the most common being 23, 30, 45, 60 and 90cm (9, 12, 18, 24 and 36in) square. They are also available in almost every colour imaginable.

The size and shape of a thimble make it a perfect object for performing sleight of hand. One of the earliest known references to thimble magic is in *The Art Of Modern Conjuring* by Professor Henry Garenne, published in 1879. The trick was entitled "The Travelling Thimble". Since then magicians have invented many ways to make thimbles multiply, change colour, penetrate handkerchiefs, appear and disappear. Many beautiful routines can be performed with thimbles, and several of the more basic sleights and tricks can be learnt in this chapter. Magicians who perform a traditional stage act often feature thimbles as part of their programme. Although small, they are visible from a distance and provide a great example of digital dexterity.

Paper comes in every shape and size and is, therefore, often an ideal medium with which to work. One of the most popular paper tricks is Torn and Restored Newspaper. A description of the effect is unnecessary as the title says it all! This chapter will reveal a simple version which allows

Above: Thimbles can be used for close-up magic or as part of a larger stage act because they can be seen for quite a distance.

Below: This wood engraving shows the early nineteenth-century French master magician Robert-Houdin producing plumes of flowers and showers of candy from a silk handkerchief.

Above: Learn The Trick Which Fooled Houdini and make a spectator's watch vanish under a silk handkerchief in impossible circumstances.

Above: Baffle your audience by magically producing a thimble from a banknote. Thimbles are wonderfully versatile objects for using in tricks.

Above: Is it really possible to move an object with the power of the human mind? Your audience will believe so when you show them the Telekinetic Paper.

you to cut a strip of newspaper into two pieces and magically join them back together again. You will also learn how to perform the classic effect, Snowstorm in China. Versions of this are still being used by many professional magicians around the world, and will finish any act in a truly spectacular fashion. Many of the tricks you will learn here can be strung together to produce a very effective act, and when you have had a little experience, you will also find that you can adapt a number of the techniques to create tricks of your own.

Below left: Snowstorm in China is a spectacular trick that makes use of – among other things – an ornamental Chinese fan and coloured tissue paper torn up to form confetti. The air is filled with a snowstorm of confetti at the end of the trick.

Below: Turn a jug of milk into a large silk handkerchief in Milk to Silk.

silk magic

There are literally thousands of tricks you can do with handkerchiefs, and some of these are described here. You should not aim to put together a whole show of handkerchief magic, as this may be a little tiresome for your audience. However, handkerchief tricks can be very spectacular, and if you use them as part of your act you can make a big impression on your audience.

simple silk production

There are dozens of ways to produce a silk from thin air. This version and the Mid-Air Silk Production which follows are two of the easiest and most magical. For extra effect, sprinkle confetti or glitter into the folds as you prepare the silk.

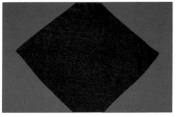

1 To prepare, place a silk handkerchief in front of you, completely flat and with one corner towards you.

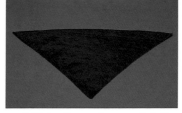

2 Fold the silk away from you, in half and along the diagonal.

3 Begin rolling the silk from the fold. Try to make the roll as tight and neat as possible.

4 Continue rolling the silk until you reach the far corner.

5 Roll the silk from one end to the other, again trying to ensure a tight, neat roll.

6 Leave a tiny "ear" of silk at the end, as shown here.

secret view

7 Grip the rolled silk in the right-hand Finger Palm position (see Money Magic chapter) so that the "ear" of the silk is clipped tightly between your right thumb and first finger.

8 Viewed from the front, if the hand is held naturally, the silk is completely hidden. With your right hand, point to an imaginary spot in the air to your left, at about chest level.

9 Reach up to that point and simultaneously, with a gentle jerk of the right hand, let the silk unroll, ready for use in another trick.

mid-air silk production

The magician's hand is shown unmistakably empty but as they reach into the air a beautiful silk appears! Practice is required to make this *always look good, but the result is so spectacular it is well worth the effort. It makes an ideal opening trick.*

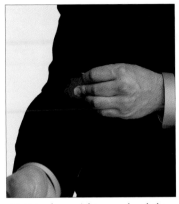

1 For this trick you must be wearing a jacket or long-sleeved shirt. To prepare, bunch up a silk handkerchief in your left hand. The bundle should be very small.

2 Extend your right arm and push the silk into the crook of your elbow, covering the silk with a fold of cloth from the sleeve.

3 Keeping the right elbow slightly bent will ensure the silk remains hidden. You are now ready to begin performing the trick.

4 Show that both hands are completely empty. Keep the arms bent just enough to prevent the silk from being exposed. (This restriction of movement is the reason why the mid-air silk production is a good trick to open with.)

5 This side view shows what happens next. The right hand quickly and sharply reaches up into the air, snapping open the fabric at the right elbow. The silk is catapulted up into the air and is caught by the right hand.

6 From the front, the silk seems to appear from nowhere!

production tube

A roll of card, which is opened and shown to be empty, is rolled back into a tube and used to produce silk handkerchiefs from thin air.

You can use this simple prop to make anything that fits inside the tube appear or disappear.

1 To make the tube you will need a piece of red card (stock) approximately 30 x 60cm (12 x 24in), a piece of black card approximately 10 x 15cm (4 x 6in), some double-sided adhesive tape, a pair of scissors, a rubber band and a pen.

2 Fold the red card in half across its width, making a sharp crease.

3 Attach a length of double-sided tape to one of the shorter sides of the black card. Starting from the opposite side, roll the card into a tube and secure it neatly with the tape.

4 With the red card still folded in half, roll it up tightly from the folded edge.

5 Secure the tube with a rubber band and leave overnight, so that when the band is removed the tube holds its shape.

6 Use a piece of double-sided tape to secure the black tube to the centre of the red card alongside the crease, as shown. This is a secret compartment that will never be seen by the spectators.

7 Mark a black dot on the red card, on the edge of the section with the secret compartment. Ensure the tube is oriented as shown here before you mark it.

8 Place the rubber band around the tube to hold it in place as you insert three coloured silks, one at a time, into the secret compartment.

9 Twist the ends of the silks together as they go into the tube. This will make it easier to remove them during the performance.

10 Once you have put all three silks inside the secret compartment remove the band and you are ready to perform the trick.

11 Begin by showing the tube of red card to the audience.

12 Pull the tube open, making sure that your right hand holds the edge with the black spot you made earlier.

13 The view from above shows exactly what is happening.

14 When the tube is fully unrolled it will look like a plain piece of card.

15 The secret compartment is hidden on the back.

16 Roll the card back up into a loose tube again.

17 Reach in and remove the first of the silk handkerchiefs.

18 Then remove the other silks and once again open the tube to show the audience that it is empty.

blended silks (version 1)

Four separate silks are pushed into an empty card tube. They come out joined together as one blended square. This is another trick you *can do using the production tube with the secret compartment that is described on pages 264-5.*

1 Using double-sided adhesive tape, carefully join the edges of four silks to make a large square. Insert this special silk into the secret compartment of your production tube.

2 When you perform the trick, have four separate silks in the same four colours displayed in a wine glass and show the tube empty as described previously.

3 Pick up the separate silks one at a time, and insert them into the secret compartment on top of the prepared silk.

4 Slowly pull out the blended silk from the bottom of the tube.

5 Open it out to show that the four different-coloured silks have joined together as one.

6 Finish by opening the tube to show it empty. The separate silks are safely hidden in the secret compartment.

blended silks (version 2)

Four separate silks are placed in the empty bag. They come out joined together as one blended square. Some magic shops stock "Blendo" silks, which are made up of a mixture of colours specifically for tricks like this one, and are a good investment.

1 Using double-sided tape carefully join together four silks, in four different colours, along the edges to make one large square.

2 Neatly put this blended silk into one side of your prepared switching bag (see page 447).

3 Turn over the cuff so that the empty side is open.

4 Display four silks, matching the four in the blended square, in a wine glass.

5 Turn the bag inside out to show the audience that it is empty.

6 Now place the separate silks in the bag's empty compartment one at a time.

7 When the silks are all inside the bag make a magical gesture.

secret view

8 At the same time as you open the bag, switch compartments. ▶

10 Hold up the silk by the edges and wait for the applause!

9 Reach into the secret compartment to pull out the blended silk with a flourish.

silk through glass (version 1)

A silk handkerchief penetrates the bottom of a glass. This is one of a variety of methods for performing this trick, and it is very effective.

Try practising in front of a mirror so that you make appropriate facial gestures, and work on your patter before you perform.

1 You should use the thinnest, most invisible thread you can find for this. Fishing line works very well. Prepare a silk handkerchief by attaching a short length of thread to one corner. This thread should be knotted at the end.

2 Display the silk in one hand (with the thread hidden in your hand) and a glass in the other.

3 Insert the handkerchief into the glass, allowing the thread to secretly trail out of the glass.

4 This secret view shows how the thread should be positioned.

5 Show a second silk handkerchief in the other hand.

6 Place this on top of the first silk in the glass. Pick up a larger handkerchief.

7 Place the large handkerchief over the whole glass. Secure it with a rubber band around the mouth of the glass.

8 Lift up the large handkerchief to show the silks inside the glass.

9 Reach underneath and feel for the trailing thread. Begin to pull down on the thread. ▶

10 The bottom silk will be pulled out of the sealed glass, under the band and down towards your hand. Grip the corner of the silk and continue to pull it down. It will appear to be penetrating the bottom of the glass.

11 Lift the handkerchief to show the other silk still in position in the top of the glass.

12 Finally, remove the large handkerchief and the rubber band.

silk through glass (version 2)

This is a variation of the method used for the previous trick. This version uses no gimmicks at all. It can be performed totally *impromptu, as you should be able to find a glass and a few handkerchiefs or napkins in most places.*

secret view

1 Display a silk handkerchief in one hand and a glass in the other.

2 Insert the silk into the glass and prepare to cover everything with a larger, opaque handkerchief.

3 As soon as the glass is hidden out of sight by the handkerchief, secretly allow it to swivel upside down.

4 Wrap a band around the base of the glass. (Your audience will assume it is the top of the glass.)

5 It is now easy to pull the silk down, creating the illusion that it is penetrating the base of the glass.

8 You can finish by handing out everything for examination, if you wish.

6 Pull the band and the handkerchief off the glass.

7 At the same time turn the glass back to the upright position while it is still concealed by the handkerchief.

rose to silk

A red rose worn on the magician's lapel is dramatically changed into silk. It would also be possible to add the prepared silk to a

bunch of real roses. The magician could then pluck the top of a rose off a specially prepared stem as an alternative to his lapel.

1 You will need to wear a jacket with a buttonhole on the lapel. To prepare, lay a silk handkerchief flat, with one of the corners pointing towards you.

2 Begin rolling the silk towards the top corner. Try to make the roll as tight as possible. The neater you roll the silk, the better the rose will look.

3 Continue rolling until you reach the opposite corner.

4 At one end, bend the corner at right angles to create an "ear".

5 Starting at this end, tightly roll the silk to the opposite end. You will start to form a small bundle.

6 The finished bundle should resemble a rose. Leave a small amount of silk at the end of the roll.

7 With a match or similar object, tuck the loose end into the fold to hold the bundle in position.

8 Push the loose end all the way through to the back of the silk, being careful not to ruin the folds that make up the rose.

9 Take this loose end and push it through the buttonhole in your lapel. You are now ready to perform. At a glance, it will look just as though you are wearing a rose in your buttonhole.

10 With your left hand, hold the rose in place by gently squeezing the sides. With your right fingers, grip the centre of the rose (the "ear").

11 Gently pull the "ear" outwards, and the rose will visibly start to transform into a large silk.

12 Stretch the silk between both hands and wait for the applause! Try using some glitter or cutting up some tissue paper into small confetti-sized pieces and inserting them into the silk when you fold it. As the silk is pulled from the lapel, the contents will cascade to the floor, adding an extra magical effect.

Milo the mouse

A handkerchief is rolled to resemble a mouse, which then crawls around and eventually jumps out of your hands entirely. This is great if you are entertaining children. The most charming aspect of this party trick is that the mouse is created in front of their very eyes and it is your skill that brings it to life. Children in particular will love this trick – whether they are performing it or being performed to.

1 Start the trick with a handkerchief unfolded in a diamond shape on the table in front of you.

2 Fold the handkerchief diagonally so that the corners are pointing away from you.

3 Fold the right and then the left side of the handkerchief into the centre so that they overlap slightly.

4 Start to roll up the handkerchief from the bottom.

5 Continue rolling until you reach the top of the folded sides.

6 Turn the handkerchief over and fold the right side in to the centre.

7 Fold over the left side so that the two flaps overlap.

8 Roll upwards from the bottom again until you reach the edge of the folded part of the handkerchief.

9 Tuck the top triangular part of the handkerchief into the gap at the top of the roll.

10 Insert your thumbs into the opening at the bottom and turn the whole thing inside out.

11 Keep turning the handkerchief inside out until two corners appear.

12 Pull out the sides of one of the corners, as shown.

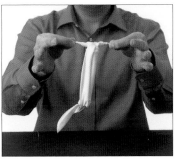

13 Twist the material down towards the rest of the handkerchief.

14 Make a small knot in the two ends of the twist.

15 Introduce the spectators to Milo the Mouse. To make him move you need to insert your right middle finger into the rolled-up handkerchief under the tail.

16 Stroke the mouse with your left hand as the right fingers flick up and down. The movements, if executed well, make it look as if the mouse is alive.

17 You can even make him crawl up your body and if you give the handkerchief a flick with your right hand you can catch Milo by the tail and pull him back with the left. A good way to finish the routine is to ask someone to stroke Milo. As they approach him give a big flick with your right fingers and send the mouse flying off your hand entirely. If you scream in mock horror as this happens the spectators will jump out of their skin.

pencil through silk

A silk handkerchief is draped over a pencil, which is pushed straight through the centre of the silk. The handkerchief is displayed to show *that it is completely unharmed. This kind of impromptu magic gives you the ability to perform a miracle with objects that can be borrowed.*

1 Hold a corner of a silk handkerchief in your left hand and display a pencil in your right fingertips.

2 Drape the silk over the top of the pencil so that the centre lies on the point of the pencil.

3 Close your left hand around the pencil so that the shape can clearly be seen through the fabric.

secret view

4 At the same moment, secretly bend your right hand at the wrist to bring the pencil back to a position outside the silk. From the front, this move is unseen and the silk continues to hold the shape of the pencil.

secret view

5 Immediately manoeuvre the pencil back up to a position behind the silk and under the left thumb. The moves in steps 3 and 4 are achieved in one swift motion, and should only take about one second.

6 Give the pencil a push upwards and the tip will appear to penetrate the silk. In reality the pencil simply slides up against the silk and into view.

7 From the front, the illusion is perfect and your audience will believe the pencil has really been pushed through the middle of the silk handkerchief.

8 Pull the pencil completely free of the silk and once again display the pencil in your right fingertips.

9 Open the silk between both hands to show that it is undamaged. You can hand both the silk and the pencil to your spectators for examination, and then perhaps use the same items for your next trick.

silk vanish

A silk handkerchief is pushed into the left hand. After a suitable flourish, the hand is shown completely empty! There are many ways to "vanish" a silk. This trick uses what magicians call a "pull" – a secret holder worn out of sight, usually under a jacket. The item to be vanished is placed inside. The holder is then pulled back into the jacket by a piece of elastic. Pulls are available from magic shops in a variety of shapes and sizes, but you can easily make your own. Pulls can also be worn within the sleeves of a jacket.

1 To make the "pull", remove the lid from a 35mm film canister and cut a hole about 2cm (¾in) in diameter. Pierce a small hole in the bottom of the canister and, with a simple knot inside, attach a piece of elastic approximately 60cm (24in) long. (The length depends on your waist size. For greater strength, cut double the length and fold the elastic in half.) Attach a safety pin to the free end of the elastic. Put the lid back on the canister.

2 Thread the elastic through your belt loops from your left side around to your right side. Attach the safety pin to a loop on the right of your body. It may take several attempts to find the correct position for the "pull" and the elastic may need to be cut down or adjusted.

3 The canister should rest at a position approximately in line with your trouser pocket, and the tension of the elastic should hold it loosely but firmly against the belt loop. Test the operation of the "pull" by pulling the canister away from the belt loop to a position in front of your chest. Let the canister go, and it should return to the position it started in. If not, readjust the gimmick.

secret view

4 In performance, hold the "pull" in your left hand. Stretch out the elastic so that your left hand can maintain a position just in front of your body. Be careful not to pull open your jacket and reveal your secret – this is an exposed view of the position you should be in.

5 Show the silk handkerchief in your right hand. Pretend to insert it into your left hand. In reality, you are pushing it into the canister through the hole in the lid.

6 Continue pushing the silk into your hand until it is completely contained within the canister.

7 This exposed view shows the position after the silk is inside the gimmick. At this stage, allow the elastic to pull the canister through your fingers and back into your jacket. Keep your hand in a position that still looks as though it holds the silk. Your spectator's view remains as in step 6.

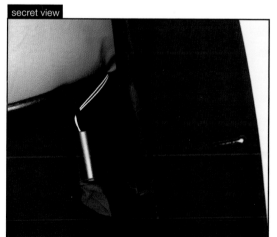

8 The canister rests back where it started, in a position under the jacket by your left pocket.

9 Move both hands to a position in front of your chest and slowly show that they are completely empty. The silk has vanished!

milk to silk

Milk is poured from a jug into a large cup. The cup is turned upside down but the milk mysteriously fails to fall out! The magician reaches into the upturned cup to reveal that the milk has changed into a white silk handkerchief. This trick creates a beautiful effect and is ideal for larger audiences. For added effect, cut white paper into confetti-size pieces and place them in the folds of the silk before placing the handkerchief in the cup. While performing this effect, it is important that you are aware at all times of the position of the cup in relation to your audience. If you hold the cup too low, the secret will be revealed. A cocktail shaker is the ideal size cup to use.

1 To prepare, carefully measure and cut a piece of board that will divide a cup internally in two. The height of the partition should be about three-quarters the height of the cup.

2 Mould some reusable adhesive around the bottom and side edges of the partition.

3 Push the partition into the cup and secure it to the sides with the adhesive. The idea is to create a watertight compartment. If you perform this trick on a regular basis, make the partition longer-lasting by using a sheet of plastic and a silicone sealant.

4 Insert a piece of sponge into one side of the cup. You may need to cut the sponge to shape and experiment to determine how much to use. The best sponge to use is the "super-absorbent" type which holds many times its own weight in liquid.

5 To complete the preparation, push a white silk handkerchief into the other compartment. One corner should be near the top, but make sure it is pushed down out of sight.

6 Place the prepared cup on to a table, along with a jug full of milk.

7 Begin your performance by carefully pouring some milk into the sponge side of the cup. Once again, experimentation will determine exactly how much milk to use. The milk is absorbed by the sponge.

8 It is wise to wait for a few seconds to ensure that the sponge soaks up all of the milk. Place one hand over the mouth of the cup and get ready to turn it upside down.

9 The slickest way to turn the cup is to allow it to swivel between your left fingers and thumb. When it is upside down, freeze for a few seconds as if something might have gone wrong. This creates a moment of tension and humour if acted well.

11 Slowly pull the silk out completely, allowing it to cascade from the cup.

10 Take away your hand from under the mouth of the cup and show that the milk has mysteriously defied gravity. Sometimes a small piece of silk will begin to fall from the cup but this helps to create the illusion that the milk is turning into silk.

obedient handkerchief

A handkerchief moves about at the prankster's command. This can look really funny if your acting skills are good enough. Britain's late *Bob Read performed this better than anyone and always had his audiences in stitches.*

1 Stretch a handkerchief between your hands. You will find that by holding it through your closed left fist it will stand up on end quite easily with 10–12.5cm (4–5in) protruding.

2 With your free hand, pull the handkerchief higher and once again let go. To make it more convincing, look as though you are concentrating on making the handkerchief remain upright.

3 Do this once more until more than half of the handkerchief is upright.

4 With your free hand, motion toward the handkerchief as if you are putting it into a hypnotic trance. Let it fall down, apparently put to sleep as a result of your hypnotic powers.

5 Fold the handkerchief in half and once again hold it with a section raised through your fist.

6 Pretend to pull a hair from your head, perhaps grimacing as you do so.

7 Wrap this invisible hair around the top of the handkerchief and pretend to pull the hair. At the same time, push your thumb up and the handkerchief will bend to the left.

8 Now mime pulling the hair the other way and this time pull down with your thumb and the handkerchief will bend the other way.

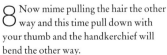

the trick which fooled Houdini

A borrowed watch is placed under a handkerchief and several spectators confirm its presence. In an instant the watch disappears without a trace. Just as mysteriously, the watch can be made to reappear. Rumour has it that one of the world's most famous magicians, Harry Houdini, was fooled by this trick back in the 1920s!

This is one of the few tricks you will learn which requires an assistant, or "stooge". Choose someone who can act well and whom you can trust to keep the secret.

1 Borrow a watch from a spectator. Place it under the centre of a handkerchief. Ask several people to reach underneath to verify that the watch is indeed still there.

secret view

2 The last person to reach under the handkerchief is your stooge, who secretly takes away the watch. To add a simple piece of "misdirection", move the handkerchief away from your assistant's hand as the secret steal takes place. All eyes will follow the handkerchief.

3 Make a magical gesture and whip the handkerchief away to show that the watch has well and truly gone!

thimble magic

A thimble is compact enough to be carried wherever you go and will generate interest as soon as it is made to appear. By linking several of the effects together, a nice routine can be developed. For instance, after performing the Linking Paper Clips, you could produce the thimble from the banknote (see opposite) and continue your routine with the Jumping Thimble, finishing with the Vanishing Thimble.

jumping thimble

A thimble magically jumps back and forth between two fingers. Although this is a simple stunt, it is amazing how well the illusion works. The trick can also be performed with a finger ring, and is a good impromptu stunt to remember.

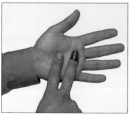

1 Place a thimble on the tip of the right second finger. Hold the first and second fingers against the palm of your left hand.

2 Tap your fingers against your palm three times. After the second tap, the fingers come approximately 10cm (4in) away from the palm.

3 The first finger quickly curls in and the third finger uncurls.

4 As the fingers reach the palm of the hand, it seems the thimble has jumped. The thimble can be made to jump back by reversing the procedure.

thimble from banknote

A banknote is shown on both sides and rolled into a cone. From within the cone, a thimble is produced. This makes a very startling and highly unusual production. As mentioned previously, stringing various effects together is a nice way to present a small impromptu show, and this is an ideal opening effect. It introduces the thimble unexpectedly and will command interest from your audience.

secret view

1 Place a thimble on your right second finger. Hold a banknote with both hands, between your first fingers and thumbs. Curl in your other fingers.

2 From the front, your spectators can see the whole surface of the banknote and the thimble is completely hidden.

secret view

3 Turn the note so that you show both sides completely. Be careful not to prematurely expose the thimble.

secret view

4 Open your second finger so that the thimble rests on the top right of the banknote. The note is clipped against the thimble, between the first and second fingers, and starts to curl in a cone shape.

5 The left hand lifts its end up and over the thimble. It continues to roll the note over and around the second finger, the first finger lifting out of the way.

6 The result is a cone, formed around the second finger of the right hand.

7 Pull out your finger, leaving the thimble within the cone.

8 Dip your finger back into the cone and push it securely into the thimble.

9 Remove your finger from the cone and display the thimble.

thimble thumb clip

A thimble is caused to disappear and then reappear from the tip of the fingers. Anything that fits on the end of your first finger will work perfectly well. For a really impromptu performance, try using a candy wrapper fashioned into a thimble or a hoop-shaped potato chip. The Thimble Thumb Clip is one of the main sleights necessary to master in order to perform many thimble tricks.

1 Place a thimble on the tip of your right first finger. Curl your first finger inwards so that the thimble rests in the crotch of your thumb.

2 Squeeze your thumb against the thimble and uncurl your finger, leaving the thimble clipped between the base of your thumb and first finger.

3 From the front, the thimble is hidden from view and the hand looks perfectly empty. In performance you will need to be aware of angle restrictions.

vanishing thimble

Once you have learnt the Thimble Thumb Clip, you can try the following routine. When executed correctly, the illusion is superb. When you have mastered the trick of making the thimble reappear from behind your hand, you can easily use the same sleight to make it reappear from anywhere you choose, for example from behind the ear of a child or from inside someone else's pocket.

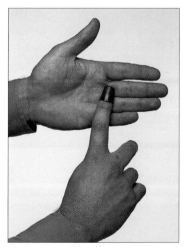

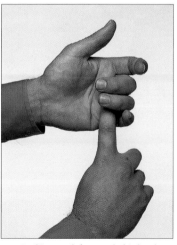

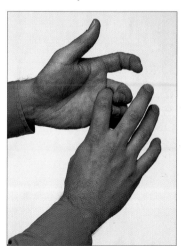

1 Place a thimble on your right first finger, and hold it against the base of the left fingers. Your left palm should face the audience.

2 Curl in your left second, third and fourth fingers. Open the fingers again to show that the thimble is still there, then start to close the fingers as before.

3 Just as the fingers cover the thimble, begin to remove the right first finger, simultaneously raising the hand and placing the thimble into a Thumb Clip. ▶

4 This view shows the right hand as it moves upwards.

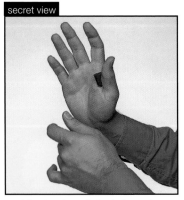

5 The view from the back shows the thimble in the Thumb Clip.

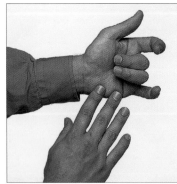

6 Bring the right hand back down to the position shown.

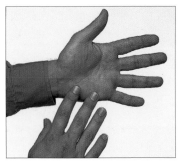

7 Open the left fingers to show that the thimble has vanished. These actions should happen smoothly and briskly. The spectators should not be aware that the thimble has gone from the left fingers until they are opened.

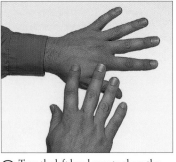

8 Turn the left hand over to show the back of the hand, then show the palm once again.

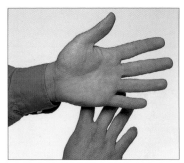

9 The right hand reaches behind the left and secretly replaces the thumb-clipped thimble on the first finger.

10 This view from the back shows the thimble being recovered.

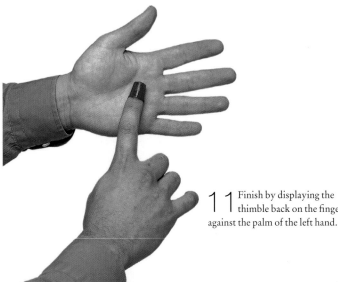

11 Finish by displaying the thimble back on the fingertip against the palm of the left hand.

thimble from silk

A thimble is produced from a silk, ready to be used for other amazing tricks such as Thimble through Silk. Even though you might not think *this is a startling piece of magic, it is a nice visual way to introduce a thimble; better than simply pulling a thimble out of a pocket.*

secret view

1 Hold a thimble in the right-hand Thumb Clip position. Display a silk handkerchief, stretching it between the two top corners with both hands.

2 From the front, all the fingers and the entire silk can be seen, and the thimble remains completely hidden.

3 Cross your arms to show the back of the silk, then uncross your arms again.

secret view

4 Hold the silk by a corner in the left hand. Your right hand reaches under the silk and retrieves the thimble from the Thumb Clip.

5 Drape the silk momentarily over your right first finger.

6 Whip away the silk to display a thimble on your fingertip.

thimble through silk

A thimble is placed under a silk and visibly melts through the fabric. This trick is the perfect follow-up to Thimble from Silk. Although it is *not easy to learn or perform, it is beautiful to watch when performed well. Use a thimble that contrasts with the colour of the silk.*

1 Hold a silk handkerchief with your left hand. It should be clipped between the first and second fingers, draping down the inside of the hand. The right hand displays a thimble on the first fingertip.

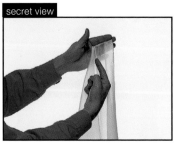

secret view

2 Hold the silk about chest level and start to move the thimble under the silk. As it passes the left hand, the thimble is secretly placed into the left-hand Thumb Clip position.

secret view

3 Without hesitation, continue to move the finger under the silk to a position in the centre. Under cover of the silk, extend your second finger and bend your first finger backwards. This can be seen here through the silk for ease of explanation.

4 Make a gesture with your left hand, which positions itself directly behind the right hand.

secret view

5 During this gesture, push the thimble from the Thumb Clip on to the first finger through the silk. In this view, the silk is lifted for ease of explanation.

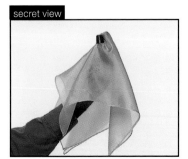

secret view

6 The first finger straightens behind the second finger. Care must be taken to keep the thimble hidden.

7 From the front, the thimble remains totally unseen.

8 With a shake of the hand, lower the second finger so that the thimble pops into view.

paper magic

A most versatile material, paper is easily available and comes in a wide variety of shapes, colours, sizes and thicknesses. Of the many tricks that use paper, a few are given here which are simple to prepare, and very enjoyable to watch. Cut and Restored Newspaper, together with Snowstorm in China, are perfect for a platform or stage show because they can be seen from a distance.

telekinetic paper

A small piece of paper is folded and stood upright on a table. Apparently using nothing but the power of the human mind, the paper is made to fall over. Is this a true demonstration of telekinesis? No, but it certainly looks like it!

1 For this trick, you will need a small piece of paper, approximately 6 x 3cm (2¼ x 1¼in). The exact size is unimportant but the success of this trick depends on the height of the paper being sufficiently more than the width. Fold the paper in half along its length.

2 Open up the fold to form a "V" shape and position the paper about arm's length in front of you. Due to the height of the paper, it is relatively easy to secretly offset its balance and make it fall over. Rub your first and second finger on your arm, explaining that you are harnessing some static electricity.

3 Gently swing your arm to a position directly in front of the paper but about 15cm (6in) away. As your arm swings around, the air will move and cause the paper to become unstable. As you are a little distance away, the change in air current will take one or two seconds to reach the paper – this will also help to disguise the method to this trick.

4 The paper will fall to the table. Try experimenting with the distance you place between your fingers and the paper. The further away you are, the better the illusion looks. Despite the fact that the method is very simple, the trick itself is extremely baffling – as you will see when you try this out for yourself.

cut and restored newspaper

A strip of newspaper is unmistakably snipped into two pieces, yet is instantly shown to be restored. This is an ideal trick for a larger audience. It can be performed for a group of children or adults with equal success.

To add to the presentation, invite a member of the audience up on to the stage with you. Give them a pair of scissors and a normal strip of newspaper and ask them to follow your actions carefully. You will always succeed and they will always fail. This can be very comical.

If you plan your moves carefully, after a few demonstrations you could switch your strip with theirs and have the spectator "unexpectedly" succeed. This would be a great finish to the routine.

1 To prepare, cut a strip of newspaper from the financial section. The content of such a page will help to camouflage the join. Place the newspaper on top of a scrap of paper to protect the table. Apply a thin layer of rubber cement glue to the middle section of the strip, as shown here.

2 Wait for the glue to dry completely, then apply some talcum powder to the covered area. This will stop the glued surface of the strip prematurely sticking at the wrong moment. Blow any excess powder off the newspaper so that everything looks normal.

3 The final piece of preparation is to fold the strip in half with a sharp crease.

4 To begin the performance, display the strip of newspaper in one hand and the scissors in the other.

5 Fold the strip in half along the crease and clearly snip off about 1cm (½in) from the centre. Try to make the cut as straight as possible. Because of the rubber cement glue, the two separate pieces will be glued back together at the join.

6 Open the strip and the paper will have magically restored itself. You can stop here or repeat the cutting and restoring process. It all depends how much of the strip you covered in glue.

7 Instead of cutting the paper straight, experiment by cutting it at a right angle. You can also place the glue at strategically placed points on the strip of newspaper so that you can begin by actually cutting the strip into two pieces. Then place the two pieces together, cutting again to re-join them.

walking through a postcard

Give someone a postcard and a pair of scissors, and tell them it is possible to cut a hole in the card big enough for you to step through.

See if they can figure out how. Unless they know the secret it is unlikely they will succeed.

1 Fold the postcard in half lengthwise. You can use a plain card, or one with a picture on it.

2 Make straight cuts in from the folded edge approximately every 1cm (½in). Notice how each cut stops approximately 1cm (½in) short of the opposite edge.

3 Turn the card round and cut more slits (marked here in red) between the slits you have already made, this time starting from the open edges rather than the fold. These slits stop 1cm (½in) from the folded edge, as before.

4 Now trim off about 3mm (⅛in) along the fold, except for the sections at each end.

5 When you open up the card you will find it now has a hole in it large enough for you to step through.

6 If you want to show this stunt but don't have a postcard with you, you can use a business card or playing card instead, with the challenge: "Cut a hole big enough for me to put my head through."

snowstorm in china

Several sheets of tissue paper are displayed and torn into strips. They are soaked in a glass of water and squeezed dry. An ornamental Chinese fan is used to aid the drying process and the paper begins to turn into confetti, creating a mini snowstorm that fills the air and covers the stage. This is a spectacular closing effect for a show.

There are several versions of this traditional trick. The following method is the invention of a wonderful Hungarian magician, the Great Kovari. We graciously thank him for allowing us to share his method with you. Many top professional magicians feature versions of this trick in their act.

1 To prepare, cut a strip of flexible plastic, approximately 1 x 10cm (½ x 4in). Pierce a small hole in the centre with a sharp point.

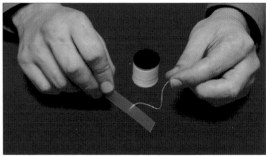

2 Attach a short length of thread to the plastic strip by tying it in a knot through the hole.

3 Use adhesive tape to attach the thread to the back of a fan so that the plastic strip hangs down behind the centre.

4 Make a hole in the top of an egg and empty the inside. Wash it out and let it dry completely before continuing.

5 Cut some coloured tissue paper into confetti-size pieces. Carefully pack them into the egg.

6 Bend the plastic strip in half, then place it carefully into the hole in the egg so that when the strip expands it grips the sides of the egg securely.

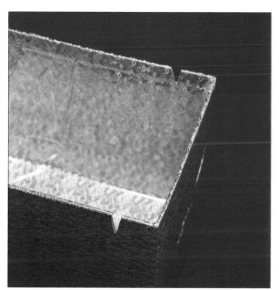

7 Cut two notches into the sides of a box. These will function as a display stand for the fan, as well as a secret holder for the wet tissue.

8 Set a table with the fan displayed in the box, a glass of water to the left and some tissue paper sheets at the back of the box. From the back, you can also see the egg hanging from the fan.

9 From the front, there is a pretty display of props and the egg remains hidden behind the fan.

10 To perform, display the various coloured sheets of tissue paper and clearly tear them into shreds. ▶

11 Roll up the shreds into a ball and drop it into the glass, soaking the paper thoroughly.

12 Replace the glass on the table and display the wet ball of paper in your right fingertips. Squeeze it dry.

13 Now make a fake transfer into your left hand. Place the ball of paper against the fingers of your open left hand and close it as your right hand comes away with the ball hidden behind the fingers.

secret view

14 This close-up view shows the position of the hands as they come together. Your body movement should suggest that the ball of paper is really in the left hand.

15 The right hand drops the wad of soggy paper into the box as it reaches for the fan.

16 This view from the back shows the paper being dropped as the hand reaches for the bottom of the fan.

17 Hold the fan up with the left hand hidden behind it. Say that you are going to dry the paper by fanning it.

18 With the left hand, secretly pull the egg off the plastic strip. The fan provides a great deal of cover for this.

19 Squeeze the egg tightly, breaking the shell, as you rapidly wave the fan to distribute the confetti pieces as far and wide as possible. The broken eggshell will drop to the floor with the paper, and the evidence will not be noticed. All that is left to do is tidy up!

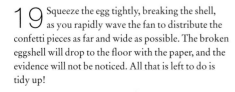

Jacob's ladder

With a little adhesive tape, a few scraps of paper and a pair of scissors you can make an amazing ladder that looks very impressive. Both *this and Jacob's Tree can be made from newspaper rather than coloured paper, although it won't look as nice.*

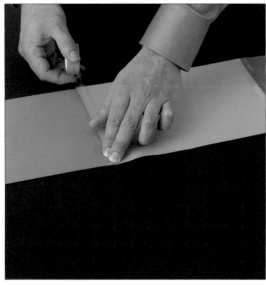

1 Tape several pieces of paper together to make a long strip. We used five sheets of colourful A4 paper but newspaper would also work well.

2 Carefully roll up the long paper strip into a reasonably tight and neat tube.

3 Use a small amount of adhesive tape to secure the rolled up strip of paper.

4 Use a pair of sharp scissors to cut halfway through the width of the tube, about 7.5cm (3in) from either end.

5 Now cut a slit along the length of the tube between the two cuts you have just made.

6 Open out and flatten the tube along the slit. Bend the ends down.

7 Carefully tease out the paper from the tubes on either side and watch the ladder grow before your eyes.

8 The completed ladder is impressive considering it is made so quickly from just a few pieces of paper.

Jacob's tree

This is similar to Jacob's ladder, except this time you make a tree. Coloured paper is reasonably expensive, so if you want to make a *really huge tree, then it may be better to tape sheets of newspaper together so that the trick doesn't cost too much.*

1 Tape several pieces of paper together to make a long strip. We used five sheets of colourful A4 paper but newspaper would also work well.

2 Carefully roll up the long paper strip into a reasonably tight and neat tube.

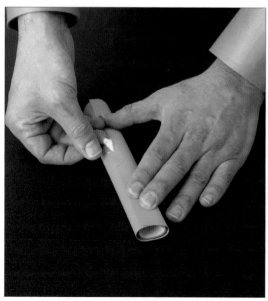

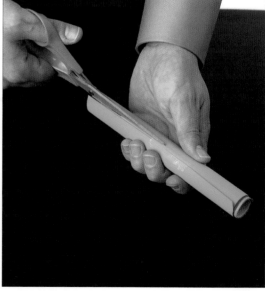

3 Use a small amount of adhesive tape to secure the end of the rolled up strip of paper.

4 Use a pair of sharp scissors to cut halfway down the length of the tube.

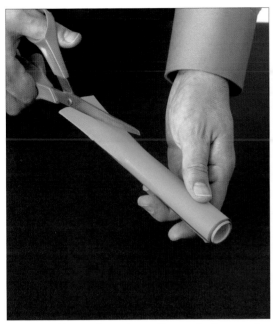

5 Repeat this cut at three other equally spaced points around the tube.

6 Bend the cut sections down, as shown in the picture.

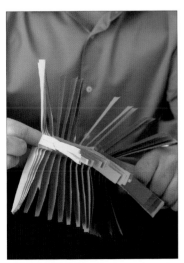

7 Carefully tease out the paper from the middle of the tube.

8 The completed tree will take shape before your eyes.

party
tricks

The dinner or party table is an ideal place to perform magic for your friends and family. If you take the time to learn a few clever routines, you will be able to entertain and astound people at any time. Most of these tricks can be performed without any set-up or preparation other than a bit of practice, and the items you require can be found in most homes, classrooms and restaurants.

life of the party

Glasses, napkins, cutlery, straws, cups and sugar cubes are just some of the objects often found on tables at meal times and at parties. It is a good idea to learn some magic tricks with these items so that whenever you are out with other people you are in a position to entertain. An ordinary dinner party or casual drink can become a very memorable occasion with an impromptu performance, and if your guests do not know each other magic is an ideal icebreaker. You can be sure that your performance will lead to conversation and no doubt speculation as to how you achieved your miracles.

One magician known for his love of intimate performances was Max Malini. Born Max Breit in 1873 on the borders of Poland and Austria, he was taken at an early age to live in New York. Between then and his death in 1942, Malini made a name for himself in many countries around the world. While other magicians were busy performing in theatres and music halls, Malini would work for small intimate groups, often at top hotels, and for the most distinguished dignitaries of the time – including royalty and numerous world leaders. One feat of magic that will always be associated with his name is the production of a huge block of coal or

ice from under his hat. His table guests, who had been in his company for several hours, were understandably astounded by the sudden production of the block, and in the case of the ice were most curious as to how such an item could be stored and hidden without melting! However, if he deemed the time and mood to be wrong, he would sometimes decide not to perform at all, despite having prepared for the trick hours in advance.

Another great story is that of Malini bending, ripping and soiling an old playing card that he would then throw face down in the gutter. Later that day, while walking with a friend, Malini would boast about his ability to name any playing card just from looking at its back. His friend might then spot the dirty card in the gutter and challenge Malini to name it. Such elaborate preparation may seem like a lot of work considering the friend might not have spotted the card in the gutter, but this kind of magic and the response it

Below: *L'Escamoteur, sur le Boulevard, Près le Chateau d'Eau* is a late 19th-century engraving which shows a street magician in mid-performance of one of the greatest tricks of all time – the legendary Cups and Balls.

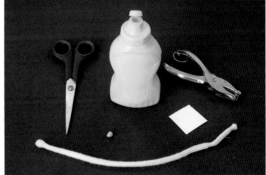

receives is what reputations were, and still are, made on. Using Malini's philosophy, why not practise and prepare the Torn and Restored Napkin trick for your next dinner party? Wait for the right time in the evening to perform it, and cause a sensation.

Once you have experimented with the collection of party tricks in this chapter you may find that you can get the best reactions when you perform them without calling attention to them. For instance, Loose Thread, in which someone who thinks they are removing a piece of thread from your clothing finds that they are apparently unravelling all the stitching in your shirt, wouldn't be nearly as funny if you pointed out the loose end of the thread and asked them to remove it. The best reactions occur when you are having a conversation with a friend and they think they are being helpful trying to smarten up your shirt or jacket. Use these party tricks in the right situation and at the right time and you will receive a tremendous amount of satisfaction from the fun and laughter you will generate.

Above left: Max Malini, the early 20th-century conjuror, caused a sensation whenever and wherever he performed.

Top: A 1950's Davenports' magic catalogue reveals how to do some simple and well-loved tricks, the props for which would have been available in-store. L. Davenports & Co have been makers of magic since 1898.

Above: Tricks such as Snag! or Jasper the Ghost can be performed at the drop of a hat, while other tricks, such as Saucy Beggar and Torn Wallpaper, require a small amount of preparation.

Explained in the following pages are several effects which can be strung together (for example, Sugar Rush and Sugar Rush Uncovered). This allows you to make your performance short or long depending on how responsive your audience is. Floating Bread Roll, Trip to China and both versions of Bending Knife are quick, off-the-cuff stunts, while Vanishing Glass, All Sugared Up and The Cups and Balls are longer routines that can form part of a small, impromptu after-dinner show. Some, such as The Shirt off Your Back, require some preparation and the use of an accomplice.

rolling straw

A straw is set on the table in front of you, and you then rub a fingertip against your sleeve. As you hold your finger above the straw, it rolls forward as if repelled by a magnetic force. The best kind of straw to use is one of the type that are supplied free in fast food restaurants. As will become apparent when you read through the method to this *trick, it may be a good idea to fail a few times before finally succeeding. Your audience will become accustomed to watching you rub your finger on your sleeve and this will provide you with perfect misdirection. If a drinking straw is not available, this quick stunt will work just as well with a cigarette.*

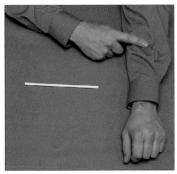

1 Place a straw in front of you on the table and rub your first finger on your sleeve. Explain that you are generating static electricity.

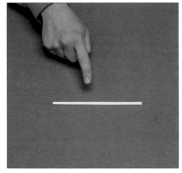

2 Hold your finger directly above the straw.

3 Move your finger forward and, as you do so, secretly blow at the table in front of the straw. The breeze will cause the straw to roll forward. Try not to change the shape of your face as you blow; all eyes should be on your finger.

Jasper the ghost

This very simple and strange party trick will leave someone wondering if ghosts really do exist, after they feel a tap on their *shoulder while no one else is around. For reasons that will become obvious, this trick works best one-on-one.*

1 Tell the person that you know a friendly ghost who would like to meet them. Hold the first finger of each hand about 10cm (4in) away from their eyes, then ask them to close their eyes.

secret view

2 As soon as their eyes close, move your right hand away and spread the first and second fingers of your left hand as shown. Lightly touch their eyelids with these two fingers. They will feel the sensation of a finger on each eyelid and will assume that both your hands are occupied.

secret view

3 Call out for your ghost friend "Jasper" and tap the person on the shoulder with your free hand.

4 Immediately bring your hands back to the original position and when the person opens their eyes everything will look as it did before.

straw penetration

Two drinking straws are wrapped around one another and clearly tangled. Yet with a magical gesture the straws are pulled apart, *leaving both intact. We have used coloured straws in the photographs so that the moves are clear and easy to follow.*

1 Hold a drinking straw vertically in the fingertips of your left hand and another horizontally in the fingertips of your right hand. The horizontal straw is held in front of the vertical.

2 Wrap the bottom of the vertical straw up and away from you, around the horizontal straw.

3 Continue wrapping it around the horizontal straw, bringing it back over until it is back where it started.

 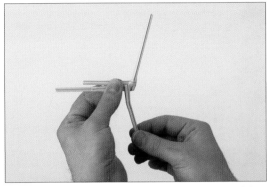

4 Now wrap the right end of the horizontal straw away from you and around the top half of the vertical straw, bringing it back to where it started.

5 Wrap it back over one more time so that the two ends of the horizontal straw meet on the left.

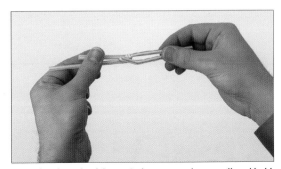 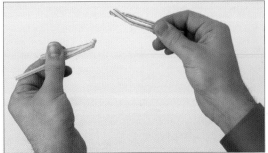

6 Bring the ends of the vertical straw together as well, and hold one straw in each hand.

7 Pull your hands apart and incredibly the straws separate, seemingly penetrating each other. In fact the order and direction of the twists undo the previous twists, so while they look hooked together they are really not.

trip to China

Next time you have to serve a cup of tea try this out and you'll make your friends jump for sure. But don't try it if someone is already *holding a hot drink, as they will spill it. Always be sensible when you try a practical joke of this type.*

secret view

1 Hold an empty teacup and saucer in your right hand. You will also need a teaspoon.

2 Put the spoon handle through the handle of the cup. Grip the spoon handle firmly between your thumb and the saucer.

3 Approach someone as if you were going to offer them a cup of hot tea. Grip the saucer and spoon tightly and pretend to trip. The cup will fall forward and make a big noise, but it won't fall as it will be trapped by the bowl of the spoon.

clinging cutlery

This is a perfect dinner table stunt. It is easy to perform, yet completely mystifying. A fork is made to cling to the outstretched palm of your hand. The secret is explained, but moments later it *transpires that you were not being entirely honest, as the fork is once again made to cling to your hand in an even more amazing fashion! The set-up takes just a few seconds.*

secret view

secret view

1 Hold a fork in your closed left fist. Grip your left wrist with your right hand and open the left fingers wide. The right first finger secretly stretches out to hold the fork in place.

2 From the front, it looks as if the fork is stuck to your hand. You can stop the illusion here, but you can also go a step further. Turn your hands around, exposing the method to the trick. Return to the same position.

3 The right hand is now removed completely, yet the fork still stays suspended from the left hand. How?

4 This exposed view shows how a knife is held under your watchstrap from the outset. When you pretend to reveal your secret, the knife is covered by your first finger (*see* step 1).

bending knife (version 1)

A knife is held between the fingertips and gently shaken up and down. The metal seems to turn to rubber and the illusion is created of the knife bending. This illusion also works with rulers, nails, pens and many other objects. It is the perfect effect to show just before the even more impressive Bending Knife (Version 2), described next.

This optical illusion dates back a long way and is a good example of "retention of vision", which is the term used to describe the effect whereby an image remains in view a few milliseconds after it has been moved away.

At about chest level, hold a knife loosely by one end, between the thumb and first finger of the right hand. Quickly and continuously move your right hand up and down about 10cm (4in). As the knife begins to shake, it appears to become wobbly, as if made of rubber.

bending knife (version 2)

This is a great follow-up to Version 1. A knife is bent in half at right angles, then straightened out again. The optical illusion is perfect.

It is not necessary to use a coin, as seen below, because the trick works almost as well without it, but the coin does give conviction to the illusion.

secret view

1 Hold a knife in the right hand with the tip against the table. The fourth finger should rest behind the handle and the other fingers in front. Hold a coin at the top of the knife between the finger and thumb. Only the tip of the coin is seen, and it is mistaken by the observer for the top of the knife.

2 The left hand closes around the right hand as shown. The knife is supported entirely by the right hand. The left hand simply helps to hide the method.

3 The knife is pushed against the table and although the hands stay straight, the knife is allowed to fall flat pivoting between the right third and fourth fingers, as seen in this exposed view.

4 From the front, with both hands covering the method, this is how the illusion looks. Finish by raising the hands, therefore straightening the knife and showing that it has unbent itself.

floating bread roll

Under the cover of a napkin a bread roll starts to float off the table and away from the dinner guests! This fun and easy-to-perform trick *is a greatly simplified version of a famous magic trick called the "Zombie Floating Ball".*

1 You will need a bread roll, a thick napkin and a fork.

secret view

2 Hold the napkin by the top two corners. You can see here that a fork is secretly held behind the napkin between the thumb and index finger of your right hand, parallel to the top of the napkin.

3 The fork is not visible to spectators from the front.

4 Cover the bread roll with the napkin, making sure they do not see the fork.

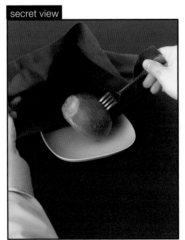

secret view

5 As you do so, stab the prongs of the fork into the roll.

6 Lift the fork upwards and from the front the roll will look as if it is floating underneath the napkin.

7 Make the roll travel left and right, seemingly out of control. This is where your miming and acting abilities come in.

8 Reach up to the roll with your left hand and subtly pull it off the fork.

9 Bring the roll back to the plate and uncover it, secretly dropping the fork into your lap.

10 With the fork safely hidden you can toss the napkin to the table with a flourish.

bouncing bread roll

A bread roll is picked up off the table and apparently bounced on the floor, like a tennis ball. It shoots up into the air and you catch it as if it was the most natural thing in the world. This trick would work *equally well with a piece of fruit such as an apple or orange, and even a pool ball at a pool table! As long as you use an object that would not ordinarily bounce, the effect will register well.*

1 This trick is easiest to do sitting at a table, although once you understand the principle you can also do it standing. Hold a bread roll in your right hand, at about shoulder height.

2 Bring your hand down below the table's edge, exactly as if you were about to bounce the roll on to the floor.

3 As soon as your hand passes the edge of the table it will be out of sight. This is where you have to work with split-second timing if the illusion is to be a success. Notice how the foot is ready to tap against the floor, simulating the sound of the roll hitting the ground.

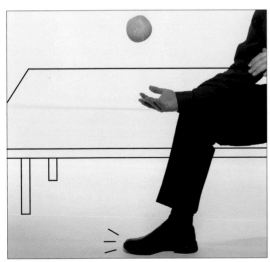

4 The moment the hand is below the table's edge, it turns at the wrist and flicks the roll up into the air as straight as possible. There should be no movement from the arm itself; only the wrist should move. A split second before you toss the roll, tap your foot on the ground.

5 Follow the movement of the roll with your head. The combination of sounds and visuals will provide the perfect illusion of the bread roll bouncing.

vanishing glass

In this amazing impromptu trick a coin is covered with a glass, which in turn is covered with a paper napkin. While the audience's attention *is focused on the coin, the glass is somehow caused to disappear. You can also make it pass straight through the top of the table.*

secret view

1 Perform this sitting at a table. Place a coin on the table in front of you, then place a glass, mouth down, on top of it. Cover the glass with a paper napkin from the top downwards so that the paper is stretched around the top and sides and would hold its shape even if the glass were removed; the bottom should remain open. Ask a spectator if the coin on the table is heads up or tails up.

2 Lift the covered glass up and back towards the edge of the table with one hand, exposing the coin. Bring attention to the coin by pointing to it with the other hand. This is simply misdirection to divert the attention of the spectators away from what happens next.

3 The glass should be resting on the edge of the table in front of you. Allow it to slip out of the napkin and safely on to your lap. There is no "move" as such – simply lift the glass away from the coin and allow it to fall silently. The napkin will hold its shape so a casual glance should not arouse any suspicion.

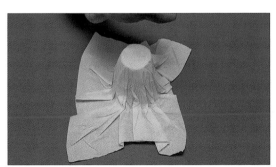

4 Carefully place the napkin shell back over the coin and remove your hand.

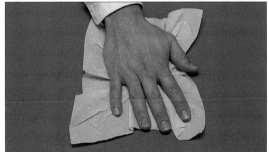

5 Tell the audience to watch as you proceed to smash the "glass" flat to the table under your hand. This sudden noise will create the moment of impact you should strive for. One moment the glass is there, the next it has completely disappeared!

tip *As a variation, ask the spectator to hold their hand out just above the "glass". Place your hand above theirs and bring your hand down on to theirs as the paper is flattened. This directly involves the spectator, who is expecting to feel the glass. Instead* *of creating the illusion of the glass disappearing, you can also finish by telling the audience that the glass went straight through the table. Simply produce the glass from beneath. If a glass is not to hand, you can do the same trick with a salt shaker or pepper grinder.*

torn and restored napkin

A paper napkin is torn into small pieces and squeezed between the hands. The pieces magically weld themselves together again. The napkins in the photographs are shown in different colours for ease of explanation.

A little experimentation with napkins will reveal that the paper is easy to tear in one direction because of the direction of the grain. Try to orientate the napkins correctly when you set up this trick so that the tearing is made easier for you.

1 To prepare, apply a small amount of glue to the top right corner of a paper napkin (at the point here marked "X").

2 Glue a second napkin to the first at this point. Wait for the glue to dry.

3 Scrunch up the top napkin into a ball. Neatness is not important.

4 Continue to squeeze the ball, making it as small as possible. You are now ready to start performing the trick.

secret view

5 Hold the flat napkin in both hands so that the duplicate ball is at the top right corner on your side of the paper. Begin to tear the napkin in half down the centre.

6 From the front, the duplicate ball is hidden completely and must remain so. The napkin provides lots of cover.

secret view

7 Place the left half of the napkin in front of the right half. Tear the paper down the centre as before.

secret view

8 Place the left pieces in front of the right, then turn the strip sideways so that you can tear the strip down the centre.

secret view

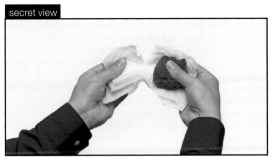

9 Place the left pieces in front of the right again, then make one final tear down the centre.

secret view

10 Place the final pieces of paper in front of the right-hand pieces as before and squeeze the edges together.

secret view

11 While you are squeezing the napkins, secretly turn them over so that the duplicate napkin is facing the front. As the real napkins are the same colour, this move will be invisible.

secret view

12 Start to open out the napkin along the top edge, smoothing out the wrinkles as you go.

13 Continue to straighten it out until the entire napkin is revealed to be restored.

secret view

14 The torn pieces are safely hidden behind the duplicate napkin at the top right corner. To finish, crumple all the paper into a ball and discard it.

sugar rush

This is a very popular effect in magic which is also known as "Matrix". Four sugar cubes are set out in a square formation. Two playing cards are shown and used to cover the cubes briefly. The sugar cubes jump about, seemingly of their own free will, until they all meet in one corner. This is similar to the next routine, Sugar Rush

Uncovered, but it does not require difficult sleight of hand because of the extra cover created by the two cards. If no playing cards are available, you could also perform the trick using coasters or even menus – whatever is to hand. If you learn both routines, you will have a nice set piece to perform at a dinner table.

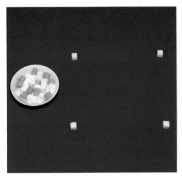

1 Set out four sugar cubes in a square formation. The cubes should be about 30cm (12in) away from each other.

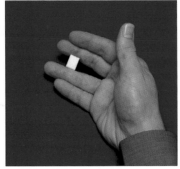

2 Grip an extra sugar cube between your second and third fingers, as shown. In performance, there will always be a card on top of your fingers so this cube will remain hidden.

3 Hold a playing card in each hand, so that they both look the same and the extra sugar cube cannot be seen. Cover both the upper right and left cubes.

secret view

4 This exposed view shows how the right hand is about to let go of the hidden sugar cube while the left hand is getting ready to take a cube away under the card.

secret view

5 Move both cards to show that one cube has supposedly jumped. (Be careful not to expose the hidden sugar cube.)

6 Cover the upper right and the lower right cubes, repeating the same move as before. Both hands should move together and at a constant pace.

7 Move the hands back to show that a second cube has moved across to join the others. Do not pause for long, but continue to move your hands to the next position.

8 Cover the upper right and lower left corners, in preparation for the final sugar cube to travel.

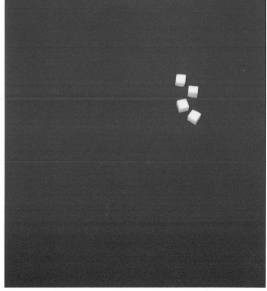

9 Repeat the move one last time and show that all the sugar cubes are together at the top right corner.

sugar rush uncovered

Four sugar cubes are placed in a square formation on the table. The hands cover the cubes for the briefest of moments and they start to jump from corner to corner until all four cubes join together in one corner. This routine is a perfect follow-up to Sugar Rush. The order of moves is basically the same, but instead of using cards as cover, this *version relies entirely on a convincing Classic Palm. Palming a sugar cube is as easy as palming gets, which is why they are ideal for this trick. You could also use upturned bottle tops, which are equally easy to palm because of their shape and easy-to-grip edges. In order to achieve success with this effect, some dedicated practice is required.*

secret view

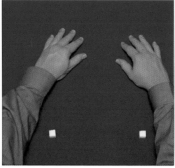

secret view

1 For this trick you will need a bowl of sugar cubes. Take five cubes from the bowl, secretly palming one in the right hand (*see* Money Magic chapter for a description of the Classic Palm technique). Set the bowl off to your left-hand side and set out the remaining four cubes in a square formation in front of you.

2 Cover the furthest two cubes with your hands. As you will notice, the sequence of moves is similar to that of Sugar Rush, so once you are familiar with that trick this one will be easier to learn.

3 Drop the palmed cube in your right hand and palm the one under your left hand. This should take no more than a second, and both moves must happen simultaneously. With practice, you will be able to palm and drop the cubes without any noticeable movement from the back of your hand.

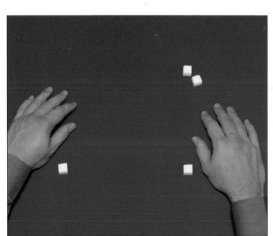

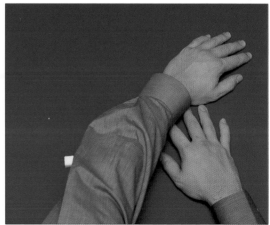

4 Move both hands away to reveal that one of the cubes appears to have jumped.

5 Without hesitation, cover the top right corner with your left hand and the bottom right corner with your right hand. Do the same move again, dropping the left-hand cube and picking up the cube at the lower right in a right-hand Classic Palm.

 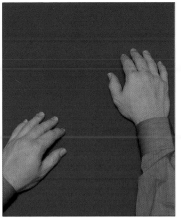 

6 Move your hands to show that the second cube has moved.

7 Finally, cover the top right corner with your right hand and the bottom left corner with your left hand.

8 Perform the move one more time to show that all cubes are now at the top right corner.

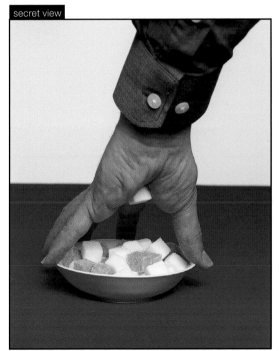

9 You will finish with a sugar cube palmed in the left hand. This is easy to get rid of. Simply pick up the sugar bowl to your left-hand side and, as you lift the bowl up, allow the cube to fall in, along with the other cubes.

10 Pick up the remaining cubes on the table and openly drop them back into the sugar bowl. The great thing about this routine is that you finish completely "clean"; that is, you destroy the evidence of the extra cube when you drop it back into the bowl.

all sugared up

A number is chosen at random and written on the side of a sugar cube. The cube is then dissolved in a glass of water and the written image is made to appear on the palm of the person who chose the number. You will need to use a very soft pencil and a sugar cube that is smooth on all sides. This routine will cause massive reactions because the effect actually happens in the spectator's hands.

secret view

1 Before you begin the trick, secretly dip your right second finger into a glass of water to moisten it. If the liquid is cold, you may be able to moisten your finger by touching the condensation on the outside of the glass. Either way, you must ensure there is some moisture on your fingertip.

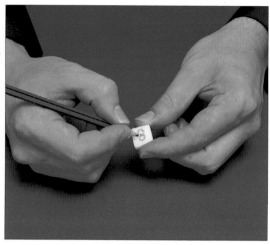

2 Ask a spectator to choose a number. Using a pencil, clearly print the number on one side of a sugar cube.

3 Squeeze the cube between your right thumb and second finger as your left hand moves the glass into view. The written number should be pressed against the moist second finger. Drop the cube into the water.

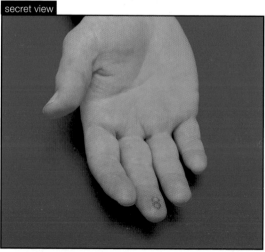

secret view

4 You have secretly transferred the graphite in the pencil to your fingertip. Now you must secretly transfer this to the palm of the person who chose the number.

5 Ask them to hold out their hand, then take hold of it and move it to a position above the glass. As you do so, lightly press your second finger against their palm.

6 This will transfer the image without their knowledge. The spectator should not notice because you are touching them for a reason, that is, under the pretence of repositioning their hand.

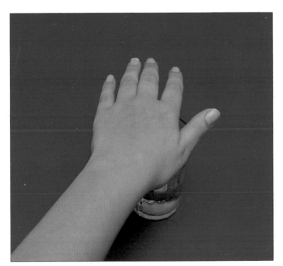

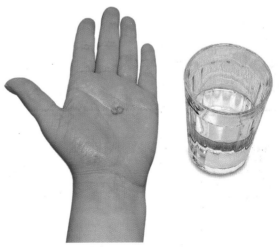

7 Ask the spectator to move their hand up and down above the glass. Explain what is going to happen: "As the sugar cube dissolves, the graphite will float to the surface of the water and the heat of your hand will cause the particles of graphite to turn into a vapour which will rise from the glass and attach itself to the palm of your hand."

8 Ask the spectator to turn their hand palm up and they will see the duplication of their number, drawn on the sugar cube moments before.

two in the hand

Three sugar cubes are displayed. Two are put into the left hand and one is placed in the magician's pocket, yet there are still three cubes in the left hand. This little mystery is repeated several times, culminating in the disappearance of all three!

If you enjoy this type of magic, then it may be worth investing in some magicians' sponge balls from a magic shop. They are quite inexpensive and come in a variety of different sizes and colours. They are the ideal prop to use for sleight of hand such as this, although you will find that it is also possible to use other small objects for an impromptu performance.

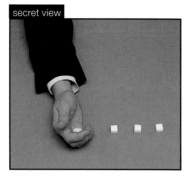

secret view

1 Place three sugar cubes in a row on the table and have an extra cube secretly hidden in your right-hand Finger Palm. This cube must remain hidden throughout.

2 Pick up the cube at the far right and display it in the right fingertips. Hold out your left hand flat and count "One", placing the cube in your left palm.

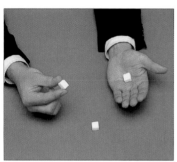

3 Display the second sugar cube in the right fingertips and count "Two".

secret view

4 As the second cube is placed into the hand, drop the extra cube along with it.

secret view

5 Immediately close the left hand and say, "Two sugar cubes in my left hand."

6 Say "One in the pocket." Suiting your action to these words, pick up the remaining cube from the table. Display it and pretend to put it in your right jacket pocket, but secretly retain it using the right Finger Palm.

7 Ask how many cubes are in your left hand and the response should be "Two". Say "Close!" as your left hand sets out the three cubes in a row on the table. Repeat steps 1 to 7, however at step 6 really place the cube in your pocket and leave it there.

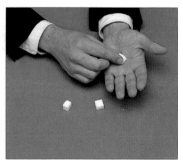

8 The third time, change the routine ever so slightly. Pick up the cube at the far right and place it on to your left palm. Count "One".

9 Pick up the second cube and display it in your fingers as before.

10 Count "Two" as you supposedly place this in your left hand along with the first cube. Continue your patter by saying, "Two cubes go into my left hand."

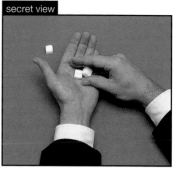

11 What you actually do is secretly pick up both cubes by pinching them against your fingers with your thumb. There must be no hesitation.

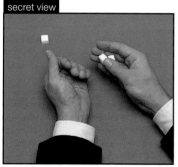

12 As the right hand comes away with the two hidden cubes, the left hand closes as if it still contains them.

13 Pick up and display the third cube. Say "One in the pocket", but in fact place all three cubes in your pocket.

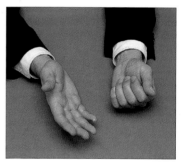

14 Ask how many cubes are in your hand. The audience may assume two, or even three.

15 Open your left hand, showing that both your hands are completely empty and all of the sugar cubes have mysteriously disappeared!

16 This trick will work with a variety of small objects. You could, for example, tear up a paper napkin and roll the pieces into small balls. As mentioned in the introduction, magicians' sponge balls are also perfect for this trick.

knife and paper trick

Paper spots are stuck to the blade of a knife on both sides. The spots are removed, but reappear at the magician's command. The sleight taught here has been used by magicians for decades and is still popular today. It includes the Paddle Move, which involves showing the same surface of an object twice while the spectator thinks they are seeing two different sides. This move has many applications.

1 Tear off six tiny pieces of paper from the corner of a paper napkin.

2 Dip the tip of your finger into a glass of water, then touch the blade of the knife to transfer the spot of liquid.

3 Repeat this at two more points on the knife, then place a paper spot on each wet point – the water makes them stick.

4 To practise the sleight you will use throughout this trick, hold the knife between your fingers and thumb with the blade pointing downwards. The paper should be on the top side of the blade.

5 Twist your wrist towards you so that the knife turns over and the blank side can be shown to the spectator.

6 Twist your wrist back again, reversing the action of step 5.

7 Repeat this wrist action once more but, as your wrist turns over, push the handle of the knife with your thumb so that the knife turns over at the same time as your hand. This time the spots will appear to be on the back of the knife as well. This is the Paddle Move. Turn your wrist back again, using the Paddle Move to flip the knife over at the same time.

8 To proceed with the trick, after step 3 add three more pieces of paper to the blank side of the knife. This completes the preparation.

9 Now that you are familiar with the Paddle Move, you are ready to learn the sequence of moves for the routine. Display the knife in the right fingertips as shown.

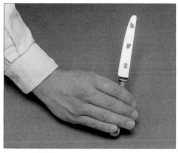  

10 Twist the wrist (without performing the Paddle Move) and show three spots of paper on the other side of the knife blade.

11 Bring the knife back to the start position and pull off the lowest spot. Pretend to slide off the spot on the underside of the knife at the same time.

12 Perform the Paddle Move, which allows you to show that the spot on the underside has also apparently been taken.

13 Repeat these moves with the second spot, in fact only taking the spot off the top of the knife.

14 Execute the Paddle Move again to show that both spots have supposedly been taken.

15 Repeat once more for the last spot remaining on the knife.

16 Using the Paddle Move, show that both sides of the knife are now blank.

17 With a shake of the wrist, quickly twist the knife between your fingers and thumb to make all three spots reappear. These can be shown to be apparently on both sides, using the Paddle Move one last time. Finish by removing the three spots, thus destroying the evidence.

the cups and balls

It has been said that a magician's abilities can be measured by the performance of this great trick, of which there are many versions. Some use just one cup, others two or three, but the effect is always similar. A number of small balls are caused to vanish, penetrate and reappear under the cup or cups, often changing into fruit and even live mice and chicks along the way! This basic version uses three balls and three cups. It is easy to perform and amazing to watch. Professional sets of the cups and balls are available from magic shops.

1 You will require four small ball-like objects. You can use sugar cubes for an impromptu performance, or you can fashion balls from a paper napkin torn into four strips.

2 Roll each strip into a ball. Although you will be using four balls, the audience will only ever be aware of three of them.

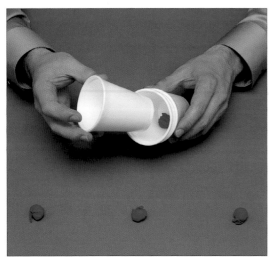

3 Stack three cups together, secreting a ball in the centre cup. Set the other three balls in a row in front of you. You are now ready to perform the incredible Cups and Balls.

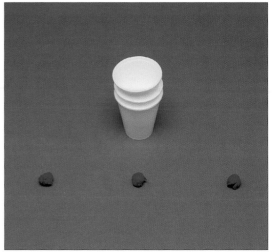

4 This shows the preparation completed and is how the cups should be set before you begin the routine.

5 Pick up all three cups in a stack with your left hand. The right hand takes the bottom cup from underneath and pulls it off the stack. Keep the mouth of the cup away from the spectator.

6 Turn this cup upside down next to the ball on your far right, as shown above.

7 Repeat step 6 with the second cup. Although there is a ball hidden inside this second cup, it will remain unseen and will not fall out if the cup is turned at a constant speed.

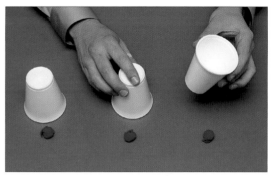

8 Place the second cup next to the centre ball, with the secret ball hidden beneath it. You must practise this until you can position the cup without fear of the extra ball falling out.

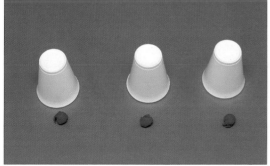

9 Finally, turn over the third cup and place it next to the ball at the far left. The extra ball is hidden under the middle cup.

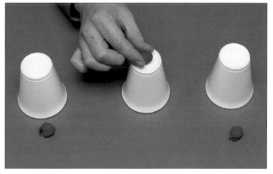

10 Pick up the centre ball and place it on the base of the middle cup. ▶

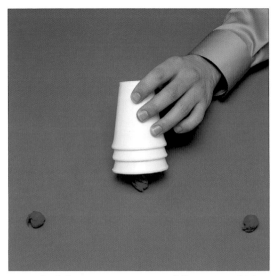

11 Stack the outer two cups on top of the centre one. Make a magcial gesture, then tilt back the stack of cups to show that the ball has apparently penetrated the centre cup and is now on the table. Pause to let this effect register with your audience.

12 Pick up the stack of cups and turn them mouth upwards again. Now repeat the set of moves and turn each cup over again. Place the first cup at the right, next to the ball. Place the second cup (containing the extra ball) over the centre ball.

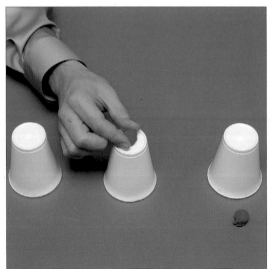

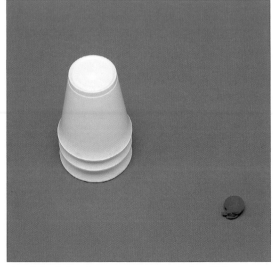

13 The third cup goes next to the ball on the left. Pick up the right ball and place it on top of the middle cup. This sequence of moves is almost identical to the sequence at the start of the routine.

14 Stack the other two cups on top as before. Make a magical gesture above the cups.

15 Tilt the cups back to show that the second ball has arrived to join the first.

16 Repeat the moves one final time. Place the first cup to the right, the second cup over the balls already on the table, and the third cup to the left.

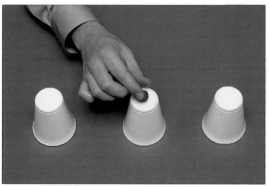

17 Pick up the last remaining ball and place it on the underside of the centre cup (*see* Tip for an alternative move).

18 Stack the cups one last time and make another magical gesture over them.

19 Tilt the cups back to reveal all three balls together.

20 That is the mystery of The Cups and Balls!

tip *When you reach step 17, instead of placing the final ball on the cup you can "vanish" it using a Fake Take (see Money Magic chapter) or any other technique that you are familiar with. The final ball will then be shown to have magically reappeared under the final cup.*

removal man

After a bottle of wine has been finished, push the cork right into the bottle. The challenge is to remove the cork without breaking either the cork or the bottle. It seems an impossible task, but it is actually quite easy when you know the secret of how it is done.

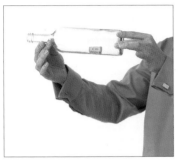

1 When you have finished a bottle of wine, rinse it out, dry it and then push the cork into the empty bottle.

2 Twist a table napkin until it is rope-like and insert it into the neck of the bottle. Keep pushing the napkin in until it is as far down as you can get it.

3 Turn the bottle upside down and shake it until the cork is caught up in the folds. You may need to try several times until the cork is upright rather than side-on. Slowly pull out the napkin; the cork will remain trapped within the folds.

4 Continue to pull until the cork comes out of the bottle.

5 Show your audience what you have achieved and take a bow!

tip *As with most tricks in this book, the more you practise this trick the easier it becomes to do well. So don't be disheartened if you find it difficult initially – it will get easier and you will soon be able to perform with ease.*

defying gravity

In this easy trick you raise a bottle from the table in a seemingly impossible fashion. No one else will be able to do it, which is likely to

both infuriate and amuse them. Make sure that you use a a a coloured bottle with a label on it so they can't see what you are doing.

1 Hold your hand in a fist and place it next to a bottle.

2 Touch your fist to the side of the bottle.

3 Lift the bottle off the table, seemingly without gripping it at all.

4 This view makes it clear that as soon as your fist is out of site behind the label your little finger stretches out to provide the necessary grip.

sticky fingers

This trick makes a good follow-up to Defying Gravity. Many objects can be made to cling to your finger using this simple technique. You

will find that some objects will work better than others. Experiment with different items and select the one that works best.

secret view

1 Point your first finger and touch it to a box of playing cards, a packet of cigarettes, a mobile phone, or any other box-shaped object that you are holding in your left hand.

2 Let go of the box with your left hand. It will cling like a magnet to the first finger of your right hand.

3 This view shows how your little finger extends under the object. It is completely covered by the object and cannot be seen by the spectators.

saucy beggar

This is a really good practical joke, perfect for when you're enjoying a meal with friends. If you don't want to go to the trouble of making *this prop yourself at home, there are often ready made ones available in magic stores or on the internet.*

1 You will need an empty squeezable mustard bottle, some thick yellow cord (the cord in these pictures was coloured with food dye), reusable putty adhesive, a small piece of card (stock), a hole punch and a pair of scissors.

2 Open the lid of the empty bottle by unscrewing it and thoroughly clean and dry the lid and bottle. Punch a hole in the piece of card.

3 Trim the card around the hole to make a collar that will sit neatly inside the lid of the bottle.

4 Use reusable putty adhesive to stick the collar to the inside of the lid.

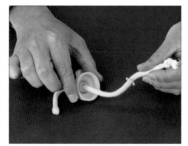

5 Before sticking the collar into place, thread the length of yellow cord through the hole in the lid and through the collar. Tie a knot in the end, which will eventually sit in the bottle.

6 In this view you can see that the hole in the collar is the same diameter as the cord, in order to provide the support needed for the trick.

7 Insert the prepared cord into the bottle and screw on the lid.

8 You are now set to make your friends jump out of their skins.

9 When the situation is right, simply squeeze the bottle hard and the string will launch itself out of the bottle, looking exactly like a stream of mustard.

magnetic credit cards

Have you ever wondered what the magnetic strip on the back of a credit card is for? Did you know that if you rub the strip on your *sleeve it will become magnetic? It doesn't really, of course, but your spectators will think so when they see what you do with it!*

secret view

1 Hold two credit cards and rub the magnetic strips on your sleeves as you explain to the spectators that you are generating static electricity.

2 Bring the two credit cards together, back to back. The card in your right hand should go behind the one in your left hand.

3 Notice how the edge of the credit card is touching the tip of your thumb. Push the cards together and as you do so allow the card to snap off your thumb and on to the other card. It will look and sound as if they are magnetized.

secret view

4 Pull the cards away from each other, reversing the movement and pulling the card against your left thumb.

5 Show the audience that the cards are no longer magnetized. If you wish to involve the audience even more, you can borrow the credit cards from a spectator and hand them back afterwards.

unburstable balloon

We all know what happens when you push a sharp point into a balloon – it goes POP! Well, with this simple stunt you can push sharp sticks into the balloon without it bursting. This trick can be used as part of a routine with Needles through Balloon.*

1 Blow up a balloon and apply two strips of clear adhesive tape in a cross, as shown. Apply another patch on an area directly opposite.

2 Display a sharp wooden skewer in one hand and hold the prepared balloon in the other.

3 Carefully and slowly push the skewer into the balloon, through the centre of the tape cross.

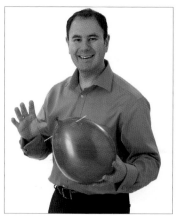

4 Direct the skewer so that it exits from the balloon through the second prepared patch.

5 If you prepare enough tape crosses on the balloon you can use several sticks at once.

torn wallpaper

Once you know how to make the simple gimmick you can do this trick anywhere. Experiment with different sized pieces of paper. It is *best to prepare this when nobody is looking and then watch people's faces when they see it – especially the person whose home it is!*

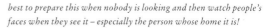

1 Take a piece of white paper and fold it in half. Make the fold with a sharp crease.

2 Tear out a triangular shape from the folded edge. It does not have to be neat. In fact the more jagged the tear, the better the illusion works.

3 Open up the folded paper and curl one half upwards. Wet the back of the straight half with a tiny amount of water and stick it on to a flat surface such as a wallpapered wall or a picture.

4 At a glance it will look as if the paper has been torn and is peeling away. Try to position the paper so that the folded edge is at an angle and therefore hidden from the direction from which people will see it.

secret view

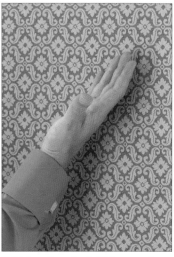

5 When someone finally spots the tear, say that you can fix it. Cover the paper with both hands – the right hand flat and the left preparing to secretly remove the paper from the wall.

6 The right hand rubs the wallpaper and the left comes away from the wall with the paper hidden inside. (This is an exposed view.)

7 After a few rubs, finish by removing your right hand to show that the wallpaper has been completely restored.

bottomless mug

This is a simple gag that makes it look as though there is a hole in the bottom of a mug. It is a quick stunt and fun to do, perhaps as part of *another trick that requires a cup, stick or knife. Despite the simplicity of this party trick, it is very effective and will catch people's attention.*

secret view

1 Hold a mug in your left hand with the palm up, and the mouth of the mug pointing to the right. Hold a wand, stick or knife in your other hand.

2 Hold the wand, stick or knife with the right first finger extended along its side. Tap inside the bottom of the mug a few times to show that it does not have a hole in it. Each time you tap, remove the wand from the mug and re-insert it.

3 On the third or fourth tap push the wand behind the cup, with your first finger inside the cup. This is the view from the front.

4 This view reveals what is really happening. As soon as the wand passes "through" the bottom of the mug, pull it back out again and hand the mug round for inspection.

relight my fire

In this trick, you show how a blown-out candle can be relit without touching a flame to the wick. This works because the smoke is *combustible. The flame ignites the fumes from the smoke and travels back down the plume to relight the wick.*

1 Position an ordinary candle on a candle holder and light it.

2 Leave it to burn for a couple of seconds, then blow out the flame.

3 Immediately hold a lit match to the smoke from the candle, about 2.5cm (1in) above the wick, and the wick will relight, as if by magic.

lighter than light

You strike a match and it floats briefly between your hands. It's best to practise this with an unlit match. You should always take great care when using matches and fire, and children should not attempt this trick unless they are closely supervised by an adult.

secret view

1 Take a match from a box and secretly dig the nail of your right middle finger into the base of the matchstick until the wood splits slightly.

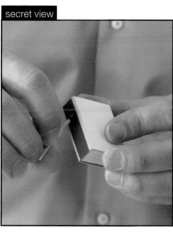
secret view

2 Steady the match with your thumb and first finger. Now strike it.

secret view

3 The match will remain securely wedged on your fingernail.

4 Lower your right middle finger and then interlock your fingers as shown. The match will appear to float behind your interlocked fingers.

5 From behind you can see how the finger supporting the match remains hidden from view. This is the secret to the trick. By wiggling your finger you can make the lighted match appear to float from side to side.

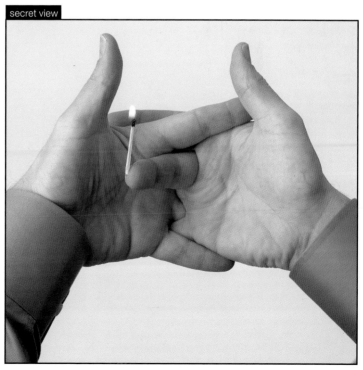
secret view

comedy rising match

You open a box of matches and a match pops up in a comical way. This is sure to raise a smile when you use it. You might be able to think of a funny picture you could draw on the cover of the box, incorporating the pop-up match.

1 Use a hole punch to make a small hole about 6mm (¼in) from the end of the matchbox cover.

2 Close the box and insert a match through the hole so that only the head remains outside the box.

3 Push open the box with your fingertip and the match will pop up through the hole in a comical way.

Robin Hood meets his match

Your friends will credit you with the skill of Robin Hood when you demonstrate this clever stunt. It is not quite as difficult as it seems but looks mighty impressive. You may need to start off quite close to the target until you get used to the trick. Once you are good at it you can begin to increase the distance between your hand and the matchbox, which will make it look even more impressive.

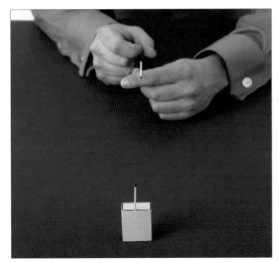

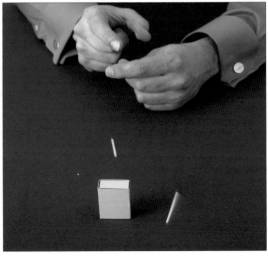

1 Remove two matches from the box and carefully trap one in the drawer. Only the bottom of the matchstick should be caught in the box. Set the box about 30cm (12in) away from you and balance the other match on your left forefinger and thumb.

2 Flick the match off your finger with your right hand and you will knock the other match out of the box. The reason for this is that the match will spin and turn sideways as it leaves your left hand, but it happens so fast that no one can see how it works.

matchbox challenge

It sounds easy to drop a matchbox from a short height and have it land on its end, but no one will be able to do it unless they know the secret. It may take a few attempts to perfect the technique, but once you've got the hang of it you should succeed every time.

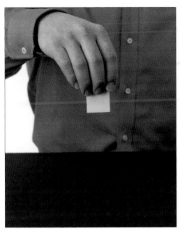

secret view

1 Hold a matchbox between the tips of your right fingers approximately 15cm (6in) above the table.

2 You have secretly pushed about 1cm (⅜in) of the drawer out. It is hidden by the backs of your fingers.

3 Let the matchbox drop: it will land on end. When anyone else tries it they will fail, as the matchbox will bounce and fall over.

uncrushable!

In this interesting demonstration you show an audience how to make the drawer of a matchbox virtually uncrushable. Experiment using matchboxes of different sizes and types, as these factors may affect how well the stunt works.

1 If you place the drawer of a matchbox on top of the cover and bang your fist down, both parts will be damaged. However, if you place the cover on top and try the same thing you won't be able to crush the drawer

2 Try it! The drawer of the matchbox will spring away from you and remain undamaged.

finger mouse

A small mouse appears inside your cupped hands and then disappears just as fast. This is a lovely little trick to show young children. If you *want to perform this as an impromptu trick, then you should carry the mouse around with you in your pocket.*

1 To make the mouse you will need a small piece of brown paper, a black pen, a needle and black thread, a pair of scissors and some adhesive tape.

2 Wrap the paper around your finger to form a cone and hold it together with a small piece of tape.

3 Trim off the open end of the cone so it is about 4cm (1½in) long.

4 Draw two eyes and a nose on the mouse with a black pen.

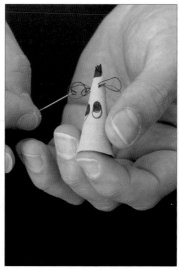

5 Use the needle and thread to make some long loops just above the nose.

6 Clip the loops into separate strands to create whiskers.

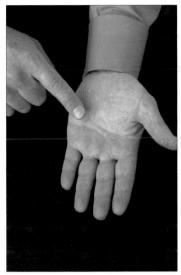 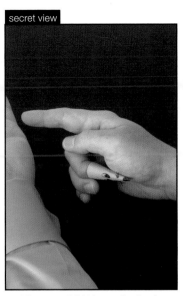 

7 To begin the trick, casually show your left hand to be empty. Your right hand points to your empty left palm.

8 The mouse is hidden on the tip of your right middle finger, which is curled inwards. From the front the mouse cannot be seen.

9 Cup your hands together as if there is something inside them.

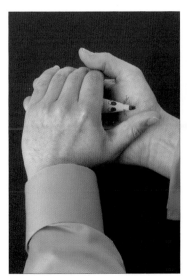 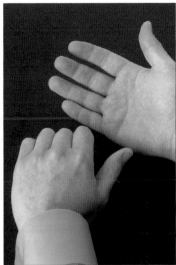 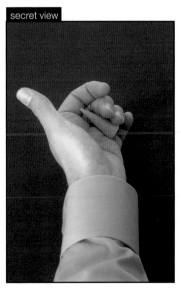

10 Slowly extend your second finger so that the mouse's head pops out from between your hands. Wiggle this finger in and out so that the mouse looks alive.

11 To make the mouse disappear, grip it in your closed left fingers and remove your right hand, showing that it is empty.

12 The mouse, now held secretly in your left fingertips, can be pocketed without anyone seeing it.

bumblebee eggs

You show your friend an envelope, which you say contains a rare breed of bumblebee eggs. When your friend's curiosity gets the better *of them and they peek inside the envelope they will jump out of their skin with surprise!*

1 You will need two rubber bands, an envelope decorated with bumblebees, a sheet of thick cardboard, a craft knife and a washer.

2 Make a special bumblebee noisemaker by cutting a large hole in the board. Then make two flaps at either end.

3 Attach two rubber bands to a washer.

4 Loop the rubber bands over the flaps in the board.

5 Twist the washer until the bands are wound as tightly as possible and insert the prepared board inside the envelope. The sides of the envelope will stop the washer from unwinding.

6 Show the envelope to your victim and explain that you recently found some bumblebee eggs that are very rare and worth a fortune. Your friend will be eager to see what they look like.

7 When they pull the board out of the envelope, the rubber bands will instantly unwind and the washer will hit the sides of the envelope, making a loud noise that will scare the wits out of your unsuspecting victim.

banana splitz

An unpeeled banana is magically cut into a number of pieces chosen by a spectator. Cards are used to make the trick more interactive and *allowing the spectator to choose how many times you slice the banana adds another layer of impossibility.*

1 Prepare the banana by inserting a thin needle into the skin at three equally spaced intervals along its length and secretly slicing it by moving the needle in an arc. The banana should look quite normal when you have finished.

2 Place the banana on a plate in front of you and show five cards: an Ace, Two, Three, Four and Five of any suit. The Ace should be the top card.

3 Shuffle the cards, dragging one card off at a time, simply reversing the order. Then repeat, bringing the order of the cards back to how they were before you shuffled them. Now you need to make a spectator choose either the Three or the Four. Magicians call this a "force". Deal the cards face down and ask the person to say "Stop" at any time as you do so. Time things so that while you are telling them what to do, you deal past the first and second card. They will say "Stop" before the last card is dealt and therefore will stop you either at the Three or the Four.

4 If you are stopped at the Four, explain that you will magically chop the banana into four pieces. If you are stopped at the Three explain that you will make three magic karate chops. Mime three karate chops over the banana.

5 Peel the banana and allow the three or four pieces to fall on to the plate.

invisible coin catch

You hold an empty paper bag open in your right hand and throw an invisible coin into it with your left hand. Although no one can see the coin, they can hear it when it lands in the bag with an audible thud. This was one of the British comedian Tommy Cooper's favourite stunts.

secret view

1 Show the audience that a paper bag is empty and hold it with the fingertips of your right hand. Notice how the first and second fingers overlap each other.

2 Throw an imaginary coin up in the air with your left hand and follow with your eyes its imaginary parabola across to the bag.

3 When it is about to reach the bag hold your hand to your ear, non-verbally cuing the spectators to listen.

secret view

4 Flick your second finger off your first finger: the flicking noise against the paper bag will sound exactly like a coin being landing inside.

tip *If you want to show a real coin after it has landed, start the trick with one hidden between your right-hand fingers and the bag. Then, after you have shown the bag empty, let the coin fall silently to the bottom. Continue with the trick and once you have made the snapping noise invite someone to reach inside and remove the coin.*

laughter lines

Trick a friend into covering their face with dirty marks. Be careful not to roll the coin too near the victim's eyes as you don't want graphite to get in them. You should also be prepared for quite a dramatic reaction once they realize what you have done!

1 Secretly run the tip of a soft pencil around the edge of a coin. Have an identical clean coin to hand.

2 Give your friend the prepared coin and tell them to copy every move you make with the clean coin. Hold the edge of the coin at the top of your nose and run it down to your chin in a straight line. Next roll it from ear to ear.

3 Continue rolling the coin for as long as you like. By the time your friend has finished their face will look a complete mess!

a good head for money

You stick a coin to a friend's head and they can't shake it off, no matter how hard they try. The reason that they are unable to shake *the coin off is that you have already secretly removed it and hidden it in your hand or in a pocket.*

1 Take a small coin and stick it to your own forehead by pushing quite hard. Now hold your hand out under the coin and knock the back of your head with the other hand.

2 The coin will fall off your forehead after a few bangs.

3 Tell a friend they are not allowed to touch the coin, but all they have to do to dislodge it is bang the back of their head, as you did. Press the coin against their forehead and hold it for about five seconds.

secret view

4 As you remove your hand secretly remove the coin and conceal it in your hand or transfer it to your pocket. You may find this easier if your fingernail is under the coin from the start. As you pushed the coin quite hard your friend will think they can still feel the coin stuck to their head.

5 Of course they can bang their head as much as they like because there is no coin there to fall off.

the shirt off your back

You ask for a volunteer and sit them down in front of the spectators. Your helper is wearing a shirt and jacket. You ask them to undo their cuffs and the top few buttons. With a sharp tug you pull off their shirt, *even though they are still wearing their jacket! This trick requires the help of a stooge: in an informal situation like a party this could be a friend who is dressed ready for action.*

`secret view`

1 An accomplice puts on a shirt in a special way. First, drape it over the shoulders like a cape and button up the top four or five buttons. Then button the sleeves around the wrists.

`secret view`

2 This is how it looks from the back. Try to arrange the shirt neatly so that the fabric is not bunched up in a way that will show through the jacket.

3 Finally put a jacket over the top of the shirt and adjust the clothing so that the shirt looks natural.

tip *If you have not already done so, check out Tie Through Neck, which could be combined with this trick to make a nice little routine.*

4 When you perform the trick, invite the supposedly random volunteer to sit down on a stool or chair. Stand behind them and ask them to unbutton the first four buttons of their shirt and their cuffs. The shirt is now loose and all you need to do is pull with one quick jerk to remove the shirt in an apparently impossible manner. If your friend reacts appropriately it can be extremely funny.

snag!

You supposedly pull a loose thread from a friend's tie and the tie wiggles as though it is being unravelled! This is a really fun gag that is perfect for raising a quick laugh. Don't make a big thing of it however – it is much funnier if you just do it and then move on as if nothing has happened. It is particularly good for a party, or in an office or school where people are wearing ties.

1 Hold the end of the tie in your left hand. Your thumb is on top and your fingers are underneath.

2 The fingers flap up and down very quickly as you mime pulling a thread with your right hand. The end of the tie will flap frantically and should result in a slick gag that will raise an instant smile.

tip *It is worth practising this trick a few times in front of a mirror to ensure that you position your fingers correctly so it really looks as though the tie is unravelling.*

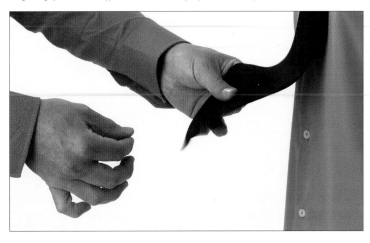

loose thread

When someone tries to pull off the loose thread on your shirt they will get the shock of their life when your shirt starts to unravel! This gag also works really well on a tie. Never draw attention to the thread; wait for your friend to spot it, then ask them to remove it for you.

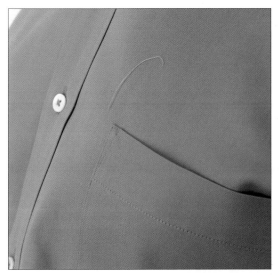

1 Take a 1.2m (4ft) length of thread that is a similar colour to your shirt and thread a short piece through the fabric just above the breast pocket. The remainder of the thread stays inside the shirt. Leave the end hanging and wait!

2 Eventually someone will try to remove the thread for you, and when they pull it the thread will just get longer and longer, as if the stitching is coming undone.

blow your nose

You blow your nose into a handkerchief, which flips up into the air. Like many of the pranks in this section, this should be impromptu.

If you call people's attention to such a small joke it will not be as funny as when people see it happen out of the corner of their eye .

`secret view`

1 Secretly hold a pencil under a handkerchief as you bring the handkerchief to your face.

2 Position the handkerchief as you would if you were going to blow your nose. Under cover of the handkerchief prepare to point the pencil up into the air.

3 Pretend to blow your nose and as you do so flip the pencil up. The handkerchief will rise up in a comical fashion. When you stop blowing your nose let the pencil drop back down and keep it hidden as you put the handkerchief away.

broken arm

As you shake someone's hand your arm makes a bone-crunching noise, which is sure to get a reaction from your unsuspecting victim. A little bit of acting will go a long way to making this prank really

funny. Don't overdo it, just make out that you are in a little pain when the cup is crushed. The louder the noise when the cup is crushed, the better the illusion will be, so experiment with different cups.

1 Secretly place a disposable plastic cup under your right armpit and shake someone's hand.

`secret view`

2 As you shake their hand crush the cup under your arm so that a horrible crunching sound can be heard.

broken nose

While we are on the subject of broken body parts, here is an audible illusion that will convince people your nose is broken.

secret view

1 Begin the trick by holding both hands palm to palm, covering your nose. Make sure that you are directly face on to the audience.

2 Under cover of your hands, put your thumbnail behind your front tooth. Now bend your hands to the left as if pushing your nose and at the same time click your thumbnail off the tooth. It will sound as though the bone is cracking.

popping your joints

For one last bone breaker, try this out and create the illusion of popping your joints. It is a brilliant illusion and will make people squirm.

secret view

1 Hold a finger as shown here. Gently bend your finger back a couple of times.

2 As you bend your finger a third time simply click the finger and thumb of your right hand underneath. It will sound just as if you are popping your joints loudly.

tip *Believe it or not you can do this to someone else. Just tell them to hold out their hand and click your finger and thumb under their finger. Be sure not to hurt them in any way.*

dead man's finger

This stunt results in a weird and slightly scary sensation. You and a friend can make your fingers instantly feel numb. This is because you are not touching both sides of your finger, but half of your finger and half of the other person's. Furthermore, the back of your finger is not a very sensitive area so you will hardly feel anything on that side. It is hard to appreciate how strange it is until you try it out yourself.

1 Hold hands with someone as shown. Notice how both first fingers are extended.

2 Pinch the first fingers with your finger and thumb and you will get the sensation that your finger is numb.

tie through neck

After calling attention to your tie you give it a quick tug and it passes through your neck, leaving your head still attached to your shoulders.

You could set this trick up with a friend and then follow it with The Shirt Off Your Back, making a nice impromptu-looking routine.

1 Without putting it round your neck, knot the tie neatly leaving a large loop at the back, which you flatten to form two flaps.

2 Feed both flaps around the collar, then fold the collar down to hold the flaps in position.

3 With the collar neatly in position the tie will look normal. When you are ready to have some fun, point out your tie and give it a sharp tug downwards.

4 It will look just as though the tie has passed right through your neck.

beer money

A banknote lies trapped beneath an upturned bottle. The challenge is to remove the banknote without the bottle falling over. The bottle must not be touched at any time. This trick must be performed on a smooth surface or it will not work.

1 Set an empty glass bottle upside down on top of a banknote.

2 Carefully roll up the banknote from one end.

3 As you continue to roll the banknote, the bottle will gradually slide off the other end of the note.

4 Once the bottle is clear of the banknote you can pick it up and pocket it.

fake scars

Here are two simple ways to make realistic-looking scars. The techniques are useful for fancy dress parties and to play pranks on *your friends. As you will be using glue, you should make sure that you work over a suitable surface, such as an old cloth or newspaper.*

1 Smear a small amount of rubber cement on your skin.

2 Thin it out by rubbing it gently with your fingertip.

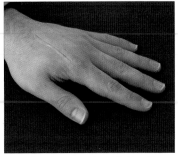

3 When the cement has dried it will become clear. Now pinch the skin in the glued area and a realistic scar will form.

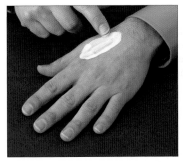

4 Here is another style of scar. Apply a dollop of rubber cement to your skin, as before.

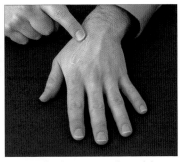

5 Wait for the cement to dry and then roll in the sides.

6 For a final touch use a red felt pen to colour the centre.

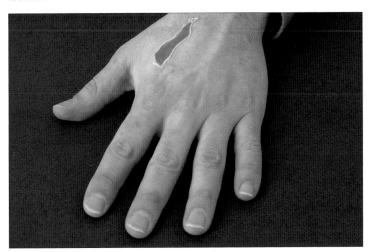

7 The result is a realistic-looking scar that will roll or wash off very easily when you have finished playing pranks on people.

tip *Wait until the cement dries and becomes translucent before creating the folds. You can create the scars on many different parts of your body, but do not put glue near your mouth or eyes.*

smiling Queen

This quirky trick with a British banknote uses origami to make the picture of the Queen smile or frown. You may well be able to find a banknote of a different currency for which this technique works too – try it out on various currencies to see.

1 Place a banknote in front of you with the Queen's head uppermost.

2 Make a sharp vertical fold precisely through the Queen's right eye.

3 Now make another sharp fold through the Queen's left eye.

4 Make a final fold between the previous two in the opposite direction, so that the banknote looks like this.

5 If you open the banknote and look down from the top, the Queen looks as if she is frowning slightly.

6 As you tilt the note away from you and look up at it the Queen slowly begins to smile.

origami rose

A paper napkin is twisted and folded to resemble a beautiful and realistic rose. While this is not a magic trick, it is a great origami *model to remember. People always enjoy watching the rose being made, and they can also keep it as a memento of the evening.*

1 This works best using a single layer of thin paper. So if you have a multi-ply napkin, strip one layer from it.

2 Lay the napkin in front of you and fold over a strip 3cm (1³⁄₁₆in) wide down one side.

3 Hold the top of the fold between the first and second fingers of your right hand and roll the paper over your fingers along the fold until you reach the end.

4 Ensure that this is done neatly, as it will form the head of the rose.

5 Space out the rolled section a little by twisting from the centre to enhance the look of the petals.

6 Pinch and twist the tissue just below the folded section to form the top of the stem.

7 Once you have twisted about 2.5cm (1in) of the stem, take hold of a corner of the napkin from the bottom.

8 Pull this corner about halfway up the stem to form a single leaf and tightly twist the rest of the napkin below it to complete the stem.

9 Adjust the folds as necessary to produce a perfect paper rose.

stunts and puzzles

This chapter will test your ability to think laterally and logically. All of the puzzles require a degree of patience and thought, and once you have learnt the answers you can try setting the problems for other people. Some of the amazing stunts will make you look much cleverer than you actually are, while others will give you a huge advantage when issuing a simple challenge or bet.

puzzle it over

A *stunt* is a feat displaying unusual strength, skill or daring. These can range in scale from the very small to the very large. One of the most famous magicians known for his large-scale stunts was none other than the great showman Harry Houdini (1874–1926). In order to promote his forthcoming shows at theatres across the world he would often challenge the local police to lock him up in their apparently "escape-proof" handcuffs. He would then generate immense publicity by promptly escaping from them.

There is a wonderful story that dates from 1904, when Houdini visited London. He was challenged to escape from a pair of cuffs that had been specially commissioned by *The Daily Illustrated Mirror* and were said to have taken five years to design and make. The event took place at the London Hippodrome and garnered huge editorial space from the *Mirror* (presumably selling lots of papers for them) and at the same time ensuring that Houdini was very much in the media spotlight.

Houdini managed to escape from the "Mirror Cuffs" in just over an hour, and the watching crowd went crazy. There are those who believe that the whole stunt was a set-up designed to be mutually beneficial to both the newspaper and Harry Houdini. Could the cuffs, apparently made to withstand escape, have been secretly fixed so that Houdini could open them without a key? Either way, the stunt succeeded in its purpose and it is easy to imagine the kind of sensation it would have caused at the time.

In recent years, the American showman David Blaine has resurrected the genre of publicity stunts. In one of his latest enterprises, in 2003, he starved himself for 44 days, sealed inside a 2 x 2 x 1m (7 x 7 x 3ft) transparent box suspended over London's Tower Bridge, and in New York, in 2006, he unsuccessfully attempted to spend a week submerged in a water-filled sphere. These dangerous stunts have earned him millions of dollars and worldwide fame. The stunts you will learn in this chapter are unlikely to earn you millions or make you famous and are a little more modest than Houdini's or Blaine's. However, they are still a lot of fun to perform and for your friends to witness.

When you think of puzzles, a number of images may spring to mind. There are jigsaw puzzles, puzzles that require lateral thinking, even puzzles made of wire of the kind found in Christmas crackers. You could even say that magic tricks are puzzles, since every magic trick, like a puzzle, has a solution. The major difference between the two is that the solution to a magic trick should always remain hidden, and while the spectator may wonder about how the trick works, it should not be necessary to know this in order to appreciate the value of the trick.

A magic trick often incorporates humour and a degree of entertainment; a puzzle is designed to test the brain, and thoughtful analysis is usually required in order to solve it successfully. That is not to say that puzzles cannot be fun or entertaining. Indeed many of the puzzles in this chapter will be the source of much enjoyment as you try to find solutions and present the puzzles to your friends.

There are some puzzles that require no interaction at all. They are simply visual treats for us to enjoy. A classic example is a ship in a bottle. It seems

Left: Jeff Scanlan's impossible bottles include this amazing creation, in which a large glass container with a narrow spout is packed with 13 tennis balls, each with a circumference bigger than that of the spout.

impossible that such an object could ever have been assembled, but there it is before us and we are intrigued by the conundrum of how it could have been made.

Very often there is more than one way to arrive at the solution to such a puzzle. In the case of the ship in the bottle, the bottom of the bottle might be removed; the ship inserted into the resulting hole and the base of the bottle resealed by a glassblowing expert. Another solution would be to construct the ship from pieces small enough to fit through the neck of the bottle, joining the individual pieces once they are inside. Of course this would require a steady hand and a lot of patience. Yet another solution is to construct a ship that has hinged masts, so that the whole thing can fit through the neck of the bottle with the masts and sails down. Once the ship is inside the bottle the sails can be carefully pulled upright and glued into position.

How would you go about getting a fully grown apple inside a bottle? This feat is actually possible, although it is a little impractical, and you need access to an apple tree in order to do it. All you do is tie the neck of a bottle to the twig of an apple tree at the beginning of the growing season and wait until the apple grows inside the bottle before carefully removing it from its stem. This leaves you with a real, fully grown apple inside a real glass bottle. Of course, before long the apple will begin to rot, so if you go to the trouble of doing this you should show as many people as possible as quickly as you can.

The world's most famous creator of impossible bottles was Harry Eng (1932–96). He managed to insert all kinds of objects into bottles, including scissors, decks of cards, ping-pong balls, golf balls, packs of cigarettes, padlocks, tennis balls, baseballs, books, dice and even a pair of shoes! Harry's work inspired Jeff Scanlan, an American who assembles a wide range of impressive impossible bottles. In some cases he has developed new techniques to create original masterpieces, some of which take weeks to make and seem totally impossible.

On the pages that follow you will find over fifty stunts and puzzles that will test your problem-solving abilities and show off various skills. Some are easier than others and some are really effective. Be warned: many of the most impressive stunts require lots of practice, just like magic tricks.

follow the leader

No matter how closely people follow your movements they are unlikely to be able to replicate what you do here. While you will *succeed every time, most of your audience start off with their fingers in the wrong position and will therefore fail to replicate your actions.*

1 Tell everyone to copy every move you make. Cross your arms in front of you, hold your hands palm to palm and interlock your fingers. The key to this trick is to make sure that the right arm goes over the left and the right little finger is on top.

2 Now bring your hands in to your chest and up towards your face. Stick out your first fingers.

3 Explain to the audience that you must use the back of the first finger of each hand to touch either side of your nose. This is quite awkward, but entirely possible.

4 Finally, without taking your fingers off your nose, you untwist your fingers and open your arms to reach the position shown.

still following the leader

Again, tell everyone to copy every move you make. Hold your hands out in front of you, palm to palm, and interlock your fingers. As the others copy you, unlock your fingers and comment that the right arm *should be over the left (use your hands to gesture as you speak, to justify taking your hands apart). This excuse enables you to reposition your arms as follows.*

1 When you interlock your fingers again, twist your left hand anti-clockwise instead of clockwise, so that when your hands come together, although it looks as if your arms are crossed as they were before, they aren't really.

2 Tell the spectators to follow your movements. Slowly give your hands a quarter turn clockwise, bringing you to the position shown. Everyone else will be in a muddle and won't be able to replicate your simple move.

tip *If you find it difficult to get into the position in step 1, simply lock your hands together as in step 2 and twist your hands anti-clockwise until you can't turn them any more. This is the position you need to get into.*

hypnotic, magnetic fingers

You apparently hypnotize your subjects as you demonstrate how the power of the mind can cause the body to do things against its will, making the volunteer's fingers close together involuntarily.

Although this stunt is not really hypnosis, some stage hypnotists do try it out on an audience before a show in order to see how susceptible people are to the power of suggestion.

1 Ask the spectators to interlock their fingers and hold their first fingers out in front of them. They must separate their fingertips as much as possible. Explain that you are going to hypnotize them, and tell them a story about very strong magnets being implanted in the tips of their fingers, drawing their fingertips closer together until they lock together. You could also mime binding people's fingers together with invisible thread.

2 Believe it or not, the spectators will find they can do nothing to resist their fingers getting closer together until they touch. Why does this work? The fingers are being stretched apart at the beginning and after a few moments muscle fatigue sets in and the muscles have to contract.

wand twist

The challenge is to copy the trickster with a simple move that seems easy to replicate. However, unless they know the secret few will be

able to succeed. Make it clear at the beginning that they are not allowed to let go of the wand or stick at any time.

1 With your hands held palm to palm, hold a magic wand, pencil or other stick-like object with your thumbs as shown.

2 Cross your thumbs, right over left. This will make the wand start to twist to the right.

3 The right hand turns downward and the left upward, palms wiping against each other. The stick remains between the thumbs.

4 Carry on turning the hands until the palms are facing the floor. When these moves are all put together the crossing of the thumbs goes unnoticed and people will get themselves into a muddle, ending up with their hands pointing in opposite directions.

floating arms

This weird stunt is something I used to do all the time as a teenager. It is very effective and creates a really strange sensation. As with *many of the stunts in this chapter, you have to try it yourself in order to realize how odd the experience is.*

1 Stand behind someone and hold their arms to their sides. They must push their arms outwards for about 45 seconds.

2 When you let go, the other person's arms will rise upwards as if they are being pulled up by invisible strings.

pepper-sepper-ation

A small quantity of pepper is sprinkled on to the surface of a glass of water. The trickster touches the water with the tip of a toothpick and *the pepper reacts by moving away from the toothpick in the most dramatic way. When anyone else tries to copy the stunt, it won't work.*

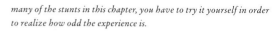
secret view

1 Coat the tip of a toothpick with a dot of liquid soap.

2 Sprinkle some pepper into a glass of water.

3 There should be enough pepper to cover the surface. Now touch the tip of the toothpick to the centre of the surface of the water.

4 Watch as the pepper jumps away from the toothpick. Remove the toothpick from the water and wipe the end dry, removing all traces of soap as you do so. When someone else tries the trick, either with the same or a different toothpick, it won't work.

tip *Use a pen instead of a toothpick. If you keep a tiny piece of sponge soaked in washing-up liquid in the cap of the pen it will be ready to work at any moment. In fact, when you put the lid on the pen to put it away, it will recoat itself for your next performance.*

table lock

If you really want to make a friend look silly, try this the next time you are out for a drink. Be prepared to make a hasty exit!

Ask your friend to place both hands palm down, flat on the table. Now take two full glasses and carefully balance them on the backs of your friend's hands. They will now be unable to move their hands without the glasses falling and the drinks spilling everywhere. This is a good time for you and your other friends to walk away and leave your victim sitting alone in this rather awkward predicament!

tip *Is is not advisable to perform this stunt on a surface that could be damaged by the spilled drinks.*

broom suspension

This cheeky trick leaves your victim left high but not necessarily dry. Only try it in suitable surroundings and never without the permission of the person who lives there. It is especially funny when you trick somebody who is a bit of a know-all or show off.

1 You will need a plastic cup (it must be plastic, never glass) full of water and a long stick. A broom handle is perfect but a snooker cue might also do the job. Stand your victim up and ask them to hold the stick in the air. Now climb on a chair and trap the plastic cup between the end of the stick and the ceiling.

2 That's all there is to it: you can just walk away or continue your conversation some distance away and your victim will be stuck wondering how to move without getting soaked. If they find a way to do it, let me know!

time for a shower

This party challenge could result in someone getting very wet, so you should only attempt it in an area that can easily be cleaned and won't *be damaged by liquid being spilled. You may have to practise the stunt a few times before you get it right.*

1 Place a plate over a glass full of liquid. Here we have used coloured liquid so you can see what is happening.

2 Hold the glass firmly to the plate and turn everything over. Put it back on the table. The challenge is to drink the liquid inside the glass, but you are allowed to use only one hand.

3 The secret to achieving this is to hold the plate and push your forehead firmly against the base of the glass.

4 Now slowly and carefully stand upright and make sure the glass is balanced properly.

5 Once the glass is vertical and balanced, remove the plate.

6 Now you can put the plate down and lift the glass from your forehead, leaving you in a position to drink the liquid normally.

inverted glass trick

In another funny stunt you turn a glass of liquid upside down, without the liquid leaking out. It is now impossible to turn the glass the right way without the liquid spilling and making a mess. Only perform this stunt on a suitable surface.

1 Cover a glass of liquid with a piece of card (stock). Here, we have used coloured liquid so you can see what is happening, but it can be anything.

2 Quickly turn everything upside down, holding the card firmly against the mouth of the glass to stop any of the liquid escaping.

3 Place the glass and the card upside down on a table.

4 Slide out the card and the glass will remain full, but upside down. It is now impossible to move the glass without creating a complete mess, so don't try this in the dining room or in someone else's home without their permission.

suspended animation

A mug dropped from a height is expected to hit the floor and shatter, but instead it stops short and remains suspended in the air. As with many stunts, science plays a key role, enabling you to harness the laws of physics and perform an extraordinary feat.

1 Prepare by tapping a nail into the side of a pencil.

2 Tie one end of a long piece of cord to the handle of a mug and the other end to a washer.

3 Hold the washer in one hand and the pencil in the other. The cord hangs over the pencil.

4 This close-up view shows how the string sits alongside the nail.

5 The cord is released and the mug plunges towards the floor.

6 Amazingly, the cord winds itself around the pencil, stopping the mug from hitting the floor and breaking.

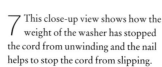

7 This close-up view shows how the weight of the washer has stopped the cord from unwinding and the nail helps to stop the cord from slipping.

straw bottle

The challenge is to pick up a bottle with a straw. There are several ways you can achive this, including tying the straw around the neck of the bottle, but the solution shown below is more fun and less obvious and, therefore, more impressive.

1 Display a bottle and challenge the spectators to lift it from the table using just a drinking straw.

2 The solution is simple. Bend the straw about one-third of the way up and then insert it into the bottle. The fold in the straw will spring open inside, and it will lock into place, enabling you to lift the bottle off the table.

the rice lift

How do you lift a jar of uncooked rice with a single chopstick? You can also use a pencil or knife in place of the chopstick. Other types of container can be used but the important factor is the shape: the container must have a "shoulder" below the neck.

3 When you can physically feel the resistance, give the chopstick one last push all the way down to the bottom of the jar and then lift the jar slowly from the table.

1 Fill a jar with short grain, uncooked rice. Put the lid on the jar and bang on the table to pack the rice down as far as possible. Remove the lid and push the chopstick down into the rice.

2 Work the chopstick up and down 30–50 times. This motion will pack the rice tightly against the sides of the jar. The more you "stab" the rice the harder it will become to pull the chopstick free.

balancing skill

Two forks are suspended from the top of a bottle on the tip of a match in an amazing display of balance. Ask members of your audience to have a go for themselves before you show them how it is done. It is very unlikely that they will be able to do it.

1 Give the audience enough time to try this out for themselves, then lock the prongs of two forks together.

2 Insert a match through the middle, between the prongs so that it joins them together, as shown.

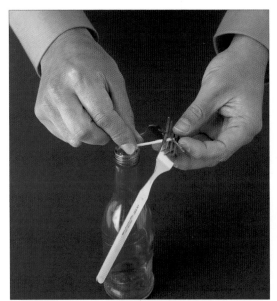

3 Carefully balance the tip of the match (the non-striking end) on the rim of a bottle. You may need to adjust things until you find the centre of balance.

4 Once you have balanced the match and forks properly you can walk away and allow the audience to come and have a closer look at how you have achieved this feat.

floating banknote

A banknote is held in the fingertips and caused to float away from the hand without any visible means of support. There are many versions of this trick, and nearly all of them are difficult to master.

However, this particular version is surprisingly easy to learn and can be performed at the drop of a hat with only a few seconds of preparation before you begin.

1 To prepare, take a piece of reusable adhesive and attach it to the centre of a banknote.

2 To begin the performance, pick up the note so that the adhesive sticks to your right second fingertip.

3 Rub the note between the palms of both hands, explaining that you are generating static electricity.

4 Slowly remove your left hand, showing the banknote adhering to your right fingers. Begin to spread the right fingers, simultaneously bending your second finger inwards, which will move the note away from the palm of the hand. From the front, it appears as if the note is floating away from the hand and hovering in mid-air. Watch this in a mirror to see how good it looks.

5 When your second finger is fully extended, the note seems to be floating quite a long way in front of the hand.

6 This view from above shows what is really happening. To finish, slowly bring both hands together again as in step 3, then put the note in your pocket or secretly remove the adhesive and hand out the banknote for examination.

card flick

Have you ever seen a tablecloth whipped off a table, leaving all the glasses and cutlery in place? This is a scaled-down version and is *considerably easier to achieve after a little practice, although no less impressive than the larger scale version.*

1 Begin by balancing a coin on top of a playing card on the tip of your finger.

2 Get ready to flick the card away from you.

3 If you are quick, the card will shoot out from under the coin, leaving it neatly on the tip of your finger.

immovable

As a demonstration of your superhuman strength, you touch your first fingers together at the tips and challenge someone to pull them apart. *Nobody can do it! You could combine this trick with Move My Fists or Try and Stand Up as they work nicely together.*

Touch your fingertips together, holding your arms as shown. As long as your challenger holds your wrists they will fail to move your fingertips apart. Their energy is dissipated and leaves your fingers unaffected.

tip *These stunts look especially impressive when the challenger is a child or someone who is smaller and clearly weaker than the person they are challenging.*

try and stand up!

You prove you are incredibly strong by stopping someone from standing up using just one finger. This effective trick is particularly *funny when a child pins a parent or other adult to their chair, and it can easily be incorporated into any show.*

Ask someone to sit down on a chair and hold your first finger against their forehead. Tell them they are not allowed to remove your finger. They now have to try to stand up. They won't be able to do it because their centre of balance is above their lap and they can't move their head forward to compensate for that.

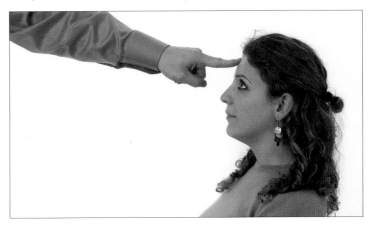

surefire bet

Ask someone to stand with their back to the wall. You place a large denomination banknote in front of their feet and explain that they *can keep the note if they can pick it up without losing contact with the wall. They will be unable to do it, and you will keep the money.*

1 When you position the person ensure their heels are touching the wall. Explain that their heels must not lose contact with the wall. Place the banknote just in front of their feet.

2 They will be unable to pick up the note without losing their balance. Shifting their centre of gravity causes them to fall away from the wall, and there is nothing they can do about it.

lift me if you can

How is it possible to drain someone of their strength in a split second? Easy, just read on! It is even more impressive if you train a small child to do this stunt so that they can flummox an adult.

1 Stand with your arms folded up and your elbows locked in to your sides.

2 Get someone to lift you off the ground holding you by your elbows. In this position it is relatively easy.

3 When you want to create the illusion of making the person seem instantly weak, simply move your elbows out to the position shown. It is a subtle difference but one that really matters.

4 Now it is impossible for them to raise you off the ground at all, because moving the elbows out has shifted the centre of gravity.

Superman

In yet another demonstration of your superhuman strength, you hold a broomstick or a pole in both hands and challenge anyone to push *you off your spot. Nobody, no matter how big and strong they are, will be able to do it.*

1 Hold a broom handle or other long stick with both hands and ensure that your feet are shoulder-width apart and your elbows are bent. Your challenger takes hold of the broom with both hands outside yours and try as they might they cannot push you off the spot.

2 This stunt also works if you hold the ends of the broom and they place their hands in the middle. Bending your arms simply dissipates all the energy that is being thrown at you.

x-ray vision

While your back is turned a coin is placed under a mug. When you turn around you are able to determine what denomination of coin it is. This trick also requires a stooge or confederate, which means that *you must teach it to a friend, who will be your secret helper when you perform it. The two of you need to practise the trick a lot so that you can get it right every time.*

1 The handle of the mug can be turned to point in any direction. Take one coin of each denomination used in your currency and lay them out around the mug like a clock. Put the lowest denomination at the 1 o'clock position, with the others equally spaced. This photograph shows British currency, which has eight different coins.

2 In performance you ask someone to place any coin on the table while your back is turned. Then you ask for the coin to be covered with the mug. This is when your friend picks up the mug and positions it so that the handle points in the correct direction for that coin. If you both always assume that the 12 o'clock position is where your friend is standing you will always get the orientation of the mug correct. Which coin do you think is under the mug in this example?

3 It was the 20 pence coin. Did you get it right?

penny pincher

The challenge is to remove both coins balanced on a glass at the same time, with one hand and without making direct contact with the *glass. This may require some practice but you will soon be able to perform it perfectly every time.*

1 Balance two coins on the rim of a glass, arranging them on opposite sides, as shown here.

2 Place the tip of your thumb on one coin and the tip of your forefinger on the other coin.

3 Drag the coins on to the outside of the glass, being careful not to touch the glass with your hand or fingers.

4 Now raise your hand quickly, pinching your finger and thumb together. The coins will momentarily stick to your fingertips and you can remove both coins together.

the great olive challenge

How can you move an olive from a table to a cocktail glass without the olive ever touching your hands? The shape of the glasses is important, but since both types can often be found in bars and restaurants, this is a perfect stunt for either location.

1 As well as the cocktail glass and the olive you will need a second, tulip-shaped glass.

2 Pick up the second glass and invert it over the olive.

3 Spin the glass around so that centrifugal force keeps the olive whizzing around the inside of the glass.

4 Without stopping, move it over the top of the cocktail glass.

5 Slowly bring the glass to a halt and allow the olive to drop into the glass below.

the trapdoor card

This superb puzzle is the brainchild of Robert Neale, from the USA. There have been many versions of this trick over the years. I use a version in my professional work as it is absolutely baffling and one of
the very best puzzles you can learn. Do not underestimate the effect it will have on spectators. Thanks to Robert for allowing me to share his idea with you.

1 You will need some adhesive glue, a handkerchief, a craft knife and two pieces of card (stock) approximately 12.5 x 7.5cm (5 x 3in) in different colours (we used green and red in this example).

2 Glue the coloured cards together back to back then cut a trapdoor in the card. You should cut three sides, leaving one of the short ends intact for the hinge. The border should be about 2cm (¾in) wide. Crease the hinge sharply.

3 With the red side upwards, ask someone to hold on to the trapdoor. Notice that the opening is facing away from them.

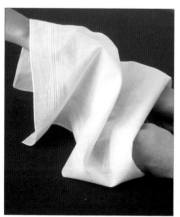

4 Explain that you are going to turn the card over, even though they will not let go of the card or turn their hand over. It doesn't sound possible. To keep the secret, throw a handkerchief over their hand and the card.

secret view

5 The handkerchief has been removed in these pictures so you can see what is happening, but you must leave it in position while you make these moves. First, bend the end of the card underneath.

secret view

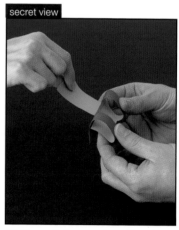

6 Now roll the top underneath so that the folds overlap.

secret view

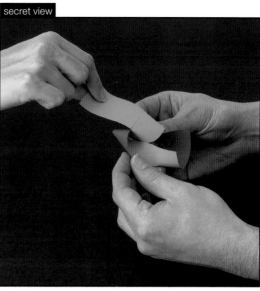

7 Roll the sides of the card back and bring them through the hole in the middle.

8 As you do this, the card will slowly begin to turn inside out. Do not rush this movement or you may tear the card.

secret view

9 Carefully pull the rolled edges all the way through the hole and open them out.

10 Now remove the handkerchief and show that the card is now upside down!

salt and pepper separation

How can you sort out a mixture of salt and pepper? This stunt makes use of static electricity to cause the particles of pepper to separate *instantly from a pile of salt, and demonstrates once again how you can harness the laws of science to perform fun stunts.*

1 Pour a quantity of salt on to a surface, which should preferably be dark so that you can see what is happening clearly.

2 Now sprinkle some powdered pepper on top of the pile of salt on the paper.

3 Rub a balloon on your hair to create a static charge and hold the balloon just above the pile of salt and pepper. The pepper will jump up and cling to the surface of the balloon while the salt stays on the table.

tip *You can use a plastic comb instead of a balloon, if you prefer. Simply run the comb through your hair a few times, then position the teeth close to the salt and pepper mixture. Try to use a white comb if you can, so that you can see the particles of pepper clearly.*

crazy corks

You make a simple move with two corks and ask the spectators to copy you. While you can make the move with ease, they will get themselves in a tangle. The corks in the photographs have red dots on one end and you should do the same to make the trick easy to follow.

1 Pick up a cork in either hand, holding it in the crotch of the thumb as shown.

2 Turn your left wrist back towards you so that you can place the thumbs of both hands on the ends of the corks that do not have spots.

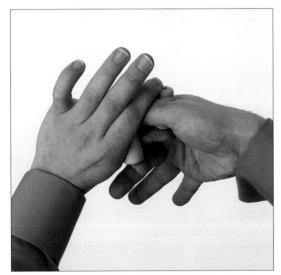

3 Now place the first finger of each hand on the ends of the corks that do have spots.

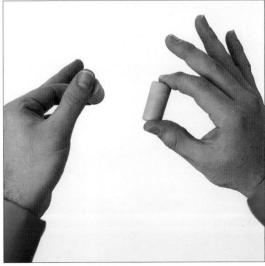

4 Untwist your left hand from your right and the two corks will be separated. Of course, they were never really linked but when others try to copy your moves they will find themselves in a muddle.

quickness of the hand

Have you heard the expression, "The quickness of the hand deceives the eye"? This little stunt proves the exact opposite. You see the money fall but you can't close your hand fast enough. This surely proves the eye is quicker than the hand.

1 Hold a banknote at the very top and ask someone to hold their finger and thumb open, ready to catch it. The idea is simple: you will drop the money and if they catch it they can keep it! Don't worry: your money is safe, as long as you ensure their fingers are open and halfway up the banknote.

2 Their natural response will be too slow. The only way they will catch it is if they guess when you are going to drop it.

love match

The challenge here is to remove a coin without the matches that are balanced on it falling. The trick gets its title because the two matches look as if they are kissing. Whenever you handle matches you should exercise great care, and children must always be supervised by an adult.

1 Remove two matches from the box and, working on a plate, carefully trap one in the drawer. Rest the other match on a coin and balance it against the head of the first one.

2 In order to do this you will need another box of matches or a lighter. Ignite the heads of the balanced matches.

3 Wait a few seconds and the head of the match resting on the coin will fuse to the other and curl upwards. Blow out the matches and pick up the coin.

drink problem

How can you drink from an unopened bottle? Next time you are at a table where there is an unopened bottle of wine or mineral water, try *challenging your companions. You will need to have some wine or water already poured in a glass.*

1 Show an unopened bottle of wine or water and pose the problem.

2 Turn the bottle upside down and pour some wine or water from your glass into the dimple at the bottom.

3 Now take a sip from the dimple and you have shown how to drink from the unopened bottle!

a cutting problem

The solution to this simple puzzle requires a little lateral thinking, and the solution is guaranteed to make your audience groan.

It would work very well as part of an act in conjunction with Suspended Animation since both use the same props.

1 Tie a piece of string to the handle of a mug and hold it up high. The challenge is to cut the string between the handle and your hand without the mug falling.

2 Tie a medium-size loop in the piece of string.

3 Snip through the loop and the mug will stay where it is!

letter of resignation

Can you draw the design in step 5 without taking your pen off the paper and without going over any line twice? Even though there are *only a limited number of ways this can be attempted, it is surprising how long it takes to work it out.*

1 Start at the bottom right corner and smoothly draw the shape shown.

2 Continue to draw, as shown, making sure the pen doesn't leave the paper.

3 Complete the outside of the shape as shown in the picture.

4 Finally, complete the cross in the middle of the box. Practise a few times before you try to challenge anyone else to do it.

5 When you try this out on someone else you will need to show them a picture of the final design, so make sure that you have one to hand before you begin.

bullseye

Or try this puzzle – can you draw a dot in the centre of a circle without taking your pen off the paper? This is possible, but only if you cheat a little, which will both infuriate and amuse the people who you challenge to solve the puzzle.

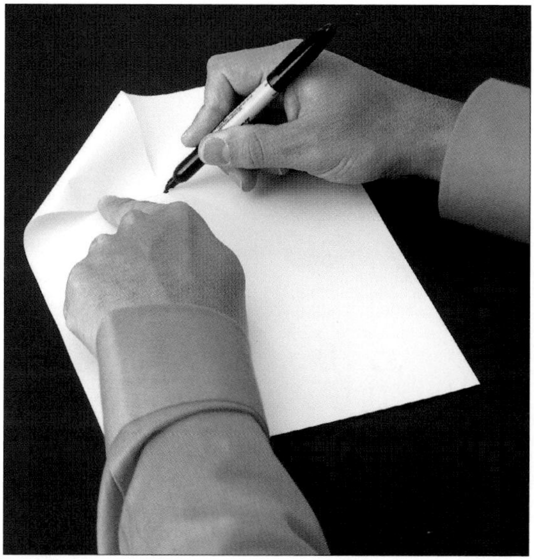

1 Loosely fold over the top corner of a piece of paper. Make a dot where the corner meets the page.

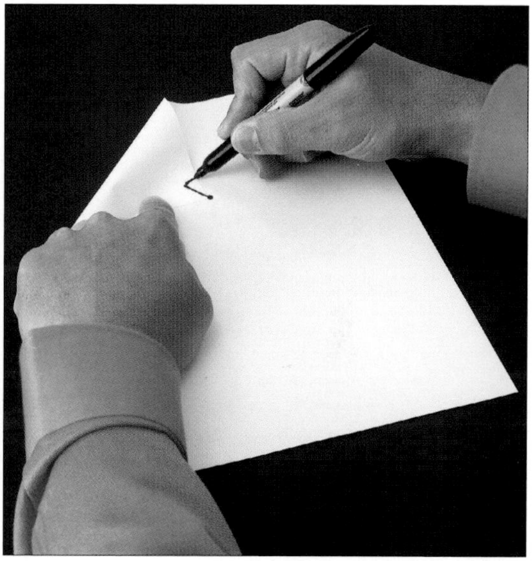

2 Now run the pen across the folded corner and back on to the front of the sheet.

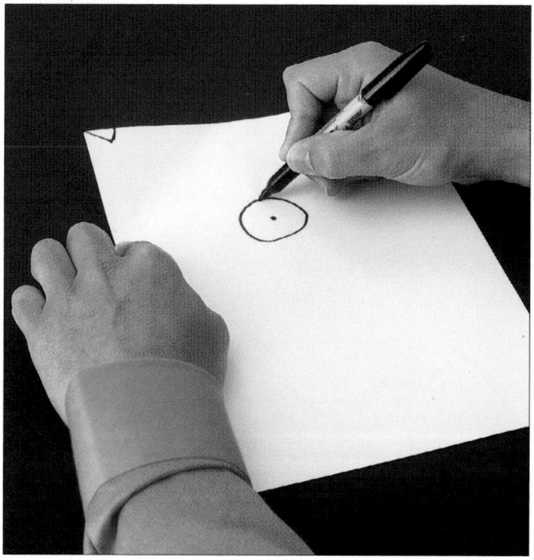

3 Allow the paper to unfold and draw the circle around the central dot.

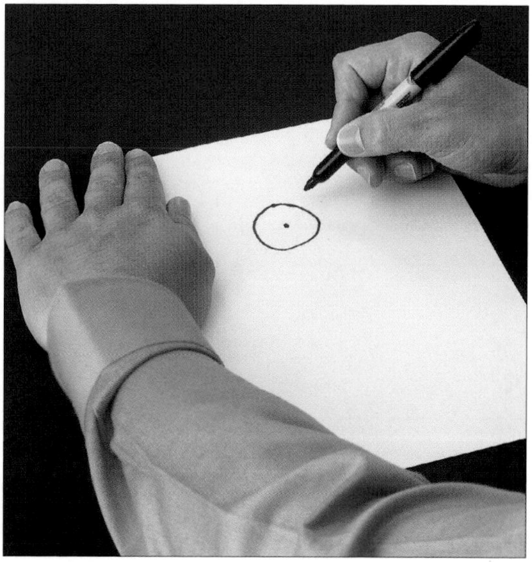

4 This completes the picture. You are now ready to challenge someone else to try and do it.

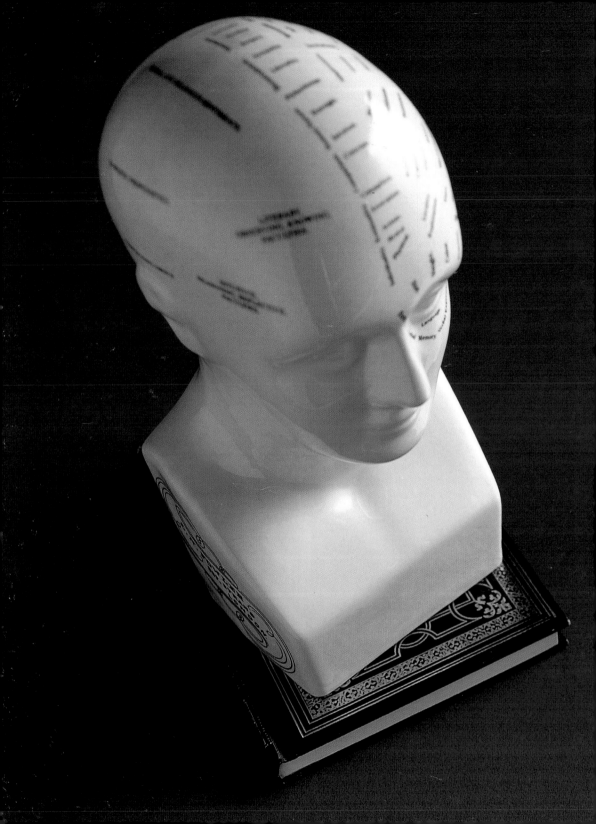

mind magic

Scientists have long subscribed to the belief that humans only use a fraction of their potential brainpower. Many people believe we have, and some even claim to have, a sixth sense with which to read people's minds and make predictions about forthcoming events. Do paranormal powers really exist? People will believe they do when you show them some of the routines in this chapter.

a meeting of minds

Inspired by the performance of a fortune-telling act at the turn of the twentieth century, American-born Joseph Dunninger became one of the greatest performers of mind magic. He originally toured with a large illusion show, but soon realized the impact his mental effects were having on his audiences. Sections of his evening show became dedicated to mind magic until he decided he wanted to be known solely as a mentalist. He subsequently worked for some of the richest and most important people in America. In the early 1940s Dunninger presented a regular radio programme and continued to do so until the late 1940s, when the world of television became an attractive opportunity to spread his reputation even further. In the 1960s Kreskin, a fresh, young American mentalist, stole the limelight from Dunninger and continues to amaze both television and live audiences with his seemingly supernatural powers.

In the 1940s, on the other side of the Atlantic, British radio audiences were being mesmerized by The Piddingtons, a husband-and-wife team many people believed were truly psychic, although they themselves

Above: A publicity poster used by the successful early twentieth-century mind-reader and magician Joseph Dunninger. Take a look at the clever design of the face and you will find the eyes and nose take on a shape of their own.

Above: David Berglas became known as television's "International Man of Mystery" following the broadcast of his series throughout the UK and Europe. Performing astounding memory feats, unusual psychological experiments, manipulation and pick-pocketing, he is one of the world's most versatile magical entertainers. He is also a past president of The Magic Circle.

never claimed this to be the case. Other prominent British mentalists between the 1940s and 70s were Maurice Fogel, Chan Canasta, Al Koran and David Berglas. Berglas has only recently retired after an incredibly successful career performing magic.

In the late twentieth century American Max Maven became one of the foremost creators and performers of mental magic. Graham P. Jolley, although not so well known, is without doubt one of Britain's finest mentalists, mixing superb mental magic with rapid-fire humour and leaving audiences enthralled, entertained and utterly astounded.

None of these performers ever claimed any real psychic ability, but there is one person who does – and as a result has become a household name. Uri Geller, known predominantly for bending spoons with nothing more than his mind, also tries to convince the public of his paranormal powers by stopping watches and duplicating drawings made by volunteers – all effects which can be replicated by known magical methods. American James Randi is one of the world's leading debunkers of phoney psychics and is well known for his numerous exposures of what he believes to be Geller's methods. The famous Harry Houdini was also known for his anger against those who claimed real psychic ability. In the early 1900s he publicly challenged anyone to show him an act of

Above: Graham P. Jolley is one of Britain's funniest and most baffling mind-readers. He is billed as "The Man You Can't Keep out of your Mind" and, among other things, will make a glass shatter with mental energy, make a table levitate, and reveal the telephone numbers of names freely selected from a huge directory.

Above: Uri Geller, the world-famous Israeli who can apparently bend cutlery and other metal objects with the power of his mind. Even scientists have marvelled at his abilities, which have been studied under test conditions on a number of occasions.

Below: One of the most popular effects for a mind-reader to perform is called a Book Test. It involves a word or selection of words being chosen from a book, which are then revealed by the performer either in the form of a prediction or as a demonstration of mind-reading.

psychic power or telekinesis that he was not able to explain. Such a challenge was bold, but only helped to increase the publicity of perhaps the greatest showman and publicist the world has ever seen.

In the following pages you will learn how to create the impression of mind-reading and even of being able to predict future events. Correctly divine a number chosen at random from the roll of a pair of dice (Dice Divination) or predict a word chosen at random from a book (Double Book Test). Transfer your psychic powers to a third party (Black Magic and Temple of Wisdom) and cause the name of a chosen card to spookily reveal itself on your arm (Ash on Arm).

Whether you choose to perform in a serious or a more relaxed style depends on your personality, but do not be put off by the simplicity of some of the methods. Remember, the simplest tricks to perform are often the most astounding.

coin under bottle tops

A coin is placed under one of three bottle tops. The caps are rearranged while your back is turned, yet you find the coin immediately. The method to this trick relies on a short length of thread or hair which remains unseen by the spectators. Experiment with different surfaces to work on. A tablecloth with a "busy" design would be perfect.

1 Haberdashery shops sell a thread that is almost invisible to the human eye. You will need to find some of this "invisible thread" or use a substitute such as a hair. Attach a small piece of this thread or hair to the underside of a coin with a piece of adhesive tape. (White thread is used here for ease of explanation.)

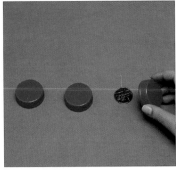

2 It is a good idea to have this coin among others in your pocket and to casually bring it out, putting the others away. Make sure that the taped side of the coin is against the table. Place three bottle tops on the table, and ask a spectator to choose any one of them to cover the coin.

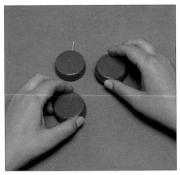

3 Ask the spectator to slide the bottle tops around while your back is turned. Explain that when you turn back you will try to divine which bottle top the coin is under.

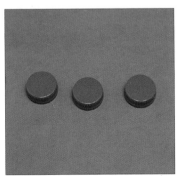

4 When they have finished mixing the bottle tops, turn around and casually glance down in order to spot the thread. Try not to make this glance too obvious.

5 Act as though you are receiving psychic vibes, perhaps hovering your hands just above each bottle top in order to feel the heat rising from the coin. After suitable byplay, lift the appropriate bottle top to reveal the coin.

the pyramid game

Can you turn the pyramid upside down by moving only three coins? Many people have access to enough coins for this puzzle, whether ones that they happen to have in their pocket or that are borrowed from friends, making this a great impromptu trick.

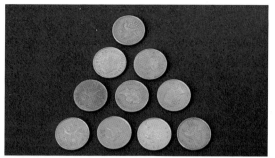

1 Lay ten coins, preferably of the same denomination, on a table in a pyramid shape.

2 Pick up the coin at the bottom right of the triangle and position as shown here.

3 Move the coin at the top of the triangle and put it at the end left of the top row.

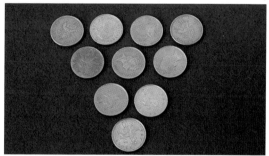

4 Move the bottom left coin and position so that it completes the upside down triangle.

riddle me this

Ask your friends this riddle and see if they can work out which card is where. This simple conundrum is particularly good when you pose it at a party or other social occasion where a group may not know each other, as it will get people talking.

1 The riddle is: "To the left of a Club is a King.
To the right of a King is an Eight.
The Diamond is not the Four or next to the Four.
Home is where the heart is."

2 And here is the answer. Did you get it right? Now try challenging friends and family to solve it.

just chance

This is similar to the next trick, Money Miracle, but is more suitable for a large audience or a formal show. Three envelopes are displayed on a plate and two members of the audience are given absolute freedom to choose one envelope each. The remaining envelope is left for the magician. After the choices have been made, the magician explains that before the performance a banknote was placed inside one of the envelopes. The envelopes are opened one at a time. Each of the spectators finds a blank piece of paper inside theirs, yet when the magician's is opened a banknote is revealed.

Practise this trick in a mirror to be sure that the banknote remains hidden throughout the trick. You can also replace the plate with a newspaper or magazine.

1 To prepare for this trick, you will need three pieces of blank paper the same size as a banknote. Fold the pieces of paper into eighths. Put one in each of three envelopes, sealing the flaps. Display the envelopes on a plate, flap side down.

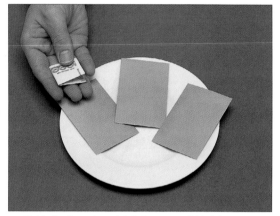

2 Fold a banknote into eighths just as you folded the paper. Hold it in your right hand, thumb on top, fingers below.

3 Place a plate on top of the note, secretly hiding it. Before the performance, put the plate on a table with the banknote just overlapping the edge. This will enable you to lift everything at once, without suspicion.

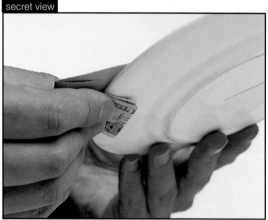

4 Explain to the audience that each of the three envelopes contains something. Offer the plate to two spectators and invite them to choose an envelope. Stress their freedom of choice. Also mention that the remaining envelope will be yours. Wait until they have removed their two envelopes. As your left hand steadies the plate, your right hand drags the remaining envelope off the plate, along with the banknote which is hidden underneath.

5 Orientate the remaining envelope so that the flap is towards you and the note is still hidden. Explain that before the performance you put some money into one of the envelopes and that, even though you said you would not influence the spectators, you used non-verbal communication to subconsciously direct their actions! Build up this moment so that people really do wonder if you somehow managed to make the spectators choose a particular envelope. Ask them to open their envelopes; they will find nothing but blank paper inside.

6 Open the flap of the remaining envelope and pretend to reach inside. In reality you insert your first and second fingers in the envelope while your thumb pinches the banknote on the back of the envelope. Slowly pull out the note.

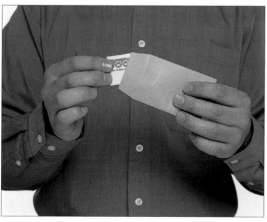

7 From the front, the illusion is perfect. It looks as if the banknote was inside the envelope the whole time.

8 Finally, unfold the note and display it at your fingertips.

money miracle

Three envelopes and two pieces of blank paper are introduced. A banknote of high value is borrowed from a trusting member of the audience. The paper and the banknote are folded in an identical manner and inserted into the envelopes. While the magician's back is turned, the spectator mixes the envelopes until even they are unsure which envelope contains the note. The three envelopes are set on the table. Immediately the magician picks up two envelopes and, without

any hesitation, tears them up into shreds and tosses the pieces aside. The final envelope is opened carefully by the spectator and inside is the unharmed banknote, much to the relief of the lender!

You could use your own banknote, but one of the most important aims in magic is to make the audience care about what you are doing. If you borrow a large sum of money, there is a lot of fun to be had from this situation.

1 To prepare, secretly mark an envelope on both sides, using a pencil. The marks should be small and very light, but clear enough for you to see. (Manila envelopes often have a natural grain with an identifying feature so you may not need to make a mark at all.)

2 Fold a banknote and two pieces of blank paper in quarters. Try to make sure that all three look identical.

3 Hand the two pieces of folded paper and the banknote to a spectator and ask them to insert each one into an envelope. Be sure to hand over the secretly marked envelope and the banknote last and watch as the note is sealed inside.

4 Turn your back and have all three envelopes mixed by the spectator so that even they are not sure which one contains the banknote.

5 Ask for all three envelopes to be laid in a row on the table. The reason you marked the envelope on both sides is because you are not sure how the spectator will set the envelopes on the table, and it is better if you do not rearrange them.

6 Turn around and, without a moment's hesitation, spot the marked envelope. Slam your hands down on to the other two envelopes. Pick them up off the table and rip them to shreds. The success of this trick relies on the speed with which you make your decision. The faster you tear up the envelopes, the more amazing the finale and the more amazed your spectators will be.

7 Ask the lender of the note to carefully open the remaining envelope and remove the contents.

topsy-turvy mugs

In this classic puzzle you line up three mugs with one upside down, then by turning two mugs at a time you manage to get all three the right way up in just three moves. When you challenge others to do the same, they just won't be able to do it. Why not? Because you cheat!

1 Line up three mugs, placing the mug at each end mouth down and the centre mug mouth up. This is the starting position for the puzzle.

2 Pick up the left-hand mug and the centre mug. In one swift movement turn both mugs over and place them back where they were. This is move 1.

3 Now pick up the end mugs. Once again turn them both over and replace them where they came from. This is move 2.

4 Finally turn over the left hand mug and the centre mug (repeating move 1). This third and final move will result in all three mugs being mouth up.

5 Turn over the centre mug and challenge a spectator to do what you just did. Here is the sneaky bit; the mugs are in fact now laid out in the exact opposite to the way it was when you did it. The spectators won't notice this small change and will be baffled as to how you managed to get all three mugs facing up in just three moves.

hide and seek solo

While your back is turned an object is placed under one of three mugs and the position of the two empty mugs is switched. When you turn around you know where the object is. You can repeat this trick again and again. It will fool even the brightest people.

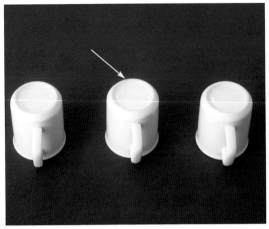

1 You will need three opaque cups or mugs, of which one must have an identifying feature on its base. Any tiny mark or blemish that you will recognize will work. Put the three mugs upside down in a row, with the marked mug in the centre.

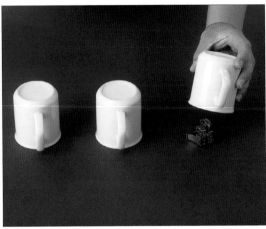

2 Turn your back and instruct someone to place an object such as a coin or watch under any mug.

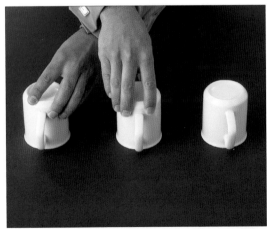

3 Tell the volunteer to switch the positions of the two empty mugs while your back is turned.

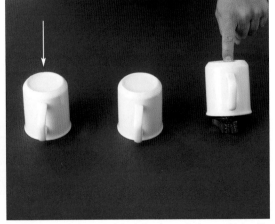

4 When you turn around, look for the marked mug. If it is still in the middle, that is where the object must be. If the marked mug is now at one end of the row, the object will be under the cup at the opposite end.

tip *You may find that borrowed mugs already have small identifying features, such as chips or scratches, if you look closely enough. If you want to use your own cups it is easy to mark one of them, but be sure to make it subtle.*

hide and seek

While your back is turned an object is placed under one of three mugs. When you turn around you are able to pick the correct mug *every single time. This trick requires a confederate, whom no one will suspect. Do not to glance at your helper in an obvious way.*

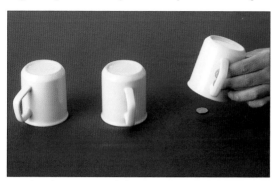

2 Your confederate watches carefully and indicates the correct mug by holding up the relevant number of fingers. In this example the object is under the third mug.

1 Place three mugs upside down in a row on the table. Turn your back and ask someone to place a small object under any of the mugs. Then turn around.

calculation sensation

Someone thinks of any number between 1 and 63. With the aid of six cards (each with a huge list of numbers on it) the magician can reveal *what the number was that the spectator thought of. It is one of the oldest mathematical puzzles, and is still very effective.*

1 Use a computer to make the six cards you will use for the calculation. These are the numbers you should type on each :

Card 1: 1 3 5 7 9 11 13 15 17 19 21 23 25 27 29 31 33 35 37 39 41 43 45 47 49 51 53 55 57 59 61

Card 2: 2 3 6 7 10 11 14 15 18 19 22 23 26 27 30 31 34 35 38 39 42 43 46 47 50 51 54 55 58 59 62 63

Card 3: 4 5 6 7 12 13 14 15 20 21 22 23 28 29 30 31 36 37 38 39 44 45 46 47 52 53 54 55 60 61 62 63

Card 4: 8 9 10 11 12 13 14 15 24 25 26 27 28 29 30 31 40 41 42 43 44 45 46 47 56 57 58 59 60 61 62 63

Card 5: 16 17 18 19 20 21 22 23 24 25 26 27 28 29 30 31 48 49 50 51 52 53 54 55 56 57 58 59 60 61 62 63

Card 6: 32 33 34 35 36 37 38 39 40 41 42 43 44 45 46 47 48 49 50 51 52 53 54 55 56 57 58 59 60 61 62 63

As long as you keep these groups of numbers together you can make cards of any shape you like. Just make sure the first number is always top left.

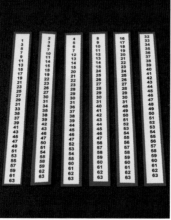

2 Ask a volunteer to think of a number between 1 and 63. Show them the cards in any order and ask them to tell you if their number appears upon it. If it does, remember the top number. Continue showing the cards, asking the same question each time. Each time they say "yes", add the number at the top of the card, keeping a running total in your head.

3 After all the cards have been seen, the total in your head is the number that the person is thinking of. In this example that number is 37.

total this sum

This is the perfect puzzle to show a maths teacher or accountant. Try it yourself and see how deceptive it is. Simply add up the numbers *listed below. If you get a total of 5,000 then you are wrong and you will need to try again.*

Write down the following numbers: 1,000; 40; 1,000; 30; 1,000; 20; 1,000; 10. Add them up and see what total you get.

tip *The reason that people get a total of 5,000 is because they begin to count in a rhythm that makes them incorrectly anticipate what the answer is.*

impossible numbers!

Write down the following number on a piece of paper as quickly as possible: eleven thousand, eleven hundred and eleven. Tricky, isn't *it! Now try asking your friends and family to have a go – you will be amazed how few people get it right first time.*

1 Did you write down 11,1111? If so then you are incorrect and should try again.

2 The reason this is so difficult to write is because of the way the number is said. "Eleven hundred" is, of course, one thousand, one hundred, but most people write a string of ones in an attempt to write it as quickly as possible.

human calculator

Six-digit numbers are selected by the spectator and the magician. Impossible as it may sound, the final total is found to have been predicted well in advance. This is a very clever mathematical trick.

As you will see, the simple formula of subtracting and adding 2 does all the work for you. The great thing about the Human Calculator is that you finish with a different number every time.

1 Give a piece of paper and a pen to a spectator and ask them to openly write down any six-figure number. Let us assume it is 2 1 7 3 4 9. You base your prediction on this number. Simply deduct 2 from the last digit and add 2 in front of the first digit. In our example, you would write down 2 2 1 7 3 4 7. Place this prediction to one side, out of view. This is written while you ask the spectator to write another six figure-number underneath the first. As soon as they start writing, jot down your prediction.

2 Let us assume their two numbers are:
217349
613948
Now you write a six-digit number underneath. Each number you write must total 9 when added to the number above. So you would write:
217349
613948
386051
Ask the spectator to write another number below yours:
217349
613948
386051
129306
Finally, you write one last number in exactly the same way as before:
217349
613948
386051
129306
870693

3 Give the spectator a calculator and ask them to work out the total:
2217347
You can now reveal that your prediction matches the total. If the last digit in the first number is either 0 or 1, subtract 2 from the last two digits, that is, 3 5 7 8 3 0 would give you a prediction of 2 3 5 7 8 2 8.

dice divination

While the magician's back is turned, two dice are rolled a number of times and the numbers totalled. When the magician turns around they are instantly able to reveal the total.

It is a little-known fact that the two numbers on the opposite side of any die always add up to 7. Using this principle, you can gain the knowledge you need to discern the total.

1 Turn your back to a spectator and ask them to follow your instructions carefully. Ask them to roll a pair of dice, adding both numbers on view together. In our example it is 6 + 1 = 7.

2 Ask them to pick up one of the dice and to add its bottom number to the total (7 + 6 = 13).

3 Tell them to roll the first die again and to add the number that lands uppermost (4 + 13 = 17). Turn back and glance at both dice. Simply add 7 to whatever numbers you see facing upwards. In our example, 6 + 4 + 7 = 17.

1089

*A number is chosen at random and is shown
to match an earlier prediction. This is an
interesting mathematical principle with
many uses. The number will always be 1089.*

1 Ask somebody to write down any
three-figure number, for example:

8 3 2

Ask them to reverse the number and to
subtract the smaller number from the larger:

```
  8 3 2
- 2 3 8
  5 9 4
```

Now ask them to reverse the total and to
add both numbers together:

```
    8 3 2
  - 2 3 8
    5 9 4
  + 4 9 5
  1 0 8 9
```

2 Try this with various numbers. It is
possible that when you reach the final
stage the spectator only has a three-digit
number. If so, the number will always be
198. Ask how many digits are in their final
number. If they say "Three", simply add
another stage. Ask them to reverse their
total once again and to add them together
again. This will ensure the total is 1089.

Because the number is always the same,
you cannot repeat this trick to the same
audience. However, you can take advantage
of this knowledge, as follows.

1089 – book test

*Here the distraction of the book is a
smokescreen, a layer of "misdirection"
designed to take the audience's attention
away from the true method, which is
clearly mathematical.*

1 To prepare, take a book and look up
page 10. Go down eight lines and look
at the ninth word. Write this word on a
piece of paper and seal it in an envelope.

2 At the beginning of your
performance, introduce the sealed
envelope containing your prediction,
and ask a spectator to look after it.

3 Perform 1089 as detailed above, but
do not ask the spectator to reveal the
total out loud. Show your book and ask
that the first two digits be used to find
a page. Ask the spectator to turn to that
page (page 10). The next digit, you explain,
is to represent a line on that page and the
final digit is to represent a word on that
line. Once the word has been found, ask
the spectator to read it out loud. Take
back the book and have the envelope
opened to show that your prediction
matches the chosen word.

tip *For an extra subtlety, choose a
book in which the eighth line down on
page 10 does not exist. When your spectator
tells you there isn't a word there, ask them
to turn to the next page instead. This little
hiccup makes it seem unlikely that you
knew which page was going to be chosen.*

double book test

*A book is chosen from a stack of books and
a page and line are chosen completely at
random. The magician leaves the room so it is
impossible to cheat. From the chosen line, one
word is decided on. The book is closed. The
magician comes back into the room and, using
the hidden powers of the human mind, is able
to write down the word being thought of.*

1 You can use as many books as you
wish, but for every book you must
have a duplicate copy hidden in another
room. Ask a spectator to choose one of the
books and note the title. Ask for a random
page number to be called out, and also a
line number. Then ask for a small number
between 1 and 10, to indicate the word on

the line. Explain that to avoid any cheating,
you will leave the room until the book has
been looked at. Once the door is closed,
simply look up the corresponding page,
line and word in the duplicate book.

2 When you re-enter the room, act like
a mind-reader and theatrically reveal
the chosen word – you could write it
down on a large sheet of card and ask the
spectator to shout out the word first
before you show your prediction.

tip *It is also possible to do this trick
while remaining in the same room. You
will need a friend at the back of the room.
They look up the word for you and write
it down on a large sheet and hold it up so
that you can see it. Everyone else is looking
at you, so they will not look behind them.*

black magic

This is one of the few tricks for which you need a "stooge" or assistant, someone you can trust to keep the secret. The stooge is asked to leave the room (out of earshot) while a member of the audience names any object in sight. The stooge returns and the magician explains that, using the power of the human mind, he will send his thoughts across the room so that this person will be able to reveal which object was chosen. The magician points at various objects in the room – maybe ten in total – and the stooge is indeed able to choose the correct object single time.

You can repeat this trick without fear of the secret being found out if each time you change the objects and the number of things you point to.

method
The secret to Black Magic is in the title! As with many tricks, the method is very simple. Simply tell your assistant beforehand that you will point to a number of items. One of them will be black. The next object will be the chosen object. This is a very adaptable trick because you can use absolutely anything, anywhere. The stooge should act as if trying to read your mind.

Left: A number of objects, which can easily be found on a desk in an office, could be used for this trick – for example, a stapler, scissors, envelope, pen, cup and adhesive tape.

temple of wisdom

The magician explains that mind-reading requires someone to act as the sender and another to act as the receiver. A spectator is chosen to act as the receiver and leaves the room. While they are out of the room, the rest of the audience decide on a small number. Let us assume it is 12. The participant comes back into the room and places their fingertips on the temples of the magician (the sender), who pretends to send the number psychically. The receiver concentrates hard, then correctly reveals the chosen number. This can be repeated as many times as you wish.

The method relies on a "stooge" whom you have briefed before the performance and whom you can trust to keep the secret. This trick can be repeated as many times as you wish.

method
When the stooge touches your temples, pass on the chosen number by the subtle action of clenching your jaw. Your temples will pulse each time you squeeze, without anybody else noticing. Try thinking of other ways to signal the number such as the position of your feet or the number of fingers you are holding open in your lap. These subtle codes can be very baffling and are great party tricks.

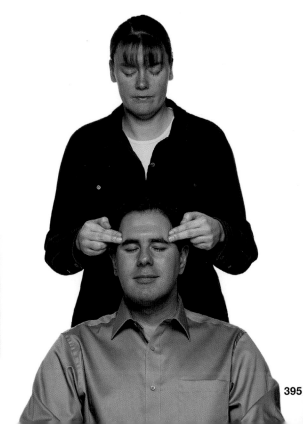

ash on arm

A card is selected and replaced into the deck. The name of the card is written on a piece of paper and the paper is burnt. The charred ashes are rubbed on the magician's bare forearm and the name of the card *appears in the ashes. There are few more effective ways to reveal the name of a chosen card. With a little imagination, you can reveal lots of other information in this manner also.*

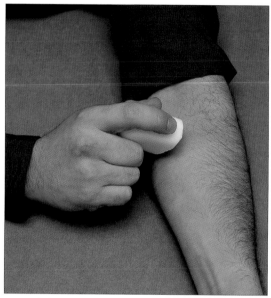

1 To prepare for the trick, slice a bar of soap with a scalpel to create a point at one end, in a similar fashion to sharpening a pencil with a knife.

2 With the point of the soap, write the name of a card on your left forearm. In our example, it is the Four of Diamonds. This writing will remain invisible until the moment of the revelation.

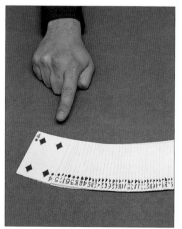

3 You will need to force the Four of Diamonds, so position that card at the bottom of the deck in preparation for the Hindu Force.

4 To begin performing the trick, start the Hindu Force (*see* Card Magic chapter) and continue cutting until the spectator stops you.

5 Show the bottom card (the force card) to the spectator.

6 Give the spectator a pencil and paper and ask them to write down the name of the selected card, then to fold the paper into quarters with the writing on the inside.

7 Light a match and burn the paper in an ashtray. As with all tricks involving matches and fire, you should be extremely careful.

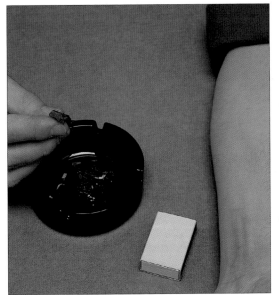

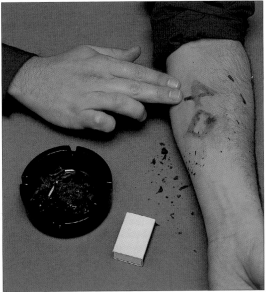

8 Roll up your sleeve (the soap will still be invisible at this point) and pick up some of the ashes in your right hand.

9 Rub the ashes on your forearm. The ash will adhere to the area you coated with soap earlier, and the name of the forced card will clearly be seen on your arm.

"X" marks the spot

A deck of cards is placed on the table in full view. It is explained that one of the cards has been marked and the spectator has to guess which one. A card is named – it can be any card at all. This card is *removed from the deck and is shown to be the only one marked with a large "X". This is a superb card trick. It will only take a few minutes to prepare, and a little practice to learn.*

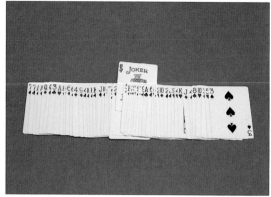

1 Prepare the cards by dividing the deck into two packets of 26 cards. Mark one packet with an "X" on the front of every card and the other packet with an "X" on the back of every card. While the "X" should be bold and clear, it should not fill the entire card, and must be positioned in the centre.

2 Arrange these cards so that (from the top down) you have the front-marked cards followed by the back-marked cards, with a Joker dividing the two packets. Square up the deck and place it back inside the card box.

3 In performance, say "Before the show I marked one of these cards with an "X". I am going to try to influence your decision and make you think of the card of my choice. The only clue I will give you is that it is not the Joker! Name any card in the deck." There are two possibilities. The first is that the chosen card will have an "X" on the back. Let us deal with this situation first.

Remove the deck from the box and spread the cards face up to find the chosen card. Do not spread the cards too wide because after the centre point of the deck you will risk exposing the "X"s. Find the chosen card (in our example, the Four of Hearts). Remove the card, keeping it face up. Spread through the first half of the deck face up, explaining that any card could have been named.

4 Turn the deck face down and display the top half of the deck in a spread or fan, subtly showing the backs of these cards. Again, do not spread too far down the deck.

5 Keep the top few cards spread wide as you reveal that the back of the chosen card has an "X" printed on it.

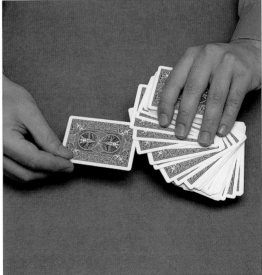

6 The second possibility is that the chosen card has an "X" on the front. Again, carefully spread through the cards until you find the one selected. The spread must be tight. Begin to pull out the card.

7 Before the "X" is revealed, turn the fan face down. Deal the chosen card face down on to the table. ▶

8 Casually spread the top quarter or so of the cards, displaying the backs, and turn the deck face up. Spread them widely, explaining that any card could have been chosen.

9 Turn the selected card face up to display the "X". The great thing about this trick is that the audience are convinced that they saw the backs and fronts of all the cards.

Whispering Jack

Any five cards are removed from the deck and placed face down on the table. A spectator looks at and remembers one. The five cards are then mixed and once again placed face down on the table. Despite the fact that even the spectator is now unsure where their card is, the magician is able to find the one selected. Whispering Jack is a great

trick to perform with a borrowed deck because the owner will know that the cards could not be marked in any way and therefore will be even more baffled. You can use any number of cards for this trick, but five seems about right. Once you read the method you will realize that the older the deck of cards, the easier this trick is to perform.

1 Remove a Jack from a deck of old cards. Explain that this card represents Sherlock Holmes, the world-famous detective. Ask a spectator to remove any other five cards from the deck and to lay them face down in a row on the table.

2 Ask the spectator to pick up any of the five cards, to remember it and then replace it. This card represents the villain. Although you do not see the face of the chosen card, you must see which position the card is taken from.

3 Explain that the detective must interview each of the suspects. As you say this, tap each card with the corner of the Jack.

4 Your reason for doing this is to create "misdirection" while you look at the back of the chosen card in order to find a mark or blemish that you will be able to recognize later. Study the cards secretively and quickly, or someone may see you staring at them.

5 Ask the spectator to mix the cards until even they cannot know where their card is. Ask them to lay out the cards on the table as before.

6 Explain that Sherlock Holmes will now interview each suspect again and find the villain. Tap the corner of the Jack on to the back of every card as before while you secretly look for the mark you spotted earlier.

7 Turn over the card – the great detective has found his man!

tri-thought

Three spectators are asked to make a choice. One chooses a number between 1 and 100, the second chooses a shape, and the third chooses a card. The magician has predicted all three choices. Tri-Thought uses the "one-ahead" principle. As its name suggests, you are always one step ahead of your audience, which is how you are able to predict their choices. This routine will baffle people completely if performed with confidence and boldness. It does require you to perform well, and is not a trick for someone of a nervous disposition!

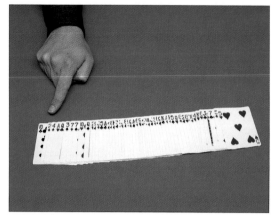

1 The "one-ahead" principle requires you to know what the final choice will be. This is why you use a deck of cards. You must know what card is on top of the deck before you begin. In our example, it is the Ten of Clubs.

2 Ask a spectator to think of a number between 1 and 100. Pretend you are reading their mind and explain that you are writing down a prediction. What you actually write on the paper is the card that was at the top of the deck (the Ten of Clubs). Fold up the paper into quarters and explain that it represents prediction number "1". However, instead of writing "1" on the folded paper, secretly write "3".

3 Drop this piece of paper into a mug so that it is temporarily out of sight. It is vital that the spectators do not see that you have incorrectly numbered the paper. The mug also prevents anyone from being able to keep track of which paper is which.

4 Ask the spectator to confirm the number they were thinking of. Let us assume they say "43". Act as though you knew all along "43" was their number and say "That's uncanny, let's try to get two out of two." Ask another spectator to think of a shape and once again pretend to read their mind as you write a second prediction. What you actually write is the number you just heard: "43". Fold this paper into quarters and write "1" on it, but say that it is your second prediction.

5 Drop the second paper into the mug. Ask the spectator to confirm their chosen shape. Let us assume they say "Square". Once again, act smug and say you will try one more prediction.

6 Now force the card, using any force method you are comfortable with. Shown here is the Slip Force (*see* Card Magic chapter). Begin by riffling down the edge of the deck until a spectator stops you, then cut the deck at this point, slipping the top card to the chosen position.

7 Offer the forced card to the spectator, but ask them not to look at it for the moment and to place it face down, off to one side.

8 Write your final prediction, but instead of writing the name of a card, write or draw the shape mentioned in step 5 – in this case, a square. Fold the paper into quarters and write "2" on it as you explain to your audience that this is the third and final prediction.

9 Drop the paper into the mug with the other predictions. Using the one-ahead principle, you have made three predictions which now match the three choices of the spectators.

10 Ask the spectator to reveal the chosen card. It will be the card you wrote at the start. Act pleased with yourself once again and tip the papers out on to the table, arranging them in numerical order.

11 Open your predictions one by one, showing your perfect mind-reading capabilities!

the big prediction

A large prediction is shown to the audience and displayed in full view. Then a card is chosen from a shuffled deck. The prediction is shown and, after some comical byplay, is proved to be correct. This effect is most suitable for a large audience. It shows how a simple idea can be *made to work for a big crowd using few props – a classic example of "Packs Flat, Plays Big". If you begin in a very serious manner, the moment of comedy – when the cards are seen stuck to the back of the board – can be very funny indeed.*

1 To prepare, make a prediction by folding a board (A1 size) in half. On one of the outer sides draw a large question mark. On the other, glue one set of cards in four rows. The cards should be in suit and numerical order, and each index should be visible.

2 The inside of the board should be made to resemble a giant playing card (in this example the Ace of Clubs). Use a computer to generate the image, then cut and paste it on to the board.

3 Take another deck of cards and place a duplicate of the prediction on the bottom of the deck, in preparation to force this card on a spectator.

4 Force this card, using any force method you are confident with. (Seen here is the Hindu Force; *see* Card Magic chapter for more details.)

5 In performance, show the prediction (with the question mark towards the audience) and place it to one side. Take the deck of cards and give them a quick shuffle, making sure the force card remains in the appropriate position. Force the Ace of Clubs, then give the spectator the cards to shuffle and mix. You no longer need the cards anyway.

6 Once again show the prediction and ask the audience if they would be impressed if the chosen card was on the other side of the board. Turn over the board and show the complete deck. Appear to search for a few seconds, then point out the selected card.

7 After the laughter subsides, open the board completely to show that your prediction really does match the chosen card. Try this out the next time you get a chance to perform for a large group of people. It is a good example of how the presentation is sometimes more important than the trick itself, which in this case is fairly basic.

impossible prediction

Three cards are displayed and a spectator is asked to choose one of them. It is a completely free choice and the spectator can change their mind as many times as they wish. The magician reveals a prediction that has been in view throughout, which matches their choice. The method to this trick relies on a principle known as a "multiple out". All three possible outcomes can be displayed as three separate predictions, but the audience is only ever aware of one of them so the prediction seems impossible. You cannot repeat this particular trick to the same audience twice, but it is one of the most baffling tricks you will ever perform.

1 To prepare the three predictions, draw a large "X" on the back of a picture card. Photocopy two other cards, reducing the size, and cut them out. Glue one of the mini photocopies on the flap side of an envelope. Keep the other photocopy loose.

2 Place all three cards, face up, inside the envelope together with the loose photocopy. With this envelope in your pocket, you will always be ready to show a miracle.

3 Casually introduce the envelope and explain you have three cards inside. The photocopy glued to the back must remain hidden. Remove the cards, taking care that the loose photocopy does not fall out, and lay them out, face up, keeping the "X" hidden. Place the envelope to one side, but in the spectator's field of vision. Ask them to choose one of the cards.

4 Give the spectator the opportunity to change their mind. There are three possible outcomes. First, let us assume the picture card is chosen. Explain that before the performance you marked the back of just one of the cards with an "X". Slowly turn over the cards one by one to reveal the "X" on the back of the selected card.

5 In this example, the second scenario would be the Five of Spades. Explain that you gave the spectator every opportunity to change their mind and that this is the card you were sure they would choose. Slowly turn the envelope over to show your prediction pasted to the back.

6 The final scenario is that the Three of Clubs is chosen. Once again explain you had a prediction, which has been in full view the entire time. Slowly tip up the envelope so that the loose photocopy falls from within the envelope. It matches the selection.

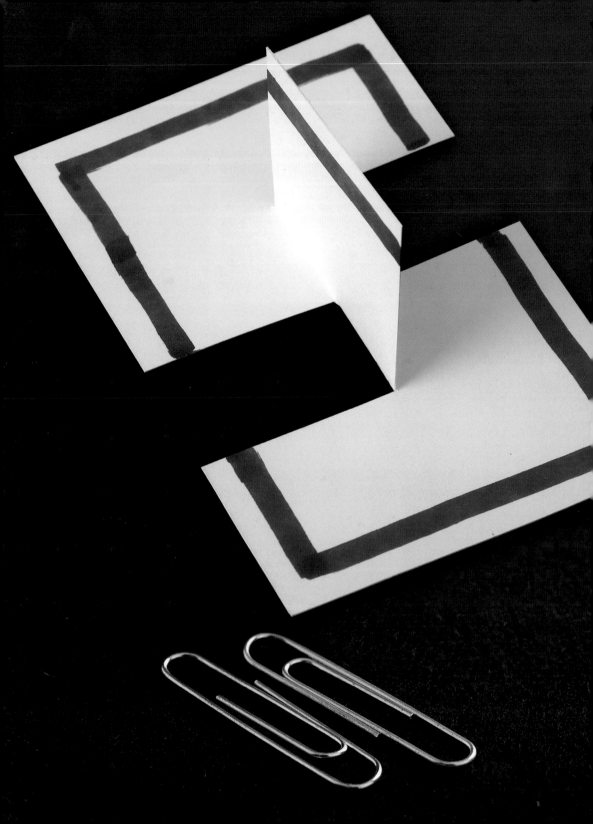

optical
illusions

This chapter contains a variety of optical illusions, including two-dimensional images that will confuse your brain, and those that require your input to make the illusions happen. Those that can be performed make ideal party tricks, or can be incorporated into a stand-up show to add an extra dimension. One thing is certain, as you proceed through this chapter you'll find it hard to believe your eyes!

don't believe your eyes

How we see things, and how we interpret the images we see, is ultimately determined by two organs– our eyes and our brain. It has been said many times that "seeing is believing", but magic tricks and optical illusions achieve their effects by defying this otherwise rational comment.

The brain is the most complex organ in the body. Everything the body does is linked to messages sent to and from the brain through approximately 100 billion nerve cells. There are two sides to the human brain, the left hemisphere and the right hemisphere. While the left side of the brain deals with all things logical, such as mathematics, speech, writing and reading, the right side of the brain tends to dominate when we are dealing with more creative processes, such as storytelling, artistic pursuits, acting, imagination or dreaming.

Occasionally, we see an image with our eyes that our brain cannot make sense of. This may be due to the fact that while the right side of the brain is creating an image, the left side of the brain is simultaneously trying to find some logic in what we are looking at to explain an apparent anomaly. This clash of thoughts seems to cause the confusion that ensues.

Above: Water sometimes has a strange effect on our perceptions of depth and distance. Here, the boat appears to be floating in mid air rather than on the surface of the crystal clear water.

We can often see natural optical illusions all around us. For example, have you ever seen a mirage in a desert? If not, you may have seen a similar phenomenon on a road on a hot summer's day.

Below: Mirages that occur in deserts are amazing natural optical illusions that have been known to drive people lost in the desert to madness. The mirage appears as liquid, but those desperate for a drink can never reach the water.

When the sun is beating down on the sand or road it heats it to an extreme level; the heat then rises from the surface and creates a layer of hot air that reflects the light in a different way to the slightly cooler air above it. These reflections are visible to the human eye, as the layer of air acts like a mirror reflecting the sky above, creating the illusion of a pool of water shimmering in the sun.

Another common optical illusion can be seen if you look at the wheel of a car when it is moving fast. The hubcap seems to be turning in the opposite direction to the wheel. And have you ever been sitting on a stationary train when the train next to you slowly starts to move? You sometimes get the weird sensation that *you* are moving backwards and that the other train is standing still.

Of all the artists who have specialized in creating optical illusions in art, the Dutch graphic artist M. C. Escher (1898–1972) was perhaps one of the most famous, using tricks of perspective to draw "impossible objects", which could not exist in three dimensions, although at first sight they seem to make sense.

In more recent times, the British pavement artist Julian Beever, who is based in Belgium, has been gaining worldwide fame as photographs of his unbelievable works of art are sent to millions via email. His chalk drawings often work from just one particular angle, but from that optimum viewing point he creates unique, original and believable three-dimensional images. Viewed from other angles, it can be seen that the drawings are in fact distorted.

One of the most famous optical illusions in art is Salvador Dali's *Reflections of Elephants*. In this wonderful painting the reflections of three swans swimming on a lake form the images of three elephants – the effect of which is quite remarkable.

Magicians often take advantage of optical illusions. For instance, the way props are painted can suggest that a box is smaller than it really is, and this means that there can be enough room to hide something or someone inside.

In this chapter you will discover some fascinating optical illusions that you can enjoy immediately, while others require some physical input from you

in order to make the illusions happen. You may well find that you can incorporate some of these simple but effective illusions with your magic tricks to enhance your presentation, but they are also great fun to try out on your friends. Enjoy the sensation of these illusions and look around you next time you are out and about to see if you can spot other natural optical illusions.

Right: Believe it or not both people are real and there are no camera tricks. This clever illusion by Julian Beever uses perspective to make the man look small when he is simply far away from the camera: the bottle is actually sketched on the ground and is around 9m (30ft) long.

common optical illusions

There are many different types of optical illusion, some of which occur naturally, and others that have been created. Certain optical illusions trick the brain into believing that objects are smaller or larger than another object of the same size. Others are images that can be viewed in more than one way. They all distort our ability to apply rational thinking to a given problem.

which is longer?

Although the top line appears to be shorter than the bottom line, they are in fact the same length. This is called the Müller-Lyer illusion, and was first made famous in 1889.

how many shelves?

Can you see three shelves or four shelves? How many you see depends whether you look from the left or the right.

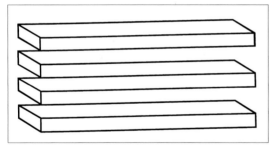

shrinking haze

If you stare at the spot in the middle of the grey haze, the haze will appear to shrink.

small, medium, large

Take a look at these three images. Which do you think is the tallest – 1, 2 or 3? Actually they are all identical. The converging lines distort the images and as the lines get closer together the images seem to grow.

connecting line

In this rather odd optical illusion it is difficult to work out which of the bottom two lines connects with the top line. Use a ruler or straight edge to check which line does join the top one.

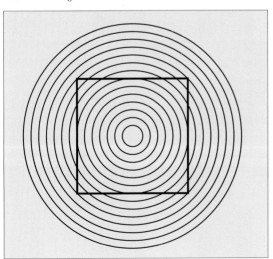

full to the brim

Is the hat below taller than it is wide? Or wider than it is tall? Both the width and the height are actually identical, although you probably won't believe it until you check with a ruler!

all square

Have a look at the square below. Are the sides parallel? Are they perfectly straight or do the sides bow in? Believe it or not all of the sides are straight. The concentric circles appear to "pull" the lines inwards creating the illusion that the sides are bowed.

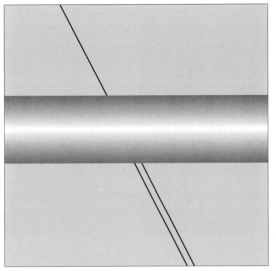

odd ball

This optical illusion is similar to All Square. The smaller circle looks as though it is not perfectly circular, although in reality it is. The rays emanating from the centre distort the outline and make us perceive the circle as irregular.

straight or crooked?

Take a look at the lines below. Even though they look like they converge in both directions, they are in fact absolutely parallel! Check with a ruler, if you like.

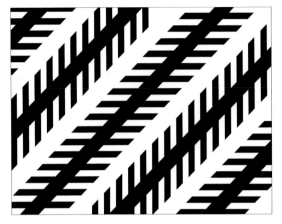

scintillating illusion

Look at this image for a couple of seconds. Do you see flickering black dots at the intersections of the squares? This effect, called scintillation, was first observed and reported in the early 19th century.

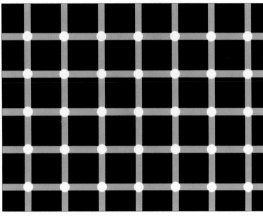

parallel lines

Are the horizontal lines parallel or do they slope? They are actually absolutely parallel, but the offset squares create the optical illusion that the lines converge and in some places bulge. This effect is sometimes seen on tiled walls or floors.

Inuit or Warrior?

Have a look at this picture. What do you see? Hint: The Native American warrior is facing the left, the Inuit is facing the right.

young or old woman?

What do you see when you look at this famous optical illusion? Hint: The old woman's nose is the young woman's cheek.

rabbit or duck?

Which do you see, a rabbit or a duck? This famous illusion is thought to have been drawn by psychologist Joseph Jastrow in 1899.

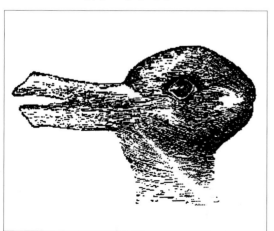

towards or away?

Is this open book facing towards you or away from you? There is no correct answer to this simple optical illusion.

shrinking pen

This fascinating optical illusion makes a pen or pencil shrink in size before your eyes. Watch yourself in the mirror and you will see how good it looks. The illusion is best when it is viewed from the front.

This is a quick and easy illusion that can easily be incorporated into a magic show, or simply demonstrated at a party. It works best if the pen is a different colour to the top that you are wearing.

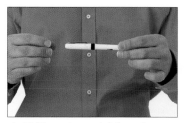 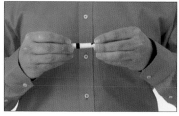 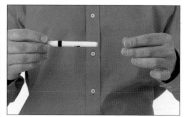

1 Hold a pen in your left fingertips so that your left hand covers just under one-third of the pen when viewed from the front.

2 Now transfer the pen to the fingertips of the right hand.

3 The right hand's grip is identical to the left hand's grip. If these movements are repeated at a speed of about four transfers per second the pen seems to shrink when viewed from the front.

floating sausage

This popular illusion is an example of a stereogram. This effect occurs when two images, one from each of your eyes, are incorrectly combined in your brain, causing them to overlap and – in this case– create a third finger floating between the two real fingers.

Hold the tips of your first fingers about 1cm (½in) apart and about 20cm (8in) from your eyes. Now stare at your fingers and bring them slowly towards the tip of your nose. You will see a sausage-like shape floating in the air between your fingers. There is of course nothing there. What you are seeing are the fingertips of each hand in reverse (as you are crossing your eyes). The result is a sausage shape where the two images overlap.

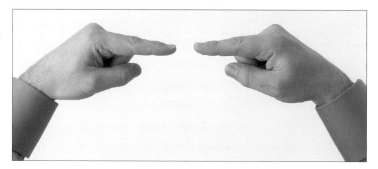

hole in hand

With a piece of paper or card you can create an instant x-ray machine that enables you to see straight through your hand as if there were a hole in the middle of it.

Take a piece of paper or card (stock) and roll it into a tube. Hold the tube to your right eye with your right hand and keep both eyes open. Now hold up your left hand beside the tube with the palm towards you, and you'll see a hole appear in it!
  This is another example of a stereorgam illusion, which occurs when your brain fuses two images, one from each eye, to create a single, combined image.

ship in a bottle

On one side of a piece of card draw a ship, on the other side draw a bottle. Simply by rotating the card you can make it look as though the ship is inside the bottle. The images move so fast that they are retained for a fraction of a second in the mind's eye, thus merging together to become a single picture. You could try this illusion using other pictures, such as a bird in a cage, or maybe a goldfish in a bowl.

1 To create this optical illusion you will need a piece of card (stock) measuring 7.5 x 5cm (3 x 2in), a pen, a hole punch and two rubber bands.

2 Punch a hole centrally at each end of the card.

3 Push a rubber band through each hole, and loop one end through the other to attach them, as shown.

4 On one side of the card draw a big, empty bottle.

5 On the other side of the card draw a ship. The images must be centred and the ship must be small enough to fit inside the bottle. If you hold the card up to the light you will be able to check that the positions are correct.

6 Hold a rubber band in each hand and quickly twist the card back and forth. The spectator will see the ship appear inside the bottle.

Emily's Illusion

I discovered this illusion while playing with one of my daughter's toys. It is a good example of how our eyes are slower to see than we think. Just like Ship in a Bottle, here the human eye sees two images and blurs them into one.

1 Draw thick parallel lines across the width of a piece of card (stock). Hold it at your fingertips.

2 Throw the card up in the air, spinning it as fast as you can. Notice how the lines seem to be going in two directions. It seems that the card has a checked rather than a lined pattern on it.

stretching arm

As you pull your arm it seems to stretch in the most peculiar way. Of course your arm is not actually stretching, but the effect is *surprisingly effective. If you reverse the moves you can also appear to make your arm shrink back to its normal length.*

1 You need to be wearing a long-sleeved shirt for this illusion. Stand up, with your left side to the spectators, then raise your left arm in front of you. Ensure your elbow is slightly bent and that your sleeve is pulled right down to your wrist.

2 Pull your left wrist with your right hand and stretch your arm just a little. Your sleeve will stay where it is but your arm will move forward.

3 Repeat this movement in short bursts, moving your left shoulder forward slightly as you do so.

pinkie down

The little finger of your left hand shrinks until it is tiny. The more slowly you perform this illusion the more amazing it is. American *magician Meir Yedid performs a whole act in which each of his fingers appears to shrink and then disappear, one by one.*

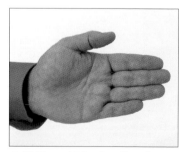

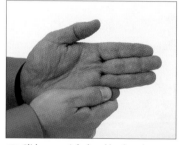

1 Hold your left hand out flat, palm facing the spectators.

secret view

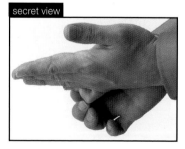

2 Grip your little finger with your right thumb covering all but the last 6mm (¼in) at its tip. Wrap the fingers of your right hand around the back of your left hand.

3 Slide your right hand back and as you do, so bend the little finger at the joint, but ensure that its pad stays in line with the rest of your left hand. Keep sliding the thumb back until you can go no further. It will look as if your little finger is shrinking. Reverse the action to stretch it back to normal size.

4 This is an exposed view of how your hand looks from beneath.

thumb stretch

You hold the tip of your thumb in your teeth and stretch it until it is more than twice as long as it was before! All the moves happen very fast and the stretched thumb is seen for only about half a second. Of course, the illusion must only be viewed from the front.

1 Hold your left thumb to your mouth and lightly bite the very tip of it.

2 Bring your right hand up and insert the tip of the right thumb in your mouth, exchanging thumb tips. Reposition your left thumb inside your right fist.

3 Now stretch out your right thumb (with a groan of pain) and simultaneously pull your left thumb out of your right fist, creating the illusion that it has stretched.

4 From the side you can see what is really happening. Now reverse the moves and finish in the same position you started in.

thumb off

You apparently unscrew the top of your thumb and then screw it back on. This is one of the oldest and most popular tricks in existence and you may have seen it done before. However, few people do it properly. When done well it is an amazing optical illusion.

1 Form a circle with the thumb and index finger of your right hand and insert your left thumb into the hole.

2 Twist your left hand back and forth, explaining to the audience that you are unscrewing your thumb.

3 With a quick shake of your hands adjust them by bending in your left and right thumbs. Then use your right forefinger to cover the area where the thumbs meet. This is an exposed view.

4 From the front the illusion is perfect. Wiggle the tip of your right thumb, which people will assume is still your left thumb.

5 Now slide your right hand along the side of your left forefinger. Slide it back again.

6 Finish with a quick shake of the hands to readjust them to the position in step 2, as you supposedly screw your thumb back on.

impossible!

A piece of card is placed on the table. It has three cuts in it, yet the spectator cannot work out how the shape is formed from one piece of

card alone. This is a very clever trick and is guaranteed to baffle most people the first time they try to work out how it is done.

1 Take a plain piece of card (stock) approximately 12.5 x 7.5cm (5 x 3in) and fold it in half lengthwise. With a pair of scissors, cut a slit from the middle of one edge to the central fold, then turn the card round and cut two more slits on either side of the first slit from the opposite edge.

2 Holding the right half of the card steady, twist the left half through 180 degrees.

3 Fold down the centre section and you will have a most interesting optical puzzle: a shape that seems impossible to form from a single piece of card.

 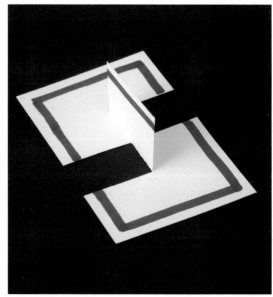

4 To add a really convincing touch, draw a border around the edge with a thick felt-tipped pen and then fold over the centre flap and draw the border across the gap too.

5 This is how it should look when it is finished, and it is ready to try out on people.

boomerang cards

Two boomerang-shaped cards are displayed side by side and it is clear that one is longer than the other. Yet, as you move them around, the *cards seem to change size so that the smaller one becomes bigger and vice versa. Try it and discover for yourself how convincing it is.*

1 Cut out two cards of identical size and shape, as shown here. Use two different colours if you wish.

2 Place one card above the other, curving down. The card at the bottom will look bigger.

3 Pick up the top card and move it to the bottom. Amazingly, it now looks as if it is the bigger one.

4 Try drawing a stick man on each card. The focus is then on the drawings rather than the cards themselves.

5 Switch the positions of the cards slowly and the illusion seems to happen right before your eyes!

stamp it out!

In this clever optical illusion the principle known as refraction, or the bending of light, is responsible for making a stamp disappear from *underneath a glass. Try it out with the props in front of you and you will appreciate just how clever and amazing this illusion is.*

1 You will need a small jug (pitcher) of water, a glass (the taller the better) and a postage stamp. Place the stamp under the glass.

2 Slowly pour water into the glass until it is almost full. Watch the stamp and you will see it disappear.

3 If you look straight down into the glass from above you can still see the stamp, so if you want to stop people from doing this place a plate on top of the glass after you have poured the water. It is now invisible from all angles.

tip *If you want to make this into a magic trick, you could prepare the face of the stamp with double-sided tape so it adheres to the glass. In this way you can lift the glass at the end and the stamp really will be gone from the table!*

east meets west

The direction of an arrow, drawn on a piece of paper can be changed without touching it, but how? Water bends light and refracts it in a *weird and wonderful way. This experiment shows just how strange nature can sometimes be.*

1 Fold a piece of card (stock) in half and draw a large arrow on one side. Stand the card up on the table.

2 Place a glass in front of the card and view the arrow through the glass.

3 To change the arrow's direction simply pour some water into the glass.

two in one

Two glasses are shown to contain liquid. Tell the spectators that the question is whether the contents of both glasses will fit into just one *glass? Although it looks impossible you prove that you can indeed fit the contents of both glasses into one.*

1 To set up this stunt you need two identical conical glasses. Fill one to the brim and then pour half its contents into the other glass. The illusion is perfect. It seems very unlikely that all that liquid will fit into just one glass but of course you know it can.

2 Slowly pour all of the liquid from the full conical glass to the empty conical glass.

3 Amazingly all of the liquid fits into one glass. The optical illusion is created by the shape of the glass. The wider part at the top can hold far more liquid than the same depth lower down the glass. It is very deceptive.

height of failure

You ask someone to guess which is longer, the circumference of the mouth of a glass or the height of the glass. It is easier to understand how this optical illusion works if you imagine a football field: it's obvious that running all the way around the edge back to where you started is far longer than running straight down the field once. The same principle is at work here.

1 This illusion works best if you use a reasonably short glass with a wide mouth. Pose the question: "Which do you think is longer, the height of the glass or the circumference?" Most people will initially guess the height.

2 You can now raise the glass on objects such as boxes, books, playing cards and wallets, until it is really high.

3 Add these things slowly, each time posing the question: "Now which do you think is longer?"

4 Each time you add something the spectators will probably still think that the height is longer, although the circumference is really still quite a bit longer.

5 You can prove this by winding string around the circumference and holding your finger to mark the length.

6 Then hold the string up against the glass to compare lengths.

clip the Queen

As easy as it seems, spectators will not be able to put a paperclip on the Queen card when you present it to them turned face down. Even when you know how the trick works it is very difficult to put the

paperclip on the correct card. This is an easy trick to make up and is fun to keep in your bag ready for those occasions when someone asks you to do an impromptu trick.

1 Glue five old playing cards together in a fan. They should all be spot cards except for the middle card, which should be a Queen.

2 Hold the fan of cards face up and ask someone to remember where the Queen is. Give them a paperclip.

3 Turn the fan face down and ask them to put the paperclip on the card they think is the Queen. It is most likely that they will put the paperclip on the centre card.

4 When you turn the fan over again you will see the paperclip is quite a distance away from the Queen.

5 In order to find the Queen the paperclip needs to be in a position you just wouldn't expect, and people certainly won't think of it the first time they see this.

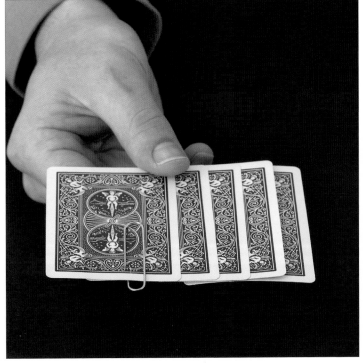

shrinking wand

Make a magic wand shrink until it disappears completely. The wand is then found inside a tiny matchbox. This optical illusion can easily *be used as a trick as part of a larger show. The shrinking principle is one that is used in many tricks, including big stage illusions.*

1 Prepare a matchbox drawer by cutting a rectangle out of the bottom. Put this drawer back in the box and keep it in your left pocket.

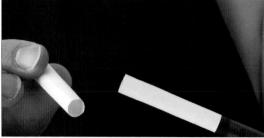

2 Prepare your magic wand by slipping a white tube of paper over one end. The tube should be the same length as the white tip of the wand and loose enough to slide along easily.

3 Display the wand, holding each end at the fingertips with the sliding tube covering the end in your right hand.

4 Slowly move your hands towards each other. The right fingers slide the paper tube down the wand.

secret view

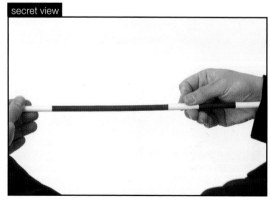

5 The end of the wand starts to go up your sleeve, as shown here. The audience will not be able to see this.

6 From the front the wand looks as if it is shrinking. Make suitable facial expressions so that it is more convincing.

7 When the wand gets really short, start shaking your hand up and down while secretly pushing the entire wand up your sleeve. The smaller motion of pushing the wand up your sleeve will be covered by the larger up-and-down motion of the hands.

8 Hold your empty hands up to show the audience that the wand has disappeared from sight.

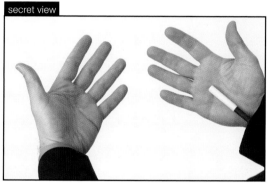

9 The wand is hidden up your sleeve and the end is hidden behind your hand.

10 To make the wand reappear, show the prepared matchbox, holding it in your left fingertips.

11 Transfer the box to your right hand and open it, making sure that the hole in the bottom remains hidden from your audience.

12 Reach into the matchbox, grasp the end of the wand through the hole and slowly pull it out.

13 The illusion is perfect. It looks as if a long wand is magically coming out of a tiny box!

stand-up magic

You will need to choose material that can be seen and understood from a distance when performing stand-up magic. This is because the audience is likely to be larger than one you would perform stunts or tricks to. So, as a rule, small props should be avoided, but as you will see from the material in this chapter, many of the props are ordinary, everyday objects that many people already own.

steal the show

The kind of performance described by the all-encompassing term "stand-up magic" could also be described as "cabaret magic", "parlour magic" or even "stage magic". Performances of this type may take place on a stage, a dance floor, in a hall, perhaps even in someone's living room, but the defining characteristic of all tricks in this genre is that they are suitable for a large audience. Often these performances make use of large props and sometimes members of the audience may be required to assist with the tricks.

Some of the tricks described in this chapter may well be suitable for close-up performances as well, but generally tricks are included in the stand-up magic category because they look better from a distance and, occasionally, distance is actually required to hide the method. Square Circle Production, for example, requires a small distance between the prop and the audience if the illusion is to be convincing.

As you begin to put an act together you may find that one or two of the items in the chapters on illusions can be included to complement your choice of tricks from this chapter. In fact sometimes there is

a fine line between what constitutes a piece of stand-up magic and what should be defined as an illusion. The key to choosing material for your stand-up magic act is *visibility*. What you are doing must be highly visible to everyone watching.

However, your choice of material will also depend on the style of performance you choose to adopt. Will you be creating a comedy act? If so, you will want to make sure there are lots of visual effects throughout the show that can be presented in an amusing way. Items such Paper Balls over the Head, Candy Caper and Crazy Spots would all be perfect for this kind of act.

If you're going to try to convince your audience that you are a mind reader, your choice of material will definitely need careful planning. Incredible Prediction, Picture Perfect and Multiplication Sensation could be ideal for this scenario. Perhaps you have decided that your act will be silent and that you will perform to music. If so, Square Circle Production, Blended Silks and Vanishing Glass of Liquid could be seamlessly linked together to make a nice little routine.

If you have the benefit of an assistant, other options are available to you. The Incredible Blindfold Act, for example, could be incorporated with one of the illusions in the next chapter, to create a smoothly flowing and varied routine.

It is almost impossible to pinpoint the beginning of stand-up magic, since the very term means different things to different people. To some extent, changing performing environments have dictated the prevailing style of magic. Nowadays the world's leading magicians have theatres in which to perform, but before variety became fashionable in the theatre magic was often performed on the streets.

An early street magician who was perhaps one of the first successful stand-up performers in recorded history was Isaac Fawkes (1675–1731). He was a frequent attraction at outdoor fairs (including the famous Bartholomew Fair in London), where his performances would have enthralled the masses. It was perhaps at this time, as a result of Fawkes' success, that stand-up magic began to catch on and gather pace.

By the late 18th century it was not uncommon for audiences to enjoy a magic act at a theatre. The Italian magician Giuseppe Pinetti (1750–1800) was one of the first to perform in such a venue when he appeared in London. In the vaudeville era, which

MR. DEVANT.

Above: England's David Devant, the first president of The Magic Circle and regular performer at The Egyptian Hall in Piccadilly, London.

began in the mid-1800s, a large number of regular acts toured the world with their stand-up magic performances, stunning and delighting audiences everywhere. The late 19th and early 20th centuries were exciting times for conjuring and the period is known today as the Golden Era of Magic.

Dozens of renowned stand-up performers have featured in magic's rich history. Among the best were Chung Ling Soo (1861–1918), T. Nelson Downs (1867–1938), David Devant (1868–1941) and Okito (1875–1963). In more recent times the names of Cardini (1895–1973), Roy Benson (1914–77) and Fred Kaps (1926–80) are just a few of those whose manipulation and magical artistry ensure that they will always be remembered.

Among today's stars of stand-up magic there are several names that represent the peak of this type of work. Britain's Paul Daniels is one of these, and he has enjoyed more than ten successful years on television. Geoffrey Durham became famous during the 1980s in the guise of his comedy character the Great Soprendo, but he is now a star in his own right and a familiar face on television and in theatres across the UK.

Above: Stand-up magician Mac King combines family-friendly comedy with sleight-of-hand and visual gags to create a show that keeps everyone entertained. He performs regularly in Las Vegas, and has also appeared on several television shows.

Left: Derren Brown regularly appears on British television. This charming and stylish performer has the apparent ability to read people's minds and control their responses, and his remarkable abilities have made him a household name in the UK.

Wayne Dobson is another of Britain's finest magicians. Although he is now confined to a wheelchair after developing multiple sclerosis, he continues to perform and receives standing ovations from audiences all over the world.

One of my favourite stand-up magicians from the USA is Mac King. He performs his show daily at Harrah's Casino in Las Vegas. His act is clever, funny and amazing. Other superb stand-up magicians include the USA's Michel Finney, Mike Caveney and Jon Stetson, Britain's premier psychological illusionist Derren Brown and the comedy magician John Archer. In truth there are dozens of world-class stand-up magicians around now and maybe after working on some of the items in this chapter you will aspire to join them. Good luck!

genie in a bottle

A bottle and a pencil are handed out for examination. The pencil is then dropped into the neck of the bottle and the genie is summoned. The genie, apparently with supernatural strength, holds on to the other end of the pencil so that the bottle remains suspended as it swings like a pendulum in the air. On the magician's command the

genie releases the pencil and once again everything is handed out for examination. Not surprisingly, no genie is found. A semi-transparent bottle has been used here so that you can see how the trick works, but you should use an opaque bottle to ensure that no one can see how it is accomplished.

1 To prepare, begin by cutting a small cube from an eraser.

2 Sculpt this into a ball using a craft knife. The ball must fit comfortably inside the neck of the bottle you are going to use.

3 In performance, hand out the bottle and a pencil for examination. Meanwhile, secretly hold the ball loosely in the fingers of your right hand. This is called a "finger palm". Your hand must be held naturally and should not arouse any suspicion.

secret view

secret view

4 This view shows how the ball is hidden in your hand. There is no way it will be visible to the audience.

5 Take back the bottle with your left hand and insert the pencil into the bottle, allowing the rubber ball to fall inside at the same time. The reason the ball is made of rubber is so that it does not make a noise as it falls into the bottle.

6 Use you acting skills and say some magic words to summon the genie in the bottle.

7 Turn the bottle over: the ball will fall into the neck of the bottle and the pencil will trap it there.

8 Holding the pencil, let go of the bottle to show that the pencil is held inside, and swing the bottle from side to side.

9 To release the pencil simply push it down slightly and the ball will drop back into the bottle. Immediately remove the pencil.

10 As you offer the props for examination, turn the bottle upside down and allow the ball to fall out into the fingers of your left hand.

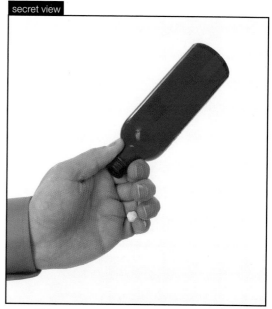

11 This secret view shows how the ball is held when it comes out of the bottle.

needles through balloon

A cardboard tube is shown empty. A long modelling balloon is inflated inside the tube so that both ends can be seen. Several long needles or skewers are pushed through the centre of the tube at all angles but the balloon does not burst. The needles are removed and the balloon is popped to finish the routine. There is more than one way of performing this trick; two of them are explained below.

1 You will need a modelling balloon, a piece of card (stock), a ruler, a pencil, a knife, adhesive tape, skewers and some adhesive glue.

2 Mark out the card into five equal sections using a ruler so that you can create a square-section tube. (The size of this tube will depend on the size of the balloon you are using.)

3 Apply glue to the inside of the last section and glue it over the first section to create the tube.

4 The finished card tube should look like this, and should be secure.

5 Using a craft knife, carefully make several star-shaped cuts in the card at different locations. Look at steps 10 and 11 to see the exact locations.

6 You can decorate your tube with a piece of coloured tape, if you wish.

7 In performance, show the balloon and the tube.

8 Blow up the balloon through the tube and knot the end. The balloon should be a snug fit in the tube but not too tight.

secret view

9 Secretly twist the balloon so that the twist is hidden inside the tube.

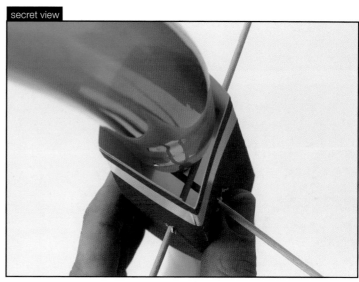

secret view

10 You can now push a skewer through one of the star-shaped cuts in the tube and out the other side. The twist in the balloon provides the space needed by the skewer.

11 Push another skewer in at a different angle. It looks as though it is impossible to do this without bursting the balloon. This secret view shows how the skewers go around the balloon inside the tube.

secret view

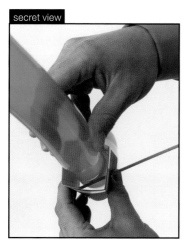

12 Modelling balloons are naturally flexible, so instead of twisting the balloon inside the tube (step 10) you can simply use the skewers to push it out of the way as they pass through the tube. This secret view shows how the skewer avoids the balloon as it enters. Notice how the balloon is pushed to one side.

13 The effect is identical. You can use either method – both work perfectly.

vanishing glass of liquid

A glass is filled with liquid from a jug (pitcher). The glass is covered with a handkerchief and tossed in the air, and both the glass and the liquid vanish instantly. This stunning trick requires two gimmicks to be made. The first is a special cloth, made from two identical layers stitched or glued together, with a disc of cardboard in the middle. When held from above the illusion of a glass under the cloth is perfect. The second gimmick is a specially prepared jug, which only takes a few minutes to modify.

1 Draw around the glass you will be using on a piece of thick cardboard and cut out this circle.

2 Stick the cardboard disc to the centre of a small square of cloth. Then stick an identical cloth on top, sandwiching the disc in the middle.

3 The jug must be opaque, and should be big enough to hide the glass inside it. Line the inside of the jug with a bubble wrap bag. Leave the section nearest the spout unstuck.

secret view

4 This is how the prepared jug looks when you have lined it.

5 To prepare, pour some liquid into the jug between the unstuck portion of bubble wrap and the side of the jug.

6 Have the cloth folded, next to the prepared jug and the glass.

7 Pour the liquid into the glass, ensuring that the inside of the jug remains hidden from view.

8 Put the jug down just to the left of the glass. Pick up the prepared cloth, open it and turn it to show both sides.

9 Lay the cloth over the glass so that the cardboard disc (known to magicians as a "form") lies perfectly on top of the glass.

10 Lift the glass from above with your right hand and move it to your left. Note how the cloth passes directly over the jug. As it does, secretly drop the glass inside the jug and carry on moving to your left. The form will hold the shape of the glass beneath the cloth. Hold it between the right fingers and thumb.

11 You should now be moving away from the table and to the front of the stage. Count to three and toss the cloth into the air. The "vanish" is startling.

12 Catch the cloth and show it on both sides before putting it away and continuing with your programme.

going into liquidation

A glass of liquid vanishes, reappearing inside a box that was previously shown to be empty. This trick was originally performed *using a spectator's hat, but the box makes a good substitute. This trick uses the same gimmicked cloth as the Vanishing Glass of Liquid.*

1 Set the folded, gimmicked cloth inside a small box and have a glass of liquid to hand.

2 Show the glass of liquid to the spectators then cover it with your special cloth.

3 Pick up the box and show that it is empty.

tip *Because of the similarity of this trick with the Vanishing Glass of Liquid you will not want to have both in the same programme. However, when you are learning it is interesting to see how the same effect can be achieved using a variety of methods. Knowing more than one way to make something happen allows you to choose the best method for any given show.*

4 Say that the glass is going to fly to the box. As you say this, mimic the flight of the glass, holding it from above, and place the covered glass inside the box.

5 Leave the glass inside, removing only the cloth, which will maintain the shape of the glass. Move away and prepare to throw the glass up into the air.

6 Throw the cloth high above you, vanishing the glass of liquid.

7 Catch the cloth and show both sides to the audience.

8 Finally, reveal to your audience that the glass of liquid really is in the box as you promised it would be.

liquidated assets

Liquid is poured into an empty cardboard box, which magically remains totally dry. Like Going into Liquidation, this routine originally used a borrowed hat. It is very effective, and uses cheap and easy-to-make props.

1 Construct a simple gimmick by cutting the rim off a plastic cup.

2 Now cut the base out of a second plastic cup.

3 When these two cups are nested together they look like one.

4 Have your special cup and a jug (pitcher) of liquid on one table and the box on the other. Hold the cup and show the box empty and dry.

5 Explain to the spectators that there is an old trick during which the magician pours water into a cardboard box without damaging it. The secret, you go on to explain, is to sneak an empty cup into the box when no one is looking. Show the cup empty and put it into the box.

secret view

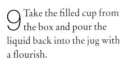

6 Now explain that you are going to do the trick without the cup! Reach into the box and remove the bottomless cup only (the inner cup). Make sure you do not "flash" the bottom of the cup to the spectators.

7 Pour some liquid from the jug, apparently into the box, but actually into the hidden cup. Suitable expressions help to sell the idea that the liquid is sloshing around the bottom of the box.

secret view

8 Take the cup and say you'll perform some magic. Put the cup into the box and in doing so, nest it inside the other one, which is now full of liquid.

9 Take the filled cup from the box and pour the liquid back into the jug with a flourish.

10 Finish by showing that the box is both empty and completely dry.

magic photo album

A photograph album is seen to be completely empty, only to be shown filled with pictures a few seconds later. This clever trick utilizes a principle called "short and long", which can be put to all sorts of uses in stand-up magic and card tricks.

1 Slice the edge off every other page in a photograph album. The first page should be cut short, the next left long, the next cut short, and so on.

2 Insert photographs into every other pair of pages, starting with pages 2 and 3, then 6 and 7, and so on.

3 Hold up the prepared album and explain to the spectators that you have some holiday snaps you would like to share with them.

4 If you open the album and flick through the pages from the back to the front, every page will appear blank. This is because you made every other page short and therefore the pages fall in pairs. The photographs are all located on the pages that are not seen.

5 Explain that the album is empty but you will use your magic to fill it up. Make a magical gesture and then open the album once again, but this time flick through the pages from the front to the back. Once again the pages will fall in pairs but now the blank pages will remain hidden and the album will appear to be full of pictures.

multiplication sensation

The last six digits of the number on a credit card are read out loud and multiplied by a number chosen by a spectator. The magician shows a prediction, which was made before the show started. It matches the total exactly.

1 You will need a slip of paper, a marker pen, a calculator, a pair of scissors and some adhesive tape.

2 Write the number 142857 on the paper, ensuring that you leave a small space between each digit.

3 Now carefully tape the edges of the paper together so that the digits are on the outside of the hoop. Use a pair of scissors to cut the tape neatly and apply it to the back of the paper only, so that the join is imperceptible.

4 In performance, display your prediction at your fingertips. No one should be able to see that the paper is one continuous loop of numbers. Place the prediction to one side or in a pocket.

5 Now take a credit card from your wallet and explain that you will read out the last six digits of the number. Pretend to read from the card, but instead call out the number 142857. Ask a spectator to enter this number into a calculator.

6 Ask your helper with the calculator to multiply the number by any whole number from 1 to 6. The secret is that no matter which number they multiply by, the answer will consist of the same six digits but in a different, cyclical order. It will be 285714, 428571, 571428, 714285 or 857142.

secret view

7 Once the answer is read out loud, secretly and quickly tear the paper between the appropriate numbers.

8 Display your prediction, which will match the total on the calculator.

spiked thumb

You cover your thumb with a paper napkin and display three long spikes. You proceed to skewer your thumb with these spikes and finally show your thumb to be perfectly healthy. This is a simple trick that will elicit a huge response from your audience.

1 All you need for this gory and wonderful trick is a large raw potato, some wooden skewers, a paper napkin and a sharp knife.

2 Use the sharp knife to cut a chunk of potato into the approximate size and shape of your thumb.

secret view

3 To begin the trick, show the napkin in your right hand, with the potato hidden behind it.

4 From the front the potato cannot be seen. Hold up your left thumb in a "thumbs up" position.

secret view

5 Slide the napkin over your left hand and as you do so grab the potato in your fist so that it sticks up in place of your thumb.

6 Seen from the front it looks just as if you have your thumb stuck up under the napkin. The illusion is perfect.

7 Show the first skewer and prepare to push it into your "thumb".

8 Act as though you are in pain as the skewer goes right through.

9 Repeat this action several more times with more skewers.

10 Finally remove the spikes, and prepare to whip off the napkin.

11 As you do so, pull the potato away unseen and at the same time stick up your undamaged thumb to complete the illusion.

tip *If you wanted to be really gross you could wrap a sachet of tomato sauce, like the ones you find in fast food outlets, around the potato before beginning the trick to give an added touch of realism.*

square circle production

For this trick you need to make a clever prop that has endless uses. It is an ideal way to make something appear – anything that will fit inside the box. It has been used by magicians for generations and is incredibly deceptive. Its great advantage is that, unlike many other *production boxes, you can use this one when surrounded by spectators. The illusion is so versatile that you can even make a giant one from which you can produce a person. You can also buy professional square circle production boxes from many magic shops.*

1 You will need several sheets of cardboard in different colours, adhesive tape or glue, a pair of scissors or a knife and some black paint. First make a tube from a sheet of black cardboard.

2 Now make a larger tube from a sheet of blue cardboard: it needs to slip easily over the black tube and to be about 2.5cm (1in) taller.

3 You now need to construct a square tube that is the same height as the black tube and that will fit easily around the blue tube. Cut some slots out of the front panel of the box so the spectators will be able to see inside it.

4 This square tube should be painted black inside.

5 These are the separate pieces you should have: a square tube painted black inside, a blue tube that fits inside it, and a black tube that fits inside the blue one and is a little shorter.

6 Set up the trick by placing the blue tube over the black tube and the red tube over everything. Place the box on a table. The surface should be black, so you will need a black tablecloth or a mat large enough to set your Square Circle Production on. Put whatever you wish to produce by magic inside the black tube.

7 To begin, pick up the red tube and move it around to show the spectators that it is empty. Replace it in position around the blue tube.

8 Now pick up the blue tube and once again show that it is empty by pushing your arm through it. While you are doing this you can see that the black inner tube is invisible, as it looks like the inside of the red tube. This principle is called "black art" and is used in numerous magic tricks. When it is used properly no one should ever know there is anything there.

9 Replace the blue tube between the red one and the black one, say the magic words and then lift all three tubes together to reveal the item.

mini flip-flap production box

This small box can be shown empty and then used to produce anything that will fit inside it. In the next chapter you will see how

a larger version of the box can be used to make a person appear. If you are good at craft projects, you could make this box out of wood.

1 You will need some double-walled corrugated cardboard to make the box. Cut a rectangular panel as shown, approximately 15 x 30cm (6 x 12in) and fold it in the middle. Cut the centre out of one side: this will be the top of the box.

2 Now cut a second, identically sized panel and fold as before.

3 Tape the two panels together to make a box that will hinge flat.

4 Cut two 15cm (6in) square doors that fit the open sides of the box perfectly.

5 Make a second, smaller box approximately 5 x 5 x 7.5cm (2 x 2 x 3in) and glue it to one of the doors.

6 Attach the doors to the front and back of the box using adhesive tape, so that they flip open in opposite directions. The small box should be inside the main box when the door is closed.

7 Load the small box with the items you are going to produce. In this case it is silk handkerchiefs, and the ends are twisted together in order to make them easier to remove during the trick.

secret view

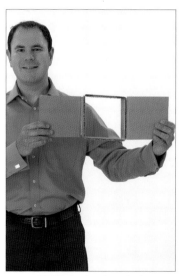

8 To begin the performance hold the box up with the loaded section on the back of the front door.

9 Open the box by moving your left hand to the left while your right hand stays where it is. This ensures that the loaded box is always shielded from view behind the door.

10 This is the view from the front. It looks as if you are showing a completely empty box. ▶

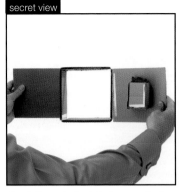

11 From the back the box now looks like this.

12 Continue to move the box all the way around, always keeping your right hand still so the box pivots around the loaded door.

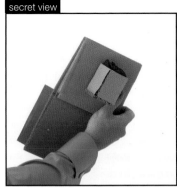

13 Grip all the sections with your right hand to flatten the box, proving that it is empty.

14 From the front it looks as if it would be impossible to hide anything inside the box.

15 Reverse the moves to reassemble the box. Now make a magical gesture with your hand.

16 Reach into the hole in the top of the box and start to produce the silk handkerchiefs one at a time.

17 If you wish, you can replace the silks in the box to finish the trick.

18 Open the doors to show the silks have vanished again.

19 Don't forget to flatten the box as this will enhance the effect.

switching bag

This clever bag can be used to switch objects, make things appear and even make them disappear. The bag is extremely simple to make,

and if you wish to make a more professional looking, longer lasting bag, you could stitch rather than glue the material together.

1 Make the bag from felt. Start by cutting out a rectangle approximately 25 x 30cm (10 x 12in) and a smaller piece just a little less than 25cm (10in) square. Apply glue to the areas shaded in black.

2 Fold the rectangle in half, with the smaller square sandwiched in between. Ensure the pieces are securely glued so the bag won't fall apart during tricks.

3 You now have a bag with two sections. The central piece of fabric should be a fraction shorter than the two sides so that it cannot be seen.

4 To hide the central section turn the top 2.5cm (1in) of fabric inside out to create a "cuff" around the edge. This completes the bag.

picture perfect

In this trick the switching bag is used for a very simple yet effective mind-reading stunt in which you appear to be able to predict what

someone will draw before they have drawn it. You could draw any common object, such as a flower or a smiley face.

1 Prepare by cutting approximately 24 small slips of paper. Half should be left blank and the other half should each have a house drawn on them. Make a larger picture of this house and seal it inside a prediction envelope.

2 Rest the envelope against a wine glass containing the blank slips of paper. Fold all the pre-drawn slips and place them inside one compartment of your switching bag. Fold back the top edges to form a "cuff", as previously described. ▶

3 Show your prediction envelope and the slips of paper in the glass. Set the envelope down on the table and distribute the 12 blank slips, along with some pencils. Ask everyone to draw something simple on their slip of paper and then fold the paper in half.

4 Collect the slips of paper in the empty side of the bag, making sure that they can only put them in the empty side and that they can't see the secret compartment.

5 Bring the sides of the bag together and then shake to mix up the papers.

secret view

6 Stop shaking the bag and open the bag. As you do so, unfold the cuff and switch sides so that the slips of paper that you wrote on are accessible and the other predictions in the secret compartment are completely concealed.

7 Fold the edges over the opposite way to hide the extra layer in the bag. Now ask someone to reach in and choose one of the slips. It will of course be one that you drew earlier.

8 Ask them to open the slip and tell everyone what it is. When they say, "A house," open your prediction envelope and show that you have drawn a house too. (Someone is likely to draw a house as there are only a few things people will draw off the cuff. Even if no one draws a house they will assume someone else did!)

candy caper

This is my favourite use for the switching bag. A glass of confetti is poured into the bag. A magic word is said and the confetti changes into colourful candy that you can share with your audience. This trick is perfect for a children's show.

1 Prepare the switching bag by filling the secret compartment with small candies. Fill a glass with paper confetti and have it on your table. Show the audience that your bag is empty.

2 Let the colourful confetti fall from a height into the empty side of your bag.

3 Give the bag a shake and simultaneously switch the sides.

4 Pour out the candy from a modest height, so that everyone can hear it hitting the sides of the glass.

5 There's only one thing left to do: offer the candy to your audience and help them eat it.

magic circles

One of the most famous magic tricks of all time is *Chinese Linking Rings*. In this simplified version, hoops of cloth magically double in size and join together. Use plain woven cotton that will tear easily along the weave – a strip from an old bed sheet would be ideal. This is very cost effective as you will be able to make up several sets of hoops from just one sheet.

1 You will need a strip of cotton 10cm (4in) wide and 1.5m (5ft) long. Prepare it by making a cut approximately 10cm (4in) deep in the middle of one end. Repeat this at the other end.

2 Apply strips of double-sided adhesive tape along the edge at one end.

3 Twist the right-hand side of the strip through 180 degrees (a half twist) before joining it neatly to the opposite end of the strip.

4 Twist the left-hand section through 360 degrees (a full twist) before joining it to the opposite end.

5 Finish the preparation by making 7.5cm (3in) slits through the centre of the divided sections on each side.

6 In performance show the hoop of cloth, hiding the prepared section in your hand.

7 Tear the hoop exactly in two by pulling the two halves apart, starting at the divided section.

8 This is the view as seen from the front.

9 When you have torn the strips the result will be two separate hoops, one in each hand.

10 Place the fully twisted hoop over your shoulder and tear the half-twisted hoop into two again. Your tear should start from the slit you prepared earlier.

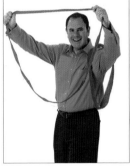

11 This will result in a giant hoop, twice the size of the original.

tip *If you prepare two cloth hoops, one regular and one with your special twists, you can invite a spectator to copy every move you make. While they keep halving the size of their hoops you can link and grow yours.*

12 Tear the remaining, fully twisted hoop in half.

13 Two hoops will form, one linked to the other.

crazy spots!

A normal, flat piece of card is shown to have four sides! This clever trick also has a great surprise ending. It is called a "sucker effect" as your audience thinks you are explaining how the trick works and then you surprise them with a twist at the end.

1 To prepare the trick you need to begin with three sheets of black card (stock), all identical in size: about 20 x 15cm (8 x 6in) is perfect.

2 Fold two of the pieces of card in half and glue them together as shown.

3 Glue this T-shaped piece on to the third sheet of card to create a flap that can be positioned up or down.

4 Cut out 15 circles from a sheet of white paper. These will be the domino spots.

5 Glue two spots on to one side of the flap, as shown.

6 Fold the flap over and glue eight spots on this section.

7 Place a tiny piece of double-sided tape at the top of this side. When you fold up this flap it will be held shut by the tape.

8 Turn the whole thing over and glue five spots on this side, as shown.

9 To perform the trick, start by holding the "domino" in your right hand so that your fingers cover the blank space. It will look as though you have six spots on view.

10 Bring your left hand up to the card from behind, to cover the blank space at the bottom of that side.

11 Turn the card with your left hand to show "three" spots on that side.

12 Grip the domino with your right hand so that your hand hides the centre spot on the reverse side.

13 Turn the card to show the audience "four" spots.

14 Your left hand hides the bottom spot on the other side and once again turns the card.

15 This time only one spot can be seen by the audience. ▶

16 Now you explain to your audience how the trick works by showing how three spots or one spot can be seen depending on where you place your hands.

17 Turn the card over and repeat the explanation for six spots or four. At the same time, secretly detach the tape from the flap and carefully flip the secret flap down.

18 All this should remain unseen by your audience, who are looking at the front of the card.

19 As you finish your explanation, turn the card over to reveal eight spots all over it!

incredible prediction

Three coloured cards are shown and a spectator is asked to choose one. You prove that you knew beyond a doubt which colour they would opt for. It is based on the principle known among magicians as a "multiple out", as the trick can end in a number of different ways.

It has been applied to thousands of tricks and is extremely effective and supremely baffling. Of course you must never perform this trick again to the same audience as they will be aware of the various outcomes and will work out how the trick is done.

1 You will need an envelope and some sheets of coloured card (stock): two orange, two blue and one yellow. Prepare the envelope by sticking one orange card to the back.

2 Put a large "X" on the back of the yellow card.

3 Insert the two blue cards, one yellow card (with the "X" on the back) and one orange card into the envelope.

4 Draw a large question mark on the front of the envelope and explain to your audience that you are about to prove that you can accurately predict a future event.

5 Reach into the envelope and remove three cards (orange, blue and yellow), leaving the duplicate blue card secretly inside.

6 Keep the envelope in view, being careful not to flash the orange card on the back of it. Fan out the three colours and ask a spectator to choose which colour they want. Make sure you give them a chance to change their mind.

7 If they choose blue, ask someone to reach inside the envelope and remove the contents. It will be a blue card and you will have proved you knew what their choice would be. (Again, be careful not to flash the orange card on the back of the envelope.)

8 If orange is their choice, turn the envelope around to reveal your prediction on the back.

9 Finally, if yellow was chosen turn all the cards around and show the large "X" on the back of the yellow card, again proving you knew which one it would be.

trooping the colours

Although you try to sort small balls into their different colours, they seem to get jumbled up in the most bizarre fashion. This is quite a *long trick to remember, but lots of practice will ensure a smooth and baffling performance. Patter will help to keep spectators entranced.*

1 You will need three coloured boxes and three small balls of each colour. Rolled-up tissue paper works perfectly. Set out the props as shown here.

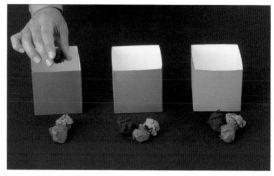

2 Pick up the blue ball in the fingertips of your right hand and prepare to drop it inside the blue box.

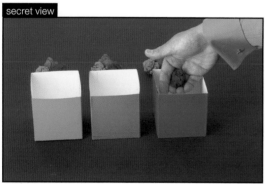

secret view

3 As your hand goes into the box and out of sight, secretly position the ball behind your fingers and remove your hand.

4 With the blue ball still secretly palmed, pick up the orange ball and prepare to place it in the orange box.

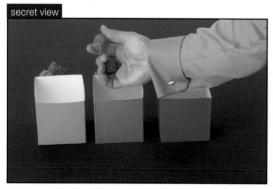

secret view

5 As your hand goes into the box switch balls and drop the blue ball inside.

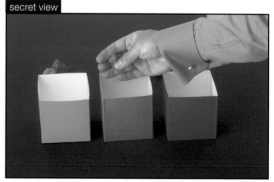

secret view

6 The orange ball now remains hidden in your hand as you lift your hand up.

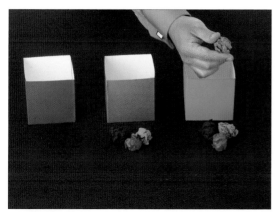

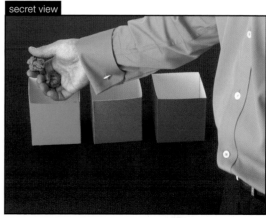

7 Pick up the green ball and supposedly drop that inside the green box.

8 In fact you switch balls once again, and drop the orange ball, retaining the green one secretly in your hand.

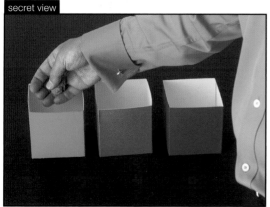

9 Remove your hand, secretly holding the green ball. Start the sequence again. First pick up the blue ball and put it in the blue box, switching it for the green ball, then pick up the orange ball and actually drop it in. Now pick up the green ball and switch it for the blue ball in your hand. The final time, you pick up the blue ball and actually place it in the blue box, pick up the orange ball and switch it for the green ball as it goes into the orange box, and finally pick up the green ball and actually put it in the green box.

10 The right hand still secretly holds an orange ball. Add this to the blue box as you tip the outer boxes upside down and let the contents fall out.

11 Finally tip the balls out of the centre box. The balls should all match their boxes but it seems the colours have mixed themselves up again.

paper balls over the head

Three paper balls vanish one at a time in the most impossible way. This trick was made famous by one of magic's greatest exponents, Tony Slydini. He was a master of misdirection and in his hands this one magic trick could entertain the biggest audiences. The trick can be done with

all sorts of objects, but it needs careful practice and rehearsal with a friend. It is a strange routine in that the only person fooled by the tric is the volunteer who is on stage with you. Your whole audience will s how this trick is done.

1 Invite a spectator on to the stage and sit them side-on to the audience. Give them a paper ball to hold in each hand and hold a third in the fingertips of your right hand.

2 Explain that you are going to put the paper ball into your left hand and that it will disappear on the count of three. Actually place the ball in your left hand as you speak. Take it back into your right hand and start the count.

3 Each time you count out loud, raise your right hand just above the volunteer's eyeline. On "Three", gently toss the ball over their head as your hand moves up.

4 Immediately pretend to place the ball in your left hand and close it as if it contains the ball. If you have succeeded, your volunteer will not have seen the ball tossed over their head and will believe it is in your left hand.

5 Open both hands to show they are empty.

6 Repeat the sequence with one of the balls the volunteer is holding.

7 And one final time. Each time it seems to be more impossible than the last time.

8 The volunteer will be amazed.

vanishing mug of liquid

A mug filled with liquid is turned upside down on a spectator's head. The liquid disappears, leaving the mug empty. Be careful not to show the inside of the mug when you do this trick, and make sure your helper receives a round of applause for being such a great sport.

1 Cut out the absorbent section of a disposable nappy (diaper). This contains crystals that are able to absorb many times their own weight in liquid.

2 Add some double-sided adhesive tape to the underside of the nappy and stick it inside a mug with a white interior. The nappy will be a tight fit so you will need to pack it in.

3 Set the prepared mug and a jug (pitcher) of liquid on a table with a sheet of card. Invite a spectator to join you on stage and sit them down next to you.

4 Slowly pour about half a mugful of liquid into the mug. The nappy will absorb everything.

5 Explain to everyone that you are going to demonstrate a science experiment with some liquid and some card.

6 Lay the piece of card on top of the mug of liquid.

7 Turn everything upside down, using a quick but smooth action. ▶

8 Place the mug and the card on your volunteer's head.

9 Slip out the card, but then admit that you've forgotten exactly how the experiment works!

10 However, as you're a magician it is easy to make the liquid disappear. Simply say some magic words and slowly lift the mug up into the air. The liquid will have vanished.

incredible blindfold act

This routine is really offered for laughs rather than as a serious mind-reading illusion. Even so, right until the end your audience will wonder how your assistant is able to tell which objects are being held up in the air while they are blindfolded. When you ask your assistant what you are holding, they should not just say, "You are holding a watch," but something like, "I am getting the sense of movement,

a sweeping motion, yes, of something moving but very small movements. In fact I see time passing slowly. Yes, the movement I see is a hand on a watch. This is a watch." Building it up like this adds a believability factor to the magic trick, which only makes it funnier when the spectators see how it was done. The success of the trick depends on how good your assistant's acting skills are.

1 Your assistant is seated side-on to the audience and blindfolded with a thick black cloth.

2 Objects are borrowed from various members of the audience and held up in the air in front of the assistant. Despite being blindfolded, the assistant is able to explain which objects have been chosen.

3 When you stand and take a bow with your assistant at the end, everyone laughs as they see a big hole in the side of the blindfold that was hidden until this point.

watch this!

A watch disappears, only to reappear on your wrist moments later. The cloth used in this trick is known as a "Devil's handkerchief".

It can be used to make lots of things disappear in a very convincing fashion and is used by professional magicians.

1 Make a double cloth by stitching two identical cloths together around the edges, leaving half of one edge open.

2 Prepare for the trick by placing two identical watches on your wrist. One should be hidden up your sleeve and the other on view.

3 Position the cloth over your shoulder so that your fingers can immediately grasp the unstitched section.

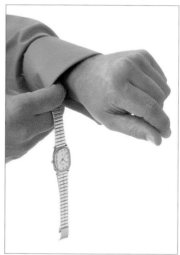

4 When you start to perform the trick, remove the visible watch.

5 As you pull your sleeve down, secretly pull the other watch further down your arm to your wrist. No one will notice this.

6 Pull the cloth off your shoulder with your left hand, ensuring that you grip the open section. Hold the cloth open to display it. The watch is held between the fingers of your right hand. ▶

7 Gather up the corners of the cloth to form a little bag.

8 Drop the watch into the secret pocket. It looks just as if it is dropping into the folds of the cloth.

9 Drop all the corners except for the one in your left hand (which is the prepared corner).

10 Show the cloth back and front. The watch is safely and totally hidden in between the two layers.

11 Finally, drape the cloth over your right arm and pull back your left sleeve to show the watch back on your wrist.

second sight

A shuffled deck of cards is placed in a brown paper bag and held high above the magician's head. Despite the apparent fairness of the shuffling procedure, the cards are named one at a time before being removed from the bag. This is a very deceptive trick and extremely baffling. You could also make an interesting presentation by pretending that you can see with your fingertips.

1 Cut a small square out of the bottom right corner of a brown paper bag.

2 When the bag is folded flat the hole is hidden perfectly.

3 You can open the bag and show that it is empty. Just put your finger over the hole and keep the bag moving. No one will notice the tiny piece missing.

4 Have a deck of cards thoroughly shuffled and then clearly place them inside the paper bag.

5 Hold the bag up high over your head and explain that you will be using a technique called second sight to establish which card you are going to pull out.

secret view

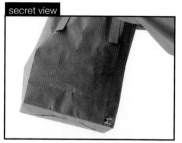

6 As you reach into the bag, glimpse the bottom card of the deck through the hole. This is the card you will remove.

7 Call out the name of the card and then remove it from the bag in order to show your audience you are correct. Repeat this as many times as you wish, each time naming a card before removing it.

Excalibur's cup

A plastic cup is placed on top of a book and a child is asked to lift it. They do, without a problem. You place a silk handkerchief in the cup and explain that you will hypnotize an adult into believing that the silk weighs a tonne and they will be unable to lift the cup. Unbelievably, they can't! You can enhance the presentation by creating a story that provides a reason or "plot" for the effect.

1 Cut a small hole, big enough for you to fit your thumb through, in the bottom of a plastic cup, as shown.

2 Set the cup on a book with the hole hidden at the rear and ask a child to lift up the cup. They do. Ask them to replace it.

secret view

3 Insert your thumb into the hole and secretly pin the cup to the book. Show a silk and place it inside the cup.

4 Now ask someone else to raise the cup off the book. They will be unable to do so.

anti-gravity glasses

Two ordinary glasses, which can be examined by the spectators, are placed on a book but don't fall off when it is turned upside down, *apparently defying gravity. This is a very old trick, which has baffled audiences for many years.*

1 You will need two plastic tumblers, two beads, some fine thread, a handkerchief, two silks, a pair of scissors and a hardback book.

2 To prepare the trick, tie the two beads together with thread, leaving a length of approximately 2.5cm (1in) between them. (This length may need adjusting to suit the size of your hand.)

3 Make a small slit in the hem of a handkerchief, or open a little of the stitching, and insert the two beads. Work them down to the middle of one of the edges.

4 To perform, show the tumblers to the spectators, then insert a silk into each one. Show the handkerchief, then lay it flat on the table. The beads should be at the edge opposite you. Place a hardback book horizontally in the centre of the handkerchief on the table.

5 Fold the left side of the handkerchief neatly over the edge of the book, as shown here.

6 Now fold the other side of the handkerchief over the edge of the book too.

7 Bring the side of the handkerchief nearest you up over the edge of the book.

8 Finally the side with the beads should be folded over.

9 Pick up the book, gripping it and the handkerchief as shown. Place your thumb directly between the two beads. ▶

10 Take one of the plastic tumblers with a silk inside.

11 Turn it upside down and position it on the book so that the rim goes over one of the beads and rests against your thumb. Notice how a small corner of silk is protruding from the tumbler. Repeat with the second tumbler.

12 Turn everything upside down, supporting the tumblers with your other hand, but then let go.

13 The tumblers are pinned in place between the beads and your thumbs, so they will remain suspended.

14 Slowly pull out one of the coloured silks to prove the tumblers are not connected to the book.

15 Repeat the action and remove the other silk.

16 Pause for a moment to add drama to the performance.

17 Turn the book over and remove the tumblers one at a time.

18 Unwrap the book. Everything apart from the handkerchief can be examined.

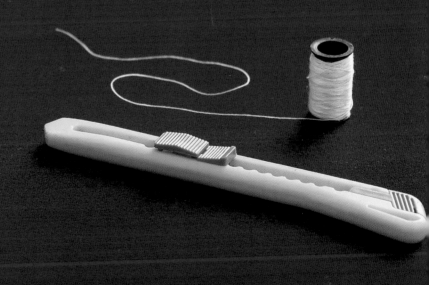

stage illusions

The term used to describe big, choreographed tricks is an "illusion". Cutting an assistant in half or making them appear to levitate are both good examples. Although this category of magic can be an expensive one to specialize in, it need not cost you much to make a few illusions for yourself. Here, you will discover the secrets of several basic tricks that look impressive when performed with confidence.

show stoppers

As a specialized area of magic, illusion pertains to the performance of magic tricks on the largest scale. Often involving at least one other person, in many cases several, and sometimes animals such as doves, tigers and even elephants, illusions usually require large props such as cabinets and boxes. They include sawing people into two or more pieces, defying gravity by suspending or levitating a person, animal or object, and causing objects or people to vanish into thin air or appear from nowhere. The scope of illusions is huge, and they have seen a resurgence in popularity in recent times, not least as a result of them being televized.

It is generally agreed among magicians that there are seven categories of illusion, namely, *production*, *vanish*, *transformation*, *restoration*, *teleportation*, *levitation* and *penetration*, although some magicians think that *penetration* is a separate category of magic, while others think it falls in the *teleportation* or *restoration* categories. All illusions, whatever their scale, are based on one or other of these seven basic elements. Some may incorporate more than one, but essentially every illusion you will ever see could be pigeon-holed into one of these categories.

Above: Although this magician is using minimal props to apparently levitate his assistant, this trick would still be reasonably expensive to perform.
Below: An old picture of a magician suspending his assistant from a broomstick at an impossible angle!

Morritt (1861–1936), Charles Carter (1874–1936), Howard Thurston (1869–1936), Harry Houdini (1874–1926), Dante (1883–1955) and many more.

The story of Harry Houdini's Metamorphosis stunt is a great example of the way in which illusions have evolved over a period of time. Before Houdini became best known as an escapologist, he performed this act with his brother, Theo. Harry would be handcuffed and would then step into a large cloth bag before being locked inside a huge chest or trunk. This was in turn bound with rope and padlocked. A large curtain would then be closed around the chest and Theo would step behind the curtain. Three seconds later the curtain would open to reveal Harry, having escaped from the chest. The rope was then untied, the box and bag unlocked and opened and out stepped Theo.

This great trick was invented by the British illusionist John Nevil Maskelyne, around 1860. Houdini gave it the name Metamorphosis and made it his own. Since then the illusion, also known as a substitution ("sub") trick, has featured in just about every illusionist's act at one time or another. It is definitely one of the most amazing illusions ever

Above: A female magician impaled on a giant screw during a recorded performance for German television. This is a good example of how effective large scale stage illusions can be. The techniques used for this stunt are a closely guarded professional secret, and this should never be attempted at home.

Illusions can be expensive to stage. It is not unusual for an illusionist to require elaborate props that must be built to suit their unique specifications, and then, of course, there is the storage and transportation of these items to consider. The magician must also take into account the number of assistants that are needed to set up, perform and stage an entire illusion show, as well as any technicians that may be required to operate lighting or other stage effects.

The way in which this sphere of magic has developed and evolved since illusion shows first became popular during the 19th century is particularly interesting. Among the first illusionists to entertain audiences with their novel spectacles were Jean Eugène Robert-Houdin (1805–71), John Nevil Maskelyne (1839–1917), Buatier De Kolta (1847–1903), Harry Kellar (1849–1922), Charles

Right: British magician John Nevil Maskelyne was one of the most famous illusionists of the 19th century, and he is credited for inventing the trick that was later called "Metamorphosis", which Houdini performed with his brother before he became a global phenomenon. In addition to his prowess as a magician, Maskelyne also invented the lock system used in London toilets, which required a penny to be inserted in order to unlock it and allow access.

created. Modern touches and twists are countless, as different performers experiment with the shape of the box, the method and the curtain, to name just a few of the changes that have been tried.

There is one act that performs Houdini's Metamorphosis faster than anyone else in the world to date. The Pendragons from the USA have taken the illusion so far forward that it would probably even stun Houdini if he were alive to see it. In the Pendragons' version, members of the audience are invited to check a box, before the magician is tied securely in a sack, then chained and locked inside the box. The assistant then steps up on top of the box and raises a curtain.

This is where the Pendragons' version of the trick surpasses all others. The curtain is thrown into the air for literally a fraction of a second before being ripped in two to reveal that the transformation has occurred and the assistant has disappeared. The box is then opened and the assistant steps out, having somehow found the time to change costumes as well.

The Pendragons remain one of the most successful and incredible illusion acts of our times. Other current major illusionists include the Americans David Copperfield and Lance Burton, Hans Klok of the Netherlands, Portugal's Luis de Matos and Italy's Silvan. Las Vegas is considered to be the magic Mecca of the world. Most major illusionists have performed their show at one or other of the myriad hotels that line the strip.

The world-famous illusionists Siegfried and Roy performed at the Mirage in Las Vegas for 13 years until one of their white tigers attacked Roy during a performance on stage on 3 October 2003. This near-fatal incident led to the closure of their show after nearly 6,000 performances during an incredibly successful 30-year partnership.

While many illusions cost vast sums of money to create and perform, it doesn't have to cost a lot to build and make your own illusion. Among the pages that follow in this chapter you will find many simple, cheap illusions that require only a little searching for the right equipment and some time to make the props.

The New York magic dealer and inventor U. F. Grant published a booklet called *Victory Carton Illusions* in the mid-1900s, which contained many illusions that could be achieved using cardboard boxes. Some of the ideas in this chapter stem from that collection of illusions.

Above: Lance Burton is one of America's foremost magicians. Having performed in Las Vegas for nine years, he went on to win the F.I.S.M., and makes regular television appearances as well as performing daily in Las Vegas.

Above: Las Vegas legends Siegfried & Roy with one of their rare and frighteningly powerful white tigers before their accident in 2003. They are among the best-known illusionists in the world.

It is unlikely that you will want to make or perform every trick in this chapter, and nor should you feel you have to. Simply choose one or two illusions that will help to make your show more substantial and give it a professional look. You will probably find that some of these illusions are more suited to your requirements than others.

You should think about who you will be performing to when you select an illusion, and you could perhaps adapt the props accordingly. For instance, you could decorate the boxes used in several of the tricks.

Whatever your preference, I think you will enjoy reading and learning how to cut someone in half with ropes, how to make someone float, and how to make your assistant magically appear on stage with you.

Right: An old Thurston promotional poster from the early 1900s. Original magic posters are very desirable collectables and often sell for vast sums of money at auctions and on the internet. This one illustrates Thurston's latest show-stopping illusion – the floating lady.

Below: South African-born Robert Harbin performing Sawing a Lady in Half. Harbin created some of the most popular illusions used by magicians today, including the Zig-Zag Lady, in which a woman's middle is inexplicably pushed over to one side during the course of the performance.

comedy levitation

Your audience will gasp in amazement when they see you levitate your assistant – and laugh too if you show them how you did it. It is generally bad practice to expose a magic trick for the sake of a laugh, but this is more of a gag than a serious illusion.

1 To prepare the illusion, cut two full-size leg shapes out of an old cardboard box.

secret view

2 Put a pair of your assistant's shoes on the ends of the fake legs and get them to hold the legs out in front of them, parallel to the ground. They will also need to lean their head back as far as possible to look as if they are lying down.

3 Cover your assistant in a sheet from the neck down. The sheet must cover the point where their feet touch the floor. The illusion of levitation is uncanny. You can either float your assistant across the stage and off the other side, or "accidentally" step on the sheet so that when your assistant moves across the stage the cloth is pulled off to reveal the method.

tip *Your assistant can be prepared off-stage and float on to the stage at any point during your performance. If they bend their knees and bob up and down it will enhance the illusion of weightlessness.*

mini me

This is another funny routine to use as part of a larger act. The curtains open, and there on the stage is a miniature, dancing, moving mini version of your assistant or yourself, depending on who is standing in front.

1 Stand in front of a table and put your arms into a pair of trousers. The waistband should rest on your shoulders. Put your hands into a pair of shoes.

2 Now drape a jacket, back to front, around your shoulders.

3 Have your assistant who is kneeling behind you put their arms through the arms of the jacket. From the front they will remain unseen.

4 If the two of you coordinate your movements you can devise some really funny things for your Mini Me to do. Even simple things like running your hands through your hair look strange.

5 Try levitating off the table by simultaneously lifting the shoes up and fluttering your hands.

6 You can move from side to side and play with different objects. This is good fun to try out.

Houdini outdone!

Houdini was famous for escaping from locks, chains, prison cells and mailbags. In this version of one of his tricks, the escapologist is tied up inside a sack but manages to escape in double-quick time. This trick is incredibly simple to learn as well as being a real show stopper.

secret view

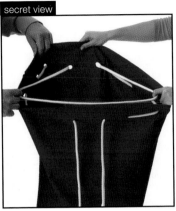
secret view

1 You will need a sack large enough for your escapologist to climb into. If necessary you can simply make your own from some cheap, porous opaque fabric. There should be a number of holes around the top of the sack through which you need to thread a rope.

2 Leave some slack in the rope, and hide this extra length inside the sack.

3 The extra loop should be equal to the circumference of the sack.

4 Prepare by arranging a screen on stage, and lay the sack out on the floor ready to step into.

5 The escapologist climbs into the sack and crouches down.

6 The assistant pulls the sack up over the escapologist's head.

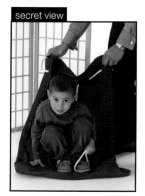

7 This is what happens inside the sack: the escapologist steps on the extra loop of rope hidden inside.

8 The assistant pulls the rope ties the bag up. (The extra rope is still held under the escapologist's foot in the sack.)

9 Now the assistant places a screen in front of the sack and waits.

10 The escapologist releases the loop of rope and uses the slack to open the sack to escape.

11 After escaping, the escapologist reseals the sack by pulling on the rope.

12 The excess rope is then slipped back into the bag, leaving the knots at the front intact.

13 The escapologist walks in front of the screen holding the sack and receives the well-deserved applause.

flip flap production

Illusions don't have to be expensive to build. Here is a way to make someone appear using nothing more than a large cardboard carton.

Now all you need to do is find a willing assistant and teach them how to perform this impressive trick.

1 Start with a tube of cardboard, simply made by cutting the top and bottom flaps off a large carton.

2 Tape a door to the front so that it swings freely in both directions.

3 Tape another door to the back, which should be hinged from the opposite side of the box.

4 Sit an assistant inside the box and close the doors. The illusion is ready.

5 Start the performance by opening the back door of the box.

secret view

6 As you can see from this secret view, your assistant is inside but unseen by your audience.

7 As you open the back door, the assistant crawls out of the box and behind the door, being very careful not to be seen.

8 When the front door is opened the box looks perfectly empty. Remember, your assistant is completely hidden behind the back door.

9 Crouch down at the back so everyone can see you through the box.

10 Close the front door of the box. Your assistant now crawls back inside the box.

11 Close the back door and make a magical gesture over the box.

12 Open the front door once again to reveal your assistant.

bowl vanish

Your assistant walks on to the stage carrying a big bowl on a tray. You show the audience a jug (pitcher) and pour its contents into the bowl. After covering the bowl with a large cloth you lift it off the tray and walk to the front of the stage. On a count of three you throw the cloth into the air with a flourish: the bowl of liquid vanishes completely! This clever illusion has been used by many of the world's *greatest magicians and although you need to prepare several gimmicks, they are easy to make and the illusion is not too difficult to perform. Its success depends on how well you make the props and how much you rehearse with your assistant. Teamwork is the key word here. Although your assistant doesn't seem to do much, in reality they do most of the work while you take all the credit.*

1 Draw around the top of the bowl you are using, then cut out a disc of stout cardboard just a tiny bit larger – 3mm (⅛in) all round.

2 This "form" needs to be attached to the centre of a large square of cloth. You can do this using double-sided adhesive tape. Attach a second identical cloth, so that the cardboard form is sandwiched between the layers. You can stitch around the edges but it is easier and quicker to use iron-on fusible bonding web.

3 Fold the cloth neatly around the form so that it cannot be seen, and place the cloth to one side while you prepare the other props.

4 Cut out the absorbent section of a disposable nappy (diaper). This contains crystals that can absorb many times their own weight in water.

5 Use double-sided adhesive tape to secure the nappy inside the bowl. Push it well down below the rim so that it will not be seen.

6 Apply a big ball of reusable putty adhesive to the underside of the bowl.

7 Position the bowl in the centre of a tray, pressing it down firmly to make sure it is securely attached.

8 To complete the set-up, place a jug (pitcher) of liquid and the prepared cloth on the tray beside the bowl.

9 In performance, your assistant walks on stage carrying the tray. It is important that no one can see the nappy inside the bowl.

10 You take the jug of liquid, hold it aloft and slowly pour it into the bowl. Unknown to your audience, the liquid is being absorbed by the nappy. ▶

11 Give the jug to your assistant, who holds it in one hand while holding the tray with the other. Pick up the cloth, flick it open and display it front and back.

12 Cover the bowl so that the cardboard form sits precisely on top of it. You must practise this move so that it happens smoothly and without hesitation.

13 Hold on to the form between both hands as your assistant lowers the tray. The tray is allowed to fall with its underside to the audience. The bowl, with the soaked nappy inside, is safely attached and hidden by the tray.

14 Your assistant now walks offstage holding the tray and the jug while you walk forward, supposedly holding the bowl between your hands. Mime this so that it looks as though the bowl has some weight.

15 Get ready to throw the cloth in the air. Count to three.

16 On "Three!" toss the cloth high into the air.

17 Aim to catch the cloth by the corners as it comes back down, and flick it out a few times, turning it from back to front to show that it is truly empty.

18 Receive a round of applause.

victory cartons illusion

In the mid-1900s a magician called U.F. Grant created many illusions that could be performed using props made of cardboard cartons. One of his most successful ideas was this one, which is used by professional magicians to this day. It is a great illusion, and you should practise hard to do it justice. You will find that the boxes last longer if you reinforce the edges with brown tape.

1 Cut the top and bottom flaps off a large carton, or make one to the exact size you need from four separate pieces of double-walled corrugated cardboard taped together.

2 Now find or make a second carton, which should be about 2.5cm (1in) taller than the first. Cut off the top and bottom flaps of this too, and cut a large hole in one side, leaving a border of approximately 7.5cm (3in) all around.

3 Flatten the cartons and set them down, as shown here. The box with the hole goes at the front, with the hole concealed at the back.

secret view

4 Your assistant is hiding unseen behind the back box.

5 Pick up the front box. This is the one with a hole in one panel, so be careful not to let it show.

6 Open it out and place it next to you. Notice how the box overlaps the one behind it.

7 As you position this box your assistant sneaks carefully inside, keeping low and entering the box as quickly and quietly as possible. If you are busy positioning the box at the same time, any extra movement of the box as the assistant enters will be unnoticed.

8 Pick up the remaining box, open it and hold it up high to show the audience that it is empty.

9 This is how things look from the back at this stage.

10 Place this second box over the first. Once you have done this you can even spin both boxes right round, as long as you are careful not to lift them off the ground.

11 Finally, make a magical gesture and your assistant pops up into view.

cutting a person in two

One of the most famous illusions of all time is Sawing a Lady in Half. The first version was invented by P.T. Selbit and it was first performed in the early 1920s. In this version two ropes pass through the middle of a volunteer from the audience.

1 Prepare a pair of 2m (6ft) ropes by loosely tying them together in the centre with a loop of cotton thread.

2 Invite an audience member on to the stage to be your assistant. Give them one end of the ropes while you hold the other and tug them to prove their solidity.

3 Invite another audience member on to the stage. As they approach, readjust the ropes in your hand by exchanging the ends so that you hold the centres of both and they are looped back on themselves but held together by the thread.

4 Pass the prepared rope behind the volunteer and hand the ends to your helper. This secret view from the back clearly shows what is really happening with the ropes.

5 Bring one rope from either side in front of the volunteer and tie a single overhand knot, apparently making things even more secure.

6 This is the view of what is going on as seen from the back.

7 On a count of three, pull the ropes. The thread will snap and it will seem as if the ropes have passed right through your volunteer's body. (The reason this works is that you switch the ends at step 3 and then switch them back again by tying the knot at step 5.)

metamorphosis

This is another of the most famous illusions in the world. This simple version is a very serviceable alternative for the aspiring amateur illusionist. Like the Victory Cartons Illusion, it was introduced to the magical fraternity by U.F. Grant. Make sure that you work against a dark backdrop to avoid light spilling through the back of the box and showing through the front air holes.

1 You will need a cardboard box big enough for you to get inside. Cut out eight air holes, four in the front and four in the back. Show the box to your audience.

2 Your assistant steps into the box. The assistant must be equipped with a retractable craft knife in their pocket. ▶

3 Close the lid of the box and set about sealing it up with parcel tape, explaining what you are doing to the audience.

4 While you are sealing the top of the box, your assistant cuts through the back panel, cutting between the air holes. The noise of the tape being applied and you talking to the audience will cover the noise of your assistant cutting.

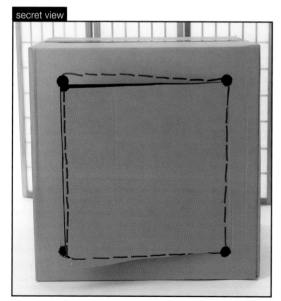

5 Arrange a screen in front of the box. From behind you can see that the hole has already been cut along three edges in the back by the assistant inside the box.

6 Stand in front of the screen and tell your audience to watch carefully. Talking will give your assistant more time, and will also help to cover any noises they may inadvertently make.

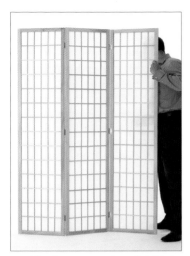

7 After about 30 seconds, walk behind the screen.

8 As you do so your assistant should be crawling out of the box.

9 Without hesitation the assistant walks round to the front of the screen as you crawl into the box.

10 The screen is immediately pushed to one side and your assistant starts to pull the tape off the box.

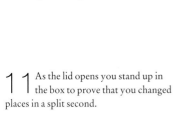

11 As the lid opens you stand up in the box to prove that you changed places in a split second.

tip over box

This illusion is also used by magicians the world over and is incredibly deceptive. A cardboard box is shown to be empty, but *the top bursts open and the magician's assistant jumps out. You can make this style of box any size and use it to make any object appear.*

1 Cut off the top and bottom flaps of a large carton if you have one, or make your own to the size you need by taping four sheets of double-walled corrugated cardboard together.

2 Cut a cardboard panel to act as a lid, and tape it on so that it will open and close with ease.

3 Cut another cardboard panel and tape it to the bottom. It is hinged along the edge that is diagonally opposite the hinge of the lid to form a flap that folds inwards.

4 Tape a strip of cardboard along the bottom edge opposite the hinge of the flap, as shown here.

5 Securely fasten a handle to the flap using tape, so that it will be on the inside of the box, and the box is ready.

secret view

6 To perform the illusion have your assistant already inside the box, with the secret flap folded up inside it.

7 Tip the box forward until the front panel reaches the floor. Your assistant stays still and holds on to the handle on the flap. The lower front edge does not move at any time.

8 From the front no one can see that your assistant is now behind the box.

9 Open the lid, which is now at the front, so that the audience can see that the box is empty.

10 This is the view of what is happening from the back.

11 Close the lid and tip the box upright again. Your assistant will now be back inside the box. ▶

12 Open the lid of the box at the top and build the suspense.

13 Your assistant makes their big entrance by jumping up and out of the box.

out of thin air

If you want to make an impact at the start of your show, this is a great way to achieve it. You show a large cloth and with a shake your assistant appears underneath. The whole illusion takes only seconds *to perform but the element of surprise makes it very impressive. No one is expecting a person to appear. This trick will work with any large prop as long as it completely hides your assistant.*

secret view

1 Your assistant will need to hide behind a large prop covered with a cloth. If your act includes any of the illusions in this chapter that utilize a carton, that would work well.

2 Say to the audience, "I bet you're wondering what's underneath this cloth?"

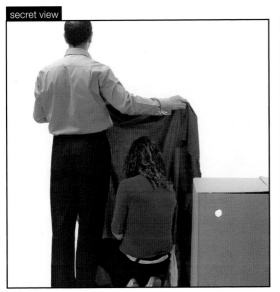

3 Pull the cloth off the prop with both hands and bring it in front of you. Position yourself so that the edge of the cloth just overlaps the edge of the box when viewed from the front. Your assistant quickly and silently crawls behind the cloth. Continue your patter, saying, "It's a box."

4 Now you raise the cloth and as you do so your assistant stands behind it.

5 This is how it looks from behind. Raise the cloth only for an instant: the faster you can make the raising and lowering of the cloth the better this illusion will look.

6 Lower the cloth with a magical flourish and say: "And this is my lovely assistant!"

putting on a show

Learning all the stunts, magic tricks and illusions in this book is one thing, but putting them together to create a show is something else entirely. Here you will find a number of things to consider before you begin this exciting task. With a little planning and a lot of rehearsal, you will soon learn to create a customized act for your next audience.

practical considerations

So, you've worked hard to learn a selection of the tricks in this book and have practised and rehearsed until you know your routines back to front. Have you noticed anything missing? An audience of course! Practising magic in the privacy of your own home or in front of close family or friends is good fun, but it doesn't compare to the thrill of performing in front of a live audience who are entertained, amazed and baffled by your skills.

Putting together an act or a show involves some careful planning, and there are several things you will need to consider before you can start to put a routine together. While it is not the intention here to cover all aspects of performance, you will find a number of useful tips to guide you as you start to plan your first big show.

When planning your routine you must be sure to take into account the kind of audience that will be watching. Will you be performing at a children's party or in a school? If so, how many children will be there? How old will they be? Will there be a mix of adults and children? Maybe your audience will be made up of adults only. Will you be the only act, or will there be other performers?

Why are these considerations so important? Well, children are usually entertained by things that are colourful and simple to follow, such as Blended Silks, Square Circle Production or the Unburstable Balloon. While these tricks are also entertaining for adults, an older audience also likes to see some things that are a little more sophisticated and may prefer an item such as Escapologist or Watch This! You will also need to assess and modify your patter so that is appropriate for the audience. You should avoid adult humour or subtle puns when performing to children.

The next consideration is the amount of space that will be available to you. If you are performing on a stage in a hall, for example, you can plan to include a few large-scale illusions, such as the Tip Over Box or Comedy Levitation. However, these may prove difficult or impossible if you are performing in someone's living room, where the limited space will restrict the material you can choose to include in your act.

Below: A magician entertains a large audience of children and adults at a school. Audiences of a mixed age group can be the hardest to entertain since they have different requirements.

There is no right or wrong length of time for a magic show, but you should remember the old showbiz saying: "Always leave the audience wanting more." It is far better to perform a really good 10-minute act than to work your way through a 20-minute sequence that is long winded, drawn out and has the potential to bore your audience.

If this is the first time you have put a show together, working out an act that lasts 10–15 minutes would be a good starting point. This doesn't sound like a long time, but when you are performing in front of an audience you will find that it feels quite long enough! As you build up confidence and get to know more and more material you can expand the act and make it last 20–30 minutes.

Unless you are putting on a whole evening's show, this length of act is likely to be as much as you will ever need to perform. Of course, there is nothing wrong with creating several acts so that you can choose the best one for each event, and you should always have something to fall back on should anything go wrong, such as a prop breaking at the last minute or an assistant becoming unavailable.

How should your act be shaped? It is good practice and, indeed, vital to have a strong beginning and a strong ending, and any act must be constructed with this in mind, although the bits in between are also important. Very often audiences decide whether they like an act within the first minute at most, so your opening trick or your arrival on the stage must pique their interest and create a strong impact. If you are performing for your friends and family it is likely that they will be a much more forgiving audience: as they know you anyway you won't have the additional pressure of making the spectators warm to you quickly. It may be an idea to either perform to them the first time, or at least use them as a test audience for your dress rehearsal. They will then be able to give you feedback before you face an audience of strangers.

What will you wear? Just as the contents of your show have to be well prepared, you also have to think about your costume. You may wish to don traditional evening dress, or perhaps you want to look a little more modern and opt for a more casual outfit. Either way, make sure you never look scruffy and are always presentable. You can be trendy and fashionable without looking a mess.

Above: Never underestimate the importance of first impressions and your overall appearance. A snazzy jacket, shirt and tie will complete your image and help to make you look more professional. Your outfit should reflect your individual style, however, so if your act is "in character", you will need to fit a costume that is suitable for such a character.

If you plan to send out invitations to your show, it is a great idea to set the tone and impress your audience by taking the trouble to create a magical looking invitation. You can do this very easily on a home computer by simply printing an area of black on a sheet of paper, as shown in the pictures below, and then printing the details of the show on the other side of the paper. When the paper is rolled up and secured with one or two rubber bands (preferably small black ones), the finished invitation will look like a magic wand.

Adding music before, during and after your act can help to give another dimension to the show. An exciting piece of music that builds to a crescendo before you make your big entrance is an easy way to get the audience really excited. If you are performing a mind-reading trick, some spooky music in the background can help to add a surreal and dramatic atmosphere as you probe your spectator's thoughts. You could enlist the help of a friend to start and stop the music for you, but with many mini-disc and MP3 players you can use a remote control to do it yourself.

magic wand invitations

These invitations are simple to make, impressive and functional. You could also try making other themed invitations, such as cutting the shape of a rabbit popping out of a top hat from paper and writing on one side, or making large playing cards out of card (stock) and paper and writing or printing on one side. Allow your creativity to blossom and apply your own ideas according to the type of show.

1 On a home computer, print an area of black on a sheet of paper, as shown, and then print the details of the show on the other side of the paper.

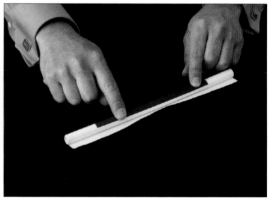

2 Roll up the paper and secure with one or two rubber bands (preferably small black ones).

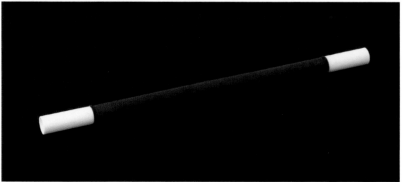

3 The finished invitation will look just like a magic wand.

setting the stage

Working out how you are going to move about the stage and where your props should be placed is known as blocking. *Make sure that during your rehearsals you are clear where all your props are situated, and that you can easily find them when you need them and have a place to store them after each trick is over. It is well worth having a dress rehearsal before the show.*

Screen used to hide props 'off-stage'. Ideal for props that are not to be used until later in the act.

Bowl Vanish

Victory Cartons Illusion (assistant hidden behind box).

Table set with ropes and hanky for Escapologist, book for Coin Cascade (extra coins in your pocket), Production Tube and silks for Blended Silks (Version 1).

It is considered bad practice to turn your back on the audience (unless it is a necessary part of the action). You should rehearse your moves around the stage so that you know where you will be at any given moment, and how you will get to the props you need for each trick without turning away from the spectators. This is a subtle but very important piece of advice that will help you look more professional when you are performing.

Finally, when looking at your audience ensure that you make eye contact with them. Try to look at people near the front as well as the middle, sides and back of your audience. It is all too easy to fall into the trap of looking at the same person or area throughout your show and this will distance you from the rest of the audience. Your performance should be an inclusive, interactive experience and you will want people to feel they are part of the show and that you know they are there.

Above: It's show time! Here the stage is set with every prop necessary for the act, so that you know exactly where everything is and where it is going to be placed once you have finished with it. You should always do a dress rehearsal with your assistant, if you are using one, before the show. This not only helps to settle any nerves, but means you can check everything is in place in advance.

Remember to smile and look as though you are enjoying yourself. You may well be nervous but don't let your audience see that. If you are unsure of your performance then the audience will pick up on these feelings, which will make it an uncomfortable viewing experience for them. An audience feels comfortable and relaxed when a performer is clearly in control and "at home" on the stage, so this is how you need to appear. When putting together a show there is much to think about apart from the actual tricks themselves. To give a really professional performance you will need to plan and practise your routine or act with all of the above factors in mind.

a sample act

Let's take a look at a sample show that can be created from the material in this book. This simple act will last for about 15 minutes.

After suitable music that builds to a crescendo, you make your entrance and greet your excited audience. A new music track begins – there is eager anticipation as you begin to execute your first miracle. After showing that two cardboard boxes are empty you magically produce your assistant. The crowd goes wild. The Victory Cartons illusion was a sensation.

The music continues and, as the applause subsides, your assistant ties your hands firmly together with a handkerchief in preparation for Escapologist. A long piece of rope is threaded between your arms and you prove you're a modern-day Houdini when the rope seems to melt through the handkerchief that binds your hands together. The music ends and you both take a quick bow to signify the end of that particular section of your act.

Your assistant walks off behind the screen and you thank your audience for their generous applause. Your carefully scripted patter leads you to your next miracle, Blended Silks. As you finish this neat little trick, you pass the props off-stage to your assistant in order to clear the stage of any unwanted items.

Above: Your assistant magically appears inside the Victory Cartons. This makes a great opening to an act as it introduces your assistant, as well as immediately engaging the audience with a professional-looking trick.

You invite an audience member on to the stage and perform Coin Cascade. Even though it is a close-up trick, this particular routine works very nicely for a larger audience. You are pleasantly surprised and head into your closing trick – the Bowl Vanish. Your assistant walks on-stage with the appropriate props as your music begins to kick in once more. You pour the liquid into the bowl. You pick up the bowl, walk to the front of the stage and throw the bowl high into the air. As it vanishes the music reaches its final dramatic ending, as does your act.

You take a well-deserved bow and then invite your assistant back to the stage to join you in yet another.

Your first show has been hard work but the adrenalin rushing around your body makes you feel great and you know you can't wait to perform another show soon. Your journey in magic has well and truly begun!

Left: In a demonstration of escapology you magically release yourself from the rope which is trapped around your tied wrists. Houdini would be proud of you! This is a good trick for getting the audience involved, as you not only bring one of them up on stage with you, but the rest of the audience can see from their reaction how impressive the trick is.

sample running orders

With so many tricks to choose from, it can be difficult to decide which to perform. You should consider all of the points raised in this chapter, such as the age of the audience, the venue and so on, before finally deciding which tricks are suitable. You must also, of course, be confident that you are able to perform the tricks in a convincing manner. This means that you must practise them many times, both individually and in a running order, until you have perfected them and are confident of your patter.

stand-up show 1	stand-up show 2	close-up show
Victory Cartons Illusion	Watch This!	Coin through Coaster
Houdini Outdone	Obedient Hanky	Vanishing Coin in Handkerchief (signed)
Cutting a Person in Two	Escapologist	Take Cover
Crazy Spots	Needles through Balloon	Love Match
Second Sight	Spiked Thumb	Spiked Thumb
Incredible Prediction	Coin Cascade	Marked Coin in Ball of Wool
Picture Perfect	Anti Gravity Glasses	
Multiplication Sensation	Candy Caper	
Magic Circles	Blended Silks (version 1)	
Bowl Vanish	Card on Wall	

glossary

There are many specialist words used within the magic fraternity. The meanings of some of the most common terms are explained here.

Book test
A word or words chosen at random from a book which are revealed by the magician either as a prediction or through thought transference.

Cabaret magic
A stand-up act, generally viewed from at least three sides and for a large crowd of people.

Card control
The technique of keeping track of one or several cards and secretly shifting them to another position in the deck.

Close-up magic
The performance of magic shown very close to the audience, often using small, everyday items.

Deck
A pack of playing cards.

Double lift
The showing of two cards held as one.

Effect
A description of the overall trick.

Above: Double Lift – two cards are in the right hand.

False cut
The appearance of a regular cut which leaves the deck or part of the deck in exactly the same order as at the beginning.

False shuffle
A shuffle that does not change the order of one or more cards. Also used to reposition particular cards to other locations in the deck.

Finger break
A small gap between the cards held by a finger (or thumb), often, but not exclusively, used to keep control of a certain card or packet of cards in the deck.

Flourish
A showy and often attractive display of skill.

Force
The action of influencing a spectator's choice, often pertaining to cards. The spectator believes that their choice was fair.

Gimmick
Sometimes known as a "fake". A secret tool employed, often unseen, to cause the trick to work.

Glimpse
To take a secret look at a card in the deck.

Illusion
Generally refers to large-scale magic tricks designed for a large audience.

Key card
A card used to help locate a selected card.

Lapping
A technique used to secretly and quickly ditch objects in the lap. Always performed at a table while

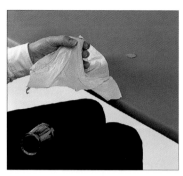
Above: Lapping a glass to make it disappear.

the magician is seated and often used as a method for the disappearance of an object.

Manipulation
Any form of manual skill, but usually associated with the highly skilful performance of sleight-of-hand on stage, such as the production of playing cards.

Mentalist
The name given to a performer who specializes in mind-reading and other psychic effects.

Method
The secret workings of a trick that need to be learned and practised before it can be performed to an audience.

Misdirection
The skill of focusing the minds or eyes of the audience on a particular point while secretly doing something else.

Optical illusion
An image that is distorted to create an untrue picture of what is being viewed, thus deceiving the eye. The impossibility of the optical illusion leads people to disbelieve or misinterpret what their eyes are showing them.

Overhand shuffle

A popular way to shuffle cards. By squeezing the front and back card every time you lift a batch to "shuffle" them, you ensure that the chosen card stays at the back of the pack.

Packet

A small group of cards that is often, but not always, separated from the main section of the deck.

Palming

The secretion of an object in the hand. There are several different palms (Back Palm, Classic Palm, Finger Palm, etc). They do not necessarily use the palm of the hand itself.

Patter

The banter that accompanies the performance of a trick. This is a very important aid to "misdirection".

Pinch vanish

A technique used to make an object disappear from view by pinching it so it is hidden by your fingers.

Practice

The rehearsal required to make a performance appear slick and without mistakes.

Above: Pinch vanishing a coin.

Above: Trimming an Ace to make a short card.

Presentation

The overall term describing the trick, patter and style given to a routine.

Pull

A gimmick made from elastic that pulls an object out of sight.

Routine

One whole trick or a series of tricks which lead from one to another.

Short card

A card that has been trimmed slightly shorter than the others so that it can be located immediately. Often used as a key card.

Silk

A piece of silk fine enough to be folded and squeezed into a small space and thus easily hidden. Silks come in all different sizes and colours.

Sleeving

The secret action of hiding an object in the sleeve.

Sleight-of-hand

The secret manipulation of an object. Often associated with close-up magic, but also very relevant to larger acts.

Slide

A tube that is used to position an object in an impossible location.

Stage magic

An act performed on stage, often using large props. Similar to cabaret magic, which was a development of stage magic after the closure of many music halls and theatres at the end of the vaudeville era.

Stooge

A secret confederate in the audience who helps to make the magic happen.

Sucker trick

An effect that seems to let the audience in on the secret and then turns the tables at the last second. Also refers to a trick that appears to have gone wrong but is later proved to be part of the routine.

Time misdirection

The technique of leaving time in between a secret move and the subsequent moment of magic.

Torn and restored (T&R)

When a magician tears an object, such as a card, into small pieces and then "restores" it, making it whole again.

Vanish

To make an object disappear.

Above: A slide can be used to position an object.

where to learn more

If you have enjoyed reading this book and would like to learn more, I highly recommend the following courses of action.

Visit your local library

Here you will find a number of magic books, which will range from those covering basic skills to ones suitable for an intermediate level. Using libraries is a cost effective and convenient way to learn more about the art of magic.

Join a local magic society

Once you have a basic grasp of magic and can perform a short act you will be able to prove your interest in magic is genuine and, therefore, may be eligible for membership of a local magic club or society. There are hundreds of these all over the world in practically every country, and you may be surprised at how close your local gathering is.

Magic clubs and societies give you the opportunity to regularly meet local people with a common interest, and very often you will be able to share and trade secrets, thus greatly expanding your magical knowledge. You may also find your society has a lending library which contains a more specialized selection of magic books that are not always available in public libraries.

Above: Coin in Bread Roll.

Join a magic organization

You may wish to join a more established or larger network of magicians. There are several national and international magic societies and clubs that may be of interest. Many will hold regular conventions and most will provide a regular newsletter or magazine, which will keep you up to date with everything related to that society.

Some of the biggest and most famous are listed below:

I.B.M (International Brotherhood of Magicians) www.magician.org

S.A.M (Society of American Magicians) www.magicsam.com

The Magic Castle, Hollywood, USA. www.magiccastle.com

The Magic Circle, London www.themagiccircle.co.uk

The Young Magicians Club www.theyoungmagiciansclub.co.uk

Magazines

There are many specialized magazines that you can subscribe to. These contain the latest news from the world of magic, interviews with some of the biggest names, magic tricks for you to learn, reviews of magic shows and magic tricks, as well as adverts showcasing the latest miracles you can buy.

In the UK there are two main magazines:

ABRACADABRA (The World's Only Magical Weekly)
Unit 3
Guild Road
Bromsgrove B60 2BY
www.davenportsmagic.co.uk

Above: Ribbon Spread and Turnover.

Magicseen
Damson Cottage
South End
Seaton Ross
York YO42 4LZ
www.magicseen.co.uk

The two major US publications that are read by thousands of magicians worldwide are:

MAGIC (The Magazine for Magicians)
6220 Stevenson Way
Las Vegas, NV 89120
www.magicmagazine.com

GENII (The Conjurors' Magazine)
4200 Wisconsin Ave. NW
Suite 106-384
Washington, DC 20016
www.geniimagazine.com

Above: Rose to Silk.

magic shops

All the magic shops listed allow you to buy online, although nothing can match the experience of actually visiting a magic shop in person. As well as being able to purchase the latest range of professional magic and magic-related publications, the sales assistants behind the counter will often be able to give you advice and demonstrations that would not be available if you buy on the internet.

Argentina
Bazar De Magia
Tacuari 237 -3er Piso
(1071) – Buenos Aires
www.magia.com.ar

Australia
Taylor's Magic Shop
11 Spring St, Chatswood
Sydney NSW 2067
www.taylorsmagicshop.com

Belgium
Mephisto Magic
Kloosterstraat 20
B-8510 Kortrijk (marke)
www.mephisto-magic.com

Canada
Morrissey Magic Ltd.
2477 Dufferin Street
Toronto M6B 3P9
www.morrisseymagic.com

Denmark
Pandoramagic
Damparken 30, 2th DK-2610 Rødovre
www.pandoramagic.dk

France
Mayette Magie Moderne
8 rue des Carmes, 75005 Paris
www.mayette.com

Germany
Zauber Kellerhof
Am Buschhof 24
53227 Bonn (Oberkassel)
www.zauberkellerhof.de

Stolina Magie
Hans-Böckler-Str. 50, 59302 Oelde
www.stolina.de

Hong Kong
Chu's Magic Company Limited
11/F, Flat 1-5
61-63 Au Pui Wan Street
Fo Tan, Shatin N.T. Hong Kong
www.chusmagic.com

Italy
La Porta Magica
Viale Etiopia 18, 00199 Roma
www.laportamagica.it

The Netherlands
Monnikendam
Gedempte Raamgracht 1-9
2011 WE Haarlem
Holland
www.monnikendam.nl

Spain
Magia Cadabra
Calle Navarros 7, Seville
www.magiacadabra.com

Sweden
Gycklaren Magic Marketing AB
Magic Center, Åldersstigen 2
Halmstad, Sweden
www.gycklaren.com

El Duco's Magic
Box 310 52, 200 49 Malmö, Sweden
www.el-duco.se

Switzerland
ZauberLaden Zurich
Hoerbi Kull
Rieterstr. 102
CH 8002 Zurich
www.zauberladen.com

UK
Davenport's Magic
7 Charing Cross Underground Arcade
The Strand, London WC2N 4HZ
www.davenportsmagic.co.uk

Above: Magnetic Cards.

International Magic,
89 Clerkenwell Road
London EC1R 5BX
www.internationalmagic.com

Alakazam Magic
Unit 113, Ellingham Ind. Estate
Ellingham Way, Ashford, TN23 6LZ
www.alakazam.co.uk

USA
Hank Lee's Magic Factory
112 South Street, Boston, MA 02111
www.magicfact.com

Hocus Pocus Magic
1492 N. Clark #104, Fresno CA 93703
www.hocus-pocus.com

Steven's Magic Emporium
2520 E. Douglas Ave.
Wichita, Kansas 67214-4514
www.stevensmagic.com

Worldwide
Marvin's Magic
www.marvinsmagic.com

These details are correct at the time of publication, but for the latest information and direct links to these and many other online magic shops visit **www.teachmetricks.com**
  Here you can contact Nicholas, and find further information about many of the magic tricks in this book.

index

Above: Blended Silks (Version 2).

Above: Sweet Tooth.

Above: Magic Papers.

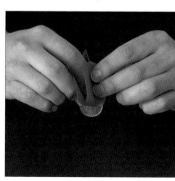

Above: Coin through Hole.

Above: Countdown.

Above: Love Match.

Genie in a Bottle 430–1
Giant Fan 140
Gibson, Walter B. 21
gimmicks 120–35, 202
Giobbi, Roberto 21
Glide 65
Gliding Home 106–7
Glimpse 64, 84
Going into Liquidation 436
Goldin, Horace 19, 27, 29, 226
Good Head for Money, A 343
Goshman, Albert 25
Grant, U.F. 472, 484, 487
Gravity Vanish 169
Gravity-defying Ring 40–1
Great Olive Challenge, The 371
Green, Lennart 25, 35

H
Handkerchief Coin Vanish 147, 172
handkerchiefs *see* silks
Harbin, Robert 19
Harris, Paul 19, 25
Heads I Win! 150
Height of Failure 422
Henning, Doug 30
Herrmann, Alexander 26
Hertz, Carl 18, 226, 227
Hide and Seek 391
Hide and Seek Solo 390
Hindu Force 117
Hocus Pocus 76–7

Hoffman, Professor Louis 20, 21
Hole in Hand 414
Hollingworth, Guy 25, 35
Houdini, Harry 17, 20, 28, 31, 34, 354, 382–3, 471, 476
Houdini, Theo 471
Houdini Outdone! 476–7
How Many Shelves? 410
Hugard, Jean 21
Human Calculator 393
Hunter Bow Knot 235
Hypnotic, Magnetic Fingers 357

I
illusion 18–19, 22, 26–9, 30–1, 59, 186, 196, 197, 210
Immovable 366
Impossible! 418
Impossible Card Location 90–1
Impossible Coin Balance 152
Impossible Knot 238
Impossible Link 254–5
Impossible Numbers! 392
Impossible Prediction 405
Incredible Blindfold Act 460
Incredible Prediction 455
Indestructible String 230–1
Indian Rope Trick 226–7
Indicator 80–1
In-Jog Dribble Control 101

Above: Rising Tube Mystery.

Above: Coin Through Coaster.

Instant Card Revelation 84
Interlocked 253
Inuit or Warrior? 413
Inverted Glass Trick 361
Invisible Coin Catch 342
Invisible Traveller 88–9

J
Jacob's Ladder 296–7
Jacob's Tree 298–9
James I 20
James, Stewart 244
Jarett, Guy 19
Jasper the Ghost 302
Jay, Ricky 21, 23, 34, 35
Johnny Carson Show 22
Jolley, Graham P. 382, 383
Jumping Match 209, 216
Jumping Rubber Band 232
Jumping Thimble 283
Just Chance 386–7

K
Kalanag 226
Kaps, Fred 24, 429
Kellar, Harry 26, 29, 226, 471
King, Mac 429
Kiss Me Quick 136–7
Klok, Hans 472
Knife and Paper Trick 322–3
Koran, Al 382
Kreskin 382

Above: The Bermuda Triangle.

Above: Instant Card Revelation.

Above: Escaping Jack.

Above: Mugged Again.

Above: Dissolving Coin (Version 2).

Above: Rising Card From Box (Version 2).

Above: Coin Cascade.

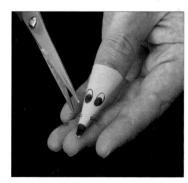

Above: Finger Mouse.

Above: Indestructable String.

acknowledgements

The author would like to thank the following, who either provided inspiration for some of the magic tricks herein or who assisted in the process of writing this book: Alan Alan, Jon Allen, Eddie Ahern, Aaron Barrie, Davenports, Milbourne Christopher, Edwin A. Dawes, Joanne Einhorn, John Fisher, James Freedman, Walter Gibson, Martin Gardner, Scott Penrose, Bob Loomis, Ali Bongo, Andrew Murray, Ian Keeble, Adam Keisner, George Kovari, Michael Ammar, Barry Shapiro, Peter Laine, Roy Lee, Jeff Salmon, Bob Read, Tom Mullica, David Hambly, Barrie Richardson, Robert Neale, David Britland, Martin Breese, Tommy Wonder, Oswald Rae, Alan Shaxon, Peter Monticup, Slydini, U. F Grant, The Magic Circle, Blue Star NC. Google.

The playing cards used in this book are Bicycle, Atlantis or Stratus playing cards. Bicycle, the Bicycle logo and the Bicycle Rider Back Design are all registered trademarks of The United States Playing Cards Company, www.usplayingcard.com, and are used with permission. Atlantis and Stratus, the Atlantis and Stratus logo and the Atlantis and Stratus Back Design are all registered trademarks of Cartamundi Ltd. and are used with permission.

Above: Chinese Coin off String.

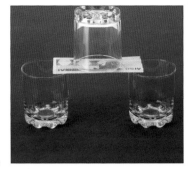

Above: Suspension Bridge.

Thank you to the following, who provided props: Carta Mundi (tarot cards), Ann Childers (money), Betty Davenport (box of tricks), Tim Ellerby (books), Jennifer Schofield (ring, money), Sarah See (money) and Amanda Wood (napkins, money).

Picture credits

The publisher would like to thank the following for the use of their pictures (l=left, r=right, t=top, b=bottom). *Alamy:* 355tl, 470t, 496; *Michael Ammar:* 35; *Frank Bemelman:* 35; *Colin Rose:* 208r; *Corbis:* 302t, 355tr, 408, 429bl, 470b, 471t, b, 472, 473; *Edwin A. Dawes Collection:* 9b, 16t,b, 17t,b, 18tl,tr, 19b, 21t,b, 23, 25b, 26bl, 27t,b, 30b, 58t, 302, 303tl, 227br, 380b; *Nicholas Einhorn* 303t; *The Fortean Picture Library:* 20t,b, 22t, 226t,b, 227t, 260b, 383tr; *Graham P. Jolley:* 383tl; *Hulton Archive:* 227bl; *The Image Bank:* 8; *Mary Evans Picture Library:* 208l, 428; *Rex Features:* 30t, 31t, 31b, 34, 409b, 429; *Jeff Scanlan:* 354 (www.bottlemagic.com); *Stone:* 9t, 11; *Telegraph Colour Library:* 10; *Vin Mag:* 18b, 19t, 25tl,tr.

Every effort has been made to acknowledge the pictures properly; however, we apologize if there are any unintentional omissions, which will be corrected in later editions.

Publisher: Joanna Lorenz
Project Editors: Lucy Doncaster and Felicity Forster
Art Manager: Clare Reynolds
Editors: Beverley Jollands and Judy Cox
Photographers: Paul Bricknell and John Freeman
Models: Aaron Barrie, Nick Einhorn, Lucy Doncaster, and Jennifer Schofield
Designers: Design Principles and Steve West
Production Controller: Steve Lang

© Anness Publishing Ltd 2008

Previously published in two separate volumes, *The Art of Magic and Sleight of Hand* and *Magical Illusions, Conjuring Tricks, Amazing Puzzles & Stunning Stunts*

Bracketed terms are intended for American readers.

The author and publishers have made every effort to ensure that all instructions contained within this book are accurate and safe, and cannot accept liability for any resulting injury, damage or loss to persons or property, however it may arise. Matches and rope should be used with caution.

For more information about Nick Einhorn and to access a host of magical hints, tips and resources visit **www.teachmetricks.com** or the author's own website at **www.einhorn.co.uk**